BASIC CHRISTIAN ETHICS

BASIC
CHRISTIAN
ETHICS

by

PAUL RAMSEY

The University of Chicago Press
Chicago and London

The University of Chicago Press, Chicago 60637
The University of Chicago Press, Ltd., London

ISBN: 0-226-70382-7
LCN: 78-56925

THIS BOOK IS GRATEFULLY DEDICATED

TO MY

MOTHER and FATHER

Mamie McCay Ramsey

(June 20, 1872–Oct. 26, 1948)

Who spent herself with serene, lavish and noble affection and who died at last of release from duty faithfully performed,

and

Rev. John William Ramsey

(Feb. 17, 1869–Oct. 26, 1948)

For nearly sixty years an ordained minister of the Methodist Church who sought by use of heart and mind to bring people to an "experimental" knowledge of God in Christ.

CONTENTS

ACKNOWLEDGMENTS TO PUBLISHERS

In most cases the footnotes give sufficient indication of permissions granted by publishers to quote from their copyrighted works. Except when otherwise noted, the quotations from the Old Testament are from *The Complete Bible: An American Translation*, translated by J. M. Powis Smith (and a group of scholars) and Edgar J. Goodspeed, copyrighted 1939 by the University of Chicago Press, and used by permission. Those from the New Testament are from the Revised Standard Version of the New Testament, copyrighted 1946 by the International Council of Religious Education, and used by permission. I am also grateful to the publishers of the following journals for kindly giving me permission to make use of the substance of a number of previously published articles: *The Journal of Religion* (University of Chicago Press), Vol. XXVI, No. 4 (Oct., 1946); Vol. XXVII, No. 3 (July, 1947); Vol. XXVIII, No. 3 (Oct., 1948); Vol. XXIX, No. 4 (Oct., 1949); *Ethics* (University of Chicago Press), Vol. LVI, No. 4 (July, 1946); *Social Action* magazine (Council for Social Action of the Congregational Christian Churches of the U. S. A.), Oct. 15, 1946; *Religion in Life* (Abingdon-Cokesbury Press), Vol. XIII, No. 4 (Autumn, 1944); and *Philosophy and Phenomenological Research* (University of Buffalo), Vol. VI, No. 4 (June, 1946).

P. R.

INTRODUCTION

In his novel *Pierre*, Herman Melville sourly defines the gospel of love as "a volume bound in rose-leaves, clasped with violets, and by the beaks of hummingbirds printed with peach-juice on the leaves of lilies." Actually Christian ethics is more like "labor and fortitude" than "sweetness and light." The task of dispelling such misunderstanding requires the same thoroughness and exactness in analyzing the principles of Christian ethics as are necessary in any other realm of thought where the issues are of vital human concern. In the end, of course, the student of Christian ethics can only know *that he knows* what the simplest true Christian vigorously "doing the truth" knows already. Yet understanding is essential no less than performance if ever we hope to comprehend the structure of the Christian life.

As a treatise on basic Christian ethics, this book endeavors to stand within the way the Bible views morality. The central ethical notion or "category" in Christian ethics is "obedient love"—the sort of love the gospels describe as "love fulfilling the law" and St. Paul designates as "faith that works through love." This volume undertakes to explain many facets of the meaning of Christian "obedient love," and its meaning for morality. This concept, basic to any understanding of the Christian outlook with the demands it places upon moral action, gives us the clue essential to understanding certain other ideas, such as "justice," "right" or "obligation," "duties to oneself," "vocation," "virtues" of moral character, "sinfulness" and the "image of God," which in turn are of crucial importance in elaborating a theory of Christian ethics.

A system of Christian ethics would be incomplete without some comparison with non-Christian moral philosophies. Many of the ethical concepts just mentioned, for example, come up for discussion in any textbook on ethics. Simply for the purpose of delineating the basic meaning of Christian ethics one needs to study it in relation to its major alternatives. Without pretending to exhaust the subject of comparative ethics, certain fundamental contrasts and connections between Christian ethics and the major philosophical theories of ethics are here rather fully explored: Platonism, Aristotelianism, hedonism, self-realization ethics, theories of value, and nineteenth-century British utilitarianism.

In addition to these viewpoints, the ethics of obedient love should also be contrasted with an ethic of mystical love or aspiration for a vision of God which too largely lay at the basis of medievalism. In the opening chapters, "obedient love" may be seen emerging from Jewish theology, Kingdom-expectation, and legalism; and the final chapter consists of a study of the biblical idea of "covenant" so important for social ethics. Thus, in the course of rooting Christian ethics firmly in its Jewish heritage, the contrasts between it and Jewish ethics, as well as similarities between them, are made plain.

Fundamental questions concerning the relevance and practicability or application of Christian ethics have been squarely faced in these pages, for example, in the chapter on Christian Vocation. Discussion of what Christian ethics means in practice must deal with concrete ethical situations confronting men. However, no complete analysis of special social problems is attempted, nor has much been said about their final solution. This is not basic; before there can be a Christian social ethic, understanding of the fundamental moral perspective of the Christian must be deepened and clarified. Nevertheless, basic Christian ethics must itself always be theory oriented toward practice. This has been held in mind throughout, and in the next to last chapter the reader will find some suggestions toward the formulation of a broad Christian social policy. He will properly regard these suggestions as quite tentative, and, if only on account of their brevity, in need of supplement.

The impulse behind some of the later chapters of this book

is the author's conviction that, especially in formulating social policy, contemporary Christian ethics must make common cause with the ethics of philosophical idealism. We must become debtors to the best insight available at the present stage of thought, instead of trying to overleap the centuries in order to embrace too closely Plato, Aristotle or the Reformers as certain of the "Neo"-orthodoxies suggest. In recent years Christian naturalism has at least been perceptive enough to see the impossibility and undesirability of going so far backward. A modern man will need to devise some Christian *employment* of the social philosophy of idealism, comparable to Augustine's *use* of Platonism and Aquinas' *use* of Aristotle which served Christianity so notably in the past. With whatever school the Christian makes common cause, however, he must first learn not to be used by it or to allow the fundamental Christian ethical perspective to suffer alteration. This can be accomplished only by his becoming quite consciously clear about what, as a Christian, he already knows of the meaning of obligation.

I submit that it would never occur to an unprejudiced mind— a mind not already greatly harmed by some wrong-headed apologetic interest—to look for the meaning of Christian ethics anywhere else than in the biblical record and in the writings of men of the past whose thinking about morality has been profoundly disturbed and influenced by what they found there. The basic principles of Christian ethics cannot be understood except from a study of the New Testament and by studying the great theologians of the past in whose reflections on moral issues Christian themes are "writ large." The reader will find in the following pages a self-contained introduction to biblical ethics, and to the moral philosophies of St. Augustine, St. Thomas Aquinas, Martin Luther, and (less fully) Soren Kierkegaard. Recurring reference is made especially to the teachings of Jesus and St. Paul. There is hardly a chapter which does not give extensive exposition of their views. Their ethic of obedient love was brought more clearly to light during the period of the Reformation than had been the case for the centuries since New Testament times. This volume, then, may equally well be described as an essay in the Christo-centric ethics of the Reformation.

A glance at the table of contents will show, however, that primary source material drawn from the Bible, and from epochal figures in the course of Christian thought, has been used systematically in the interest of setting forth a constructive theory of Christian ethics, and not at all with mere antiquarian concern. No matter how much heritage there is in it, Christian ethics has to do with the present and not with history that is past. This calls for a constructive elaboration of the way the data of morality and contemporary moral demands may be comprehended in the light of Christian faith.

In what sense is the word "Christian" used here? As an extended exercise in defining various ethical terms, here actually we are undertaking to say what, so far as ethics is concerned, the word "Christian" means. Not what the word *should* mean in order to be true and illuminating for morality, but what in fact it *does* mean—whether interesting or not in the final issue, let alone true or illuminating. Our task is not one of first discovering what in any event is true in the field of ethics, and then piously calling that Christian. It is rather the task of discovering what may properly be described as basic Christian morality. At the beginning of such a study all that is necessary to know is barely enough of the meaning of the word "Christian" in order to isolate the subject-matter to be investigated. Exactly so, at the beginning of his science a biologist knows what an animal is only in a very rough and practical way; and it is precisely by means of his researches that he comes to know somewhat more about the meaning of biological life. This is the sense in which we take it for granted that the Christian scriptures are where we should look to find out what Christian ethics means.

This book, therefore, is addressed not only to persons called by the name Christian, but also to the enquiring among the cultured despisers of this religion. To the latter, it says: "This is what Christians *as such* are talking about"; and it addresses these enquiring ones not first of all with a view to convincing them, but with a view to increasing their understanding. Addressed to the Christian reader, these pages are part of the continuing conversation among us by which we commend to one another the bearing Jesus Christ has for our ethical thought and practice. And do we not have it on rather high authority that if, in the course of this conversation, we are too easily impressed by its truth for us, then it was probably not *Christian* ethics we were talking about?

The task of coming to terms with Christian ethics is a difficult one

> due partly to the poverty of our English tongue at this point, to the fact that we have only one word [love] to cover all that the Greek employed two if not three words to express. And the distance between the two extremes becomes clear when we realize that at one end we may use the word to describe an emotional disposition which desires nothing so much as to give, at the other end one which craves nothing so much as to possess. We say of God that He "so loved the world that he gave," and equally we might say of a man, "He so loved . . . that he snatched."[1]

Understanding the meaning of words is a necessary and fundamental condition for making any sort of beginning in the study of Christian ethics, as is true also in any other scientific or philosophical enquiry.

Modern logic and mathematics, for example, begin with certain "primitive ideas" whose meaning is either quite arbitrarily devised or presumed to be known already. These fundamental notions, themselves never defined in terms of other ideas, are then used to define the meaning of other, secondary terms. In mathematics, for example, a "point" may be defined as the place where two lines cross one another, or a "line" may be defined as the path of a moving point. But you must already know what a "point" is ever to learn the meaning of "line" or else you have to know what a "line" is before learning the meaning of "point." Both words cannot have derivative meaning, one must be basic to the other, or else still a third "primitive idea" must be found,

[1] C. A. Anderson Scott, *New Testament Ethics*, Macmillan, 1930, p. 22.

itself never defined in terms of these two but used in defining
them derivatively. Newton measured the speed of light in terms
of absolute space and time; Einstein reverses the order: he defines space and time in terms of the speed of light. A totally
ignorant man would not learn much from a dictionary, for here
he finds some words defined in terms of others whose meaning
he must know already. It is impossible for every word in a dictionary to have derivative meaning; some words fundamental to
all the rest must be given meaning "primitively" by *pointing*, as
when we point and say "blue" and all people who are not color-
blind learn to say "blue" with reference to the same color sen-
sation.

Now, "Christian love" is a similar fundamental notion in the
theory of Christian ethics. Paul's Hymn in praise of Christian
love, I Corinthians 13, ought never to be read as if here a few
additional statements are made about "love" with which we are
already somewhat familiar, or as a composite definition in terms
of certain other more basic notions drawn from other familiar
experiences. This classic statement of the meaning of Christian
love defines by *indication*, pointing not to anything generally
experienced by all men everywhere, like blueness or fatherhood,
but, as we shall see, to Jesus Christ. Transcribing in unforgettable
phrases the nature of divine love seen in him, St. Paul elaborates
the meaning of perfect love for the Christian. A person reading
this chapter should bring to it a sense of reading for the first
time the definition of some new, unheard-of conception, love
seen "in the flesh" only in Jesus Christ and for the first time
formulated in language by St. Paul. In order to be certain of
putting entirely aside any other meanings which, before you read
this chapter or look toward Christ, may be associated in your
mind with the word "love," try substituting a blank space, or
"x," the algebraic symbol for the unknown, or the Greek word
Paul uses, *"agape"* (which for most modern readers has the advantage of meaning nothing at all) for the English words "love"
or "charity" in our translations:

Agape is patient and kind; *Agape* is not jealous or boastful; it is not arrogant or rude. *Agape* does not insist on its own way; it is not irritable or resentful; it does not rejoice at wrong, but rejoices in the right. *Agape* bears all things, believes all things, hopes all things, endures all things. *Agape* never ends . . . [verses 4–8].

When all is said, we shall have considered from many sides this "primitive idea" of Christian ethics, in terms of which other notions, such as "justice," "right" or "obligation," "duties to oneself," "vocation," "virtues" of moral character, "sinfulness" and the "image of God" receive derivative definition. Even the "fatherhood of God" in its Christian meaning is not merely a general religious notion but refers always to the "God who put forward Christ," "the Father of our Lord and Savior Jesus Christ." Analyzing ethical problems from the viewpoint of Christian love simply means that Jesus Christ is the center. Because this is the case, the interpretation given in this book concerning the ethics of obedient love does not rest on any merely *linguistic* study of the New Testament. It rests rather on a study of morality in the light of the religious *thought* of the New Testament.

I am most indebted to my wife, whose help for many years has been too constant for special tribute and who willingly assumed an increased number of family responsibilities during the semester I remained at home to write. Professor George F. Thomas, Chairman of the Department of Religion at Princeton University, gave invaluable encouragement and criticism, especially in the early stages of this writing. He also read the last three chapters in the final draft, and helped in organizing them. I am deeply grateful to Professor Paul L. Lehmann of the Princeton Theological Seminary and Professor Clyde Manschreck of Southern Methodist University for their constructive criticism of Chapters I–VII. In addition, I am greatly indebted to my colleague, Professor Claude Welch, for his careful and competent advice in making the final revision of the whole work, and for preparing the Suggestions for Further Reading and the Index. My teachers at Yale University, notably Professors H. Richard

Niebuhr, Roland H. Bainton, Robert L. Calhoun, Liston Pope, and Charles W. Hendel, continue to be my instructors. Since this is a first book, the author is tempted to go on indefinitely with these acknowledgments, trying to omit no one. To come to a period, let his indebtedness be summed up in a single tribute: to those who have been patient with me and to those who have not: from no one have I learned more.

A special sort of mention should be made of the students for six years at Princeton in a course now called *Religion II: Christian Ethics*. In the teaching of religion in a modern university, one too frequently is forced to admit that what is easily communicable in religious instruction is problematically Christian, and what is certainly Christian is doubtfully communicable. The students of *Religion II* have confirmed my belief that there is not much point in trying to teach *less* than what is here stated, and they have supported the hope that this book may in some measure fill the need for a first book in Christian ethics at the college and the seminary level. Aiming at the student mind has not meant aiming low, though it has required the full elaboration of many points which might have been treated more concisely, and quoting rather than simply citing passages from scripture.

Since Christian ethics did not first occur to my mind I quote unabashedly from those who have gone this way before me and from whom I have learned something. It may perhaps then be said of this volume, without presumption but with gratitude, that "unless I am deceived, it is the whole of Christian living in brief form, if you will grasp its meaning."

PAUL RAMSEY

Princeton University
Princeton, New Jersey
March, 1950

BASIC CHRISTIAN ETHICS

I

THE TWO SOURCES OF CHRISTIAN LOVE

"For you yourselves have been taught by God to love one another."—I Thessalonians 4:9.

"Will any one look a little into—right into—the mystery of *how ideals are manufactured* in this world? Who has the courage to do it? Come!"
—Friedrich Nietzsche, *The Genealogy of Morals*, I, 14.

THE first thing to be said concerning Christian ethics is that it cannot be separated from its religious foundation. This is true not because of some tender-minded belief that "supernatural sanctions" are needed to enforce right conduct which, it is thought, may be adequately defined without any reference at all to religion. The fact that God requires something of man, and stands ready to reward obedience and punish violation, is not nearly so important as the question to *what sort* of God man has obligations and what are his commandments. Religious conviction concerning God's dealing with man affects the basic meaning and content of biblical ethics. God has something to do with the very meaning of obligation; he is no merely external threat standing behind morality. The ethics of Jesus, for example, cannot be understood without some understanding of the God of Abraham, Isaac and Jacob, Moses and the prophets, the God of the people of the covenant. Biblical writers do not view ethics naturalistically as rooted in human nature or in the social environment, or abstractly in terms of some generalizations about human values. They view ethics theologically as rooted in the nature and activity of God. As a consequence, man's relation to God was thought to be of vital importance, not simply *for* ethics, but *within* ethical theory itself.

1

We must first of all discover in the strange, new religious world of the Bible the source of the ethical perspectives peculiar to the Hebrew-Christian heritage. For a proper study of the origin and nature of Christian ethics, a distinction may be made between (1) God's righteousness and love and (2) the reign of this righteousness in the Kingdom of God. These are two sources of "Christian love." Never imagine you have rightly grasped a biblical ethical idea until you have succeeded in reducing it to a simple corollary of one or the other of these notions, or of the idea of covenant between God and man from which they both stem.

I. THE RIGHTEOUSNESS OF GOD

The Bible has been called "the book of God's righteousness."[1] The "righteousness of God," his judgment and his steadfast faithfulness to the covenant he makes with men, is not only frequently mentioned in the Bible but is its main theme. Yet while pointing this out, near the beginning of his book *Justice and the Social Order* Emil Brunner announces that he intends to use the word "justice" in a different sense from its biblical, or for that matter from its ancient Greek, meaning.

> When we moderns speak of justice, of just and unjust, we do not mean the sum total of all goodness or all virtue. . . . Both in ancient Greece and in the Bible the word just has a depth and scope which it has long since lost. When we speak of just and unjust, we have something far more restricted in mind than when we simply distinguish good from evil. . . . No man of today but would find it strange if, because he was kindly, devout, charitable, grateful and God-fearing, he should be called just, as in the language of the Bible.[2]

Now we must of necessity go along with prevailing usage; and there is even something to be gained in greater precision from restricting the meaning of words and using more of them. But in shuffling words we must see to it that nothing significant gets lost. Having narrowed the meaning of "justice," Brunner then

[1]Brunner, *Justice and the Social Order*, Harpers, 1945, p. 110.
[2]*Ibid.*, p. 13.

uses the word "love" for much of the excluded meaning left over
from the biblical term and finds himself forced to write a chapter
on the interstate commerce between justice and love. No legitimate exception can be taken to his statement in this connection
that "love can only do more, it can never do less, than justice
requires." Nevertheless, it appears that restricting the scope of
the meaning of the biblical term has actually restricted the scope
of its operation and radically modified the weight and extent of
its impingement upon what Brunner calls "the world of systems."
"The state knows nothing of love," Brunner quotes Barth with
approval and himself goes on to comment:

> The man of love can only serve the state with justice. He must
> transform his love entirely [*sic!*] into justice for as long and insofar
> as he acts in the state. . . . But because no man, as a member
> of an institution, is *only* a member of an institution, but always
> and only a person, there is room for love even in the most im-
> personal of institutions, not in the actual activity of the institu-
> tion itself, but "between the lines" [*sic!*].[3]

But was not the whole nation of Israel, with all her institutions,
in every way bound to serve the cause of justice in its broadest
and deepest meaning? What man nurtured in the Bible can be
content with love effective only through the interstitial spaces?
What prophetic voice announced that "justice" need not flow
down like a mighty stream but only as a gentle spray? The biblical
conception of justice defines the purpose every institution and
social order should serve, and yet it requires a great deal more
than Aristotle thought was simply just. To re-view the biblical
point of viewing which every one is in daily danger of losing, it
may be well for us to recover something of the larger meaning
of the word "justice." This book deliberately adopts a procedure
the reverse of Brunner's. The meaning and measure of full human
obligation are to be found only in the biblical conception of righteousness, and not elsewhere in some moral norms derived from
reason operating apart from the Hebrew-Christian religious heritage.

[3]*Ibid.*, p. 129, and chap. 15 *passim.*

The righteousness of God and the justice of men are ordinarily distinguished in the Bible. God's righteousness acting in judgment is regularly designated by the word *tsedeq*, while human justice formulated by judgments in courts of law and given in informal custom is the primary meaning of *mishpat*. To comprehend the depth and scope of the biblical notion of "justice," it is necessary first to *distinguish* these two kinds of justice—God's judgmental righteousness and human justice—and then to *relate* them decisively together, so that the meaning of God's righteousness acting in judgment (*tsedeq*) becomes normative for human justice (*mishpat*).

Norman H. Snaith has conclusively demonstrated that the meaning of the righteous judgment of God (*tsedeq*) in biblical thought has been invaded by the "vocabulary of salvation."[4] It follows from this that, in so far as divine righteousness (*tsedeq*) determines the nature of human justice (*mishpat*), the meaning of justice among men should be equally understood as bound to be concerned with salvation.

"The revelation of the righteousness of God," Amos Wilder writes, "means above all the enactment of his salvation."[5]

> In thy righteousness, rescue me and deliver me,
> Incline thy ear unto me and save me (Ps. 71:2).

Commenting on petitions such as this in the Psalms, Otto Baab points out the same connection of righteousness with salvation. "The word evidently has the power to inspire in men an assurance that God will reply to their petitions for help under various circumstances. It is certainly not an abstract virtue or ethical attribute which is in question here; rather the very nature and work of God are at stake. *When the whole being of God is bent on salvation to men, then his righteousness is operative.*"[6] As a consequence of linking God's righteous judgments with his saving ac-

---

4*The Distinctive Ideas of the Old Testament,* Westminster Press, 1946, chaps. iii and iv; "invading the salvation vocabulary" (p. 87).
5"New Testament Faith and Its Relevance Today," *Shane Quarterly* (Butler University), IX, No. 2 (April, 1948), p. 98. He is here commenting on Paul's use of the term but says "it is often so used in the Old Testament."
6*The Theology of the Old Testament,* Abingdon-Cokesbury Press, 1949, p. 133.

tivity, the Bible knows nothing, or little, of any conflict between justice and love. "The antithesis which in dogmatics we are familiar with is a righteous and just God and *yet* a Saviour. The Old Testament puts it differently—a righteous God and *therefore* a Saviour."[7] The righteousness (*tsedeq*) of God, then, actually borders on the meaning of *chesed,* or God's keeping troth, his unwavering faithfulness in keeping the covenant. This word, usually translated "mercy" or "loving-kindness," means "fixed, determined, almost stubborn steadfastness," "sure love," "love unswerving," "fidelity, firmness, truth," "firm adherence" and "determined faithfulness to the covenant," "the strength, the firmness, and the persistence of God's sure love."[8] Such covenant-love of God provides the measure for the sort of fidelity men are due to give to the covenant. In like manner the righteousness (*tsedeq*) of God provides the measure of true justice for all human justice (*mishpat*).

The second part of this thesis, namely, that the idea of justice (*mishpat*) has been invaded by the vocabulary of God's righteousness (*tsedeq*), requires more extended comment, but it is equally apparent. The connecting link between divine righteousness and human justice is the covenant and the events believed to have occasioned Israel's origin as a religious nation. The covenant promulgates the justice of God on earth. God's righteousness becomes the plumb line for measuring the rightness of human relationships. Since the covenanted community has no charter for existence apart from God's act, the foundation and constitution of her justice must be laid in his righteousness. The core of Old Testament ethic, its central, organizing principle, is to be found underneath an abundance of external codes of law in God's active righteousness (*tsedeq*) which through the covenant became "the nature of the kingdom" (*mishpat*) (I Sam. 10:25). The laws and customs of the country should all be framed with decisive reference to "the God of gods and the Lord of lords; the great, mighty and awful God, who is never partial, and never takes a bribe, who secures justice for the orphan and the widow, and loves the resi-

[7]Davidson, *Theology of the Old Testament,* Scribners, 1904, p. 144, quoted by Robinson, *The Religious Ideas of the Old Testament,* Scribners, 1921, p. 70.
[8]Snaith, *op. cit.,* pp. 125, 126, 128, 130, 141, and chap. v *passim.*

dent alien in giving him food and clothing" (Deut. 10:16–18). This standard immediately becomes a measure for what is expected in human affairs, as in Jeremiah's comment on the renewal of the covenant in 621 B.C. under King Josiah:

> Do justice [*mishpat*] and righteousness [*ts^edaqah*]; deliver the despoiled from the hands of the oppressor; commit no wrong or violence against the resident alien, the orphan, and the widow.
>
> Did not your father, as he ate and drank,
> Do justice and righteousness?
> Then all went well with him.
> He defended the cause of the poor and needy;
> Then all went well.
> Is not this how to know me? (Jer. 22:3, 15–16).

If God paid particular attention to the case of an enslaved people, as he did when he "smote Egypt," if he pays special attention to the case of the poor and outcast, the widow and the orphan, the "sojourner" or resident alien, if he has "a particular regard for the helpless ones of earth to rescue them from the clutches of those that are stronger than they,"[9] then there must be a corresponding quality in the life of his people so long as they remain his people. In ancient Israel "the use of the land was subject to the welfare of the community" by laws guaranteeing family holdings in perpetuity (*cf.* the story of Naboth's vineyard) and prohibiting the removal of ancient landmarks which fixed these holdings. All this was for the "common good." Going beyond this, the laws also included a concern for those who had no holdings in Israel, making "provision for the poor, for widows, and for resident aliens (who had no allotment in Israel). Their support was secured by the laws of gleaning and the like."[10]

Numerous passages in scripture enjoin the doing of justice (*mishpat*) *and* righteousness (*tsedeq*), or define "what is good" or "what the Lord requires" as "only to do justice (*mishpat*) *and* to love kindness (*chesed*) *and* to walk humbly with your God" (Mic. 6:8). But in the face of these passages it might still be pos-

[9]*Ibid.*, p. 87.
[10]M. Burrows, *An Outline of Biblical Theology*, Westminster Press, 1946, p. 302.

sible to contend that human justice was meant to be one thing and righteousness and mercy quite different things, even when the latter are also made normative for what is done *somewhere on earth*. It may be that justice should prevail in courts of law or in the "world of systems"; while righteousness and mercy, measured according to God's righteousness and covenant-love but still enjoined upon men, should be effective only "between the lines" in personal, extra-juridical relationships. The simple juxtaposition of the words "justice" and "righteousness," no matter how many times reiterated, would not be sufficient to show that righteousness penetrates the biblical definition of justice itself. The authors may simply be enumerating two different things, justice and righteousness, both of which go to make up "what is good." Righteousness may simply do more, never less, than justice.

This suggestion falls to the ground, however, when we read of human justice (*mishpat*) in *perfect parallelism* with God's righteousness acting in judgment (*tsedeq*) or when the two words are interchanged and used *instead of* each other. The familiar words of Amos may be cited as an example:

> But let justice [*mishpat*] roll down like waters,
> And righteousness [*tsᵉdaqah*] like a perennial stream (5:24).

Here plainly justice must be understood as the same thing as righteousness, expressed differently in poetic parallel lines. Another instance of completely parallel meaning may be found in a psalm so juridical in its nature as to be entitled in the American translation, "Long Live the King!"

> Give the king thy justice [*mishpat*], O God,
> And thy righteousness [*tsidqathᵉkha*[11]] to the king's son,
> That he may judge thy people with right [*tsedeq*],
> And thine afflicted with justice [*mishpat*]!

> May the mountains bring the people peace,
> And the hills righteousness [*tsᵉdaqah*]!
> May he judge [*yishpōt*[12]] the afflicted of the people,
> And give deliverance to the poor,
> And crush the oppressor (72:1–4).

[11]Inflection of *tsedeq*.   [12]Inflection of *mishpat*.

And again in "A Homily for 'Divine' Rulers":

> Give justice [*shiphtu*¹²] to the weak and the orphan;
> Do right [*hasdîqu*¹¹] by the afflicted and wretched;
> Set free the weak and needy
> Rescue them from the hands of the wicked (Ps. 82:3–4).

Moreover, in the "charge to judges" near the beginning of Deuteronomy, the words for human and divine justice are *interchanged*, indicating to all responsible for delivering judgment "in the gate" that the only true human justice must be cut to the measure of God's righteousness. "Hear the cases between your fellow-countrymen, and judge aright [*tsedeq*] between a man and his fellow or the resident alien in his employ. You must never show partiality in a case [*mishpat*]; you must hear high and low alike, standing in fear of no man; for the judgment [*mishpat*] is God's" (Deut. 1:16, 17). Here beyond question "judging aright" in any case, true justice, receives its decisive definition by reference to the standard of God's righteous judgment. Human justice is entirely articulated with the justice of God. And the reason for this is also given: for the judgment (*mishpat*) is ultimately God's.

> For when thy judgments [*mishpātêkha*] come down to the earth,
> The inhabitants of the world learn righteousness [*tsedeq*] (Isa. 26:9).

While this passage from Isaiah may not be so exactly juridical in its import as that from Deuteronomy, it provides another instance of the confluence of divine and human justice in their biblical meanings.

In the light of these and doubtless many other crucial passages in the Bible, it cannot be denied that the idea of justice, and precisely that sort of justice secured through political and other institutions, has been invaded by what righteousness on God's part means. The connection of justice and righteousness, or justice and mercy, by simple juxtaposition in countless other passages cannot, then, be entirely fortuitous.¹³

¹¹Inflection of *tsedeq*.   ¹²Inflection of *mishpat*.
¹³For example, in Zech. 7:9–10: "Render true judgments [*mishpat*], and practice kindness and mercy [*chesed*] each toward his brother. Do not oppress the widow and the orphan, the resident alien, and the poor; and let none of you devise in your heart wickedness against your brother."

These qualities, justice (*mishpat*), righteousness (*tsedeq*), and mercy (*chesed*), which are to be distinguished on first beginning to understand the Bible, prove on closer inspection not at all clearly distinguishable in their meaning and never separable in fact. Perhaps their meanings never entirely coalesce into bare identity, but they infect one another, and this influence runs in the direction *from* God *manward*. The situation is not unlike that in the early Platonic dialogues which discuss the unity of all the virtues with one another and with the "knowledge of the good." Temperance and wisdom, courage and justice and holiness, are found at least to cohere with one another in a remarkable way, although Socrates is reluctant to draw the conclusion that they are absolutely one and the same. Laches and Socrates began by restricting their discussion to a part of virtue, namely, courage; this they thought a more manageable topic; but they are forced in the end to the conclusion that true courage, rightly understood as involving knowledge of good and evil, includes in some sense the whole of virtue. Temperance and all the other virtues, it can at least be said, are to be found somewhere in the same region with one another and "somewhere in the region" of the knowledge of the good.[14] Even more strongly for the biblical viewpoint it must be asserted that "justice" is no restricted part of "what is good" (Mic. 6:8) but definitely to be found somewhere in the region of "the knowledge of God"; and "Is not this how to know me?"—to "do justice and righteousness," to "defend the cause of the poor and needy" (Jer. 22:15, 16). In the *Republic*, when it is discovered that temperance "extends to the whole, and runs through all the notes of the scale," instead of residing in a part of the soul or in one special class in the state, Socrates announces that beyond doubt justice will also be found somewhere in this same country.[15] In like manner, biblical writers always locate justice somewhere in the same country with righteousness. Having discovered the meaning of justice, Plato defines its opposite as at once the opposite of every virtue: "Must not injustice be a strife which arises among the three principles—a meddlesomeness, and

[14]*Charmides.*
[15]*Republic,* 432 (Jowett).

interference, and rising up of a part of the soul against the whole, an assertion of unlawful authority, which is made by a rebellious subject against a true prince, of whom he is the natural vassal—*what is all this confusion and delusion but injustice, and intemperance and cowardice and ignorance, and every form of vice?"*[16] With equal eloquence a biblical author might have exclaimed, "What is *injustice* but unrighteousness, faithlessness, showing no mercy, and a famine of the knowledge of God in the land?" Without doubt, "doing justice" (Mic. 6:8) means "doing God's will as it has been made clear in past experience"[17] of his enacted salvation and covenant faithfulness. At least there is in the Bible what Plato would have called a "participation," "communion," or "presence" of justice, righteousness, and mercy with one another or "imitation" one of another; and this influence runs from God's justice toward man's justice. Justice (*mishpat*) means what we today call justice *permeated* by the character of God's righteousness (*tsedeq*).

We must wrench our minds around from supposing that all the poor and weak of the earth need is "equality before the law" or justice in the sense of equal opportunity and the devil take the hindmost. It may be they have already received this and still have "gone to the wall." Instead, partiality for them lies at the heart of the biblical notion of justice; this shows the influence of the vocabulary of salvation.

. . . His delight will be in the fear of the Lord.
He will not judge by that which his eyes see,
Nor decide by that which his ears hear;
But with justice [*tsedeq*], will he judge [*shāphat*[18]] the needy,
And with fairness *decide for* the poor of the land (Isa. 11:3–4a).

This is what Jeremiah calls "strict justice [*mishpat*]" (7:5) but not what we today call strict justice.

Morning by morning give righteousness judgment [*mishpat*]
And deliver the despoiled from the hand of the oppressor (Jer. 21:12).

16*Ibid.*, 444 (italics mine).
17Snaith, *op. cit.*, p. 96.
18Inflection of *mishpat*.

It is notable that the prophet Nathan did not rebuke King David for violating justice in some equal or narrow sense or for breaking an ordinance of nature, reason, or society. He charged him, a man of power, with violating the covenant obligation of "mercy" to one weaker than he, because, taking the words from David's own mouth, "he showed no pity" (II Sam. 12:6). A sin against "mercy," David himself acknowledged, was the same thing as a sin against the righteous Lord of Israel (II Sam. 12:13). The righteous king became the prototype for the Messiah of God; just so, there is something messianic, something of extraordinary and unexpected helpfulness, at the heart of the biblical notion of justice.

Old Testament ethics reaches perhaps its highest expression in the book of Hosea, in the Suffering Servant passages in Isaiah, and in Job's "negative confession," an *apologia pro vita sua:*

> If I set at naught the cause of my male or female slave
> When they strove with me;
> Then what shall I do when God arises?
>
> If I withheld ought from the desire of the poor,
> And caused the eyes of the widow to grow dim;
> Or ate my portion alone,
> And the orphan did not eat of it—
>
> If I saw any perishing for lack of clothing,
> And there was no covering for the needy;
> If his loins did not bless me,
> And from the fleece of my sheep he did not keep himself warm;
> If I shook my fist at the orphan,
> Because I saw my help in the gate;
> May my shoulder-blade drop from the shoulder,
> And my arm be broken from the socket.
>
> If I rejoiced at the calamity of him who hated me,
> And was elated when evil came upon him—
>
> Verily the men of my household said,
> 'Is there anyone that has not been satisfied with his meat?'
> The stranger did not lodge in the street;
> I opened my doors to the wayfarer.

O that one would listen to me!
Here is my signature! Let the Almighty answer me!
     (Job 31:13–14, 16–17, 19–22, 29, 31–32, 35).

Whoever imagines that religion adds to ethics only the threat of supernaturally administered punishment has simply never read the Bible.

Men who on their side are ordinarily only fitfully faithful to their covenant obligations derive knowledge of the true meaning of human "justice" or "righteousness" from the measure of God's righteousness and not from anything they themselves think or do. The righteousness of God gives a supernatural measure for all things just or unjust, not in some other world, but precisely in this unrighteous world of human affairs where man's faithfulness is like a morning cloud (Hos. 6:4). The Hebrew prophets are frequently praised for their *passion* or *zeal* for justice; they also are noteworthy for their understanding of the very *meaning* of justice. Prophetic morality indeed rests upon a discovery of "the neighbor" which Jesus fulfills, and this was true precisely for the reason that both Jesus and the prophets measure what is just and right by the righteousness of God and not by any human standard. The biblical norm for sound ethical conduct tends to leave behind all prudential reference to enlightened self-interest, all reference also to mutual participation in the common good, overleaping even the criterion of membership in the chosen people of God to include concern for the alien who has no holding. Justice or righteousness "shows a persistent tendency to topple over into benevolence, and easily to have special reference to those who stand in dire need of a Helper."[19] Biased in favor of the helpless, "justice" means care for the poor, the orphans, the widows, and aliens resident in the land. Why? Because the Bible measures what is required of man against the perfect righteousness of an utterly faithful, savior-God. Righteousness requires that the sojourner in the land of promise be cared for, even as God cared for Israel during her days of sojourning in Egypt when he unexpect-

---

[19]Snaith, *op. cit.*, p. 97.

edly and without their meriting it saved them from slavery. Israel is enjoined to have regard for the "sojourner" not because he is due very much but because he is in need: the standard is a super-natural measure, remembering that Israel herself was once a sojourner in Egypt and God then had a care for her which did not calculate her merit. This is the sense, the extreme sense, in which it is true to say that "the relationship between Israel and Yahweh did not begin to be moral in the eighth century; it began to be moral when it began to exist."[20]

Indeed, from the standpoint of biblical religion, the motive for righteousness cannot be limited to the respect or obedience owed to divine authority. There are reverence and obedience enough. But the people of the covenant acted primarily from a total re-sponse to God which may be described as grateful obedience or obedient gratitude; and, of the two, gratitude was more funda-mental, since God had first delivered Israel from bondage in Egypt before ever there was a nation to receive his law. This extraordinary righteousness of God which held them in allegiance and placed them under obligation gave rise in turn, when applied as standard for man's conduct, to the distinctive definition of righteousness or justice by biblical writers. It produced the suc-cession of the prophets and led to several subsequent revisions of the law code before legalism finally triumphed over righteousness in official Judaism after the Exile and in the days of Jesus.

The conception of justice in the Bible is therefore radically dif-ferent from any other which has commended itself to the human mind. In one type of justice, according to Aristotle, "the law looks only to the difference created by the injury and treats the men as previously equal" where, for example, the one commits, the other suffers, the crime of robbery. "Arithmetical" or "corrective" jus-tice demands that the "equality" of the previous relationship of private individuals with one another be exactly restored: to each according to what he had. When, however, it is a question of the distribution of common property or public benefits, the shares should bear the same proportion to one another as did the original

---

[20]Robinson, *op. cit.*, p. 65.

contributions. "For if the persons are not equal they must not have equal shares; in fact this is the very source of all the quarreling and wrangling in the world, when either they who are equal have and get awarded to them things not equal, or being not equal those things which are equal."[21] "Distributive" justice takes account of the actual proportionate inequalities of men: to each according to his contribution, according to his "stake in the community."

In contrast, the biblical notion of justice may be summed up in the principle: To each according to the measure of his real need, not because of anything human reason can discern inherent in the needy, but because his need alone is the measure of God's righteousness toward him. Such justice or righteousness is primarily neither "corrective" nor "distributive," as in the Greek view, but "redemptive," with special bias in favor of the helpless who can contribute nothing at all and are in fact "due" nothing. Justice does not depend upon a person's stake in the community. To the contrary, his stake in the community, the very fact that, although an alien or a forgotten man, he comes in effect to belong or still belongs to the community, this depends on "justice" being done. Such righteousness does not derive its nature from some already existing proportionate connection individuals have with one another in view of some common good. There took place, of course, a good deal of corrective justice "in the gate," where justice was meted out in Israel. There was also much concern through laws regulating the inheritance of family property to maintain every family's stake in the community. Still biblical justice was never primarily concerned with devising some method or other for calculating what is a man's "due."

The tradition of redemptive justice patterned after the prototype of divine justice Jesus carries on, completing the tendency of "justice" to topple over into benevolence, fulfilling the funda-

---

[21]*Nicomachean Ethics*, 1131a (Everyman ed., p. 107). Emil Brunner (*op. cit.*, Part I) uses a thoroughly Christianized form of Aristotle's "distributive justice" when he calculates "what is due" the heavy laborer, the expectant mother, or the little old crippled lady standing in line. Aristotle puts the stress on inequality of *contribution* in determining what is just, while for Brunner the accent falls on inequality of *need* and *difference*, not superiority, of function.

mental idea in the religious ethics of the Old Testament yet entirely nullifying the law. "When Jesus said 'Give to him who begs of thee, and do not turn away from him who wants to borrow from thee' (Matt. 5:42), it is . . . but an exact summary of what [the Jews] laid down as prescribed by divine law. To lend to a would-be borrower is not optional but obligatory, and no less obligatory to give to the poor according to the measure of his need and to the ability of the giver."[22] Indeed, Jesus seems to have overturned the normal human sense of justice (the law written on the heart) and to have approved what Aristotle called "the very source of all the quarreling and wrangling in the world," when he condemned the begrudging of generosity and the grumbling protests of laborers who had worked all day long in the vineyard, who bore the burden of the day and the scorching heat, and who quite naturally objected when they received no more wages than those who worked for only one hour in the cool of the evening (Matt. 20:1–16): they, being not equal, received equal pay.

This idea of justice or righteousness, which strictly speaking never first occurred to the mind of any man but represents in human thought a prolongation of the righteousness of God, found expression in moral theology during the Middle Ages in a way that must seem alien to all modern notions of basing justice on the natural rights of man and not on any supernatural measure. Almsgiving was not then considered a special deed of "charity" but a "due" part of "justice"; failure to give alms to the poor meant more than a refusal of benevolence, it was a violation of justice, the sort of justice "due *to be given*" from the controlling love of Christ to any one in need. Consequently medieval Christian theologians justified "theft" in cases of dire distress when any one who had a superfluity of goods refused to act "justly." A poor man who took by stealth or force what he and his family very greatly needed was not utterly condemned as a thief, although such an act by itself could not rightly or altogether restore

---

[22]G. F. Moore, *Judaism in the First Centuries of the Christian Era: The Age of the Tannaim*, Harvard University Press, II, 168 (1927).

the justice which in the first place should have been practiced. This viewpoint in medieval moral theology was quite in line with the teaching of Jesus in which he used almsgiving as an illustration of practicing piety [δικαιοσύνην, "righteousness," "justice"] before men (Matt. 6:1). Wherever and whenever it appears, the biblical conception of righteousness strikes contrast and awakes conflict with ordinary notions of justice on account of essentially "how much more" (Matt. 7:11, Luke 11:13) it does than others.

In line with the standpoint of the Bible generally, Jesus' conception of the righteousness required of men was cut to fit his understanding of God's love. ". . . I say to you, Love your enemies and pray for those who persecute you, so that you may be sons of your Father who is in heaven, for he makes his sun rise on the evil and on the good, and sends rain on the just and on the unjust. . . . You, therefore, must be perfect, as your heavenly Father is perfect" (Matt. 5:44, 45, 48). These words have been translated, "Be therefore all-including (in your good will), even as your heavenly Father includes all."[23] Since numerical inclusiveness is not the main point, it would be more in rapport with the immediate context to render them, "Be therefore entirely indifferent to the qualities of character in particular men which usually elicit preference or lack of preference for them"; or, what is the same thing, "Be therefore completely self-giving and redemptive in any single case of your good will, even as your heavenly Father disinterestedly cares for all." Such love finds the neighbor out and acts righteously toward him. In any case, we see here plainly the source of the strenuous perfectionism in the teachings of Jesus, the origin and foundation of love so absolutely free as his, yet so absolutely demanding.

In passing beyond Jesus to the first Christians, we have only to notice, as far as ethics is concerned, that Jesus has become "the righteousness of God" for them. Instead of simply saying "the God of Abraham, Isaac, and Jacob, the God of Moses and the covenant," Christians add a significant reference to "the God and Father of our Lord and Savior Jesus Christ." In this sense, Chris-

[23]C. C. Torrey, *The Four Gospels: A New Translation,* Harpers, 1933.

tian ethics and Christian political theory must be decisively and
entirely Christocentric. No one who thinks biblically of "the righteousness of God" and also thinks Christianly of Jesus Christ as
the righteousness of God can possibly imagine that this has reference only, or even mainly, to some matters of importance simply
for otherworldly or "interstitial" salvation. Jesus Christ was either
not the *righteousness* of God or *not* the righteousness *of God* or
else he counts for more than love "between the lines" or among
the ruins.

Jesus Christ must be kept at the heart of all Christian thinking about justice—and precisely that sort of justice which should
prevail in the "world of systems," in this world and not some
other. On this there can be no variation, as long as he discloses
the "righteousness of God" to men. Christians have varied, of
course, in ways of formulating their ideas about Christ as God's
righteousness. Yet for all their own different theologies, New
Testament authors were driven with remarkable unanimity to
affirm the lordship of Christ. This means that no limitation can be
put upon the scope of his rule. "Jesus Christ is Lord" (Phil. 2:10),
"the image of the invisible God, the first born of all creation,
for in him all things were created, in heaven and on earth, visible
and invisible, whether thrones or dominions or principalities or
authorities—all things were created through him and for him. He
is before all things, and in him all things hold together" (Col.
1:15–17), "all things were made through him, and without him
was not anything made that was made" (John 1:3). How can the
state and human justice know nothing of love, if in him *all* things
hold together? The kingship of Christ (Luther) demands the
assertion and the acknowledgment of his righteousness or justice
as the sovereign rule of no less than the whole of life and instant
practice of the same (though we have yet to see what this may
mean in actual practice). Otherwise we deny his lordship, which
was not the covenant we were commanded. "Is not this how to
know me?"—to commit no wrong or violence against the alien
Arabs resident in the land of Israeli, to defend the cause of the
poor and needy and "second-class citizens" in this "Christian"

land, to deliver the despoiled from the hands of the oppressor? (Jer. 22:3, 15–16). Is not this the cause justice should serve? Men and nations in the present day in whose memory the Hebrew-Christian ethical heritage still lives have special responsibility before God not simply for doing justice but for the *kind* of justice they do.

> "You only have I known, of all the families of the earth";
> Therefore will I punish you for all your wrongdoing (Amos 3:2).

To whom more has been given, of them more is required.

In this sense, the religious ethic of St. Paul was entirely Christo-centric. This means that he believed such love as he describes in I Corinthians 13 would have been unknown except for Jesus Christ and degrees of love in Christians derivative from him as gifts of his Spirit. What precisely was it about Jesus Christ that Paul considered so exemplary and so revealing? Paul knew a good deal, we may suppose, about the life of the historic Jesus, and was in a position to ascertain any additional information about his activities he might have judged important for a Christian to know. Yet he did not take much stock in emulating any of the good deeds of Jesus, taken in isolation, not even his final martyr's death. Jesus' entire life was one of complete humility, self-abasement, and love which sought not its own. Nevertheless Paul attached no great importance to any one of Jesus' deeds of love or to all of them together or to his last sacrificial act. It is true that in Paul's writings, religious "revivalists" can find as much reason for singing hymns about "being saved" by the humility and obedience of Jesus as by his "blood" or "the cross"; his final self-sacrifice was simply of a piece with his humility and for him obedience went as far as death. All this is properly understood only when we see that, according to Paul, the meaning of Jesus' exemplary deeds of love, even his death on the cross, was caught up in a cosmic event of infinitely greater significance. In the last analysis the significant thing for Paul was not what kind of man Jesus was or even what sort of death came to him. The significance of these elements of Jesus' human life and death was included without loss in an event of much greater import; the fact that the pre-existent Christ became a man at all was the thing of cosmic-historical importance for human salvation; this was the true prototype of divine-Christian love.

> Have this mind among yourselves, which you have in Christ Jesus, who, though he was in the form of God, did not count equality with God a thing to be grasped, but emptied himself, taking the form of a servant, being born in the likeness of men. And being found in human form he humbled himself and became obedient unto death, even death on a cross. Therefore, God has highly exalted him and bestowed on him the name which is above every name, that at the name of Jesus every knee should bow . . . and every tongue confess that Jesus Christ is Lord . . . (Phil. 2:5–10).

Of course, the kind of man who was "the Jesus of history" entirely accords with the startling fact that the Christ became a man at all. Jesus' lifetime of humility and obedience was simply a logical continuation of the great act of self-emptying love by which alone the Christ could become any sort of man. His life was but an extension into human history of a line started in eternity going down toward man. When that line came within the range of human visibility, it was an indication of its original "slope" that instead of coming as the highest man the Christ came as the lowliest, that "the Jesus of history" loved men and gave up all self-concern for their sakes, that he died not with acclaim as a hero but with mockery as a criminal. For Paul the nature and intensity of divine love for man should be measured by the divine "stoop" or "condescension" necessary for the Christ, who did not count equality with God a thing to be grasped, to make himself available to man, and of course as this sort of man. This, then, is the "mind which you have in Christ Jesus" which Paul enjoins Christians to have among themselves. God's love was manifested not just in this or that act of kindness which Jesus performed, or all of them together, but in that while men were still sinners Christ gave up all glory for himself and died for them. Christian morality means extending the life of Jesus by imitating him in our lives, yet it means this only because his life itself was a prolongation visible "in the flesh" of the humility of Christ and of the God who put him forward.

Theological statements may differ from this *kenotic* (self-emptying) view of Paul's, and doubtless will continue to vary from age to age. In and through them all, however, distinctively Christian love will always be grounded in some account of the divine condescension toward men, in the conviction that Jesus was the Word of God now in flesh appearing, that he was the act of God. Indeed, there are some not unimportant differences in theological formulation within the New Testament itself. "This is my commandment, that you love one another as I have loved you" is interpreted by the gospel and letters of John in terms of the verse, "Greater love has no man than this, that a man lay down his life *for his friends*" (John 15:12, 13). With this as proto-typal divine love, it is not surprising that Christian love in the letters of John suffers some in-group limitation, becoming essen-tially "love *for the brethren*," preferential love among Christians. In contrast, the synoptic gospels and Paul portray a "greater," or at least a decisively different, love than this. "While we were yet helpless, at the right time Christ died *for the ungodly*. Why, one will hardly die for a righteous man—though perhaps for a good man one will dare even to die. But God shows his love for us in that *while we were yet sinners* Christ died for us . . . *while we were enemies* we were reconciled to God" (Rom. 5:6–8, 10). With this as prototypal divine love, then as a consequence love for the helpless, the quite ungodly, the wholly unrighteous, those who are still sinners, and love for the enemy, become essential determinants in the nature of Christian love, in comparison with which Johannine "brotherly love" perhaps admits too close simi-larity with Aristotle's friendship for the sake of the good. As Paul points out, "Perhaps for a good man one will dare even to die"; and, as Aristotle allows, the friend of a friendly and righteous man will doubtless "give himself the greater good" of lavishing many less worthy goods upon his friend, perhaps even going so far as to die for him.[24]

[24]*Nicomachean Ethics*, 1169a.

Differences in New Testament theology, however, should not be emphasized, since in getting to know the origin, and more decisively the meaning, of Christian love the important point to see is the unanimity with which men of the Bible applied a supernatural measure to all obedient love. How to care for the resident alien is known from God's care of the sojourners in Egypt; the meaning of human justice from the redemptive righteousness of God; how to be perfect from God's care for the just and unjust, the good and evil alike; the meaning of Christian love by decisive reference to the controlling love of Christ (II Cor. 5:14).

Using the measure of divine love inverts self-love and discovers the neighbor. Not that we should do to others as we would be done by, or merely love our neighbors as ourselves (in case this standard drawn from man himself has uncertain meaning or seems to lack steadfastness or singlemindedness), but that we should love our brothers as Christ who laid down his life for his friends and for those predestined to be his disciples (the Johannine writings) or love our neighbors as Christ who, while men were yet sinners and his enemies, for their sakes emptied himself of all self-concern and himself did not grasp at being equal to God (Paul)—this is the principle *par excellence* of Christian ethics. Christian love is: to be a Christ to our neighbors (Luther). John Wesley first describes the "regenerate" man as one who loves his neighbor as himself, yet he instantly goes on to declare: "Nay, our Lord hath expressed it still more strongly, teaching us to love one another even as He hath loved us. Accordingly the commandment written in the hearts of those that love God is no other than this, 'As I have loved you, so love ye one another.' Now 'herein perceive we the love of God, in that he laid down his life for us.' 'We ought,' then, as the apostle justly infers, 'to lay down our lives for the brethren.' If we feel ourselves ready to do this then do we truly love our neighbor."[25]

Christocentric ethics stems, then, from some account of the "divinity" of Christ. Discussion of this doctrine always gets off on

---

[25]Sermon XVIII, pt. iv, sec. 3. (Thomas Jackson edition of *The Works of the Reverend John Wesley*, 3rd ed., 14 vols. London: Wesleyan-Methodist Book-Room, 1831.)

the wrong foot if it be imagined that here the issue turns on some extraordinary statement about Jesus' manhood. So far at least as concerns ethics, the real point is a revolutionary assertion about the true nature of divinity. Ordinarily it is supposed that the way to obtain a more and more perfect conception of the divine nature is to add on as much power as possible, as much impeccable self-sufficiency, as much imperturbable sovereignty, as much unqualified majesty. The Greeks had this notion of divinity in mind when they denied that God could love anything less than himself, and Nietzsche when he said, "If there were a God I could not endure not being he."

However, from a Christian point of view it is possible to think of God too highly, for Christ reverses all we expect Highness to be; the God who put him forward is one whose "grace" is only his mercy and forgiveness. Of him we cannot think too lowly. Nietzsche could not have endured being this downgoing, giving-over sort of God; indeed, living men can hardly bear being his disciples. Such radical reversal of ordinary conceptions of the divine nature follows from the basic conviction that Christ is clue to knowledge of God. Christianity does not say, "Behold the Christ, half-God, half-man, Behold glorious strength thinly disguised, Behold Superman in a business suit, Behold the majestic God you know already in a peasant's tunic." Instead the New Testament proclaims, "Behold weakness, Behold divinity divine enough to abandon divinity, Behold majesty secure enough to proceed un-majestically, Behold strength strong enough to become weakness, goodness good enough to be unmindful of its own reputation, Behold love plenteous enough to give and take not again." Some men who have seen clearly what is involved in this conviction of the Christhood of divinity have turned from it in horror. Thus, Friedrich Nietzsche called the Christian idea of God "the record god up to this time" in which "suddenly we stand before that paradoxical and awful expedient, through which a tortured humanity has found a temporary alleviation, that stroke of genius called Christianity: God personally immolating himself for the debt of man . . . the creditor playing scapegoat for his

debtor, from *love* (can you believe it?), from love of his debtor!
. . . You already guess it," Nietzsche continues, "I do not like
the 'New Testament'; it almost upsets me that I stand so isolated
in my taste so far as concerns this valued, this over-valued Scripture; the taste of two thousand years is against me; but what boots
it!"[26] Fewer perhaps than Nietzsche thought have had their religious faith and their moral behavior profoundly determined by
reference to the measure of "the righteousness of God" in Christ.

Nevertheless, first for their understanding of God, then for their
understanding of the nature of obedient love, Christians look to

> That Always-Opposite which is the whole subject
> Of our not-knowing, yet from no necessity
> Condescended to exist and to suffer death
> And, scorned on a scaffold, ensconced in His life
> The human household.[27]

Christian ethics stands therefore in decisive relation to Jesus Christ
for the strenuous measure taken of human obligation. As a consequence, Christocentric ethics contrasts both with humanism's
cutting the pattern to fit man and also with any religious or mystical ethics which may indeed be theocentric and pious enough
but in a general or cosmic sense not historically related to this
particular man, Christ Jesus. Christian ethics necessarily means
a religious ethics "about" Jesus irreducible to the so-called "simple" religious ethics "of" Jesus. The Christian, indeed, is consistently more Christocentric, considerably less merely theocentric,
in his religious and ethical outlook than was Jesus himself.

> The supreme tribute to Jesus' own humility is that no one can
> answer the question, "What did Jesus think of himself?" . . .
> There is only one inescapable conclusion. This is that Jesus was
> not concerned to make people know what he was, and the reason
> is that he was almost completely dominated by the desire to
> make known to the people what the will of God was and what
> God wanted done. This does tell us something about what Jesus
> thought of himself. It tells us clearly that he thought less of him-

[26] *The Genealogy of Morals*, II, 20, 21; III, 22.
[27] W. H. Auden, *The Age of Anxiety*, Random House, 1947, p. 137.

self than he thought of God. This is the basis for his humility. He thought much of God.[28]

Unquestionably this was true of Jesus. Unquestionably it is *not* true of the Christian. In "imitating Christ" one thing the Christian never attempts: he never imitates the fact that Jesus had no Christ to imitate. In imitating certain of the saints, St. Francis for example, one thing the Christian never forgets: to imitate in him his imitation of Christ.

II. THE KINGDOM OF GOD IN THE TEACHINGS OF JESUS

We have seen that Jesus' conception of the righteousness required of men was cut to fit his understanding of God's love, his sending rain on the just and unjust and making the sun rise on the evil and the good. Jesus' familiar teaching about anxiety provides another illustration of how an attitude disciples are asked, and enabled, to cultivate has origin and foundation in God's constant, indiscriminate care for his creatures.

> Therefore I tell you, do not be anxious about your life, what you shall eat or what you shall drink, nor about your body, what you shall put on. Is not life more than food, and the body more than clothing? Look at the birds of the air; they neither sow nor reap nor gather into barns, and yet your heavenly Father feeds them. Are you not of more value than they? And which of you by being anxious can add one cubit to his span of life? And why be anxious about clothing? Consider the lilies of the field, how they grow; they neither toil nor spin; yet I tell you, even Solomon in all his glory was not arrayed like one of these. But if God so clothes the grass of the field, which today is alive and tomorrow is thrown into the oven, will he not much more clothe you, O men of little faith? Therefore do not be anxious . . . (Matt. 6:25–31).

Although the foregoing passage concludes with the words, "But seek first his kingdom and his righteousness and all these things

[28]E. C. Colwell, *An Approach to the Teachings of Jesus,* Abingdon-Cokesbury Press, 1947, pp. 72–75.

shall be yours as well" (Matt. 6:33), the meaning of the teaching may be sufficiently understood as grounded in the divine righteousness, the present universal reign of God's love where it is largely unchallenged in physical nature. It is true the kingdom of God and the love of God are not ultimately separable in defining what is right for man. Nevertheless, certain of the teachings of Jesus have reference mainly to God's love, others to God's kingdom. It is significant that the two requirements, non-preferential love and "Do not be anxious," contained in these largely non-eschatological teachings are surely as strenuous as any of the more eschatological teachings, now to be considered, whose meaning is in some sense measured by reference to the impending end (*eschaton*) of the present age of human history and the coming kingdom of God.

Typical of Jesus' eschatological teachings is his other saying about anxiety. Of anxiety, indeed, more must be said; for,

> While far and near a fioritura
> Of brooks and blackbirds bravely struck the
> International note with no sense
> Of historical truth, of time meaning
> Once and for all, and my watch stuttered:—
> Many have perished; more will.[1]

When with the poet men turn from brooks and blackbirds, from Jesus' thought of rainfall and sunshine, from viewing the birds of the air and the lilies and grass of the field, turning from physical nature where in general "every prospect pleases, and only man is vile," when instead they begin to consider happenings in human history, the tyrannical, embattled kingdoms of this world, if then men are not to be overcome by anxiety there must be some other ground for faith than the present extent or reign of God's love in nature. Therefore Jesus said, "Fear not, little flock, for it is your Father's good pleasure to give you the kingdom" (Luke 12:32). This second injunction not to be anxious has its source and ground in Jesus' conviction regarding the coming reign of love in God's kingdom.

[1] W. H. Auden, *op. cit.*, p. 13.

Jesus held a quite Jewish view of the *nature* of the kingdom of God and a quite apocalyptic view of the *manner* of the kingdom's coming. The kingdom of God was not a "heaven" for immortal, disembodied souls, nor was it an inner spiritual quality of life men were to cultivate. Jesus opened his mission, calling men to repentance, saying, "The time is fulfilled, and the kingdom of God is at hand; repent and believe the gospel" (Mark 1:15). In this teaching, repentance depends on the kingdom; the kingdom in no sense depends on man's repentance. Other subjective attitudes of which Jesus spoke, in the Beatitudes for example, and the absolute obedience and singleness of mind he commanded, were necessary in preparation for the kingdom. The kingdom itself was quite objective; it was coming no matter what were men's attitudes or what they did.

The Beatitudes are therefore thoroughly eschatological (Matt. 5:3–12; Luke 6:20–23). Jesus was not so naïve as to suppose that by the *power* of their meekness the meek would sooner or later inherit the earth. To be realistic about the forces which triumph in the present age, if the meek ever inherit the earth, the not-so-meek would promptly take it away from them. Meekness and inheriting the earth are entirely separate matters; only the approaching kingdom brings them into connection. God's power guarantees the inheritance of the earth to the meek, and their continuation in it. "Blessed are those who hunger and thirst for righteousness" is not simply a sage saying, to the effect that people who earnestly desire righteousness are thereby employing the device best calculated to attain it. This may be so, but Jesus' teaching has altogether another meaning: Blessed are those who hunger and thirst for the coming triumph of the righteous cause, for they shall be satisfied. In every case, the blessing announced should be understood as a *prediction* depending entirely upon the occurrence of the eschatological event indicated by the final words of the Beatitude. "Blessed are the poor in spirit, for theirs is the kingdom of heaven; Blessed are those who mourn, for they shall be comforted; Blessed are the merciful, for they shall obtain mercy; Blessed are those who are persecuted for righteousness' sake, for theirs is the kingdom of heaven" (Matt. 5:3, 4, 7, 10). "Blessed are you poor, for yours is the kingdom of God; Blessed are you that hunger now, for you shall be satisfied; Blessed are you that weep now, for you shall laugh" (Luke 6:20, 21). Whether men now suffer from a physical or a spiritual hunger, hungering itself indicates only their need and readiness for the kingdom; God's kingdom alone brings the added blessing of satisfaction. No more than "losing life" are the Beatitudes directives for gaining future self-realization in the normal development of events; events are not expected to be what men call "normal," else the realization might not follow. Evidently, then, Jesus' notion of the kingdom of God, along with his understanding of God's love, were allied, yet somewhat dual, supernatural sources of his view of the absolute righteousness demanded of men.

The present decision and action of men affect only whether they shall be blessed or woeful in the days of the kingdom. Jesus seems to have eliminated from his view of the approaching end-time such notions, prevalent in his day, as a final messianic war between the forces of Satan and the angelic legions of the Son of Man. In its place he pictured a final judgment and the consignment of tares to a great conflagration. Nor was he concerned with elaborate visionary schemes for specifying in detail, if somewhat mysteriously, the time and manner of the kingdom's coming. Nevertheless, when he dismissed such speculation with the words, "But of that day and hour no one knows, not even the angels in heaven, nor the Son, but the Father only" (Matt. 24:36), he could have meant to say only that no one knows exactly when *in this or at most the next generation* the kingdom of God will finally appear. Although in these and other respects what sort of apocalyptic expectation Jesus held may still perhaps be discussed, it is not now seriously doubted that his belief was of this general type. Jesus confidently expected that God would soon, suddenly, and catastrophically intervene to disrupt the order of life prevailing in this present age and to inaugurate by his own power alone a kingdom of righteousness.

Jesus stressed *gradualness* only with respect to the *proclamation* of the kingdom's coming and the different hold the message would take on the minds of men (Parable of the Soils and the Sower). He never hoped to "evangelize the world in this generation," for even the proclamation of the message of the kingdom, which must proceed by stages and under local limitations, cannot move fast enough to avoid being overtaken by the in-breaking kingdom itself. Sending his disciples out on a missionary journey, he told them to travel light and, "When they persecute you in one town, flee to the next; for truly, I say to you, you will not have gone through all the towns of Israel, before the Son of man comes" (Matt. 10:23). To a whole multitude of people he announced, "Truly, I say to you, there are some standing here who will not taste death before they see the kingdom of God come with power" (Mark 9:1; *cf.* Matt. 16:28 and Luke 9:27). When he said, "The kingdom of God is not coming with signs to be observed," he meant not that the kingdom would be invisible or spiritual in its nature but that it would come altogether too swiftly to be predicted by soothsayers or augurers reading the entrails of fowl or other signs. ". . . Nor will they say, 'Lo, here it is!' or 'there!' for behold, the kingdom of God is *in the midst* of you." That is to say, even while men are reading the signs the kingdom will be upon them, already in their midst; these words, addressed to the Pharisees, certainly cannot possibly mean "The kingdom of God is *within* you" as an inner spiritual condition. Moreover, the gospel of Luke associates this teaching with another warning, probably spoken by Jesus on some other occasion, against predicting the kingdom's coming or its location "here" or "there." Significantly Jesus concludes this second saying with an image which vividly combines entire objectivity with catastrophic suddenness: "For as the lightning flashes and lights up the sky from one side to the other, so will the Son of man be in his day" (Luke 17:20–24).

If Jesus had wished to emphasize the gradualness of the coming of the kingdom, a process such as the aging of wine or the seasoning of wood over the years rather than the leavening of dough in a few hours, and the development of some seed such as the oak rather than the mustard plant which rushes up to maturity in a single season, would have been the subjects of his parables. What these parables teach (and a parable should be distinguished from an allegory by its having only a *single* point) is that the kingdom-power is even now *secretly* operating.[2] In the most ancient and reliable account of the Last Supper, Jesus gave bread and wine to his disciples, himself not eating or drinking, saying, ". . . For I tell you that from now on I shall not drink of the fruit of the vine until the kingdom of God comes" (Luke 22:18).[3] No wonder, then, that as Jesus set his face toward Jerusalem his disciples (instructed now in almost all the teachings they ever heard from Jesus' lips) "supposed that the kingdom of God was to appear immediately" (Luke 19:11). Without attempting to resolve all uncertainties which surround any attempt to reconstruct the whole of Jesus' belief, beyond question a quite Jewish view of the objective, social *nature* of the kingdom and a quite apocalyptic view of the *manner* of its coming must be presupposed as we now go on to inquire: What was the relationship between his kingdom-expectation and his ethical teaching?

In general, there have been three approaches taken to the question of the validity of Jesus' strenuous ethic acknowledged to be fully eschatological. Some scholars, of whom Albert Schweitzer is foremost, interpret Jesus' teachings as an "interim ethic," which is to say, they were valid for the short interval of time between the present and the expected kingdom (understood as wholly future, not at all present), valid, indeed, because of the shortness of the interval still to pass before the kingdom comes. Against both the understanding of the kingdom and the interpretation of Jesus' teachings contained in this viewpoint objec-

[2]*Cf.* E. F. Scott, *The Kingdom of God in the New Testament*, Macmillan, 1931, p. 71. Alternatively these parables may be interpreted as stressing the contrast between "apparently insignificant littleness" and "great consummations" (H. E. Fosdick, *The Man from Nazareth*, Harper, 1949, p. 170, and *cf.* Martin Dibelius, *Jesus*, Westminster, 1949, p. 68). In no case can it be supposed that gradual growth was Jesus' point.

[3]*Cf.* Rudolph Otto, *The Kingdom of God and the Son of Man*, transl. by Floyd V. Filson and Bertram Lee Woolf, Lutterworth, revised ed. 1943, pp. 265 ff.

tion can be raised. It is strange that the term "consistent" eschatology should have been applied to this position, for the only consistently eschatological understanding of the kingdom holds it to be thoroughly eschatological *but not altogether future.* Jesus' idea of the kingdom was "a case of eviction well under way."[4] As the blade of a plow sends rifts in the earth ahead of where it is, so the future kingdom already has brought about a division within every family or existing community and a crisis of decision for every individual in the present age. Jesus' loosening the sway of demon and disease manifested the effective, present power of the coming kingdom; his teachings likewise are to be understood as in some sense present demands of the kingdom of God. The teachings of Jesus about non-resisting, unclaiming love surely contain some description of the nature of relationships among men in the future kingdom itself; if so, these teachings have validity beyond the interim. Moreover, Schweitzer's own career has surely been motivated by devotion to Christ as much as by "reverence for life"; his whole life indicates his personal conviction that Jesus' teachings have bearing on the conduct even of a man who no longer believes himself to be living within the interim in which they were first borne in upon the mind of man. The striking words with which Schweitzer concludes his great work, *The Quest of the Historical Jesus,* emphasize the continuing significance of Jesus for ethics:

> He comes to us as One unknown, without a name, as of old, by the lakeside, He came to those who knew Him not. He speaks to us the same word: "Follow thou me!" and sets us to the tasks which He has to fulfill for our time. He commands. And to those who obey Him, whether they be wise or simple, He will reveal Himself in the toils, the conflicts, the sufferings which they shall pass through in His fellowship. . . .[5]

Other scholars have said that the radical ethic of Jesus has validity for the future kingdom only, and that his teaching will become fully applicable only when the kingdom of God has

[4]Amos Wilder, *op. cit.,* p. 82.
[5]Macmillan, 1948, p. 401.

been fully established. If Schweitzer and his school are correct, then the time for practicing this ethic has gone with the rejection of literal apocalypticism and "the Sermon on the Mount is a document of the past—and nothing more. Or—and this is the second explanation—its time will come and we are not yet in the right position to be true Christians."[6] Short shrift may be made of this "kingdom ethic" interpretation. Jesus' teachings obviously were intended to apply in a world in which there is striking, hostility, persecution, and oppression; not in the kingdom only, where there will presumably be no more blows on the cheek, no more impression into military service, nor need for borrowing.

By criticism, then, of the two foregoing viewpoints, it seems that in some manner or other claim for the validity of Jesus' extreme teaching must be extended to include not only life during the interim and not only in the kingdom, but both. Moreover, a Christian today must ask: Do not the teachings of Jesus contain some part of God's requirement upon men who no longer in any vivid or significant sense share the primitive perspective of apocalypse? Consequently a third answer to the question of validity almost suggests itself, and a number of interpreters of the New Testament affirm that the strenuous ethic of Jesus, generated in its extremity by apocalyptic expectation, reveals an absolute ethic valid always. However, they have sometimes put forward this point of view by sleight of hand, intended, it seems, to disguise or minimize the nature and the importance of Jesus' apocalyptic expectation, blurring the world of difference between the outlook of the historical, synoptic gospels and the "spiritualized" and already "realized eschatology" of the gospel of John. These interpreters speak of an esoteric "intuition" of God's "absolute demands" moment by moment, without giving these demands much content; or else they verge on transforming the ethics of Jesus into an "eternal idea" more appropriate to the ahistorical Greek temper.

Jesus' eschatological teachings (and they comprise the *whole*

[6]Martin Dibelius, *The Sermon on the Mount*, Scribners, 1940, p. 12.

of his teachings with a few exceptions, such as Jesus' parables in Luke 15 and his beautiful words about the lilies and the birds and about God's indiscriminate rainfall and sunshine) may be divided into two groups. The first includes teachings in which the effect of Jesus' kingdom-expectation may be seen mainly in their greater *urgency* or stepped-up *intensity,* but whose essential meaning may be translated without great loss into more moderate statements. When, along with Jewish and many other teachers of morality, Jesus condemned anger as well as murder, he did not speak calmly as if he were merely expressing some eternal truth.

> But I say to you that everyone who is angry with his brother shall be liable to judgment; whoever insults his brother shall be liable to the council, and whoever says, "You fool!" shall be liable to the hell of fire. . . . Make friends quickly with your accuser, while you are going with him to court, lest your accuser hand you over to the judge and the judge to the guard, and you be put in prison; truly, I say to you, you will never get out till you have paid the last penny (Matt. 5:22, 25, 26).

When, along with Jewish and many other teachers of morality, Jesus condemned lustful thoughts, he added:

> If your right eye causes you to sin, pluck it out and throw it away; it is better that you lose one of your members than that your whole body be thrown into hell. And if your right hand causes you to sin, cut it off and throw it away; it is better that you lose one of your members than that your whole body go to hell (Matt. 5:29, 30).

Jesus required radical separation between a man and any offending member; between a man and his possessions, willingness to sell all and give to the poor. He also required radical separation of a disciple from bondage to ordinary family responsibilities: following Jesus means loving him more than parents or children, even by comparison *hating* them. Decision must also be unwavering: "No one who puts his hand to the plow and looks back is fit for the kingdom of God" (Luke 9:62).

Now, of course, these teachings gain urgency and intensity from their eschatological background. Any one who is of a mind to do so, however, can translate them out of their mother tongue without much loss of meaning: Be not angry, avoid inward lust, decide once and for all time, with singleness of purpose, for some cause allegiance to which will be superior to all other duties and all other goods. For these moral maxims a degree of obvious and universal validity may be claimed. Jesus' two teachings on anxiety have about the same ethical significance; although one is primarily eschatological, the other not, the one is no more extreme than the other; this teaching, then, may be stated in non-eschatological terms without change of meaning.

Jesus' teaching and practice regarding observance of the sabbath were also altogether eschatological. The coming kingdom of God, he believed, would not likely pay attention to the calendar or the time of day. The Son of man may come on the sabbath as likely as on any other day, before sunset as likely as after a new day has begun, for, as Jesus said, "the Son of man is lord even of the sabbath" (Mark 2:28). The present age even now witnesses the coming triumph of God's supernatural Messiah whenever any of the power of disease or demon is loosened. "If it is by the spirit of God that I cast out demons then the kingdom of God has come upon you" (Matt. 12:28). Just as the Son of man will not wait for the sabbath to pass, so even now the cure of human affliction ought not be delayed. Even long-standing troubles which, because of their chronic nature, might in normal times wait until tomorrow for curing, even these succumb to the present operation of God's power; his kingdom is not tarrying. "And ought not this woman, a daughter of Abraham whom Satan bound for eighteen years, be loosed from this bond on the sabbath day?" (Luke 13:16). The Jewish authorities, therefore, were actually on the side of Satan. On behalf of previous revelation of God's will, they, with the demons, resisted God's present activity and his rapidly increasing assumption of power over history and the kingdoms of this world. Wait, Lord, they said, not yet, not until the sabbath has passed!

Yet Jesus' teaching concerning the sabbath may be translated from its original eschatological setting and language without any change or loss of what this means for morality. Utter obedience to God in prompt recognition of his lordship even over the sabbath proves quite equivalent to loving one's neighbor in such fashion as to ignore the claims made on behalf of other forms of righteousness: "The sabbath was made for man, not man for the sabbath." Love for neighbor comprises the full meaning of absolute, unhesitating obedience to God. Instant obedience equals perfect love. As we shall see at greater length in Chapter Two, the ethical principle which summarizes Jesus' teaching and practice in relation to the law of sabbath observance may be stated in general, non-eschatological terms: the infinite superiority of neighbor-need in comparison with legal righteousness in determining the meaning of human obligation. The expression "obedient love" points to the religious (eschatological) setting as well as to the ethical attitude fundamental in Jesus' outlook. This means that instantaneous, total obedience to the demands of God's reign and perfect love for man are in fact precisely the same thing. Obedience means no more than love and love fulfills every legitimate obedience. And as every one knows, this general principle that the sabbath is made for man (stated so forcefully and with such urgency by Jesus) may be defended as an obvious truth apart from its eschatological sanction.

The second group of eschatological teachings, however, are those whose very *content* and *meaning*, not simply the urgency associated with them, show the affect of Jesus' kingdom-expectation. These "strenuous" teachings comprise all those vivid injunctions, so distinctive of Jesus, to non-resisting, unclaiming love, overflowing good even for an enemy, unlimited forgiveness for every offense, giving to every need, unconditional lending to him who would borrow. Jesus, of course, said quite the same thing when considering the lilies and the birds and the righteousness of God through sunshine and shower; and throughout the Bible men are slanted in the direction of redemptive love where no love is due—in Hosea, for example. Still the extremity of Jesus' teachings cannot be denied and must be faced. When considering history and the affairs of men it would hardly first occur to the mind of any man to recommend these sayings as the truth, except with eschatological backing. When asked whether kindness should be returned for injury, Confucius replied, quite reasonably, "With what then would you recompense kindness? Recompense injury with justice and recompense kindness with kindness."[7] The radical content of Jesus' strenuous sayings depends, it seems, on his apocalyptic expectation. As a consequence they cannot be translated from their mother tongue without danger of serious loss of meaning. We cannot, for example, recommend non-resistance or returning good for evil as obvious to the degree in which anger or impure thoughts or even anxiety may be discouraged among men and sabbath observances set aside. Therefore, non-resistance has frequently first been turned into non-violent *resistance,* and this then generalized to fit perhaps any age or circumstance. Jesus' original teaching about non-resistance seems in contrast to suit only an apocalyptic perspective. The least that needs to be said is that there are crucial teachings of Jesus whose meaning has been so decisively affected by his kingdom-expectation that they can be torn from their context only at great peril of complete misunderstanding or with exceeding carefulness to conserve their original meaning. Persons who question the validity of the ethics of Jesus have these teachings mainly in mind.

III. IN WHAT WAY, THEN, ARE THE TEACHINGS OF JESUS VALID?

What is needed is a way of affirming the validity of Jesus' strenuous teachings always and under every circumstance, a way, indeed, for specifying the degree and, if need be, the functional limitation of their validity, which at the same time says right out loud that most Christians today diverge from the mind of Jesus on a matter that was a large and controlling element in his own thinking. This has to be said, so let it be said forthrightly: few contemporary Christians accept the kind of kingdom-expectation Jesus considered of central importance, and rightly they do

[7]*Analects,* Bk. XIV.

not. Literal eschatological belief in the end of history, Rauschenbusch remarked, is nowadays "usually loved in inverse proportion to the square of the mental diameter of those who do the
loving."[1] Of course, it may be contended that apocalypticism is
a better myth than the idea of progress prevalent since the eigh-
teenth century, and New Testament eschatology at least permits a man to recognize a catastrophe when he sees one rather
than dying in his procrustean bed of development with his illu-
sions on. There has taken place in our time a revival of highly
sophisticated and attenuated eschatology; but no amount of reflection upon the running down or explosion of the universe for
physical reasons or upon *man's* self-destructive mastery of nuclear
physics comes to the same thing as Jesus' confident expectation
that the *living God* would soon, suddenly and catastrophically
put an end to the present age. Those were the days when the
Sermon on the Mount first occurred to the mind of man. God's
final judgment was expected to separate the sheep from the goats;
whereas in the crisis of our time, at Bikini, both sheep and goats
were killed.

Whoever is of a mind not to accept apocalypticism should note
well what he does in continuing to attribute validity to the main
body of Jesus' eschatological teachings, including the Beatitudes.
Jesus himself did not think that the gospel of love would be sufficient by itself to resolve the totality of evil in many life-situa-
tions, or to defeat the demonic power of evil encompassing even
those purely personal relationships which in themselves are often
amenable to love's persuasion. As a matter of fact, remarks a
leading New Testament scholar:

> . . . The practice of Jesus' ethical teaching had in his mind noth-
> ing whatever to do with bringing the kingdom to pass. God was
> going to do that—and he was going to do it almost at once. . . .
> God was going to bring in the kingdom, and he was going to
> bring it with power. . . . Jesus, although he enjoined non-vio-
> lence upon his followers, did not attribute non-violence to God.
> Only God's power would suffice to destroy the forces of wicked-

[1]Walter Rauschenbusch, *A Theology for the Social Gospel*, Macmillan, 1917,
p. 209.

ness. Coercion would be needed, but it would be God's coercion, not man's.[2]

The same writer continues: "The moral precepts of Jesus we listen to, although we do not keep them; but the eschatological teachings we do not hear at all."[3] Yet Jesus' expectation of the immediate end of the kingdoms of this world qualifies almost all his teachings. No wonder, then, that the ethical teachings have a sentimental meaning for us, and a meaning vastly different from the significance they had when they were first borne in upon the mind of man in the context of the inbreaking kingdom. We frequently hear it said that Jesus' call to the strenuous way of limitless love lays down a method for making all the world a kingdom of God and is to be responded to with this end in view. For Jesus, however, the reverse was the case: the kingdom of God was already effective in the present age and for this reason he believed the strenuous teachings could be lived out. Since "it is God's good pleasure to give you the kingdom," men may now "fear not," their love and forgiveness be unrestricted, themselves meek. The fact that these teachings can be obeyed, and indeed that they were even announced by Jesus, are effective "signs" that the kingdom is already appearing with power. Secretly though not gradually, God has established "bridgeheads" in the present age; healings on the sabbath are one, the teachings of Jesus themselves another and more momentous vantage point for God's saving power.

Apparently Jesus did not think that the way of love, which it was his and his disciples' *vocation* to practice, would by itself be able to deal with every form of evil, or was all the action needed. It is plain that Jesus considered the area in which evil could be overcome by good to be a limited one. He thought, of course, that it was the special business of his disciples to operate only in the area where evil could be overcome by non-resistance; but this decision depended for support precisely on his expectation that God was already actively bringing this evil time to an end. Jesus

[2]John Knox, "Re-examining Pacifism" in *Religion in the Present Crisis,* ed. by John Knox, University of Chicago Press, 1942, pp. 39-40.
[3]*Ibid.,* p. 38.

believed that the general forces of evil in human history were going to be dealt with as a separate function by God himself, and were even now being decisively confronted by the kingdom-power. There is thus a specialization of tasks: while Christians exercise attitudes creative of good and love evil out of existence by extending the community of those who are ready for the kingdom, God will destroy evil with righteous vengeance, and himself bring in the kingdom. Whether by Messianic battle or day of judgment, in any case the future Jesus faced was full of Messianic woes.

Once the teachings of Jesus are lifted out of the context of his eschatology there are two directions in which Christian thought and decision may move. Both of these are alike guilty of departing from the mind of Jesus. The two alternatives can best be illustrated in the area of Christian action in wartime. In the first place, Christians can extend the field in which the ethic of non-resistance is supposed to be applicable. We can say that to love, to suffer and to do good in the face of armed injustice is "God's method of dealing with evil" in its entirety. If we do so, we say something Jesus would not have said; he did not attribute such power to love and non-resistance. Making the strenuous teachings of Jesus cover the whole ground of action necessary to restrain or eliminate evil was simply not the religious ethic of Jesus.

The other alternative is to justify the employment of force in dealing with tyrannical structures of evil. This involves the substitution of human power-controls for divine power and, it may be, humanly directed violence for the divine violence entailed literally in Jesus' eschatological expectation. God's coercive intervention to deal with general evil may be replaced by concrete legislative measures, governmental institutions, and other responsible human arrangements, which then stand in exactly the same relation to the love-ethic as did the divine intervention which Jesus expected. Although on this view the Christian will take a responsibility for the restraint of evil which Jesus himself never allowed to be a part of specialized Christian vocation, this solution has the merit of claiming for the love-ethic only the limited, if positively creative, function Jesus actually assigned it. The first step to an understanding of the validity of Jesus' strenuous teachings must involve putting a limitation upon the area of their intended application.

Besides the foregoing limitation of its function, can anything more be said for the validity of the ethics of Jesus? In what sense does his ethic have validity throughout the whole range of human affairs? Here we must have the courage to look squarely into the mystery of how ideals were manufactured in this Christian world, for obedient love for neighbor, which is the distinctive "primitive idea" of Christian ethics, had its origin and *genesis* in apocalypticism. "The late-Jewish Messianic world-view," wrote Schweitzer, "is the crater from which burst forth the flame of the eternal religion of love."[4] In face of the inbreaking kingdom, moral decision was stripped of all prudential considerations, all calculation of what is right in terms of consequences which in this present age normally follow certain lines of action. Not only all prudential calculation of consequences likely to fall upon the agent himself, but likewise all sober regard for the future performance of his responsibility for family or friends, duties to oneself and *fixed* duties to others, both alike were jettisoned from view. Preferential loves, even those justifiable in normal times, were supplanted by entirely non-preferential regard for whomever happened to be standing by, friend or enemy, bullying sergeant or indigent beggar. All that mattered was perfect obedience to God. All that mattered was complete readiness for the kingdom to come. All that mattered was the single individual a man happened to confront. All that mattered was unhesitating, total love. Thus, standing so entirely before God with all prudential righteousness gone, "the neighbor," the neighbor in any man, was decisively discovered. Under such circumstances God's reign between a man and his neighbor clearly required that a person give the name of duty to the slightest momentary claim upon him, foregoing his own and also, in face of the kingdom, foregoing the claims of those to whom he had some special

[4]Albert Schweitzer, *Out of My Life and Thought*, Holt, 1933, p. 18.

obligation in the age now being liquidated. Any individual who chanced to be standing by became father, mother, brother, or sister, in short, the neighbor of any one else.

When God's "righteousness" fully prevails in the attitude of one person toward another, there will be no consideration for enlightened selfishness in relation to him, no consideration either for finding out what may be "due" him in terms of some worth inherent in him or because of his adherence and contribution to some common good which is the goal of men's intention in the present age. All that matters is what is due him according to the measure of the righteousness of God; and there could take place no weakening of the severity of these demands out of consideration for what should righteously be done at the same time toward other people, because all neighbors except the one actually present were apocalyptically removed from view and taken care of by God. Because in his view God was now in charge of the kingdoms of this present age, not only destroying their evil but also terminating lines of fixed responsibility within them, and himself bringing in a new kingdom of righteousness, Jesus devoted himself entirely to the task of being what man was soon to become and teaching men in radical fashion to renounce their connections with this present age and in limitless love prepare for the coming great day. Thus, in him and in his teachings the kingdom established a "bridgehead." Jesus did not bring the kingdom; his sense of the kingdom brought Jesus. The urgency and wholeness of his understanding of the demands upon any one standing on the border between these two worlds confronting only God obediently and the neighbor lovingly, brought his strenuous teachings for the first time into human reckoning, and made him the absolute disclosure of what God's reign means.

In Jesus' apocalypticism we can, after a fashion, watch revelation taking place. His ethic came to light only in the context of this outlook. Christian ideals were not forged, as Nietzsche supposed, through resentment by "whisperers and counterfeiters in the corners," but in the strong light and under the urgent impulse of Jesus' kingdom-hope. Christians may well regard this as an instance of God's using the weak and foolish things of this world to confound the wise and to disclose to the minds of men his perfect will.

Whoever considers it a fault that the ethics of Jesus originated from connection with an apocalyptic view of the end of human history which modern men no longer find plausible, whoever as a consequence is tempted either to dismiss the ethic or to modernize Jesus' other views, should reflect that *genesis* has nothing to do with *validity*. We properly judge the worth of anything, whether a concept or a cathedral, not by what it came from but by an analysis of its own peculiar meaning and form, its present appropriateness and adequacy in relation to human experience generally, and to the ends it now serves. Some accounts of revelation commit the genetic fallacy just as certainly as do many contemporary sociologists and psychologists. Jesus was not less good because he came out of Nazareth; and any one making the adverse judgment upon his origins that no good thing can come out of Nazareth presumably has arrived at this opinion by virtue of his ability to tell good from bad whether it come from Nazareth or not. The ethical teachings of Jesus may be true *and* he may have said what he did *because* of firm conviction of God's approaching completion of his reign among men. What Jesus said, and said only under the stimulus of his eschatological expectation, should be weighed for its own merit or demerit alone and not by reference to psychological, historical and cultural conditions out of which his teaching arose. The origin and history of Christian love may be interesting and important in its own right, but to suppose that factors determining the origin of this conception have anything to do with its value, or affect its truth to any degree one way or another, is an instance of the "genetic fallacy" so prevalent in post-evolutionary thought.

Indeed, precisely from the utter removal of all other considerations, Jesus' ethic gained an absolute validity transcending limitation to this or that place or time or civilization. Precisely because all other neighbors were apocalyptically removed from view except this single chance individual who might be hostile or friendly, beloved child or total stranger, Christian love gained unqualified lack of concern for either preferential interests or preferential duties, becoming an attitude unconditionally required of men in spite of hostility, in spite also of friendliness, on the neighbor's part. As a consequence of his kingdom-expectation, Jesus was able to proclaim for the human realm an ethic of obedient love which he formulated so memorably and for which he easily found supernatural measure and providential ground when considering the lilies and the birds, rainfall and sunshine.

Question concerning the validity of the apocalyptically derived teachings of Jesus in large measure resolves itself into the question, Taking into account the complexity of every actual ethical situation, what value can possibly be gained from confronting man with a disclosure of his full and perfect duty in responding to the claims of the single individual? Later on we shall consider the problem of practicing Christian ethics in any actual vocation in a world of responsibilities which must be viewed largely in non-apocalyptic terms. The basic problem we shall face in transposing the ethics of Jesus to a non-apocalyptic setting is this: What possible bearing can an ethic which specifies to the full what a man should do in relation to a single neighbor, an ethic which reveals with no qualification at all what the reign of "righteousness" means in regard to any man, what bearing can this possibly have upon moral action in a world where *there always is more than one neighbor* and indeed a whole cluster of claims and responsibilities to be considered? This problem cannot be avoided by reducing Christian ethics to the status of an inner disposition. The teachings of Jesus about non-resisting love describe not only what a Christian man (or group) will be *disposed* to do but what he will *actually* do in relation to a single, chance neighbor when the situation is uncomplicated by other claims. There is no such situation in a non-apocalyptic world. How, then, can this ethic mean anything at all for actual practice?

A chief problem in morals arises from the fact that the vast network of neighbor claims tends to dim our perception of obligation and provides us with a too ready excuse for a lapse into concern for self. We need to see clearly how we should be obliged to behave toward one neighbor (or how our own group should act toward one neighboring group) if there were no other claims upon us at all. The Sermon on the Mount is "an eschatological stimulus intended to make men well acquainted with the pure will of God." We may scarcely be able to perform it in regard to a single (friend or enemy) neighbor. It was never intended to be performed as a new law for the adjudication of neighbor-claims in a settled society. Nevertheless, "we are able to be transformed by it."[5] And precisely the situation in which we constantly need to be judged and transformed by it is when, because of the very multiplicity of neighbor-claims, we are tempted to defend the interests of self more than Christian love for even a single individual would allow. In the teachings of Jesus,

> . . . The relation is always one of two men face to face, where a claim recognized becomes immediately an obligation. In actual life we are seldom so fortunate, and there are almost always other people to be considered who also have claims upon us, some of which will conflict with the claim of the man immediately present before us. . . . But Jesus intentionally makes the situation simple. It is not his aim to tell men how to reconcile different claims, he wishes only to ensure that they shall not blind themselves to the claims that exist. . . . The situation envisaged is that in which two persons are isolated, and an illustration given of how a conscientious man would act if he had no other claims to consider but those of the person immediately confronting him. . . . In actual life there is almost always a vast network of claims which, as soon as they are recognized, impose a check upon us whenever we seek to satisfy the claims of any one individual. This very fact tends, however, to dim our perception of our obligations, and provides us with a ready excuse when we do not want to be reminded of them. It is well, therefore, that we should be clear as to what are the claims of the man most closely concerned, and how we should be obliged to behave towards him if there were no other claims upon us at all.[6]

[5]Martin Dibelius, *op. cit.*, p. 135.
[6]L. A. Garrard, *Duty and the Will of God,* Oxford: Basil Blackwell, 1938, pp. 71, 73, 74.

Here human thought gains an Archimedean point on which to stand and judge the world; or rather, by this ethic men may know themselves, their customary morality, their institutions and cultures to be subjected to an ultimate criticism and found wanting in terms of an absolute standard which was never drawn from the customary morality of any people and can never be identified with the structures of any particular civilization.

Vastly more important than Jesus' miscalculation of time, or even more essential elements of his apocalyptic outlook, was his astounding claim that the Messiah of God would judge the world according to the attitude men now display toward him and his movement of preparation for the kingdom. "And I tell you, everyone who acknowledges me before men, the Son of man also will acknowledge before the angels of God; but he who denies me before men will be denied before the angels of God" (Luke 12:8, 9). That Jesus Christ is the standard for measuring the reign of God among men is essentially a correct however astounding a claim. Christian ethics constitutes a standing judgment upon all human conduct and upon every human culture, requiring of them absolute obedience to God and singleminded love for neighbor. Christianity is not, like Judaism and other forms of religious ethics, a "religious civilization," it is rather a criticism of any civilization, religious or otherwise, and of any customary code of conduct, on behalf of the welfare of the neighbor, which all civilizations and codes of conduct are absolutely bound to serve in obedient love. Christian ethics may claim to be relevant in criticism of every situation precisely because its standard derives from no particular situation and is not accommodated to man's continuing life in normal, historical relationships; and this in turn is true in point of origin precisely because of Jesus' apocalyptic view of the kingdom of God.

In the last analysis, the two sources of Christian love—God's love and the kingdom of God—are one source; the righteousness of God is one righteousness. Apocalypticism served as a burning-glass to bring biblical ethics to pin-point focus and intensity. The biblical idea of the righteousness of God was the crater from which, when stirred into renewed action by apocalypticism, burst forth the flame of the eternal religion of love. On account of his kingdom-expectation, Jesus formulated in most unqualified fashion "the righteousness of God" as it is understood by the Bible generally. Without this conception of God's redemptive dealing with man, the outlook of apocalypticism, however urgent, would have brought to focus another, quite different ethic. After all, "Eat, drink and be merry, *for* tomorrow we die" is an eschatological ethic. It was apocalypticism *within the context of biblical faith in God's saving love* which produced Jesus' decisive statement of divine righteousness as the measure and meaning of human obligation. Not only in what he said, but in what he did and in what he was, Jesus placarded before men "the righteousness of God," he became the standard for measuring the reign of God among men. Through him, Christians become those who "have been taught by God to love one another" (I Thess. 4:9), and henceforth whoever acknowledges Jesus Christ will be acknowledged before the angels of God.

II

CHRISTIAN LIBERTY: AN ETHIC WITHOUT RULES

"... *at least every one* claimeth to be an authority on 'good' and 'evil.'"
> —Friedrich Nietzsche: *Thus Spake Zarathustra,*
> II, xxvii.

"... *at least more* is required of us than we are capable of performing."
> —John Calvin: *Institutes of the Christian Religion,*
> II, v, 9.

I. ESSENTIAL ELEMENTS OF CODE MORALITY, WITH ILLUSTRATION FROM JEWISH ETHICS AT THE TIME OF JESUS

CAN a man know that he is good? A tailor in ancient Israel had an easy answer to this question. He was forbidden to go out of his house after sunset wearing his "needle," the badge of his trade. This rule held for every day of the week for the purpose of "building a fence around the Law," lest on the eve of the Sabbath the tailor forget and, by wearing his badge, be guilty of "bearing a burden" on the hallowed sabbath day. Obedience to this rule assured him of being, in this respect, right with God.

In every code-morality fences around the law serve to guarantee righteousness. In the United States today, among many Christian folk who allow that card playing and dancing are not inherently wrong, these practices are still often prohibited lest other rules be more readily broken. Rook cards may provide innocent fun, but a person goes too far if he takes in hand a pack of playing cards with spots and markings more ordinarily

46

used in gambling. Better not approve of square dancing lest some one start to round-dance, or dancing of any sort lest worse befall. In this fashion, every conventional code of conduct seeks to make itself secure by building innumerable fences around more basic legalistic definitions of right and wrong.

In ancient Israel, these more fundamental religious and ethical obligations were codified in 613 provisions of the law. No one has ever bothered to count the regulations by which conduct is governed in an average American community. These rules may be informal customs or statutory legislation protecting life and property. They may be "puritanical"—Do not drink, Do not smoke, Do not gamble, Do not go to movies on Sunday —or rules defining conventional respectability in precisely opposite terms. We, Christians and non-Christians indifferently, are all born and bred "under the Law" just as certainly as were Jews in the days of Jesus.

Serious-minded, upstanding people, in our day no less than before, support the universal conscription of Christian conscience to some new drill-master. A sect of Russian Mennonites frowns more on smoking than on drinking, on scriptural grounds, since Jesus said not what goeth into a man, but what cometh out, defiles. Ranging from this to the more significant view that Christians are not to go to law, not to take oaths, not ever to resist evil, Christian groups have frequently turned the New Testament into a new Law, the Sermon on the Mount into a new Decalogue. Primarily because need for instructing the younger generation is always urgent, Christian morality repeatedly takes form as a new legalism in which every one must be trained.

In addition to (1) the fundamental requirements of the law and (2) rules to hedge them about, every legalism or customary morality develops two other types of regulation: (3) rules defining as precisely and exhaustively as possible the meaning of the command or prohibition contained in the original law, and (4) rules establishing some order of preference among the laws in case conflict makes necessary a breach of one or more of them.

By the time of Jesus innumerable oral or unwritten laws had

been added to the written or Mosaic law, mainly for the purpose of explaining how the written law should be performed and how it might be violated. The decisions and later interpretations by the Rabbis were asserted to be no more than a rediscovery of meanings whispered in Moses' ear at the time he was given the law inscribed on tablets of stone. Oral tradition was thus invested with the same binding authority as the 613 written laws believed to have been promulgated by God through Moses: even innovations in legalism are always received as "truths once delivered."

The extent to which the meaning of particular laws needed to be given more exact definition may be illustrated by reference to the divorce law and the sabbath law, both of which are important for understanding the teachings of Jesus.

According to regulation in the Torah, a man may write out for his wife a bill of divorcement, and send her away, "if she find no favour in his eyes, because he hath found some unseemly thing in her" (Deut. 24:1). Now, clearly the entire meaning of this provision depends upon the meaning assigned orally to the expression "some unseemly thing." R. Shammai, leading conservative whose opinion prevailed in Jesus' day, said that "some unseemly thing" meant "something shameful," *i.e.*, adultery; and, he concluded, only for this cause does the Law permit divorce. On the other hand, his liberal colleague, R. Hillel, who has been much praised for being an "almost Christian" in his humanitarian views, held that it was "unseemly" on a wife's part "even if she lets his food burn"; his opinion was that for this and many other trivial causes the Law permits divorce, a viewpoint which demonstrates that it is not unqualifiedly praiseworthy for a legalist to be liberal while still remaining a legalist. In the early part of the second century R. Akiba arrived at the still more liberal opinion that a husband might initiate divorce from his wife "if he finds another woman more beautiful than she," which, if not an "unseemly thing" in a wife, clearly indicates that the earlier part of the law has been fulfilled in that she no longer "finds favour in his eyes."

The sabbath law required all faithful Jews to do no work on

the sabbath day. This provision was of unparalleled significance to the Jews, along with circumcision indicating their status as a peculiar, a chosen people. Even God Almighty had observed the sabbath on the seventh day of creation; and popular belief in the time of Jesus expected that, if all Jews everywhere observed this law in every detail for one sabbath only, God would promptly give his people the kingdom. Yet it remained for oral tradition to indicate the meaning of working, or not working, on the sabbath.

An exhaustive definition of work forbidden on the sabbath was therefore drawn up, classifying thirty-nine types of prohibited labor:

> (1) sowing, (2) ploughing, (3) reaping, (4) binding sheaves, (5) threshing, (6) winnowing, (7) cleansing crops, (8) grinding, (9) sifting, (10) kneading, (11) baking, (12) shearing wool, (13) washing, (14) beating, (15) dyeing, (16) spinning, and (17) warping it, (18) making two cords, (19) weaving two threads, (20) separating two threads, (21) making a knot, (22) untying a knot, (23) sewing two stitches, (24) tearing to sew two stitches, (25) catching a deer, (26) killing, (27) skinning, and (28) salting it, (29) preparing its skin, (30) scraping off the hair, (31) cutting it up, (32) writing two letters, (33) blotting out for the purpose of writing two letters, (34) building, (35) pulling down, (36) beating smooth with a hammer, (37) putting out a fire, (38) lighting a fire, (39) carrying from one tenement to another.[1]

Numerous other types of labor would need to be prohibited if the sabbath were really to be kept entirely free from labor. Moreover, each one of these thirty-nine kinds of work in its turn had to be explained by oral legislation. A woman tying a knot in her girdle was not considered guilty of laboring; but she violated the law by tying a similar knot for the purpose of carrying water jugs hung from the waist. A person who wrote even a single letter on two walls which form an angle, or on the two sides of his account book, was guilty of "writing two letters" and so of working on

[1]Emil Schurer, *A History of the Jewish People in the Time of Christ* (trans. by John Macpherson), Scribners and T. and T. Clark, 1898, Div. II, Vol. II, sec. 28.

the sabbath, while writing in sand or some other impermanent medium was not condemned. A Jewish householder could give alms to a Jewish beggar standing outside his door only under peril of "working" to "carry from one tenement to another." Since neither man under these circumstances was allowed to complete the operation of giving or receiving an alms, violation of the law was avoided only by a stratagem of manual cooperation. Whoever of the two men extended his arm across the threshold thereafter remained passive: if the householder put his hand out of the house, the beggar then acted to take the gift from his upturned palm; if however the beggar extended his hand into the house, the householder had then to complete the action by placing the gift in his outstretched hand. Thus, neither man was guilty of finishing the task of carrying from one tenement to another, although plainly the quality of mercy was strained to effect a real change of location in the object given away. Undeniably, it had been moved from the inside to the outside of a tenement.

For all the vast pyramiding of rules explaining the prohibition of work on the sabbath, it would be a complete misunderstanding of the motives of Israel's religious leaders to suppose that they were intent on increasing the burden of righteousness. True, their detailed and exhaustive interpretation of the meaning of scriptural law was difficult to remember. But only difficult *to remember. Obeying* the law, presuming one *remembered* its meaning, was hereby made easier, not more difficult. The most difficult thing imaginable is for a person to obey the sabbath law without knowing its meaning. Attempting to obey the sabbath law, doing no work at all on this day, while lacking an adequate understanding of what working and not working mean, is so difficult as to be quite impossible. The rabbis wanted to fill out the common man's understanding of the meaning of the prohibited labor, thereby making it easier for him not to work on the sabbath if he remembered the meaning and seriously wanted to avoid working. The way in which Christians sometimes suppose that they continue bound by this law, while not adopting the rabbinical *or some other* exhaustive and detailed legal definition of labor, manifests a lack of thoroughness in legalism, a legalism which is itself from the first a fundamental misunderstanding of Christian ethics.

Finally, those who champion conventional morality and seek to preserve any sort of legalism intact must necessarily draw up rules establishing some precise order of preference among existing customs or laws. There must be rules for the breaking of rules, rules for the keeping of rules, laws which say when a law is to be kept and when it may be broken, and indeed ought to be broken, in order to obey another more important regulation. If, in the simplest case, there are only two primary laws, a third immediately becomes necessary, a law stating which of the two comes first in case conflict makes necessary breaking one. When primary laws are more numerous, more interlocking and numerous become the secondary, and usually oral, laws governing their breach and observance. Jesus' saying about the ox falling in a ditch serves as just such a rule, freeing common-sense Christian legalists time and time again from half-hearted sabbatarianism.

On one occasion Jesus himself seems to have reinterpreted obligation under the law by merely reversing the judgment current in his day as to whether it is more important to keep one's oath or honor father and mother. Deuteronomy decrees the unconditional inviolability of oaths: "When you make a vow to the Lord your God, you must pay it without delay. . . . A spoken promise you must be careful to observe" (23:21, 23). Equally unconditional is the injunction to honor father and mother. Since both are commandments of God, "tradition" alone can assign the leading role to one or the other. Jesus sets aside one such interpretation only to formulate another:

> You have a fine way of rejecting the commandment of God, in order to keep your tradition! For Moses said, "Honor your father and mother;" and "He who speaks evil of father or mother, let him surely die"; but you say, "If a man tells his father or his mother, 'What you would have gained from me is Corban' (that is, given to God)—then you no longer permit him to do anything for his father or mother, thus making void the word of God through your tradition which you hand on. And many such things you do" (Mark 7:9–13).

No matter which is the better rule for breaking or keeping these laws, either one or the other conclusion finds support here simply by the employment of a technique essential to all legalism. This is shown by the fact that within half a century rabbinic Judaism had adopted the position Jesus maintained—without thereby ceasing to be Judaism.

More all-embracing are the interpretations sometimes given that Jesus rejected the oral law but endorsed obedience to the written law, or that he rejected ceremony while endorsing obedience to the ethical provisions of the law (whether oral or written). Did Jesus simply recodify code morality, setting rule against rule? Did he take the side of complete obedience to the written (ethical and ceremonial) laws of scripture against the development of oral interpretation? Or did he champion ethical rules at the expense of ceremony? Either of these general rules, however radical a departure from current practice, would still have been the attitude of a legalist establishing an order of preference for obeying and for disobeying existing regulations. The first was in fact the viewpoint of the Sadducees who, having their own simpler interpretation, pretended to stick to the written law and refused to go along with the more elaborate oral interpretation given by rabbis of the Pharisee party. This position did not deliver them from the necessity of assigning meaning to written law by means of *some* oral interpretation. Rather, like literalists and strict constructionists in our own day, they simply affirmed that their own special interpretation was obviously contained in the written words themselves. Under the banner of rejecting oral additions to the law the Sadducees merely rejected any other tradition than their own.

Evidently Jesus was willing to count heavily upon something more than the literal words of scripture. He did not always condemn "the tradition of men" but frequently employed it in his teaching, for example, in his permission of labor to help the ox out of the ditch on a sabbath. Jesus certainly stood more in agreement with the oral mitigation of ancient punishments than with the exact words of *lex talionis* which demand an eye for an eye.

He believed in the resurrection, which the conservative Sadducees rejected, and from their point of view rightly rejected, because, not being an original part of Hebrew religion, this doctrine is not mentioned in the first five, authoritative books of the Bible. Moreover, the synagogue system of religious instruction, the synagogue which has been called a "popular religious university," in which Jesus was trained and where he always went for services, is nowhere founded in the Torah. The synagogue became a part of Jewish tradition during the Exile when by the waters of Babylon Temple worship and sacrifice were no longer possible. This institution is traceable to Moses only as one of those words originally whispered in his ear the memory of which was lost and then regained six centuries later.

It is equally evident that Jesus was no Amos sweeping all ceremony aside, retaining only ethics. The Temple was an institution he cherished and purified. He wore the tassel, the "hem" of his garment, which was a badge of his Jewishness. There is no reason for supposing that he ever called in question the rite of circumcision. He probably never ate pork or camel or rabbit meat, foods ceremonially unclean. All these practices were of ceremonial importance only.

The attitude of Jesus toward any one form of the law—oral, written, ethical, ceremonial—was neither entire acceptance nor entire rejection. Jesus did not give another rule for living by the rules. In the strict sense of the word, he had no new *principle* for selecting among the laws. His was a greater freedom from the law, he lived more without the law than any procedure of this sort implies.

Before going more fully into the essential nature of Jesus' ethic in relation to its Jewish background, it should be observed that, if ever any consistent account is to emerge, certain of the sayings attributed to him must be decisively rejected, at least as they are ordinarily understood. Only with bitter irony and indignation could the Jesus whom we otherwise know in our gospels have said concerning the religious leaders of his day, "The scribes and the Pharisees sit on Moses' seat; so practice and observe whatever they tell you"—even as a preface to the qualifying words: ". . . but not what they do; for they preach, but do not practice. They bind heavy burdens, hard to bear, and lay them on men's shoulders; but they themselves will not move them with their little fingers" (Matt. 28:2–4). Jesus' greatness did not consist simply in practicing what the rabbis taught. And the words, "For truly, I say to you, till heaven and earth pass away, not an iota, not a dot, will pass from the law until all is accomplished. Whoever then relaxes one of the least of these commandments and teaches men so, shall be called least in the kingdom of heaven" (Matt. 5:18, 19) are either not the original words of Jesus or else they are sorely in need of a loose interpretation, an interpretation not encouraged by reference to such details as the "iota" and the "dot," the smallest letter in the alphabet and the least embellishment of the text. Profounder meaning than all this must be given to the assertion that Jesus "fulfills" the law: In both senses of the word, the Jewish religious heritage was "finished" by Jesus Christ. Jesus completes in such fashion as entirely to annul the law. This also means that Jesus Christ "finishes" any ethic of conventional respectability, any customary code of conduct into which at least every man is born, any more or less philosophic definition of good and evil in which "*at least everyone* claimeth to be an authority."

II. JESUS OVERCOMES THE LAW

Whoever wishes to gain a clear impression of the ethics of Jesus in its natural setting within Judaism must refrain from comparing the most plausible meaning that may be assigned to the one with the more unfavorable aspects of the other. This means that references made in our synoptic gospels to Jewish teachings which Jesus opposed must be supplemented by some knowledge of how these ancient teachings were currently interpreted and received in Jesus' own day. Such an approach will lead to a fairer estimate of the degree of reasonableness and humanitarianism there was in Jewish legalism, and at the same time it throws into bold and

unmistakable relief the radical meaning of the contrasting teachings of Jesus.

The gospels frequently represent Jesus' opponents as simply
dumbfounded, his hearers easily persuaded, by Jesus' replies to
criticism. As a matter of fact, an intelligent Jew would hardly
have been reduced to silence by Jesus' words, spoken on the occasion of his healing the man with the withered or paralyzed hand,
"Is it lawful on the sabbath to do good or to do harm, to save
life or to kill?" (Mark 3:4). Rabbinic instruction made a precise
distinction between doing good and saving life. Every effort necessary to save human life, or even to allay *extreme* pain, was of
course permitted on the sabbath. But doing some good of a sort
that might just as well be postponed was considered an undue
disregard of sabbath holiness. The paralyzed man was not going
to die before sunset, nor was he in great pain. Jesus could easily
have waited a few hours before performing the "labor" of curing
him. Thus mercy might have been done, but without such haste
as to discredit Jesus as a teacher among the Jews. The question
Jesus put that day was therefore not a rhetorical question having
an obvious answer, as modern readers are apt to suppose, nor a
telling retort to which the Jews themselves had no reply. Its significance lies in indicating so clearly what Jesus regarded as sufficient reason for breaking the most treasured religious custom
of his people: doing good was for him equivalent to saving life.

In the case of Jesus' healing the woman who for eighteen years
had been bent over and could not straighten herself, the ruler of
the synagogue said to the people, "There are six days on which
work ought to be done; come on those days and be healed, and
not on the sabbath day" (Luke 13:14). He must be understood
to be speaking of chronic afflictions, such as that of the hunch-
backed woman whose infirmity, however embarrassing or however much an obstacle to her personal self-expression, was physically neither painful nor perilous. On the sabbath, emergency
cases only! Let persons suffering long-standing afflictions come
on the other six days to be healed!

Making an effort to care for animals on the sabbath, if, according to a saying drawn from oral tradition, a sheep fall into a pit (Matt. 12:11) or an ass or an ox into a well (Luke 14:5), was permitted on the sabbath only if the animal were in extreme pain or in danger of dying. If a man hears a fluttering in his dovecote he may climb up to see if the trapped dove is suffering more than ordinary discomfort. If not, he must climb down again without loosening it. He may investigate the plight of his animal down in the ditch, but more work than this is justified only on account of great pain or peril of death. The persons Jesus cured of long-standing ills bore no analogy to the circumstances under which oral law permitted laboring on behalf of animals. Jesus' reference to this saying proves nothing except that he thereby expected to *prove* nothing and to convince few of his own departure from law observance. More to the point is the regular practice of people in daily caring for their stock: "You hypocrites! Does not each of you on the sabbath untie his ox or his ass from the manger, and lead it away to water it? And ought not this woman, a daughter of Abraham whom Satan bound for eighteen years, be loosed from this bond on the sabbath day?" (Luke 13:15, 16). But no adversary who is a legalist will be put to shame by this argument, for the issue turns not upon the greater worth human beings have in comparison with animals but upon the distinction between avoidable and unavoidable work whether done on behalf of animals or men.

The attitude Jesus displayed in these episodes, in contrast to the ethics of Judaism, may now be briefly summarized: A faithful Jew stayed as close as possible to observance of the law even when he had to depart from it. Jesus stayed as close as possible to the fulfillment of human need, no matter how wide of the sabbath law this led him. Judaism varied the rules so as to care for human need. With regard to sabbath observance, Jesus quite spontaneously left the rules behind in order quickly to take maximum care of those in need. Judaism expressed concern both for men and for the law. Jesus' concern for men led him to be downright unconcerned about the law. Jewish ethics was a legalism modified by humanitarianism, which meant also a humanitarianism *limited* by legalism. Jesus' humanitarianism was not at all fettered by respect for long-established custom or the preconceptions of legal definition. Love led him to be downright unconcerned about laws he had been trained to cherish. (In the preceding chapter we saw that this love was for Jesus *"obedient love,"* not simply some humanitarian ethic. It arose from his prompt and total response to the demands placed on him by God's inbreaking kingdom. Since the Son of Man might come on the sabbath as likely as on any other day, no legal impediment should be put in the way of manifesting "righteousness" on this day. Since the Lord of the sabbath will not delay his coming, there ought to be no postponement of any possible triumph over the powers of evil.)

This contrast is not of historical significance only. The statement or defense the Jews had ready to make of their position is precisely the viewpoint of conventional moralists in every age: Even when for mercy's sake you have to break them, stick as close to the rules as you can. This is the viewpoint of at least every man who considers himself an authority on good and evil. In contrast, Christians are bound by Jesus' attitude of sticking as close as possible to human need, no matter what the rules say, as the primary meaning of obligation, which, seriously undertaken, requires at least more of us than we are capable of performing and gives us no opportunity for becoming authorities. Strictly speaking, this is a new "principle" for morality only in the sense that here all morality governed by principles, rules, customs, and laws goes to pieces and is given another sovereign test. For this reason Christianity is relevant, as relevant as a revolutionary threat, to every culture yet identical with none. It announces to every age: man is not made for your institutions.

When on a sabbath the disciples of Jesus "plucked and ate some ears of grain, rubbing them in their hands" (Luke 6:1), they were technically guilty of violating two of the thirty-nine articles of sabbath religion: they reaped and threshed grain. It is worthy of note that Jesus did not contest the classification of their action as work, he did not suggest another legal definition of the prohibited labor, instead he justified their *working* on the sabbath. "Have you not read what David did when he was hungry, he and those who were with him: how he entered the house of God, and took and ate the bread of the Presence, which it is not lawful for any but the priests to eat, and also gave it to those with him?" (Luke 6:3, 4).

It is significant that the rabbis also justified the action of David, so that no simple citation of this event can make clear the difference between them and Jesus. According to Jewish commentary, David and his band of outlaws fleeing from the wrath of King Saul were famishing and in danger of starvation or of being captured on account of physical exhaustion: this alone made legitimate an unceremonious act. The difference between this and the illegal action which Jesus justified appears even greater than in the incidents of sabbath violation we have already examined. The disciples were not famishing, nor even, so far as we have reason to suppose, unusually tired. They were not accused of having walked more than a sabbath day's journey, which we may be sure would not have passed unnoticed. Clearly, then, for the most trivial reason Jesus justified their failure to observe the sabbath law.

Indeed, pointing out that "there is obviously not much connection between the hunger of a band of soldiers and the pastime of strollers," Guignebert, a contemporary French student of the life of Jesus, cites this as evidence of Jesus' "habit of being satisfied with the most rough and ready application of a text to a case it is supposed to justify" and proof of his "complete lack of capacity for abstract criticism."[1]

Now, unless making generalizations be the chief end of man, one need not hesitate to agree that Jesus lacked such "capacity for abstract criticism." His manner of thought was vividly imaginative, grounded in particular events; he shared the Hebrew sense of "happenness." Nevertheless, the supposition that Jesus knew what he was doing and meant what he said (which is the only

---

[1]Charles Guignebert, *Jesus*, Kegan Paul, 1935, p. 179. (Published in the United States by Knopf, 1935.)

way of avoiding Guignebert's conclusion) significantly accords with Jesus' thoroughgoing departure from Jewish legalism in other instances. The Jews set aside even the most sacred regulations when any one was in peril of death. Jesus went wide of the law for the sake of an increase of the simple pleasures of taste and conviviality, the freedom of men to nibble grain when strolling through the fields without hindrance from those who consider themselves moral and religious authorities. His position was as far without the law as could be, and he came to take this position, not on account of any consciously adopted antinomian program, but by preoccupation with concrete human needs, even casual and unimportant ones. Anticipating a distinction yet to be made between the infinite, inherent *value* of *human* personality in general and an attitude infinitely *valuing* the person and needs of the *neighbor* no matter what his inherent worth, Jesus' actions and teaching may be described as flowing from an orientation which valued the needs of the neighbor infinitely above all else.

Here the word "infinite" has precise meaning which may be illustrated from the writings of W. D. Ross. The British moralist and translator of the works of Aristotle holds the view that knowledge is infinitely superior to happiness and moral goodness infinitely superior to knowledge. By this he means that no amount of increase in happiness is worth even the smallest loss of knowledge; and no gain in knowledge, however great, ever equals in worth the slightest decline in moral goodness.[2] In the same sense Jesus believed serving the needs of one's neighbor to be infinitely superior to observing law. No increase of legal righteousness is worth securing at the expense of the needs of others who might be served. Any augmentation of human satisfaction and well-being, however small, equals or exceeds in worth any sacrifice whatever of righteousness according to the law and justifies the infraction of rules, however sacred. Human need and man-made regulations (indeed, as Jesus devoutly believed, *divinely* promulgated law) are never to be compared except to the infinite advantage of the former.

[2]W. D. Ross, *The Right and the Good,* Oxford, Clarendon Press, 1930, ch. vi.

This point of view Jesus resolutely put into practice in his association with those defined as "sinners" under the law and with the unwashed "people of the land" who were notoriously lax in tithing and ritual cleanliness. The strictest party in his day wished not only to enforce the tithe on every thing that was grown but also to make all God's people priests by extending to every one before every meal the regulations about ceremonial handwashing which formerly were binding only upon priests preparing to sacrifice. Moreover, since contamination came by physical contact and might therefore be accidental, whoever seriously wanted to know that he was good, those who really desired to keep themselves pure and to make Israel a pure nation, refused to eat with the common people among whom the tithe was likely not paid, dishes and hands unwashed.

Jesus' insistence in this connection that "whatever goes into a man from outside cannot defile him, since it enters, not his heart but his stomach" (Mark 7:18, 19), establishing, as it does, the inwardness of real purity and real defilement, should not cause Christians to forget the many important laws of the Jews, such as that prohibiting covetousness, which can be practiced only with inwardness. And the words, "Woe to you, scribes and Pharisees, hypocrites! for you tithe mint and dill and cummin, and have neglected the weightier matters of the law, justice, mercy and faith" (Matt. 23:23), may be an apt description of certain ones among the Pharisees or, at most, of a majority of them in Jesus' day. It is perfectly clear, however, that justice, mercy and faith were matters which a faithful Jew recognized he ought not to neglect. When Jesus said, "These you ought to have done, without neglecting the others" (Matt. 23:23) he made no new departure; in reality, these words summarize that mixture of humanitarianism and legalism which was the essence of Judaism. The gulf that separates Jesus from the best ethical viewpoint of his people can be seen only when we comprehend the lengths they were willing to go in separating themselves under ordinary circumstances from other, less worthy human beings on behalf of living up to what the law required, and in contrast the length

Jesus was willing to go, wide of the law, making himself of absolutely no reputation, in order not to separate himself from the
"people of the land." As serious-minded, religious men the Pharisees scrupulously held aloof from unscrupulous folk, publicans
and sinners. Jesus drew near them (so it was said *they* were closer
to the kingdom of God); and as a consequence he became unscrupulous about traditional regulations of behavior, and unconcerned to protect his own respectability in the opinion of those
who judged goodness in the abstract or who, out of concern for
their own merit, disconnected worth from beneficence.

Often it is said that the essential nature of Jesus' ethic is found
in his selecting from among the various rules codified in Deuteronomy and Leviticus the two love commandments, love for
God and love for neighbor, as his summary of the meaning of
Torah. This is true, when properly understood against the background of frequent use of similar summaries, indeed the same
summary, by rabbis themselves. Single verses such as "You have
been told, O man, what is good, and what the Lord requires of
you: Only to do justice, and to love kindness, and to walk humbly
with your God" (Mic. 6:8), "Seek the Lord, that you may live"
(Amos 5:6) and "The righteous lives by reason of his faithfulness" (Hab. 2:4), as well as a number of longer passages, were
said to have penetrated most deeply into the meaning of the law.
A disciple once promised R. Hillel that he would obey all the
law he could be taught while standing on one foot. To him Hillel
replied, "What is hateful to thyself do not to thy neighbor; this
is the whole law." This so-called "negative Golden Rule" plainly
had positive significance for Hillel and for many Jews. The question therefore arises how this teaching differs, if at all, from that
of Jesus, "So whatever you wish that men would do to you, do
so to them," to which Matthew (7:12) has appended the comment, ". . . for this is the law and the prophets." Summary of
the law in terms of the commands to love God and neighbor was,
indeed, not original with Jesus. The first known written selection
and combination of these two Old Testament laws occurred in
The Testament of the Twelve Patriarchs well before the time of

Jesus. That this was a current and familiar summary is further
shown by the fact that, in Luke's account of the discussion concerning the great commandment, the scribe questioning Jesus,
not Jesus himself, gives the answer: Jesus simply approves the
summary, "You have answered right; do this, and you will live"
(Luke 10:28). Jesus merely quoted, or confirmed, a quite current
opinion. The question therefore arises whether Jesus remained
ethically a Jew still or whether there is significant difference between his and the rabbinic summaries.

Dispute concerning the chief commandment among the leaders of Jewish legalism, as well as the effort they made to find
a *précis* of the whole law in a single one of its provisions,
amounted to no more than spiritual exercises, providing at most
material for edification and for instruction. "This or that Rabbi
might give it as his opinion that a particular commandment was
the most important of all but his opinion did not abate in the
least degree the importance of every other commandment, nor
did it release him or any one else from the absolute obligation
to obey every other command,"[3] or else make provision for their
possible obedience by arranging them in some order of descend-
ing importance. When R. Hillel told his enterprising disciple,
"What is hateful to thyself do not to thy neighbor; this is the
whole law, the rest is commentary," he added the significant
words, "Go and study," *i.e.*, go and study the commentary, which
Hillel regarded as also a significant and binding statement of
man's obligation under the law. Whenever Jewish rabbis "spoke
of neighborly love as the greatest or most fundamental law they
meant . . . a general or basic commandment from which all other
commandments could be deduced. The rabbi was not discriminating between the importance or unimportance of laws so much as
between their fundamental or derivative character."[4] In brief,
Jewish teachers who formulated an epitome of the law hedged
it about with the injunction, "Do this and those other laws as well."

[3]T. W. Manson, *The Teachings of Jesus,* Cambridge University Press, 1939,
pp. 303–304.
[4]Israel Abrahams, *Studies in Pharisaism and the Gospels,* Cambridge University
Press, 1917–24, 1st series, p. 24.

In his summary of the law, Jesus just as plainly taught, "Do this, and not necessarily those other commandments." We have seen Jesus' declaration, "The sabbath was made for man, not man for the sabbath" (Mark 2:27), to be the statement of one who, for reasons given, set the sabbath law entirely aside. The verbally parallel statement which may be cited from a number of rabbis, "The sabbath is given for you and not you for the sabbath," had, coming from their mouths, an absolutely different meaning. It meant: the sabbath is given *for you to keep,* in order that you and your servants and domestic animals may have rest. Legalism itself is not unnecessarily inhumane, least of all Jewish legalism. Legalists in all ages are simply antecedently convinced that it is in man's interest for the law to be obeyed; they live by the preconception that it is good for man to abide by the rules. In contrast, Jesus Christ was so wakeful to man's need that he was free from such fixed belief that sabbath *observance* is always made for man.

In similar fashion, when we look again behind the verbal agreement between Jesus and the leading opinion in his day, we find that Jesus used the familiar device of summarizing the law so as to teach, "Do this, and not necessarily the other laws." Either this was his teaching, or else Jesus still remained essentially within the ethics of Judaism, a not unpraiseworthy yet a not so original thing. How hard it is to exceed the righteousness of the scribes and Pharisees can best be grasped by noticing how some of the sayings attributed to Jesus by the gospel of Matthew go not at all beyond legal righteousness. "These (weightier matters of the law: justice, mercy, faith) you ought to have done, without neglecting the others (tithing mint and dill and cummin)" (23:23) exceeds not at all the standard of righteousness Pharisees embraced. "Do this and those" was their aim, "go and study" their slogan. Taken at face value the words with which Matthew concludes Jesus' summary of the law in terms of the love commandments, "On these two commandments *depend* all the law and the prophets" (22:24) reduce Jesus' use of the summary to entire identity with rabbinic use of the same device, their use, indeed, of the same summary. These words may mean that Jesus merely cited "a general or basic commandment from which all other commandments could be deduced"; he "was not discriminating between the importance or unimportance of laws so much as between their fundamental or derivative character"; he too enjoined, "Do this and also that." This interpretation tells us more about the rebirth of legalism within early Christianity than it does about Jesus; it is "just another indication that where the Law is in question Matthew is simply not to be trusted."[5] The fact that this was far from the view of Jesus is borne out not only by what we otherwise know concerning his relation to the law but also by the accounts given of his use of the summary in Luke and Mark. In Luke, Jesus accepts the lawyer's summary saying, "Do this, and you will live" (10:28), where a religious leader of the Jews would necessarily have answered, "You have answered rightly; go and study the commentary; obey also the other laws which depend on these; at least arrange them in some order for possible obedience." Careful comparison of the concluding words in Mark's account, "There is no other commandment greater than these" (12:31), with the concluding words in Matthew suggests the same decisive difference:

> The Marcan conclusion asserts that no other commandment can take precedence of these two . . . Mt.'s conclusion says something different, that these two commandments are the fundamental principles upon which all other commandments in Scripture are based. Mt. thus tacitly excludes the possibility of a clash between the two great commandments and the rest, whereas Mk. reckons with such a possibility and declares how it is to be decided.[6]

However, the contrast is not yet sharp enough. It may be that a naïve and undeveloped legalism tacitly excludes the possibility of a clash between any of its regulations, and contents itself with an organization of the whole body of laws into an apparently

[5]T. W. Manson, *op. cit.*, p. 304, note 2.
[6]Major, Manson and Wright, *The Mission and Message of Jesus,* Dutton, 1938, p. 519.

harmonious arrangement of basic and derivative rules. Sooner or later, however, the possibility of a clash must be reckoned with, and a mature or long-standing legalism always faces this possibility and declares how in each instance the conflict ought to be decided. There must be rules establishing not only an order of *logical derivation*, but some precise order of *actual preference* as well, among existing laws. We have seen that one chief function of oral tradition in Judaism was drawing up rules determining when a law was to be kept and when it ought to be broken in order to obey another more important regulation. Was Jesus' summary of the law in terms of the love commandments simply another rule for the breach and observance of rules, contributing to the normal course of Jewish legal development?

Jesus stands entirely outside the evolution of Jewish legalism for the reason that he taught not simply the superiority of love for God and for the neighbor over any other commandment; what is more, he taught that these commands were *infinitely* superior to all the rest. Instead of measuring love for God and man against other parts of the code and declaring the love commandments to be more important than all or any one of the remainder, Jesus in effect affirms the love commandments to be *incommensurable* with all the rest and declines to measure their importance by comparison with any other legislation. For him man's obligation did not arise from a conflict of these commandments with other equally valid though less essential commandments which were still to be obeyed when there is no clash. Jesus refused to motivate action by a cancelation of legal claims, even if the right law always proved supreme. Man's obligation arose out of these two commandments alone, there could be no conflict with other parts of Torah, this was for him the *whole* law of God. "Do this, and you will live," he said to the lawyer, without reference to anything else still to be done. As has been pointed out,

> It never occurred to any Rabbi to challenge the necessity of the thousand other requirements because they could be epitomized in two. *Jesus boldly took the view that since the Law was com-*

prised in these primary injunctions all the rest might be left aside. Nothing was necessary but to hold fast to what was essential, and the details would follow of themselves.[7]

And the "details following of themselves" involves absolutely no prediction or expectation that practice will necessarily follow the pattern laid down in the rest of the law.

It was precisely this policy of "Do this, and not necessarily those" which "finished" the law of the Jews, since by its very nature as an ethical system legalism finds support only in a policy of "Do this and that." Because the love commandments were drawn from the religious heritage of Judaism, Jesus "fulfills" the law. Because with Jesus validity ceases in principle to inhere in all the laws as such and comes to inhere in these two commandments alone (or in these and two or three others, which however never occupy the center of his attention), Jesus annuls the law. Here legalism goes to pieces, and Jewish leaders from Caiaphas to Klausner[8] could not but regard such an interpretation as a much more serious matter than mere disobedience to this or that command, much more threatening to their religious civilization than even apostasy from the whole of the law. This is a true estimate of his role whether or not Jesus himself deliberately adopted or was ever fully aware of the departure from Judaism he set in motion.

Consider next the "strenuous" teachings of Jesus, his injunctions never to resist one who is evil but to do him some positive good instead, to forgive times without number, his absolute prohibition of divorce, and the requirement of such radical decision and unconditional obedience as seem calculated to destroy family obligation and throw ordinary human communities into confusion. Typical of all these strenuous teachings is Jesus' hard saying:

> You have heard that it was said, "An eye for an eye and a tooth for a tooth." But I say to you, Do not resist one who is evil. But if any one strikes you on the right cheek, turn to him

[7]E. F. Scott, *The Ethical Teachings of Jesus,* Macmillan, 1948, p. 34 (italics mine).
[8]Joseph Klausner, *Jesus of Nazareth,* Macmillan, 1925.

the other also; and if any one would sue you and take your coat, let him have your cloak as well; and if any one forces you to go one mile, go with him two miles. Give to him who begs from you, and do not refuse him who would borrow from you (Matt. 5:38–42).

Again, whoever wishes to gain a clear impression of Jesus' relation to *lex talionis* or the law of retaliation, which he quotes and rejects, must first learn how this Old Testament regulation was currently interpreted and received in Jesus' day. The words of Jesus of course stand in contrast to the written *lex talionis*, but comparing them with the *lex talionis* as it was then orally interpreted makes most evident Jesus' bold meaning and at the same time the reasonableness and humanitarianism of current Jewish opinion. For this opinion also had long since abandoned, for rather absurd but morally admirable reasons, any literal or exact requirement of the penalty, "You must give life for life, eye for eye, tooth for tooth, hand for hand, foot for foot, burning for burning, wound for wound, lash for lash" (Exod. 21:23–25). This law itself, when enacted, had moderated the more ancient practice of seven-fold vengeance (Gen. 4:24). Down to the time of Jesus, punishments had been progressively mitigated, still staying within the law. R. Dosetai ben Judah argued that, since the eye of an offender might be larger than the one struck out, to insist upon payment in kind would be unjust. Simeon ben Yakai reached the same conclusion by considering the case of a blind man guilty of injuring the eye of another. In this instance exact retaliation is impossible, still some sort of just punishment ought to be inflicted. The conclusion therefore was well-established in Jesus' day that *lex talionis* meant monetary reimbursement for injuries, and this every one who heard Jesus, and Jesus himself, must have known, however much the actual practice of men in that day and in ours falls short of the Jewish sense of justice. Legal procedure, then, attempted to estimate the value of a wound or limb lost; just retaliation meant suit for damages.

It would seem that a law of liability for damages and ways for claiming compensation are indispensable to any society. Yet

Jesus virtually rejects *lex talionis* even in this sense. Resistance of one who is evil not only crudely by returning blows when blows have been struck, but also by availing oneself of the protection of courts of law seem pointedly excluded by the words, "If any one would sue you and take your coat, let him have your cloak as well." Far beyond merely enduring an injury by striking not again *or by refusing to claim damages,* going a second mile puts one in the way of inconvenience if not actual injury for the sake of him who is evil. Non-resisting love renounces all claims on behalf of self.

Whatever may be said regarding the practicability of the strenuous teachings of Jesus and notwithstanding perplexing problems about the sense in which they were meant to be applied, we must search fully into their nature and meaning. What has now been said should make perfectly obvious the difference between Jesus' ethic of non-resistance and all forms of non-violent resistance, to which his views have sometimes been watered down in the interest of making them more plausible. It is plain that Jesus did not substitute the milder coercion of law courts and a system of claims and counter-claims for exacting an eye for an eye. Judaism had already done that! Jesus' ethic is one of non-resisting, unclaiming love. He did not say, Go one mile and a half more, then call the sheriff! He did not say, Do not resist by violent means which necessarily bring death, but you may resist non-violently by using all means such as passive non-cooperation and civil disobedience which fall short of directly killing another man. He did not simply distinguish between the crossbow the English yeoman used, which the Pope once called a "right devilish weapon," and feudal armor and siege machinery, permitting one and not the other form of resistance, or between the degree of violence and carnage involved in alternative methods of modern total war. Significant distinctions may have to be made between atom bombs and blockbusters, between obliteration and precision bombing, between just and unjust wars, between warfare and economic sanctions, between that particular combination of physical force, "spiritual" force and chicanery by which dictators are overturned and the combination of physical and "spiritual" force and chicanery by which they come to power, between a *coup d'état* and lobbying for forcing one's will, between bullets and ballots for the correction of injustice. Every one makes such distinctions, but at this point in his teaching Jesus is not concerned with these issues. Non-violent or passive resistance and violent resistance are *equally* far removed from non-resistance. Non-resistance is incommensurable with *any form* of resistance. Resistance does not become more Christian by becoming non-violent, neither is armed resistance unchristian by virtue of its being armed but by virtue of being *resistant*. Neither active resistance nor passive non-cooperation are identical with Jesus' strenuous ethic of non-resistance, and neither one approximates closer to it than the other. It is possible, therefore, that circumstances and arguments which will justify the Christian in departing from the ethics of Jesus so far as to abandon non-resistance will also warrant his resisting with arms. The purely technical difference between spiritual and material coercion, between non-violence and violence, gives no ground for begging the question in Christian ethics in favor of either form of resistance, since any form of resistance equals any other in equally not being non-resistance and all alike resist him who is evil. Of this more later.

Love so unclaiming as to be thoroughly non-resistant manifests itself in other teachings of Jesus. "'Lord, how often shall my brother sin against me, and I forgive him? As many as seven times?' Jesus said to him, 'I do not say to you seven times, but seventy times seven'" (Matt. 18:21, 22). Forgiveness of another person times without number results from willingness to abandon all claims upon him, however just they may be, or at least from willingness to satisfy his claims whatever be his attitude of neglect or defiance toward the righteous claims you may have upon him. If you still have an unrenounced claim upon another person which you feel justified in making a precondition of his good standing with you, then he really ought not to be forgiven times without limit, and you yourself ought to forgive him no more than, say, seven times in a day. Surely that is all the scoundrel has a right to expect, more than he deserves; and moreover some limit on forgiveness by insisting upon the fulfillment of your own claims may be exactly what he needs. There is some point in retelling the story of the prodigal son so as to hold the father's forgiveness within more reasonable bounds. The son, having wasted his substance in a far country with riotous living,

> came home penniless but full of good intentions; but the father, who knew by experience what such intentions are usually worth, met his son's entreaties with implacable firmness: "My house is closed to you till such time as you have made good your position by honest work, and also replaced the sum that you have wasted"; the son then went out into the world, and turned over a new leaf, and when at last he returned to his father he thanked him for the strictness that had led to his amendment, unlike other fathers whose foolish laxity and weak acquiescence would have left him to continue in his bad habits . . .

Would not the hearer of this story have been forced to admit that "it actually happens so in life," and to proceed to the inference that "the Heavenly Father acts likewise"?[9] Jesus appears to have taught differently.

Jesus' teaching on divorce seems a case of his judging between conflicting scriptural rules. He appeals from the "Moses" who wrote Deuteronomy to the "Moses" who wrote Genesis, from Moses the sober statesman to Moses the heady idealist and prophet of God's absolute ordinance in marriage, while the Jews preferred the statesman's sober attempt to accommodate legislation to human, all too human, realities: "For your hardness of heart he wrote you this commandment [allowing divorce]. But from the beginning of creation, 'God made them male and female.' 'For this reason, a man shall leave his father and mother and be joined to his wife, and the two shall become one'" (Mark 10:5–8). Instead of regarding Jesus' teaching on divorce as an instance of such legalistic procedure of appealing from the "Moses" of Deuteronomy to the "Moses" of Genesis for establishing priority among rules, instead of regarding his view as an appeal through

[9]Anders Nygren, *Agape and Eros*, Society for Promoting Christian Knowledge, London, 1932, Pt. I, Vol. I, p. 59. (Published in the United States by Macmillan.)

and beyond scripture to some philosophical notion of an "order of creation" in which permanent monogamy is firmly written, it is possible, and preferable, to regard his strenuous views on marriage and divorce as another manifestation of unclaiming love transcending enactment into statute. Beyond question Jesus' original words are those given in Luke, "Every one who divorces his wife and marries another commits adultery, and he who marries a woman divorced from her husband commits adultery" (16:18), and again, with severe simplicity, in Mark 10:11, 12. For the hardness of Christian hearts Matthew twice inserts the qualifying words, "except for unchastity" (5:32 and 19:9). Permission of divorce for this or any other reason is not a genuine part of Jesus' teaching, although it must be admitted that only with this permission does the saying conceivably become a part of the customs and legal structure of any possible human society. As it stands in Matthew, the teaching is identical with the interpretation of R. Shammai, whose opinions were in the ascendancy in Jesus' day. If Jesus had merely voiced the prevailing opinion, his disciples would not have been surprised by what he said, much less have exclaimed, as Matthew himself reports, "If such is the case of a man with his wife, it is not expedient to marry" (19:10). This response is completely out of place where it stands after the words of Shammai have been placed on Jesus' lips; it belongs rather with the original form of the teaching in Mark and Luke. Even then, it is a misunderstanding of Jesus to suppose that he gave a new, and more utterly severe, law for marriage, rather than an ethic whose yoke of obligation is equally heavy or light whether one marries or not.

How should this be understood? Adultery as the primary reason for divorce appears to be the natural and just order of human relationships when claims, what is "due," are being considered. In polygamous societies adultery or unchastity is punished even more severely than where monogamous marriage prevails; and everywhere, whatever the form of marriage, as long as marriage endures as an institution, there has been some definition of the faithfulness due one's partner in marriage, the legitimate claim of one, the acknowledged duty of the other partner. Thus, in the order of human claims, adultery, or failure to fulfill basic claims, comes first as reason for releasing the injured or innocent party from any further obligation within the marriage. Something like this line of reasoning both should and will find acceptance as long as the normal procedure for estimating rightful claims, and weighing refusal of what is due in terms of these claims, continues to be the primary consideration for preserving a marriage or bringing it to an end. For Jesus the order of claims upon another has been supplanted by a sequence dictated by another's needs; for this reason unchastity was for him not so decisive as nature and society teach us it is in the order of claims; and for him a marriage terminated for this as well as for any other reason represented some degree of failure to achieve God's purpose. Unclaiming love will hardly find any cause for divorce, least of all will it fasten first upon what is the chief reason for divorce in the attitude of a person mainly concerned to claim his own rights.

As was said in the case of unclaiming love manifested as non-resistance, divorce on account of adultery is as far removed from the teaching of Jesus as divorce would be for any of the other reasons prevalently considered to be grounded in more or less important and just claims upon a partner in marriage. It is possible, therefore, that circumstances and arguments which will justify the Christian in departing from the ethics of Jesus so far as to divorce on account of unchastity, and marry again, will also warrant remarriage after divorce for other cause. Different degrees of seriousness in the infraction of claims are of great importance, but they give no ground for begging the question in Christian ethics in favor of divorce under one circumstance only, since divorce for any reason is absolutely different from no divorce at all. Moreover, Jesus' judgment upon the law of Moses that he permitted divorce only on account of the hardness of men's hearts remains an essential part of a Christian theory of law.

This interpretation of Jesus' meaning might also be suggested by the extent to which Jesus did not approve the place of superiority customarily assigned the husband in respect to the claims and duties within Jewish patriarchal marriage. The status of woman as a piece of property owned by the male still found institutional expression in two ways: By definition, adultery was a crime committed by a woman against her husband or by a man against the husband of some other woman, never by a man against his own wife, just as trespass is a crime against the owner of property, never against the property itself. And it was not customary to speak of a wife *initiating* divorce. Both of these Jesus spontaneously set aside: "Whoever divorces his wife and marries another, commits adultery *against her;* and if *she* divorces her husband and marries another, she commits adultery" (Mark 10:11). Scarcely relevant to anything that might happen within the Jewish community, this statement is so amazing coming from a Palestinian Jew that most scholars in fact maintain it could have been written only within the Græco-Roman environment of early Christianity.

The relation of these strenuous teachings of Jesus to the supernatural measure of morality, the love of God and the kingdom of God, has already been explored. At this point it is sufficient to summarize their relation to the law: They constitute an ethic of perfection which transcends any possible legal formulation. "You, therefore, must be perfect, as your heavenly Father is perfect" (Matt. 5:48), cannot be captured in a code. Because this is an extension of the Old Testament norm, "You must be holy; for I, the Lord your God, am holy" (Lev. 19:2), Jesus finishes the law in the sense of completing it. Because for Jesus the determination of valid obligation has shifted so far from the laws themselves (supposed by the Jews to make them a peculiar, a holy people) over to the side of this supernatural principle of perfection itself, Jesus finishes the law in the sense of destroying its very nature as law. It is as if in every one of his strenuous teachings Jesus were uttering the challenge, "Try to make a law out of this if you can! Try to make this customary, conventional or habitual!"

Or to say the same thing, "See whether in terms of these requirements any one can claim to be an authority on good and evil. See whether any one can take his measure in the mirror of these words and still consider himself among the righteous." In face of a standard which requires at least more of us than we are capable of performing, and only then, is the righteousness of those great and noble men, the scribes and Pharisees, exceeded. When Nietzsche said, "The good *must* be Pharisees—they have no choice,"[10] he was right so long as the law, any law or customary morality, remains intact, but he took insufficient account of the transcendent goodness of that single individual who was able to say, "Why do you call me good? None is good but God alone" (Mark 10:18; Luke 18:19).

III. WHAT THE CHRISTIAN DOES WITHOUT A CODE: ST. PAUL'S ANSWER

Concerning Jesus' teaching on the inwardness of real purity or defilement, the gospel of Mark makes editorial comment, "Thus he declared all foods clean" (Mark 7:19). Jesus, however, on that occasion was dealing only with the question of ritual handwashing; he himself never abrogated the food laws of the Jews. This was the work of St. Paul, who extended the principles manifested by Jesus mainly in connection with sabbath observance and ceremonial cleanliness to cover also the law of clean and unclean meats and the rite of circumcision.

> If with Christ you died to the elemental spirits of the universe, why do you live as if you still belonged to the world? Why do you submit to regulations, Do not handle, Do not taste, Do not touch (referring to things which all perish as they are used), according to human precepts and doctrines? These have indeed an appearance of wisdom in promoting rigor of devotion and self-abasement and severity to the body, but they are of no value in checking the indulgence of the flesh (Col. 2:20–23).

Except for Paul Christian liberty from Jewish legalism might not have gone so far, and only after the success of his polemic against a more conservative and more Jewish interpretation of Christianity did the author of Mark's gospel, and other Christians like

[10]*Thus Spake Zarathustra*, III, lvi, 26.

him, realize that Jesus had *in effect* if not in actuality "declared all foods clean" and circumcision unnecessary.

The letter to the Galatians was Paul's great declaration of Christian independence from legalism. Dispute now centered upon a powerful party of Jewish Christians who insisted that for a Gentile to become a Christian he must first of all become a Jew by undergoing circumcision and submitting to food laws and other requirements of Torah. In answer to those who wanted to judaize Christian ethics by *enforcing* circumcision, Paul notably did not impose a new law *forbidding* it. Instead, he went beyond any form of law, declaring that "in Christ Jesus neither circumcision nor uncircumcision is of any avail, but faith working through love" (Gal. 5:6).

Notice the far-reaching consequence of this position. St. Paul advanced significantly beyond the actual views of Jesus by nullifying laws which in all likelihood Jesus never thought of questioning, yet his ethical perspective and reasons for doing so were essentially the same as Jesus'. This means that it is of little importance for Christian ethics to know exactly what part of the law Jesus or Paul actually rejected and which laws they still retained. Their rejection of particular laws which happened to engage their attention, propelled as it was by a radically new understanding of morality, cannot be limited to overcoming this or that historical form of law. In principle every form of legalism was nullified by them from the beginning. If Paul might go beyond Jesus, Christians of a later day may go beyond Paul if in any respect Paul still considered Jewish law binding as law. Paul himself sees quite clearly that the standpoint from which circumcision and food laws are rightly declared no longer of any avail also overturns more universal rules for distinguishing good from bad, worthy from unworthy, persons. "There is neither Jew nor Greek, there is neither slave nor free, there is neither male nor female; for you are all one in Christ Jesus" (Gal. 3:28). The business of Christian ethics, therefore, does not consist in following literally the selection of rules from Torah made by Jesus or Paul. It consists rather in employing their spirit of freedom in relation to the existing morality of custom and law born anew and bred in every man.

". . . There is obviously a great deal written in the Old Testament as divine law which no Christian can regard as binding upon himself unless he ceases to be a Christian."[1] How shall permanently valid teachings be discovered in the Bible and separated from the "great deal" that is no longer binding, without recourse to some third rule or set of rules and without importing into Christian ethics some sub-Christian philosophical principle? Christian regard for the worth of human life cannot be grounded in the commandment not to kill (or in the Stoic notion of a divine spark in every human being), nor can Christian marriage be derived from the continuing validity of the seventh commandment *as a law* (or from a self-sufficient order of creation in which monogamous marriage is clearly written), not even with the support of a secondary *rule* that these rules are superior to all the rest. Brunner is correct in saying that, "When we wish to know what is just in the state, in economics, in society, marriage and the family, we receive no help from the Decalogue"—certainly not in its primitive meaning—"but can only attach to its commandments what we have learned in other ways."[2] His error is in the primacy he assigns to the "law of nature," a sub-Christian source of insight, in correcting the defects of scriptural and other actual codes of law.

There are those in every age who insist that for a person to become a Christian he must first of all become respectable by submitting to certain accepted social requirements. Yet obviously a great deal in any code of gentlemanly respectability no Christian can regard as binding upon himself unless he ceases to be a Christian. How, again, shall discrimination be made without simply revising the rules of conventional respectability or having too early recourse to some principle of philosophical ethic itself a modern Torah? "In Christ Jesus neither 'respectability' nor lack of respectability, neither conventional nor unconventional be-

[1]Emil Brunner, *Justice and the Social Order*, Harpers, 1945, p. 123.
[2]*Ibid.*, p. 122.

havior, is of any avail." With this as a starting point, we shall inquire whether from "faith working through love," and from this alone, an entirely Christocentric ethic can be elaborated. Interpreting scripture by scripture, this is the question: Is there any principle in scripture itself whereby we may leave aside the "great deal written there as divine law which no Christian can regard as binding upon himself unless he ceases to be a Christian"?

The ethics of Paul, indeed Christian ethics generally, seems always in peril of opening the floodgates of anarchy and license in the name of freedom from law. In order to avoid this danger, Christian ethics has frequently been placed in the protective custody of certain supposed ways for making ethical distinctions more forceful. Surrounded by a guard of Judaism, Aristotelianism, Stoicism, or, in recent times, personalistic idealism, "faith working through love" proves less disturbing to prevailing ethical conceptions and directions are laid down in advance for deciding what is permitted and what not. Nevertheless, in contrast to these forms of coalition ethics, the answer St. Paul himself gave to this issue is beyond doubt more distinctive of Christianity.

In I Corinthians Paul had occasion to defend his position against a party of Christian libertines who came upon him in an opposite direction from the Jewish Christians. These libertines were extreme anti-legalists or antinomians who believed Christian liberty to be quite without regulation. "All things are lawful for me," all things are now permitted, the slogan of this faction, Paul quotes several times in course of refuting it.

Paul counters with the theme, All things are lawful for me, all things are now permitted, *which Christian love permits.* " 'All things are lawful,' but not all things are helpful. 'All things are lawful,' but not all things build up. Let no one seek his own good, but the good of his neighbor" (I Cor. 10:23, 24). For Paul there is a clear connection between love and doing good works. Paul's principle may be formulated as, "Love and do as you *then* please"; this by no means implies simply, "Do as you please";

for by definition Christian love will be pleased only by doing what the neighbor needs. In place of rules for conduct, instead of "the law" which Christianity entirely finishes, comes not irregularity but self-regulation, and not merely the self-regulation of free, autonomous individuals but the self-regulation of persons unconditionally bound to their neighbors by obedient "faith working through love."

Although the practical problems with which Paul deals in this letter to the church at Corinth are those of a bygone day, as long as he sticks to teaching only what he understands love will teach them, he gives imperishable ethical instruction. Only when he appeals in sub-Christian fashion to what "nature itself teaches" does Paul adopt parochial standards about women's hairdress and such matters (I Cor. 11:14). The wonder is that Paul was so thoroughly emancipated from his Jewish background as not to appeal to Torah, or that under pressure of advising in church administration he did not "lay down the law," his own law or that which "nature itself teaches," more than he does. His exhortations generally have authority only as love's directions, and hold in view the needs and "edification" or "building up" of others. Christian love will not be limited by any previously existing regulation drawn from what society or "surely nature itself" teaches, it will not conform to preconceptions about right and wrong or conventional codes of conduct with which authorities on good and evil happen to be prepossessed.

Nevertheless, such love, far from being directionless, lays down its own directions, internal self-regulations conformable only to the needs of neighbor. While love itself never submits to external rule and does not proportion its benefaction according to some rule, it never becomes unruly, since the needs of other persons are the rule of love and quickly teach such love what to do. Serving the needs and claims of others requires discrimination and maximum self-control, yet giving the name of duty solely to the needs of neighbor has already led quite beyond law as a primary source of discriminating insight and as power regulating behavior. What should be done or not done in a particular instance, what is good or bad, right or wrong, what is better or worse than something else, what are "degrees of value"—these things in Christian ethics are not known in advance or derived from some preconceived code. They are derived *backward* by Christian love from what it apprehends to be the needs of others. Christian love which teaches the Christian what to do is itself *teachable* without restriction. Solicitous love elicits from a man conformity to its own requirements, and while these requirements vary with the neighbor's needs they are also as inflexible and "total."

"Everything is lawful, everything is permitted which Christian love permits" also means "everything is demanded which Christian love requires." The former is Christian liberty, the latter is slavery to Christ. The former, Christian leniency; the latter, Christian self-severity. Aristotelian "moderation" in all things strives to hit the "mean" between too much and too little; it is inflexible and immoderate about the principle of moderation. The religious ethic of St. Paul led him, in contrast, to become "all things to all men" (I Cor. 9:22), a principle of accommodation which lays down its own regulation as to when much or little should be done without primary reference to any principle, even the principle of moderation, standing between a Christian man and doing everything for all men. By being immoderate about this one thing, namely Christian care for the neighbor's needs, Christian ethics is *on principle* alternatively more lenient (more free from regulation) and more severe with itself (more subject to command) than any other ethic. Thus Paul sometimes became "as one under the law," at other times "as one outside the law" (I Cor. 9:20, 21).

Luther spoke of these two sides of the matter in his *Treatise on Christian Liberty*. The Christian, he said, is "perfectly free lord of all, subject to none." This is Christian leniency and flexibility in ethical behavior. "What love teaches" cannot be identified for all time and all historical or social circumstances with any particular program of action such as prohibition or socialism. In Christ Jesus, teetotalism is not of any avail, neither is the current informal regulation requiring a person to drink in order for him to be socially acceptable; socialism is of no avail, neither is private property an absolute; a rigid rule against taking life is not necessarily valid in all circumstances, as legalistic pacifism believes, neither, of course, is the opposite; forbidding card-playing or gardening on Sunday avails nothing, neither does the persuasion that a game of bridge is an indispensable right of man or that Sunday is the day a man has fully to himself.

Persons who desire rigid allegiance to certain programs for social reform, or the imposition of rules that will remove all doubt about how the individual should conduct himself, will have to go elsewhere than to Christian ethical theory. And they generally do: these are the fanatics for secular gospels and supernatural sanctions. Christian love whose nature is to allow itself to be guided by the needs of others changes its tactics as easily as it stands fast; it does either only on account of the quite unalterable strategy of accommodating itself to neighbor-needs. Indeed, only in contrast with this fundamental strategy does the word "law" receive decisive definition: that law which Christian ethics transcends and abrogates may be defined generally as *any* standard or principle which, for whatever good reasons, we do not allow to be breached even though the needs of others, when alone considered, require different actions from us.

A glance at the programs to which today both secular and religious groups are devoted leaves the impression that their inflexibility is more a vice than a virtue. They "have indeed an appearance of wisdom in promoting rigor of devotion and self-abasement and severity to the body, but they are of no value in checking the indulgence of the flesh" (Col. 2:23); they manifest, indeed, the mind of fleshly self-interest claiming to speak authoritatively on good and evil. These programs live on from pride in a position once taken, not from love sticking close to human needs which would long ago have altered them. On the surface and because of their numerous factions this seems especially true of left-wingers who live by opposing each other's proposals and *avant-garde* individuals who dearly love to be shocking. The same, however, is also true of Catholic opposition to birth control, the precise, almost murderous, practice of the principle that a mother ought to give her life for her child, and many a Protestant's legalistic championing of prohibition and total abstinence. What surely "nature itself teaches," what is taught by our own special enlightenment or intelligence, and indeed what love *once* taught must always be held suspect enough for critical re-examination in the light of present neighbor-needs and the means available for meeting them. Movements to reform human behavior as well as defenses of the *status quo ante* often gain prolonged life from "pride working through selfishness," while "faith working through love" would be a sensitive instrument responsively alert to change its doings with every real change in human affairs, always keeping itself abreast with changing needs. Such infinite willingness to learn springs from having our sensitivity to obligation in the actual situation confronting us quite freed from any slant in favor of self. Surely nature and grace both teach us that selfish partiality can best be protected under cover of some conventional ethical standard we are capable of performing easily and in which we can gain the authority of Pharisees.

Paul's way of declaring independence from law and from accepted customs stands in significant contrast to other so-called emancipated viewpoints that are more often met with. Intellectuals frequently act as if superior enlightenment gives them unqualified right to act in a different manner from what, they condescendingly concede, must still be required of ignorant people. The Corinthian Christians knew the pagan deities were nonentities, images of them idols that had no real existence, being mere replicas of nothing. Some of them declared, "All of us possess knowledge" (I Cor. 8:1), and then made a show of their freedom, ostentatiously buying meat from butcher shops next door to temples, meat which was known to have been previously offered to idols. No more than they did St. Paul believe such meat defiled: "We are no worse off if we do not eat, and no better off if we do" (I Cor. 8:8). But he taught that love would not give them such freedom as they were claiming on account of superior enlightenment. Knowledge may have its privileges, but the violation of love is not one of them. Paul's theme, Love and *then* do as you please, has little in common with, Gain superior knowledge, and *then* do as you please. All things are now permitted which knowledge permits, leads to results decidedly different from those which follow from, All things are now permitted which Christian love permits. Love takes care not to offend others, while increasing knowledge does not necessarily decrease arrogance or lead to increased concern for "edification." "Therefore, if food is a cause of my brother's falling, I will never eat meat, lest I cause my brother to fall" (I Cor. 8:13). This love-imposed restraint applies, of course, *only* to babes in Christ whose conscience may be wounded "when it is weak" (8:12), not at all to self-styled authorities who may take offense from observing some violation of their particular conception of good and evil.

On the other hand, religious people often believe that superior "spirituality" ought always freely to manifest itself in face of anything less spiritual. Some of the Corinthian Christians gave way to ecstatic seizures, speaking in tongues or unintelligible gibberish, they believed, under the impulse of the Holy Spirit. Now, just as St. Paul possessed the knowledge that an idol had no real existence, so also he did not doubt the possibility of real spiritual inspiration. He himself on occasion exercised the gift of tongues. But for him neither of these undeniable facts was basic for Christian liberty. He did not declare, Be certain you are divinely inspired and do as you *then* please, All things are lawful for me which the Spirit moves me to do, but rather: Love and do as you *then* please, All things are lawful but not all things are helpful. To be helpful the Spirit also gives the gift of interpreting unknown tongues, so that presumably a Christian speaking in tongues will, out of consideration for edification, pause awhile for the translation to be given.

> Therefore, he who speaks in a tongue should pray for the power to interpret. For if I pray in a tongue, my spirit prays but my mind is unfruitful. What am I to do? I will pray with the spirit and I will pray with the mind also; I will sing with the spirit and I will sing with the mind also. Otherwise, how can any one in the position of an outsider say the "Amen" to your thanks-

giving when he does not know what you are saying? For you may give thanks well enough, but the other man is not edified. I thank God that I speak in tongues more than you all; nevertheless, in church I would rather speak five words with my mind, in order to instruct others, than ten thousand words in a tongue (I Cor. 14:13–19).

The Christian will also recognize that there is diversity of spiritual gifts, the mystery and ecstasy behind his own behavior giving him no special claim to divine inspiration in comparison with persons whose actions and emotions are less tempestuous. Indeed, for Paul, the *holy* Spirit may always be known by its quality, not by its strength; only the spirit of Christ is the true Spirit of God. "Therefore I want you to understand that no one speaking by the Spirit of God ever says 'Jesus be cursed!' and no one can say 'Jesus is Lord' except by the Holy Spirit" (I Cor. 12:3). This also means that no one speaking by the Spirit of God ever says an unlovely thing. "If I speak in the tongues of men and of angels, but have not love, I am a noisy gong or a clanging cymbal" (I Cor. 13:1). The sophisticated freedom of enlightened people and claims to independence of spiritual inspiration made by religious people are both put in halter by Paul's "still more excellent way" to freedom.

But may not human reason or conscience comprehend right and wrong from what "nature itself teaches"? If so, then it may be asserted that the rational, moral law known to all men gives them sufficient ground for freedom from "unjust" statutory laws and from oppressive social institutions and conventions. Perhaps here, and not in some special enlightenment or special inspiration, is to be found a basis for sound morality without specific rules and for every legitimate claim to freedom. Christian liberty, it may be affirmed, cannot transcend moral law known by practical reason and sensitive conscience.

The question arises whether Paul himself did not form a coalition with another, equally primary source of valid ethical insight by his appeal to the law written on the hearts or natural consciences of men generally.

> When Gentiles who have not the law do by nature what the
> law requires, they are a law to themselves, even though they do
> not have the law. They show that what the law requires is
> written on their hearts, while their conscience also bears witness
> and their conflicting thoughts accuse or perhaps excuse them on
> that day when, according to my gospel, God judges the secrets
> of men by Christ Jesus (Rom. 2:14–16).

This passage has been made to bear the weight of an elaborate
theory of "natural law," or right naturally and generally known
to human reason or conscience. From man's native moral capacity Christian ethics might derive a system of definite and forceful
precepts and prohibitions, in short, a law. At least, it may be
asked, did not St. Paul and must not any acceptable view of ethics
in some sense trust the promptings and warnings of conscience?

Whether or not there is actually a natural morality inscribed
in every human heart, this much is certain: this law also Christian
ethics transcends. The fact that such law is inward and indeed
that God himself wrote it there in his work of creating man
would not alter its character as law or give this law primacy for
the Christian. Paul believed that *God* actually revealed Torah to
Moses no less certainly than he may have believed that God wrote
his precepts and prohibitions on the heart, giving voice to human
conscience. Divine origin either of the written law or of the
natural law (the suggestions of conscience) was simply not decisive for Paul. Tracing law home to a moment of historical revelation in the past before Christ or to creation apparently did not
altogether settle the issue he raises regarding present validity.
Regardless of what God did through Moses in the past, what he
has now done in Jesus Christ, and what he is doing, ought now
to become the one and only center of man's existence before God.
God has *now* showed thee, O man, what is good and what the
Lord doth require of thee. Through decisive historical events and
in a historical person making time A. D. quite different from time
B. C., God *now* enters into covenant with man, overcoming, to
speak of ethics only, all Do and Don't morality whether in the
form of an external law *once* valid for the Jews or an inward law

once valid for the Gentiles. Man's ethical and religious orientation focuses on the Christ, necessarily turning away from the old Law, away also from the sovereign dictates of natural conscience. The primacy of either is overcome, both must be schooled by Christ. Code morality still finds a standing point in the words of Jeremiah, "I will put my *law* within them, and will write it on their hearts" (31:33); but his use of the future tense of the verb obviously refers to some source of instruction outside the normal, universal promptings of conscience. No looking backward in time toward God's activity in creation, no delving deep into rational human nature or the human heart (which in fact he believed inscrutable) fulfills Jeremiah's expectation, but looking toward that person from whom men may learn something they do not already know merely from capacities within themselves. Whether in the old Law or the new covenant, God manifests his will in something objectively given to which man must conform rather than something conformable to man. Christian ethics is an ethics of perfection which cuts man to fit the pattern, not the pattern to fit man: how, then, can any major part of its fundamental content be drawn from man?

In striking fashion St. Augustine confirms the interpretation just given of Romans 2:14–16: these words of St. Paul's cannot be taken as ground for importing into the heart of Christian ethics a sub- or extra-Christian source of moral judgment. We must inquire with great care, St. Augustine remarks, precisely what sense it is in which the apostle attributes authenticity to the law written in natural conscience; this we must do

> *lest there should seem to be no certain difference in the new testament,* in that the Lord promised that He would write His laws in the hearts of His people, inasmuch as the Gentiles have this done for them naturally. This question therefore has to be sifted, arising as it does as one of no inconsiderable importance. For some may say, "If God distinguishes the new testament from the old by this circumstance, that in the old He wrote His law on tables but in the new He wrote them on men's hearts, *by what are the faithful of the new testament discriminated from the Gentiles,* which have the work of the law written on their

> hearts, whereby they do by nature the things of the law, *as if,*
> *forsooth, they were better than the ancient people, which re-*
> *ceived the law on tables, and before the new people, which has*
> *that conferred on it by the new testament which nature has*
> *already bestowed on them?"* [3]

Indeed, by what is Christian ethics to be distinguished from
generally valid natural morality, if some theory of natural law
becomes an authentic part and to any degree the *primary* foundation of Christian morality? This would amount to saying that the
dictates of natural conscience and morality reasoned out in terms
of the common good or some other philosophic norm (while these
are doubtless better than an ancient, external code) are nonetheless "before the new people, which has that conferred on it by
the new testament [*i.e.*, by Christ] which nature" and reason
have already bestowed upon others.

St. Augustine holds that by "the Gentiles" the apostle undoubtedly means only those Gentiles who have become Christian; these
as well as former Jews have *now* had God's law written on their
hearts by the new covenant; just as, in an earlier passage, St.
Paul speaks of the gospel as "the power of God for salvation to
every one who has faith, to the Jew first and also *to the Greek*"
(Rom. 1:16). This is poor exegesis, but good Christian ethics.
Too often "natural law" theory has been validated in such fashion
as to render the gospel ethic superfluous; Christian ethics has then
nothing *distinctive* (and also *primary*) to say about morals that
has not already been bestowed upon mankind by nature or philosophy. Undoubtedly it must be admitted that St. Paul actually
refers to the voice of natural conscience, a God-given morality
of nature, and not simply, as Augustine supposes, to the insights
conscience gains when converted toward Christ. Beyond question,
then, he refers to a ground for morality natural to all men and
within their competence as reasonable beings. *But this law also,*
he believed, Christian ethics transcends, for all its vaunted inwardness or natural spontaneity and in spite of the fact that God

[3] *On the Spirit and the Letter*, ch. xliii (*Basic Writings of St. Augustine*, ed.
by Whitney J. Oates. Random House, 1949, I, 494). (Italics mine.)

himself ordained it for the Gentiles along with special Torah for the Jews. What God has now ordained shifts morality from foundation in either of these ancient standards for righteousness.

When Paul wrote that "the law was our custodian until Christ came" (Gal. 3:24), he did not mean a division of function between inferior and superior teachers. The custodian in question did no teaching, he was a slave who conducted a young man through the bewildering streets of the city and turned him over to his one and only teacher. Whatever validity Paul assigns the law in his letter to the Romans, it never includes positive instruction in any aspect of Christian morality. Jesus Christ is the one and only teacher.

The same may be said for the validity allowed the promptings and warnings of conscience, or, in the doubtful possibility that Paul went so far, the quite secondary validity he found in a system of first principles of ethics known as natural law. They serve perhaps as custodians, performing even this function in extraordinarily self-contradictory fashion. These inner lawgivers make us acquainted with sin and awaken defiance in us; far from wanting to follow what the inner voice suggests, every man also wishes daringly to do otherwise and, "aroused by the law," bit in teeth, he often does otherwise (*cf.* Rom. 7). No law, not even an inner one, has positive moralizing power.

Moreover, it is insufficient to say that code morality written on tablets of the mind or on tables of stone has not enough control over will and action. The problem lies not only in willing what is good but also in knowing what is good among all existing customary regulations and among the equally numerous and diverse suggestions of conscience. Paul cared for the conscience of the weak who thought it wrong to eat meat offered to idols, but he by no means believed this scruple to be right. Instead of going to the voice of conscience for final instruction, the Christian, both he who is weak and still under regulation and he who is strong and not, needs to have his conscience instructed.

A Turk who hath possessed himself with a false belief that it is unlawful for him to drink wine, if he do it, his conscience smites

> him for it; but though he keep many concubines, his conscience
> troubles him not, because his judgment is already defiled with
> a false opinion that it is lawful for him to do the one, and un-
> lawful to do the other.
>
>   For conscience followeth judgment, doth not inform it. . . .
> So we confess also, that conscience is an excellent thing where
> it is rightly informed and enlightened: wherefore some of us have
> fitly compared it to the lanthorn, and the light of Christ to a
> candle; a lanthorn is useful when a clear candle burns and shines
> in it: but otherwise of no use. To the light of Christ then in the
> conscience, and not to man's natural conscience, it is that we
> continually commend men.[4]

The early Quaker theologian who wrote these words setting forth
the doctrine of the supra-natural light *within* the lantern of man's
conscience needs to be supplemented only by reference to the
decisive moment of light *for* conscience in the historical Christ
to place him in entire agreement with St. Paul's view of a source
of ethical knowledge transcending all law, a source outside the
heart toward which the heart should turn.

   Christian ethics, therefore, is not greatly concerned to prove
that there is anything in our moral intuitions not derived from
social training. It may be that there is nothing in individual conscience, no content of his moral or value judgments, that is not
normally placed there by association of ideas drawn from customary morality. It may be that we are what we are in our moral
judgments because we have been where we have been and belonged to what we have belonged to. But Lord of both conscience
and custom is Christ; he alone, standing without the law, has
become the norm for selecting among the rules that surround us,
he alone the one authentic teacher for conscience. Only love, and
not special knowledge, inspiration or clear conscience, liberates
the Christian from bondage to the laws and conventions of society.

   While love frees from the law it binds a man even closer to
the needs of others, even as Jesus Christ was bound; and precisely
that which alone frees also binds. The possession of law—any law,

   [4]Robert Barclay, *Apology for the True Christian Divinity,* 1676 (*Barclay in
Brief,* edited by Eleanore Price Mather. Pendle Hill Historical Studies. No. 3,
p. 39).

as defined above—"puffs up" the man prepossessed with it. Conventional respectability puffs up the "gentleman" with self-importance. Acting according to "the principle of the thing" puffs up. Knowledge and wisdom puff up. Appreciation of high spiritual values puffs up. St. Paul realized long before Nietzsche that at least every one considers himself an authority on good and evil, and no less than every one desires to know that he is good. But love which is not puffed up does not leave men without a directive in life such as these other views supply. As Paul says, "Love builds up" (I Cor. 8:1). Love builds up others, and so doing it also builds up its own unlegislated self-discipline in personal living. Variable as the neighbor's needs, love is constantly engaged in tearing down where need be, and again building up, directives as to how better the neighbor may be served.

Everything is quite lawful, *absolutely everything* is permitted which love permits, everything without a single exception. "Therefore let no one pass judgment on you in questions of food and drink or with regard to a festival or a new moon or a sabbath. . . . Why do you submit to regulations, Do not handle, Do not taste, Do not touch (referring to things which all perish as they are used), according to human precepts and doctrines?" (Col. 2:16, 21). Turned around, however, this ethic becomes very grim, very grim indeed. *Absolutely everything* is commanded which love requires, absolutely everything without the slightest exception or softening. *Freedom from* the law belongs only to that individual who is *free for* reason of the most terrifying obligation. So Luther could turn to the other side of the matter and say that the Christian man is in bondage to all and subject to every one, "a perfectly dutiful servant of all, subject to all." In a Christian outlook there is always inflexibility against difficult opposition or repeated rebuff which gives steadfastness in action on behalf of any need love discerns. With whatever is relevant to actual need, love changes its tactic; against what is irrelevant love stands firm. When all fellow-feeling and natural affection wither, when there are no grounds for love in the neighbor's apparent worth, when his response is not appreciative but the contrary, when "nature itself teaches" us to be repelled, when, in short, love that has only begun to be Christian would be destroyed by the enemy, a Christian in love believes against hope, even as was said of Abraham, the father of faith, "in hope he believed against hope" (Rom. 4:18). When otherwise there is no foundation or justification for love, a Christian loves on in faith; love never ends because it endures all things (I Cor. 13:7, 8). A Christian says "nevertheless" and "in spite of this" to every circumstance, persistently finding the works of love obligatory. The commands of love are as stringent as the needs of the world are urgent: sensing this, let any man *then* do as he pleases.

This, then, is the Christian solution of the problem of absolutism and relativism with which philosophers wrestle in their systems of ethics, frequently at the same time dismissing Christian and every other religious ethic as necessarily absolutistic and dogmatic. Yet, rightly understood, we here stand at the heart of the problem of relativism threatening morals, and of an adequate solution to this problem.

> Is there a possible solution beyond the alternative of an absolutism that breaks down in every radical change of history and a relativism that makes change itself the ultimate principle? I think there is, and I think it is implied in the basis of Christian ethics, namely, in the principle of love, in the sense of the Greek word *agape*. This is not said in an apologetic interest for Christianity, but it is said under the urge of the actual problem of our present world situation. Love, *agape*, offers a principle of ethics which maintains an eternal, unchangeable element but makes its realization dependent on continuous acts of a creative intuition. Love is above law, also above the natural law in Stoicism and the supra-natural law in Catholicism. You *can* express it as a law, you can say as Jesus and the apostles did: "Thou shalt love"; but in doing so you know that this is a paradoxical way of speaking, indicating that the ultimate principle of ethics, which, on the one hand, is an unconditional command, is, on the other hand, the power breaking through all commands. And just this ambiguous character of love enables it to be the solution of the question of ethics in a changing world. . . . Love alone can transform itself according to the concrete demands of every individual and

social situation without losing its eternity and dignity and unconditional validity. . . . Love, realizing itself from kairos to
kairos, creates an ethics which is beyond the alternative of absolute and relative ethics.[5]

The task of the next chapter will be to give a more systematic
elaboration of the meaning of Christian love. This, to be sure,
has already been defined in some measure by tracing in the preceding chapters its emergence from Jewish theology, apocalypticism, and legalism.

[5]Paul Tillich, *The Protestant Era*, University of Chicago Press, 1948, pp. 154–155,
156. *Cf.* also the chapter entitled "Beyond Law and Relativity" in Reinhold
Niebuhr, *Faith and History*, Scribners, 1949.

III

THE MEANING OF CHRISTIAN LOVE

"A man would no more be able to live exclusively according to the highest Christian concepts all the time than he
would be able to live by eating only at the Lord's table."
—Soren Kierkegaard, *Works of Love*, p. 39.

"I have given no definition of love. This is impossible because there is no higher principle by which it could be
defined."—Paul Tillich, *The Protestant Era*, p. 160.

I. TEACHINGS OF JESUS CONCERNING DISINTERESTED LOVE FOR NEIGHBOR

WE have seen that Christian love is unclaiming and
non-resisting, that a Christian "seeks not his own good,
but the good of his neighbor" (I Cor. 10:24). The
question which logically should now be posed, Who then is my
neighbor? is in fact that most unanswered question in the entire
New Testament! Jesus told the parable of the Good Samaritan
apparently in answer to the lawyer's question, "Who is my neighbor?" (Luke 10:29). The most noteworthy thing about the story,
however, is that it does not answer this question at all, but some
other. The question asked for a definition of "my neighbor"; Jesus
told a story defining instead the meaning of "neighborly love."
No answer at all is given to the request for a general definition
of "neighbor" which might justify loving a certain man if he
falls within the definition or failure to love him if he does not.
It may be supposed that the priest and the Levite were hurrying
along that day to a conference called to give authoritative answer
to the question, "*Who* is my neighbor?" Certainly the qualifica-
tions they had drawn up for *first* determining whether another
person was one's neighbor or not were likely as broad and inclu-

sive as any the Samaritan may have had in his head. Jesus took the weight off of concern for *first* knowing the neighbor. The question he really answered in this parable was not the one he was asked but the one which he himself addressed to the questioner: "Which of these three, do you think, *proved neighbor* to the man who fell among robbers?" and promptly turned into a requirement: "Go and do likewise" (Luke 10:36, 37). Not "which of these three, do you think, knew best who his neighbor was?" but, "which . . . proved neighbor?" Proving neighborly is one thing; setting up tests for proving the neighbor another. The question the lawyer put to Jesus was not the question Jesus put to him. In the answer the original question was radically transformed:

> Christ does not talk about knowing one's neighbor, but about one's self being a neighbor, as the Samaritan proved himself one by his compassion. For by his compassion he did not prove that the man attacked was his neighbor, but that he was the neighbor of the one who was assaulted.[1]

This parable tells us something about neighbor-love, nothing about the neighbor. What the parable does is to demand that the questioner revise entirely his point of view, reformulating the question first asked so as to require neighborliness of himself rather than anything of his neighbor. A shift is made from defining the qualities of the man who rightfully ought to be loved to the specific demand that the questioner himself become a neighbor. The parable actually shows the nature and meaning of Christian love which alone of all ethical standpoints discovers the neighbor because it alone begins with neighborly love and not with discriminating between worthy and unworthy people according to the qualities they possess. Perhaps it would be better to forgo using the expression "love for neighbor," which puts the emphasis on who the neighbor is, and use instead "neighbor-love" or "neighborly love," expressions which have the advantage of stressing what love ought to be.

[1]Soren Kierkegaard, *Works of Love*. Translated from the Danish by David F. Swenson and Lillian Marvin Swenson, Princeton University Press, 1946, p. 19.

If there is any hope of an understanding here, the failure of Jesus to answer the first question, "*Who* is my neighbor?" should not be filled in by reference to loving everybody or all mankind. Nor should the correctness of such a universal definition of neighbor be demonstrated by reference to some divine spark in every man providing an element of worth hidden underneath apparent unworth and under the many attributes which separate man from man. Unquestionably, "if it is a virtue to love my neighbor *as a human being*, it must be a virtue—and not a vice—to love myself since I am a human being too. There is no concept of man in which I myself am not included."[2] But this is not the reason for neighbor-love. Christian love, attributing worth to the neighbor's needs infinitely superior to the claims of self, does not rest upon a doctrine of the infinite, inherent value of human personality in general; such a doctrine would logically lead to subtracting from obligation as much as the just claims of self require. Response to the general worth of human personality always hesitates a little in confronting the neighbor. Hereby the full particularity of neighborly love finding the neighbor out would be lost. Never is it said that "neighbor" includes "enemy" among those who ought to be loved because they are human beings, but rather that love for another *for his own sake*, neighborly love in the Christian sense, discovers the neighbor in every man it meets and as such has never yet met a friend or an enemy. Christian love does not mean discovering the essentially human underneath differences; it means detecting the neighbor underneath friendliness or hostility or any other qualities in which the agent takes special interest. The full particularity of neighborly love, finding the neighbor out by first requiring nothing of him, should not be reduced to universal brotherhood or the cosmopolitan spirit. This is stoicism, not Christianity. In Dostoyevsky's *The Brothers Karamazov* it was "a lady of little faith" who announced grandiosely that she loved humanity so much that she often dreamed of giving up everything for mankind. Father Zossima commended these dreams only in comparison with others which

[2]Erich Fromm, *Man for Himself*, Rinehart, 1947, pp. 128–129 (italics mine).

might have filled her mind and then said to her, "Sometime, un-
awares, you may do a good deed in reality." Doing a good deed
in reality, as neighbor-love led the Samaritan to do, stands at an
opposite pole from love for mankind generally.

> "The more I love humanity in general, the less I love man in
> particular. In my dream," he said, "I have often come to making
> enthusiastic schemes for the service of humanity, and perhaps I
> might actually have faced crucifixion if it had been suddenly
> necessary; and yet I am incapable of living in the same room with
> any one for two days together, as I know by experience. As soon
> as any one is near me, his personality disturbs my self-compla-
> cency and restricts my freedom. In twenty-four hours I begin to
> hate the best of men: one because he's too long over his dinner;
> another because he has a cold and keeps on blowing his nose.
> I become hostile to people the moment they come close to me.
> But it always happened that the more I detest men individually,
> the more ardent becomes my love for humanity."[3] . . . I could
> never understand how one can love one's neighbors. It's just one's
> neighbors, to my mind, that one can't love, though one might
> love those at a distance. . . . For any one to love a man, he must
> be hidden, for as soon as he shows his face, love is gone. . . .
> Beggars, especially genteel beggars, ought never to show them-
> selves, but to ask for charity through the newspaper. One can
> love one's neighbors in the abstract, or even at a distance, but at
> close quarters it's almost impossible.[4]

Love for men in general often means merely a bifocal "self-regarding concern for others," a selfish sociability, while love for
neighbor *for his own sake* insists upon a single-minded orientation of a man's primary intention toward *this* individual neighbor
with all his concrete needs. Christian love means an entirely
"neighbor-regarding concern for others," which begins with the
first man it sees. Since this man may be *any* man, such love is,
of course, universal in compass, but only implicitly universal. It
begins by loving "the neighbor," not mankind or manhood.

The expression "love for neighbor *for his own sake*" has just
been used. Such disinterested regard for another person is one

[3]Fyodor Dostoyevsky, *The Brothers Karamazov*, Bk. II, ch. 4, "A Lady of
Little Faith" (Modern Library Giant edition, p. 56).
[4]*Ibid.*, Bk. V, ch. 4 (pp. 245–246).

of the primary meanings of "Christian love." While this may be an attitude seldom found among men, correctly understood it is no more unusual than hating some one *for his own sake,* as Thornton Wilder's Julius Cæsar discovered. Surrounded by traitors on every side he personally inquired into each new conspiracy with a strange "element of eagerness."

> Would it not be a wonderful discovery to find that I am hated to the death by a man whose hatred is disinterested? It is rare enough to find a disinterested love; so far among those that hate me I have uncovered nothing beyond the promptings of envy, of self-advancing ambition, or of self-consoling destructiveness. It is many years since I have felt directed toward me a disinterested hatred. Day by day I scan my enemies looking with eager hope for the man who hates me "for myself" or even "for Rome." [5]

Properly understood in the same sense, loving one's enemy is no more difficult than loving one's friend or the man next door with Christian love. Instances in which an enemy is excepted from neighbor-love and hated *on account of* his hostility are really no more unusual than excepting a friend from neighbor-love and loving him merely *on account of* his friendliness. In the case of a friendly neighbor it is possible in loving him to love only his friendliness toward us in return. Then he is not loved *for his own sake.* He is loved for the sake of his friendliness, for the sake of the benefits to be gained from reciprocal friendship. Thus, very often, love for a friend shows up as "enlightened selfishness," which is a very good thing, indeed, in comparison with crude selfishness, but still quite different from Christian love for neighbor. In lower forms of friendship, for profit and for utility, a person really loves only himself; this is fundamentally true also of the highest type of friendship Aristotle could conceive of, friendship for sake of the good.

> Of the good man it is true likewise that he does many things for the sake of his friends and his country, even to the extent of dying for them, if need be: for money and honours, and, in short,

[5] *The Ides of March,* Harpers, 1948, pp. 218, 113.

all the good things which others fight for, he will throw away while eager to secure to himself the καλὸν [the beauty and no- bility of the deed]. . . . And this is perhaps that which befalls men who die for their country and friends; they *choose great glory for themselves:* and they will lavish their own money that their friends may receive more, for *hereby the friend gets the money but the man himself the καλὸν; so, in fact, he gives him- self the greater good.* It is the same with honours and offices; all things he will give up to his friend, *because this reflects honour and praise on himself.*[6]

Worlds apart as they are, in common concern for self-righteous- ness Aristotle and the tailor in ancient Israel would have under- stood one another. To "give away all I have" and "deliver my body to be burned" solely with *agape*-love even for a friend goes against the grain of ordinary human nature surely no less and no more than did love for enemy in the experience of an Abraham Lincoln or a Robert E. Lee.

What is needed is some technique for disentangling self-regard- ing from other-regarding motives in concrete human relationships, some experimental device, like those the scientist uses, which will isolate one of these factors from the other and test the effect of each alone. Perhaps we may distinguish the respect in which we love our neighbors for the sake of their friendliness to us (and thus for our own sakes) from the respect and degree to which we love them for their own sakes. At least we can devise a thought- experiment in which we can distinguish these two elements, even if we never entirely separate them in actuality. Kierkegaard sug- gested that, "If the parents simply had no hope, no prospect at all, of sometime having joy in their children and reward for their loving solicitude—still there would certainly be many fathers and mothers who would always lovingly do everything for their chil- dren. [But there would be many other parents in whom love] would still be so weak or the selfishness so strong, that there would be *needed* this joyous hope, this encouraging prospect." This is still a mixed case, the elements are not as yet completely enough isolated for it to be entirely plain to what degree parents

[6]Aristotle, *Nicomachean Ethics,* 1169a (Everyman edition). (Italics mine.)

love their children or love themselves in what is called their parental affection. Kierkegaard's other, more rigorous test takes us beyond the land of the living:

> If we wish to assure ourselves that love is entirely disinterested, we must remove every possibility of requital. But this is exactly what happens with respect to the dead. If love persists notwithstanding this, then it is in truth disinterested. . . . If you therefore wish to prove whether you love disinterestedly then sometimes pay attention to how you behave toward the dead. Much love, unquestionably the most, if subjected to a sharper testing, would appear to be selfishness. But the fact of the matter is, that in a love relationship between the living, there is always a hope and a prospect of requital, at least of a reciprocated love; and generally speaking, this is what happens. But this hope, this prospect, together with the requital, produces such an effect that one cannot definitely see what is love and what is selfishness, because one cannot see quite definitely whether requital is expected or not, and in what way. As regards the dead, the observation is so easy.[7]

The dead, of course, are no proper objects of love; we are seeking, however, a way of distinguishing qualities in love itself, not accrediting persons toward whom love should be directed.

Nevertheless, what is needed is some test for discovering true love for neighbor among living men. To find this we must go to the words of Jesus.

> You have heard that it was said, "You shall love your neighbor and hate your enemy." But I say to you, Love your enemies and pray for those who persecute you, so that you may be sons of your Father who is in heaven; for he makes his sun rise on the evil and on the good, and sends rain on the just and on the unjust. For if you love those who love you, what reward have you? Do not even the tax collectors do the same? And if you salute only your brethren, what more are you doing than others? Do not even the Gentiles do the same? You, therefore, must be perfect, as your heavenly Father is perfect (Matt. 5:43–48).

If a person has love for his enemy-neighbor from whom he can expect no good in return but only hostility and persecution, then

[7]*Op. cit.*, pp. 281–282.

alone does it become certain that he does not simply love himself in loving his neighbor. If you wish to assure yourself that love is disinterested, you must remove every possibility of requital. Among relationships with living men this is exactly what happens with respect to the enemy. If love persists notwithstanding hostility, then it is in truth disinterested. If, therefore, you wish to prove whether you love disinterestedly, then sometimes pay attention to how you behave toward your enemy. Much love, unquestionably the most, if subjected to such sharp testing, would appear to be selfishness. For the fact of the matter is that in a love relationship between persons who have a personal or national affinity for one another, there is always a hope and a prospect of requital, at least of a reciprocated love; and generally speaking, this is what happens in due time. But precisely this hope, this prospect of requital in the not far distant future produces such an effect that one cannot definitely see what is Christian love and what is enlightened selfishness, because one cannot see quite definitely whether requital is expected or not or whether the neighbor is loved for his own sake or not. As regards the enemy the observation is easy. "For if you love those who love you . . . if you salute only your brethren, what more are you doing than others?" Do not even tax collectors do the same? A Christian, however, does not love his enemy for being his enemy any more than he loves his friend merely for being his friend: in either case he loves his neighbor, in spite of his hostility or, what may be just as much a hindrance, *in spite of* his friendship. Love for enemy simply provides a crucial test for the presence or absence of regard for the neighbor for his own sake.

A similar understanding of the nature and meaning of Christian love follows from a consideration of the commandment, "You shall love your neighbor as yourself" (Matt. 23:39; Mark 12:31; Luke 10:27). The words "as yourself" do not indicate how much love, or for that matter that any amount of love, may be withheld; instead, they describe the sort of love Christians should give to others. How exactly do you love yourself? Answer this question and you will know how a Christian should love his neighbor. You naturally love yourself for your own sake. You wish your own good, and you do so even when you may have a certain distaste for the kind of person you are. Liking yourself or thinking yourself very nice, or not, has fundamentally nothing to do with the matter. After a failure of some sort, the will-to-live soon returns and you always lay hold expectantly on *another* possibility of attaining some good for yourself. You love yourself more than you love any good qualities or worth you may possess. Unsubdued by bad qualities, not elicited by good ones, self-love does not wait on worth. In fact it is the other way around: self-love makes you desire worth for yourself. Regardless of fluctuations in feeling, you love yourself on one day about as much as on any other. And regardless of differences in temperament or capacity for deep emotion, one person probably wishes his own good about as much as another person wishes for his.

Christian love means such love for self *inverted.* Therefore, it has nothing to do with feelings, emotions, taste, preferences, temperament, or any of the qualities in other people which arouse feelings of revulsion or attraction, negative or positive preferences, in us. Christian love depends on the direction of the will, the orientation of intention in an act, not on stirring emotion. The commandment requires the Christian to aim at his neighbor's good just as unswervingly as man by nature wishes his own. Thus Christian ethics draws its standard *from man* only by inverting it. And moreover, if any one experiences self-love as not naturally so steadfast as here described, then no matter: he can tell better how the neighbor should be loved by using for a measure the love of Christ, "the righteousness of God" whose meaning was explored in Chapter One of this book.

Persons interested in coalition ethics frequently fasten upon the words "as yourself," interpreting them as a tribute to the positive ethical value of love for self in Christian ethics. But pointing to the existence of self-love is one thing, making it an injunction would be another. The words, "You shall love your neighbor *as yourself,*" certainly contain a reference to love for self, yet they by no means include a commandment, *"You shall* love yourself."

One of St. Augustine's chapters is entitled, "The Command to Love God and Our Neighbor *Includes* a *Command* to Love Ourselves." Yet the text of what he has to say under this heading fails to substantiate so strong a statement.

> Seeing, then, that there is no need of a command that every man should love himself and his own body,—seeing, that is, that we love ourselves, and what is beneath us but connected with us . . . it only remained necessary to lay injunctions upon us in regard to God above us, and our neighbor beside us. . . . Nothing seems to be said about our love for ourselves; yet when it is said, "Thou shalt love thy neighbor as thyself," it at once becomes evident that our love for ourselves *has not been overlooked*.[8]

Hereby men are told to apply the whole measure of self-love in love for neighbor. No more disastrous mistake can be made than to admit self-love onto the ground-floor of Christian ethics as a basic part of Christian obligation, however much concern for self-improvement, for example, may later come to be a secondary, though entirely essential, aspect of Christian vocation.

Christian ethics begins with a "leap" by which alone Christian love gives the name of "duty" to the claims of neighbor. "God's command *drives us* to our neighbor," as Luther wrote; faith "snatches us away from ourselves and puts us outside ourselves." Luther describes the leap, inverting love for self: ". . . Every one should 'put on' his neighbor, and so conduct himself toward him as if he himself were in the other's place. . . . A Christian man lives not in himself but in Christ and his neighbor. Otherwise he is not a Christian. He lives in Christ through faith, in his neighbor through love; by faith he is caught up beyond himself into God, by love he sinks down beneath himself into his neighbor."[9] However faith accomplishes this, Christian love comes into exist-

---

[8] *On Christian Doctrine,* 1, xxvi (italics mine). (Nicene and Post-Nicene Fathers edition.) *Cf.* Soren Kierkegaard, *Philosophical Fragments,* Princeton University Press, 1944, p. 30: "Self-love is the underlying principle, or *the principle that is made to lie under,* in all love; whence if we conceive a religion of love, this religion need make but one assumption, as epigrammatic as true, and take its realization for granted: namely the condition that man loves himself, in order to command him to love his neighbor as himself" (italics mine).

[9] "Treatise on Christian Liberty," *Works,* Muhlenberg Press, II, p. 342.

ence only by a "leap" which carries a man beyond all enlightened self-interest, beyond all intentional concern for self-realization, beyond the mixture of motives in pursuit of some common good; a leap which breaks entirely through the circle of self, goes bareheaded out of the "I-castle," and sets the agent fully on the side of another person, where for the first time he discovers "the neighbor" and "seeks the other's own";[10] a leap which is so self-effacing that one manages to care for another for his own sake alone and not for some ulterior purpose, even giving "so that the gift looks as if the gift were the recipient's own possession."[11]

The "as yourself" of the commandment ought never to be understood as if the individual remains somewhat on this side of the chasm separating him from his neighbor or as if he merely divides the ground between them, adjusting self-regarding and other-regarding sentiments in fifty-fifty or some other proportion. Neighbor-love, of course, contains the presupposition that every man loves himself; Christianity does not begin without this presupposition; but this is by no means a *flattering* assumption. To the contrary, the commandment has as "its intention to strip us of our selfishness," to open "the lock of self-love as with a pick lock." "Certainly no wrestler can get so tight a clinch upon his opponent as that with which this commandment embraces the selfishness which cannot stir from its place."[12] And if there is anything lacking of purity and steadfastness in self-love as a provisional measure for what ought always to be given in Christian love to the neighbor, the deficiency is made up by reference, no longer to self-love, but to the love of Christ. So far is this commandment from accommodating to the fact of selfishness; it may indeed be said that "the neighbor" is "a category which in its offensiveness is as perilous to self-love as possible."[13] "The neighbor" *in this sense* without doubt may be discovered by the leap inverting self-love; he will certainly be discovered when "the love of Christ controls us" (II Cor. 5:14).

[10]Soren Kierkegaard, *Works of Love*, p. 218.
[11]*Ibid.*, p. 22.
[12]*Ibid.*, p. 15.
[13]*Ibid.*, p. 18.

The other proof-text for an alliance between Christian and self-realization ethics, "For whoever would save his life will lose it; and whoever loses his life *for my sake and the gospel's* will save it" (Mark 8:35; *cf.* Matt. 10:39; 16:25; and Luke 9:24), affirms, it is true, an immediate connection between seeking to save one's life and actually losing it. Seeking and losing life belong together so closely that any one prudently trying to save his life might as well be intent on losing it. But turned around, the connection between losing one's life and actually saving it breaks apart upon the words "for my sake and the gospel's." Whatever else these words may mean, they certainly direct a man's whole intention and attention toward another goal than in the end saving his own life. It is significant that so often these words are entirely omitted in quoting this verse; most Christian self-realizationists do not know they are there; "whoever loses his life will save it" becomes the motto. Even so, plainly whoever goes through the motions of losing his life *in order to* save it never really intends to lose anything; whoever gives even his body to be burned in order to save his own soul loves only himself. Saving one's life may be equivalent to the imprudent intention of losing it; but losing one's life by no means is the same as prudently intending to save it. One may speak perhaps of losing *and* finding, never of losing *in order to* find one's own life. No calculating "in order to" connects these two things. If the fully Christian orientation, "for my sake and the gospel's," be not always present, at least an "and" should hold "losing" apart from the intention of "saving" one's own life in every case of truly disinterested love for neighbor.

II. IS LOVE FOR SUPERIOR VALUES PART OF THE MEANING OF CHRISTIAN LOVE?

Love so extremely self-giving has recently been subjected to searching criticism by Erich Fromm from the standpoint of contemporary psychology. He understands Christian love to be rooted not in strength but in weakness. This was Nietzsche's view, whom

Fromm quotes with approval: "Your neighbor-love is your bad love of yourselves. Ye flee unto your neighbor from yourselves and would fain make a virtue thereof! But I fathom your 'unselfishness.' . . . You cannot stand yourselves and you do not love yourselves sufficiently."[1] In contrast, "true kindness, nobility, greatness of soul . . . does not give in order to take . . . does not want to excell by being kind."[2] "The one goeth to his neighbor because he seeketh himself, and the other because he would fain lose himself."[3] Erich Fromm then summarizes the essence of this view as follows:

> Love is a phenomenon of abundance; its premise is the strength of the individual who can give. Love is affirmation and productiveness. "It seeketh to create what is loved!" To love another person is only a virtue if it springs from this inner strength, but it is a vice if it is the expression of the basic inability to be oneself.[4]

Now, it may be true that, as Nietzsche said, the Hebrew Jesus "died too early; he himself would have disavowed his doctrine had he attained to my age!"[5] It may be true that there are significant differences between these two creators of value. But the contrast between weakness and strength is not one of them. "Giving *in order to take*," "Wanting *to excell* by being kind," "fleeing unto your neighbor from yourselves and faining to make a virtue thereof," "going to the neighbor *for the sake of* losing oneself"— all these expressions precisely describe that "self-regarding concern for others" which Christianity thoroughly disavows. However, such *unwillingness* to be oneself, flight from self, is not overcome alone, if at all, by *willing defiantly* to be oneself or by positive self-love. Between these two attitudes stands a third, the product of Christian faith: simple *willingness* to be oneself before God, self-acceptance which, stripped of self-love, can still love the neighbor for the sake of nothing else.

Moreover, nothing could be plainer than that Christian love **is**

[1] *Thus Spake Zarathustra*, I, xvi.
[2] *The Will to Power*, stanza 935.
[3] *Thus Spake Zarathustra*, I, xvi.
[4] *Op. cit.*, p. 126.
[5] *Thus Spake Zarathustra*, I, xxi.

"a phenomenon of abundance." It seeks to create what is loved, and springs out of the strength of an individual who, himself quite willing to be himself, can afford to give and take not again. From the strength of self-acceptance, Christian love can afford not to take the credit for virtue, so far is it from "faining to make a virtue of fleeing unto your neighbor from yourselves." Beyond question a creative love must find its premise in the strength of an individual who can give, but the premise of this strength is not "loving yourself sufficiently" but a religious faith which enables a person to be willing to be himself and, with his own interests in view, nothing more. Beyond question distracted plunging into charitable activities and self-righteous interference in the affairs of others find their premise in weakness, but in turn the premise of such flight from self may be found not in insufficient positive love for self but in unwillingness to be oneself and in subtle self-love desperate for something more. Stripped even of too great love for self provoking apparent escape from self, Christian love proceeds from a total acceptance of self to pay full primary attention to something and some one else. Luther spoke of how Christian love "issues in works of the freest service cheerfully and lovingly done, with which a man willingly serves another without hope of reward, and for himself is satisfied with the fullness and wealth of his faith. . . . Since each has such abundant riches in his faith that all his other works and his whole life are a surplus with which he can by voluntary benevolence serve and do good to his neighbor."[6] Beyond question, the premise of such love is "fullness and wealth."

After all, the ancient Greeks, whose values Nietzsche championed, were the ones who from first to last thought of love as a manifestation of weakness, the desire for some good not yet possessed, aspiration born out of great need. The Greeks were inclined to believe that God could not properly be spoken of as "loving" man, for if God felt the movements of love for any being other than himself he would be a needy creature yearning to overcome some inadequacy in his own nature. Since God has no

[6]*Works,* II, p. 336.

need in his fully abundant being, God remains unmoved, moving all creatures by their craving desire for him. Having at hand only Plato's conception of love as born of Poverty,[7] the conclusion necessarily followed that God could not be thought of as loving. Now, the early Christians did not deny the consistency of this line of reasoning when they declared that God loves. They simply changed the notion of love to one of love born of plenitude, from a phenomenon of weakness to a phenomenon of strength, from craving desire to be filled with some good not yet possessed to what Luther called "desire inverted" giving out of abundant self-possession and overflowing benefaction. In this sense, God loves; in this sense, the Christian should love his neighbor. How strange that Nietzsche never noticed that the quality of love had already been "transvalued"!

Love as craving desire or acquisitive aspiration born of poverty ordinarily does not express itself overtly as love for self but as love for "the finer things of life." Is not proper "spiritual" love distinguishable from vulgar love according to the degree to which spiritual rather than material values have become the ends pursued? For defining Christian love do we not need first to establish some authentic scale of values, giving preference always to desire for goods higher in the scale over desire for inferior goods? If all love by its nature needs to gain satisfaction, then the difference between proper and improper, Christian and non-Christian love can be defined only in terms of what values are found satisfying. If love means desire, then love becomes spiritual or, as popular parlance has it, "Platonic" only by being directed in aspiration toward union with the highest possible good. According to Plato, love once born of poverty attains what it desires through stages of ascent toward an otherworldly realm of spiritual beauty.

[7]*Symposium*, 203–204. Another way of understanding the nature of love governs the idea of God set forth in the *Timaeus*: "He was good, and the good can never have any jealousy of anything. And being free from jealousy, he desired that all things should be as like himself as they could be. This is in the truest sense the origin of creation and of the world . . . God desired that all things should be good and nothing bad, so far as this was attainable" (30) (Jowett). But God's love, in this sense, never became fully dominant in Greek ethics.

For he who would proceed aright in this matter should begin in youth to visit beautiful forms; and first, if he be guided by his instructor aright, to love one such form only—out of that he should create fair thoughts; and soon he will of himself perceive that the beauty of one form is akin to the beauty of another; and then if beauty of form in general is his pursuit, how foolish would he be not to recognize that the beauty in every form is one and the same! And when he perceives this he will abate his violent love of the one, which he will despise and deem a small thing, and will become a lover of all beautiful forms; in the next stage he will consider that the beauty of the mind is more honourable than the beauty of outward form. So that if a virtuous soul have but a little comeliness, he will be content to love and tend him, and will search out and bring to the birth thoughts which may improve the young, until he is compelled to contemplate and see the beauty of institutions and laws, and to understand that the beauty of them all is one family, and that personal beauty is a trifle; and after laws and institutions he will go on to the sciences, that he may see their beauty, being not like a servant in love with the beauty of one youth or man or institution, himself a slave mean and narrow-minded, but drawing towards and contemplating the vast sea of beauty, he will create fair and noble thoughts and notions in boundless love of wisdom; until on that shore he grows and waxes strong, and at last the vision is revealed to him of a single science, which is the science of beauty everywhere.[8]

Lovers of wisdom since Plato have declared that wisdom or other rare values are worthy goals toward which men should aspire. Ethics has the task, according to this view, of determining as accurately as possible the proper way of proceeding onward and upward toward the realization of the highest possible good.

The question now to be faced is whether some predetermined set of spiritual values constitutes any part of the meaning of Christian love, whether the validity of some particular discrimination between higher and lower goods is prerequisite to accrediting love for neighbor. Frequent reference in the New Testament to "sins of the flesh" in contrast to things of the "spirit" has led to the widespread, though entirely mistaken, impression that

[8]*Ibid.*, 210 (Jowett)

Christian ethics chiefly opposes the goods of the physical life and wishes to withdraw men from them, setting their minds on "things that are above." For an understanding of the biblical background the word "flesh" should not be identified with "body." The dualism in the New Testament between "flesh" and "spirit" is quite another distinction than the dualism in Plato between "body" and "soul" or in Descartes between "extension" and "thought." What then do the words "flesh" and "spirit" mean, if they do not imply a rudimentary scale of value between inferior physical and superior spiritual goods?

When Shakespeare spoke of the "ills that flesh is heir to," he of course meant physical infirmities, pain and death; but much more as well, for "flesh" is also heir to mental and emotional grievances. "Flesh" includes a reference both to the physical and to the spiritual aspects of human life which ordinary language and Christian ethics refuse to separate from one another as severely as was the case in Platonic or Cartesian dualism. We even use the word "body" to indicate the whole of man's nature when we say "every*body*" and "no*body*" meaning "every one" and "no one."

St. Paul's use of the word "flesh" was not unlike this. He used this term for the human realm in its entirety, human personality as a whole, especially when he was thinking of man as man and not God, man as a finite creature subject to vanity and being less perfect than God. But the human "mind" and "soul" fall under this disparagement no less than the "body." Almost everywhere in the Bible the word "flesh" is used with this meaning. As St. Augustine noticed:

> . . . Flesh is put for man, where it is said, "The Word was made flesh;" and again, "And all flesh shall see the salvation of God." For it does not mean flesh without soul and without mind; but "all flesh" is the same as if it were said, every man.[9] . . . For any one who either does not recollect or does not sufficiently weigh, the language of sacred Scripture, may . . . suppose that the Epicurean philosophers live after the flesh, because they place man's highest good in bodily pleasure . . . and he may suppose

---

[9]*On the Trinity*, Bk. II, ch. 6 (*Basic Writings of St. Augustine*, ed. by Whitney J. Oates, Random House, 1948, II, 706).

that the Stoics, who place the supreme good of men in the soul, live after the spirit. . . . But in the sense of the divine Scripture both are proved to live after the flesh.[10]

Paul happened also to believe that sin was a power that had invaded and taken possession of "flesh," but again the body was no more in bondage to sin than the human mind or heart, for both are "flesh." Since "flesh" includes both physical and spiritual aspects of human nature, "sin in the flesh" likewise affects both equally and without distinction. Because flesh is altogether bound by sin, St. Paul ordinarily speaks of the "deeds of the flesh," telescoping the longer expression "deeds of sin in the flesh" which would more adequately convey his meaning. In any case, there is no ground here for making the body the laggard or positive principle of evil or for finding in mind or heart or conscience the source of human good. The "soul" is not inherently good any more than it is inherently immortal in the Christian view. The doctrine of the resurrection of the body means for ethics that Christianity stands in frontal opposition to any viewpoint that totally disparages the body. And the early Christians argued, against the much more "spiritual" Greek view, that an equally supernatural intervention would be required to raise the soul again and give it life as to raise the body, for both are "flesh." The distinction between material and spiritual values has no more standing in the Christian outlook than body-soul dualism. Both fall to the ground precisely in face of Paul's distinction between flesh and spirit.

Careful examination of lists Paul draws up of specific "works of the flesh" (the works of sin in the flesh) and "the fruit of the Spirit" also leads to this conclusion.

> Now the works of the flesh are plain: immorality, impurity, licentiousness, idolatry, sorcery, enmity, strife, jealousy, anger, selfishness, dissension, party spirit, envy, drunkenness, carousing and the like. . . . But the fruit of the Spirit is love, joy, peace, patience, kindness, goodness, faithfulness, gentleness, self-control. . . . Those who belong to Christ have crucified the flesh with its passions and desires (Gal. 5:19–24).

[10]*The City of God*, Bk. XIV, ch. 2 (*Basic Writings of St. Augustine*, ed. by Whitney J. Oates, Random House, 1948, II, 239–240).

Along with such obvious works of the flesh as impurity, licentiousness, drunkenness, and carousing, Paul also lists, as if they were equally "fleshly," such "spiritual" sins as enmity, strife, jealousy, anger, selfishness, dissension, party spirit, and envy. There is more of "the *mind* of the flesh" in this classification than there is of uncurbed physical impulse. Using the Latin words for "soul" and "body," St. Augustine remarks that here Paul condemns "animosities" as well as "carnalities." "Who that has enmity has it not in his soul?"[11] Along with such obvious fruit of the Spirit as love, joy, peace, patience, kindness, goodness, faithfulness, and gentleness, Paul also lists, as if it were equally "spiritual," self-control, which surely in many instances has to do primarily with restraining the passions and desires of "flesh" in the gratification of physical appetites.

What then can possibly be Paul's principle of classification? We have already seen that the holy Spirit may always be known by its quality and not by its strength—not, to be sure, by some general "spiritual" quality or value available in human experience everywhere, nor by its place on some scale of values, nor by some universal human relationship such as fatherly or brotherly love. The holy Spirit of God is the spirit of Christ. Gifts or fruit of the Spirit must, therefore, be understood by particular reference to Christ-like love. This, and not any dualism between material and spiritual values, is what leads Paul to teach that control of the body *and* kindness are equally the fruit of the Spirit. Opposite from this, sinful selfishness works, it may be, such diverse results as drunkenness or envy in the flesh. Nor can licentiousness and dissension be grouped together as "bodily," but both do in fact spring from self-centered egotism: This is the carnal mind or mind of flesh which leads Paul to cut across the common distinction between body and soul, between higher and lower values.

Intellectual and artistic people often disdain the life of the laboring man, inert and uncultured as it seems, content with merely physical pleasures, close to the clod. They find it difficult to acknowledge the essential nobility of unselfishness even on this

[11]*Ibid.* (p. 241).

level, desiring, as they do, to improve man away from these inferior goods, onward and upward, rather than to improve his dealing with them. Christianity, however, makes an opposite judgment. It feels no necessity for first transforming such a man into a cultured person before he can become a Christian. Christian ethics, of course, makes criticism of sensuality, but only on the ground of first distinguishing between the good of *sensuous* delight and physical satisfaction and the evil spirit of *sensuality*. And even understanding sensuality as a function primarily of the spirit rather than of physical impulse, traditionally Christian ethics has found more fault with pride than with sensuality.

> Pride is essentially competitive—is competitive by its very nature—while the other vices are competitive only, so to speak, by accident. . . . The sexual impulse *may* drive two men into competition if they both want the same girl. But that is only by accident; they might just as likely have wanted two different girls. But a proud man will take your girl from you, not because he wants her, but just to prove to himself that he's a better man than you. Greed *may* drive men to competition, if there isn't enough to go round; but the proud man, even when he's got more than he can possibly want, will try to get still more just to assert his power.[12]

The great sin of pride, pride of power, pride of knowledge or achievement, pride of virtue or self-righteousness, pride of religion or spiritual pride, stands close to the elbow of a cultured man—just as close as to the common man but, since both are men, no closer. And love for neighbor is as much of a task at any level where men are involved with one another and with goods they want, be they material or spiritual values. A "culture-vulture" may be a vulture still, and the chief concern of Christian ethics is not with spreading enlightenment, desirable as that may be, but with purging away vulturous self-interest.

The main line of philosophical ethics from Plato to the present arranges the problems of morality along a vertical, ascending scale of values. It counsels men to achieve life on the higher grade of "shareable goods," such as truth and beauty, individual por-

---

[12] C. S. Lewis, *Christian Behaviour*, Macmillan, 1943, pp. 45–46.

tions of which are not decreased by more widely distributed participation in them. Instead of fighting over houses, beefsteaks, and women, which are unshareable, let desire be fixed upon non-competitive goods, the finer things of life which are shareable. This solution is always put forward in some form by every ethical system built upon the foundation of a poor love which must be filled with satisfactions acquired by aspiration. Now, while truth, beauty, and goodness themselves are essentially shareable, the *prestige value* associated with these high-minded values remains essentially unshareable. The possession of truth, originating some brilliant idea, capacity for appreciating beauty may be *mine* and not necessarily *thine*. Every one may have the experience of great music, but not every one can be the conductor of the orchestra. Artists and philosophers, or for that matter theologians, are not notoriously charitable in the Christian sense. No*body*, no flesh is. The prestige value inevitably associated with any system of truth or with original insight in any area is not itself shareable. A moment's remarking upon this fact should disclose that no solution of man's chief moral dilemmas is to be found merely by ascending some vertical scale of values. There is no help from gaining values *themselves* shareable when the problem consists of making *men* share. Acquisitive desire or aspiration for goods which are essentially non-competitive in *their* nature advances us not at all in the direction of a love essentially non-competitive in *its* nature. Such love can only be born of plenitude, it is a *giving* love which already possesses the strength and beauty toward which the Greeks aspire.

Christian ethics raises no fundamental objection to definitions of *value* given by any school of philosophical ethics. Hedonism, for example, or the theory that pleasure alone is the good, may be incorrect on philosophical grounds, but if true there would be nothing unchristian about it. Christianity makes no essential attempt to transform a person who believes there is no good in life but pleasure into one who believes there are other goods besides pleasure. Its concern is to turn a hedonist who thinks only of *his own* pleasure into one who gives pleasure (the greatest good he knows) to his neighbors. When a person becomes a Christian he may also cease to be a hedonist and adopt some other theory of value, but he does not thereby become a better Christian. In fact it works the other way round: out of greater responsiveness to the entire range of his neighbor's need he may for the first time become sensitive to certain higher human values to which formerly, even in his own case, selfishness blinded him. Is pleasure homogeneous or heterogeneous? Are there significant qualitative differences among pleasures? Is poetry better than pushpin because of the superior quality, or because of the greater intensity and purity of the pleasure it gives? Was J. S. Mill still a hedonist when he distinguished pleasures according to quality? If "the good" simply means "pleasure" and "better" means only "more pleasurable," then how could Mill say it is "better" to be Socrates dissatisfied than a fool or a pig satisfied? Or, shall we follow the suggestion that, just as a man who judges wine alone good for drinking may yet prefer the taste of some wines to others, so also he may prefer the quality of some pleasures to others while still judging that pleasure alone is good? The issues drawn between quantitative and qualitative tests for pleasure and between hedonism and other theories of value doubtless are important issues, ones on which every thoughtful person must come to some conclusion, but it would indeed be strange if Christian ethics were forced to wait on their final solution. A Christian hedonist is no more anomalous than a Christian self-realizationist or Christian pursuit of any other values, since *how* things are sought, not *what*, makes all the difference. From a Christian point of view, J. S. Mill's outstanding error was not his hedonism, but his belief that in regard to distribution of goods his theory of ethics was really equivalent to Christian ethics because the slogan "greatest happiness of the greatest number" means much the same thing as the "golden rule"—an epigrammatic bit of folk-morality, passed on by sages everywhere as the essence of wisdom, universally accepted as a valid norm, rarely lived by, but, despite its presence in the New Testament, providing no approximation at all to the real and distinctive meaning of Christian love.

There are two chief questions in ethics: *What* is the good? and *Whose* good shall it be when choice must be made between mine and thine?[13] The first is the main concern of philosophical ethics, which arranges its answer to the question along a vertically ascending scale of values. If the second question is not left out altogether, it is quite subordinated. Three quarters of the way up the scale, "social values" may be written in, somewhat above material goods, somewhat below the things of intellectual, artistic, or "religious" spirit. Such "sociability" still remains overtly or covertly within the circle of self. Philosophy often undertakes to demonstrate that it is good *for the agent* to be sociable: What is this but "self-regarding concern for others," a poor love which goes to others in order to fill some subtle or plain need?

The other question, *Whose* good? is the main, perhaps the only,

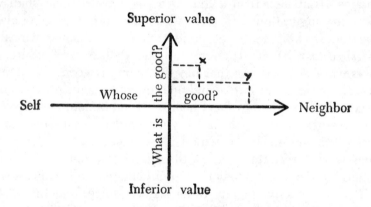

[13]St. Augustine acknowledged although he himself did not employ the distinction between these two questions: "Thus, when it is asked whether a wise man will adopt the social life, and desire and be interested in the supreme good of his friend as in his own, or will, on the contrary, do all that he does merely for his own sake, there is no question here about the supreme good, but only about the propriety of associating or not associating a friend in its participation: whether the wise man will do this not for his own sake, but for the sake of his friend in whose good he delights as in his own. . . . The questions concerning the social life . . . are different questions into none of which the question of the chief good enters." (*The City of God,* Bk. XIX, chs. i–ii, *Basic Writings of St. Augustine,* ed. by Whitney J. Oates, Random House, 1948, II, 470–471). Augustine's own view was that man finds in the enjoyment of God a *bonum commune.* Logically this places God in the same class with other shareable goods even though he be also the highest good and the only inalienable good (*summum et incommutabile bonum*)

concern of Christian ethics, which consequently finds itself in
opposition to philosophical ethics only when the latter pretends
to answer this question in terms of selfish enlightenment or by
general, value-centered appeals to the acquisitive aspirations of
some poor love. Christian ethics answers the question, *Whose*
good? by requirements which would move the agent on the horizontal plane where he happens to stand more over to the side
of his neighbor. This answer plenteous love supplies. The man
whose character-graph may be plotted at "y" is a "better" Christian than "x," even though "y" happens to be a practicing hedonist and "x" a lover of wisdom. Nevertheless, the difference between
"x" and "y" is more than a difference of method, the one gaining
what he needs through knowledge, the other gaining what he
needs through sociability. The difference rather is a quite fundamental one, strategic not tactical, between poor and plenteous
love, between craving and giving, between desire and desire inverted, between acquisition and self-sacrifice, between upward-
reaching and giving-over, between *Agape*-love which seeks not
its own and erotic love which seeks its own on earth and in
heaven.[14] Would it not be foolish to try to demonstrate the value
of such "neighbor-regarding concern for others" in satisfactions
to the self, even in terms of the great satisfaction of escaping from
oneself?

Indeed, adopting the distinction sometimes made between the
"good" and "right," "duty" or "obligation," we may say that
neighbor-love is not good, it is obligatory. Strictly speaking, there
can be no "duty" to gain the good; the good is naturally desired,
and not gaining it comes only by mistake or from ignorance, not
from failure to do one's duty. In contrast, neighbor-love defines
what is "right" or obligatory. Love for neighbor comprises "the
meaning of obligation," which some philosophers suppose was

14Anders Nygren elaborated this contrast between pagan and Christian love in
his *Agape and Eros: A Study of the Christian Idea of Love,* Macmillan, 1932,
3 vols. Not much is accomplished by pointing out that some elements in human
experience are not taken into account by this view. Christian ethics should doubtless include all things human, but not necessarily *on the ground floor* of its understanding of morality. Nor can this interpretation of Christian love be refuted by
linguistic or merely textual studies of the New Testament.

disclosed only by Rousseau and Kant, the founders of the philosophy of idealism and deontological ethics in the modern period. Certainly Christian ethics is a deontological ethic, not an ethic of "the good." Certainly it is no part of the meaning or intention of neighbor-love to be good *for me* but for me to prove good *for my neighbor,* though good may follow for me as a *quite unintended* by-product. When Christian love by a leap has set the agent fully on the side of the neighbor, when "righteousness" has been accomplished, then and then only Christian ethics becomes interested in "the good." When right relation to neighbor has been established, then and then only does Christian love need to become as enlightened as possible about what is truly good—for the neighbor. Then and then only, as a secondary though quite essential concern, does it enter into a Christian's head for his neighbor's sake to ascend whatever scale of values he may find reasonably creditable.

III. IS LOVE FOR GOD PART OF THE MEANING OF CHRISTIAN LOVE?

What, in all this concern for the neighbor, has happened to the love of God? Whoever raises this question must first be asked what he means. For "the love of God" may mean either the love of God for man or man's love for God. In the former, God is the "agent," man the "patient"; in the latter, man the agent, God the patient or recipient of love.

In favor of interpreting the love of God to mean man's love for God, there is, of course, the tradition of Jesus' words: "You shall love the Lord your God with all your heart, and with all your soul, and with all your mind. This is the great and first commandment. And a second is like it, You shall love your neighbor as yourself" (Matt. 22:37–39). Standing as they are, these two formulations of the love commandment threaten to divide Christian loyalty if ever there is difference, let alone contrast, between love for God and love for neighbor. If Christian love itself is divided into two sorts of love or love for two different objects, disunity in obligation results, and frequently Christians have spoken of religious duties due to God different from ethical duties owed to man. Christian ethics thus imitates Don Quixote dashing off at once in at least two directions.

Singleness of orientation might be maintained in either of two obvious ways, the Neo-Platonic view reducing love for neighbor to love for God or the humanitarian view reducing love for God to love for neighbor. Neither is satisfactory. St. Augustine was responsible for mediating to Christianity an understanding of "the love of God" with many ingredients of Neo-Platonism in it. His largely Neo-Platonic solution, it is true, fastens upon the words quoted by Jesus in the First Commandment, "Thou shalt love the Lord thy God," and has the tradition of Johannine mysticism behind it. Nevertheless, this is the viewpoint of general religiousness and has much about it that is not distinctively Christian. Likewise, humanitarianism is a general position within ethics, hardly a distinctively Christian point of view.

St. Augustine believed that man's "chief good" must be "something which cannot be lost against the will. For no one can feel confident regarding a good which he knows can be taken from him, although he wishes to keep and cherish it. But if a man feels no confidence regarding the good which he enjoys, how can he be happy while in fear of losing it?"[1] Only the enjoyment of God satisfies this double requirement, of being a supreme good which cannot be lost against one's will. The first commandment directs men through love to the enjoyment of an eternal good, and demands that "no part of our life is to be unoccupied, or to afford room, as it were, for the wish to enjoy some other object."[2]

Augustine observes that "as there are two commandments on which hang all the Law and the prophets, love of God and love of neighbor; *not without cause the Scripture mostly puts one for both* [the love of God alone]."[3] The truth is that, while the scrip-

[1]*On the Morals of the Catholic Church*, ch. iii (*Basic Writings of St. Augustine*, ed. by Whitney J. Oates, Random House, 1948, I, 231).
[2]*On Christian Doctrine*, Bk. I, ch. xxii (*Nicene and Post-Nicene Fathers*, Scribners, 1908, First Series, vol. II).
[3]*On the Trinity*, Bk. VIII, ch. vii (*Basic Writings*, II, 783). (Italics mine.)

ture "mostly puts one for both," the New Testament scripture mostly puts the second commandment for the first. This Augustine does not fail to notice, especially in the emphasis of St. Paul on love for neighbor, yet he explains this away with breath-taking swiftness:

> And many other passages occur in the sacred writings, in which only the love of our neighbor seems to be commanded for perfection, while the love of God is passed over in silence; whereas the Law and the prophets hang on both precepts. But this too is because he who loves his neighbor *must needs also love above all else love itself.* But "God is love; and he that dwelleth in love, dwelleth in God." Therefore, he must needs above all else love God. . . . For he knows the love with which he loves, more than the brother whom he loves. So now he can know God more than he knows his brother: clearly known more, because more present; known more, because more within him; known more, because more certain. Embrace the love of God, and by love, embrace God.[4]

Now, this point of view is not wholly wrong, it is simply confusing; and confusion results from a blending of Christian and Greek meanings of the word "love." It is plain that Augustine has grasped the biblical understanding of "obedient love"; "because he who loves God must both needs do what God has commanded, and loves him just in such proportion as he does so; and therefore he must needs also love his neighbor, because God has commanded it."[5] Such obedient love differs greatly from aspiring love. Plainly, also, in his discussion of "loving above all else love itself," Augustine acknowledges that God stands as a "middle term" between a man and his neighbor toward whom love is finally directed; the neighbor is far from being the middle term or merely a stepping stone between man and God. God, who is Love, is the "ground" from which real love for neighbor proceeds; in fact, he *is* this love for neighbor:

> . . . [The Apostle John] seems to have passed by the love of God in silence; which he never would have done, unless because he intends God to be understood in brotherly love itself. . . .

[4]*Ibid.*, chs. vii and viii (*Basic Writings*, II, 784, 785). (Italics mine.)
[5]*Ibid.*, ch. vii (*Basic Writings*, II, 783).

. . . This same brotherly love itself . . . is set forth by so great authority, not only to be from God, but also *to be God*. When therefore we love our brother from love, we love our brother from God; neither can it be that we do not love above all else that same love by which we love our brother; whence it may be gathered that these two commandments cannot exist unless interchangeable. For since "God is love," *he who loves love certainly loves God; but he must needs love love who loves his brother*.[6]

Here "the neighbor" in all concreteness does not remain undiscovered. Being interchangeable, the second love commandment is not wholly absorbed into the first; one is not quite put for both. Indeed, the concluding words of the foregoing quotation, taken seriously, give good ground for putting the second for the first, even though Augustine does not pass over in silence love for love itself. "The brother" stands forth as a final object of love; he is loved *through* God, through love; there is here none of that "loving God *in* the neighbor" which certain interpreters find in St. Augustine,[7] and none of that "loving the neighbor simply for the sake of loving God" which often seems to be Augustine's manner of speaking.

In the total thought of St. Augustine, however, the true meaning of Christian love for neighbor is blurred by its combination with love for God, interpreted not as "obedient love" but as the soul's desire for beatific union with God. Failing to find more than an incidental back-handed reference to self-love in the commandment which actually mentions it, Augustine derives from the first commandment a more positive requirement to love self.

Neither let that further question disturb us, how much of love we ought to spend upon our brother, and how much upon God: incomparably more upon God than upon ourselves, but upon our brother as much as upon our ourselves; and we love ourselves so much the more, the more we love God. Therefore we love God and our neighbor from one and the same love; but we love

6*Ibid*., ch. viii (*Basic Writings*, II, 785–786). (Italics mine.)
7*E.g.*, Albert C. Knudson, *The Principles of Christian Ethics*, Abingdon-Cokesbury Press, 1943, ch. vi, and Anders Nygren, *op. cit.*, Pt. II, vol. II, pp. 331–332.

> God for the sake of God, and ourselves and our neighbors for
> the sake of God.[8]

> For he alone has a proper love for himself who aims diligently
> at the attainment of the chief and true good; and if this is noth-
> ing else but God . . ., what is to prevent one who loves God
> from loving himself?[9]

Blunting the cutting edge of neighbor-love may be seen again
in the coalition Augustine effects between biblical and other notions of "righteousness."

> He therefore who loves men, ought to love them either because
> they are righteous, or that they may become righteous. For so
> also he ought to love himself, either because he is righteous, or
> that he may become righteous; for in this way he loves his neigh-
> bor as himself without any risk.[10]

It may be declared categorically that loving men *because* they
are righteous amounts to no more than Aristotle's friendship of
the good for one another. Here plainly Augustine makes room
for some standard drawn perhaps from natural moral law or even-
handed justice by which righteousness may be determined. Clearly
also he gives such "righteousness" primacy in eliciting and limiting the nature of Christian love. Love for neighbor, it is true,
may be vitally concerned that men *become* righteous. The neighbor comes first, righteousness is wanted for him in the second
place, for so a man ought to love himself, that he may become
righteous, whatever happens to be his opinion concerning the
meaning of righteousness. Actually we know that Augustine held
a Neo-Platonic conception of the meaning of right and proper
love. As a consequence he believed that:

> what . . . you aim at in yourself you must aim at in your neigh-
> bor, namely that he may love God with a perfect affection. For
> you do not love him as yourself, unless you try to draw him to
> that good which you yourself are pursuing. For this is the one
> good which has room for all to pursue it along with thee.[11]

[8] *On the Trinity*, Bk. VIII, ch. viii (*Basic Writings*, II, 786).
[9] *On the Morals of the Catholic Church*, ch. xxvi (*Basic Writings*, I, 342).
[10] *On the Trinity*, Bk. VIII, ch. vi (*Basic Writings*, II, 783).
[11] *On the Morals of the Catholic Church*, ch. xxvi (*Basic Writings*, I, 343).

But as this divine Master inculcates two precepts—the love of God and the love of our neighbor—and as in these precepts a man finds three things he has to love—God, himself, and his neighbor—and that he who loves God loves himself thereby, it follows that he must endeavor to get his neighbor to love God, since he is ordered to love his neighbor as himself. He ought to make this endeavor in behalf of his wife, his children, his household, all within his reach, even as he would wish his neighbor to do the same to him if he needed it; and consequently he will be at peace, or in well-ordered concord, with all men, as far as in him lies.[12]

In a most Christian fashion, Augustine here uses inverted self-love as standard for determining how the neighbor should be loved. Antecedent to this, however, stands his conviction that the chief end of man is to be found in mystic communion with God, which may be true or not but on this truth love for neighbor by no means depends.

There is true Christian love for neighbor at work here in Augustine's thought on this point. Convinced that the chief end of man was to be found only in mystic union with God, the Christian, he believed, should love his neighbor for the sake of love for God. This meant loving him for the sake of *his neighbor's* love for God, not simply loving him for the sake of one's own love for God. The neighbor should not be by-passed. To the contrary, the highest good ought to be desired for him. In similar fashion it has been pointed out that a Christian who happens to believe that pleasure alone is the good for man, loves and should love his neighbor for the sake of pleasure, *i.e.*, for the sake of *his neighbor's* pleasure, not just his own. This combines love for neighbor with another view concerning the nature of "the good" from that held by St. Augustine. Either of these views may be equally Christian, provided there is sound reason for believing either of them. An insufficiently Christianized element appears only when, in either coalition ethic, the neighbor is loved *because* he is righteous, as Augustine sometimes says, or *because* he already loves God or *because* he gives pleasure.

[12]*The City of God*, Bk. XIX, ch. xiv (*Basic Writings*, II, 490).

Interesting light is thrown on the inadequacy, from a Christian point of view, of Augustine's Neo-Platonic unification of Christian love by his distinction between "use," "abuse," and "enjoyment." This distinction was made necessary by his view that all love is acquisitive desire. If Christian love is a kind of acquisitive desire, then Augustine concludes quite properly that nothing human or mundane, *e.g.*, the neighbor, can be the final object of Christian love. The eternal good, or God, alone is an adequate object of craving love; only he should be "enjoyed" or "rested in with satisfaction for his own sake."

> . . . We are said to *enjoy* that which in itself, and irrespective of other ends, delights us; to *use* that which we seek for the sake of some end beyond. For which reason the things of time are to be used rather than enjoyed, that we may deserve to enjoy things eternal; and not as those perverse creatures who would fain enjoy money and use God—not spending money for God's sake but worshipping God for money's sake.[13]
>
> If you cling to [any good], and rest in it, finding your happiness complete in it, then you may be truly and properly said to enjoy it. And this you must never do except in the case of the Blessed Trinity, who is the Supreme and Unchangeable Good.[14]

Toward his fellow human beings, as well as toward other of God's "creatures," a Christian, according to Augustine, has the attitude of "using" them. "To use . . . is to employ whatever means are at one's disposal to obtain what one desires, if it is a proper object of desire," *i.e.*, union with God.[15] Not only do Christians in this sense mutually "use" one another and their neighbors out of the desire of each for the supreme good; God also in his love for men "uses" rather than "enjoys" them.[16] His love for men is "in order to" their love for himself, just as Christian love for neighbor is "in order to" one's own and the neighbor's love for God. Just so, also, a Christian "uses" rather than "enjoys" himself; his love for himself is "in order to" union with God who is the secret object of all his craving.

13*Ibid.*, Bk. XI, ch. xxv (*Basic Writings*, II, 167).
14*On Christian Doctrine*, I, xxxiii (*Nicene and Post-Nicene Fathers, ibid.*).
15*Ibid.*, I, iv.   16*Ibid.*, I, xxxi.

It becomes an important question, whether men ought to enjoy
or to use themselves, or both. For we are commanded to love
one another; but it is a question whether man is to be loved by
man for his own sake, or for the sake of something else. If it is
for his own sake, we enjoy him; if it is for the sake of something
else we use him. It seems to me, then, that he is to be loved for
the sake of something else. . . . Neither ought any one to have
joy in himself, if you look at the matter clearly, because no one
ought to love even himself for his own sake, but for the sake of
him who is the true object of enjoyment. If, however, he loves
himself for his own sake, he does not look at himself in relation
to God but turns his mind in upon himself, and so is not occupied
with anything that is unchangeable. . . . Wherefore if you ought
not to love even yourself for your own sake, but for his in whom
your love finds its most worthy object, no other man has a right
to be angry if you love him too for God's sake.[17]

The neighbor, the self, and for that matter any other of God's
"creatures" may, of course, be "abused," but only if they are
loved with desire for something less than God.[18] Love of neighbor for his own sake, therefore, tends to fall within Augustine's
definition of "abuse."

These opinions of Augustine are a bulwark against identifying
the inherent infinite value or sacredness of human personality as
the ground principle of Christian morality. His view that humanity, whether in one's self or in another, may be "used" for the
sake of something higher than itself stands in opposition to Kant's
imperative, "So act as in every action to treat humanity whether
in thyself or in another always also as an end and never as a
means only." Nevertheless, Christians who are not personalists,
humanists, or Kantians will instinctively feel that something has
gone wrong in Augustine's analysis. The neighbor too often seems
lost in God, love for neighbor in love for God. Augustine is entirely right in saying that the neighbor cannot be an end-term of
Christian love if the latter is understood as acquisitive aspiration.
All the great religions, including Neo-Platonism, have declared
that only God can satisfy the infinite yearning of a human heart,
that only he can be rested in for his own sake. But Christian love

[17]*Ibid.*, I, xxii.　　[18]*Ibid.*, I, iv.

is not desire; it is, as Luther said, "desire inverted." If, then, both a Christian and his God have a love born of plenitude, not out of need, God may love man for his own sake and the Christian love his neighbor for his own sake, both propositions frequently denied by Augustine. The neighbor, and moreover the neighbor for his own sake, is an entirely legitimate object for a *giving* sort of love to come to rest in, with no reference beyond to something else for the sake of which he is loved. The neighbor is never the ultimate object of aspiring *caritas*-love; he is always the end-term of *agape*-love.

This Augustine does not altogether deny. As was noticed above, Christian categories are at work in his thought along with Platonic themes. "Loving the neighbor for the sake of loving God" suggests ambiguously that the agent grasp at union with the divine by means of loving his neighbor, and at the same time it suggests that he should earnestly desire the supreme good for his neighbor. Similarly, two meanings of the word "use" lie side by side in Augustine's thought. On the one hand, to use—whether we are speaking of money, the self, neighbors, or any other "things of time"—means to have an ulterior purpose in view in employing them. We are to regard them with the moderation of employers, not with the ardor of lovers. To use means to "seek for the sake of some end beyond," "that we may deserve to enjoy things eternal."

On the other hand, Augustine defines "use" in a fashion which allows the neighbor's need to be the end in full view in all loving action. Adopting this second reading, our English translations of Augustine's words *frui* (enjoy) and *uti* (use) may certainly be objected to as prejudicial. "That use, then, which God is said to make of us has no reference to His own advantage, but to ours only; and so far as He is concerned, has reference to His goodness."[19] Presumably the same may be said of a man's "use" of his neighbor: that use, then, which one is said to make of his neighbor has no reference to one's own advantage, but to the neighbor's only; and so far as the agent himself is concerned, has

---

[19]*Ibid.*, I, xxxii.

reference only to his goodness, *i.e.*, the "righteousness" he has by faith and the love he manifests subject to the controlling love of Christ. Moreover, at times Augustine even speaks of "enjoying" the neighbor. He defines "the peace of the celestial city" and "the peace of the reasonable creatures" as consisting in a "perfectly ordered and harmonious enjoyment of God, *and of one another in God.*"[20] He also expressly distinguishes between men and inferior creatures, reserving the word "use" for the latter only, and in this connection states that we are to "enjoy" both ourselves and our neighbors:

> When, therefore, the creature is either equal to us or inferior, we must use the inferior to reach God, but we must enjoy the equal only in God. For as thou oughtest to enjoy thyself not in thyself, but in Him who made thee, so also him whom thou lovest as thyself. Let us enjoy, therefore, both ourselves and our brethren in the Lord; and hence let us not dare to yield, and as it were to relax, ourselves in the direction downward.[21]

The second definition of "use," and more especially Augustine's willingness to speak of "enjoying" self and neighbor, taken seriously, would have radically altered Augustine's belief that all love must be desire. Nothing different from this has been our meaning in defining Christian love as disinterested love, or love for neighbor for his own sake. As it is, the two sorts of love lie side by side in Augustine's thought, much as do the conceptions of love in the *Symposium* and the *Timaeus* in the thought of Plato.[22] Augustine distinguishes between *amor ex miseria* (or a love due to the dryness of need and longing) and *amor ex misericordia* (or a love that springs out of the fullness of goodness and benevolence).[23] Yet he never seriously calls in question his judgment that love should be generically defined as desire born out of

---

[20]*The City of God*, Bk. XIX, chs. xiii and xvii (*Basic Writings*, II, 488 and 494). (Italics mine.)

[21]*On the Trinity*, Bk. IX, ch. viii (*Basic Writings*, II, 798). A distinction should be drawn between "enjoying one another in God," which holds the neighbor in view, and "enjoying God in the neighbor," which loses sight of the neighbor for the sake of communing with God wherever he may be found.

[22]See note 7 to sec. II of this Chapter, on p. 106 above.

[23]*Cf.* Anders Nygren, *op. cit.*, Pt. II, vol. II, p. 251.

need. This notion that all love necessarily means some sort of desire or craving aspiration leads him to focus all such love on God, to some extent therefore by-passing the neighbor, or else loving him only, or ambiguously, for the sake of loving God. This mystical, otherworldly aspect of Augustine's thought indeed has still for most ears an extraordinarily pious and religious sound. Yet his Neo-Platonic unification of Christian morality around man's love for God, carried out with entire thoroughness, would have been as disastrous a deviation from Christian principles as many a secular system of humanitarianism.

St. Paul began with the other understanding of "the love of God." For him God was always the agent, man the recipient of divine love through Christ. Only three times in all his writings does Paul speak of men loving God. Two of these Paul promptly corrects by returning man to the patient's position before ending the sentence. "If any one imagines that he knows something, he does not yet know as he ought to know. But if one loves God, one *is known* by him" (I Cor. 8:3). This sudden shift from the active to the passive voice of the verb when he is speaking of man's relationship to God surely signifies that Paul never truly intends to make man the initiating agent in "the love of God." Man is known by God, he is loved by God. "We know that in everything God works for good with those who love him, who *are called* according to his purpose" (Rom. 8:28). Here again in all consistency men are first loved by God who calls them.

Nothing is more striking than the way St. Augustine has of wrenching St. Paul's meaning completely around to his own Neo-Platonic notion of man's yearning for God, even in quoting such a passage as "For I am sure that neither death nor life, nor angels, nor principalities, nor things present, nor things to come, nor powers, nor height, nor depth, nor anything else in all creation, will be able to separate us from *the love of God* in Christ Jesus our Lord" (Rom. 8:38, 39). "This charity, that is," writes Augustine, "*this will glowing with intensest love*, the apostle eulogizes with these words, 'Who shall separate us from the love of

Christ?' "[24] "The love of Christ" becomes *our* love for Christ, to
say the least a most unusual interpretation of what Christians
believe Jesus Christ has done to make manifest God's love. Whenever he spoke of "grace" Augustine meant "infused love"; and he
rides this doctrine into almost every New Testament passage that
speaks of "the love of God." These words are always taken to
mean *our* love for God, infused in us, of course, only by the grace
of God. Augustine's favorite Pauline scripture, the verse he perhaps quotes most frequently, was the apostle's statement that
"God's love has been poured into our hearts through the Holy
Spirit which has been given to us" (Rom. 5:5). Even this verse
he interprets in terms of his basic religio-ethical category: man's
(infused) love for God. "Now *'the love of God'* is said to be shed
abroad in our hearts," he writes, *"not because He loves us, but
because He makes us lovers of Himself."*[25] For explicitly rejecting St. Paul's real meaning Augustine is not to be excused simply
because of the ambiguity of the genitive "the love of God" (or in
the Latin *amor Dei*), which modern translations of this verse uni-
formly render, "God's love." Paul's point of view should have been
clear in any translation and in any language, for in Romans he
immediately goes on to speak of God showing *his* love for us in
that while we were yet sinners Christ died for us (5:8). Plainly,
God's love is shed abroad or poured into our hearts because he
loves us, not first of all because he makes us by infusion lovers
of himself. Augustine is not to be excused; he has to be explained,
in that before coming to study the scriptures he already had
learned too much of what love meant from the Platonists. As
Nygren remarks, he did not come to Christianity *from* Platonism,
he came to Christianity *as* a Platonist; Platonism was a school
he never left. As it stands perhaps such an unqualified statement
is too extreme. We have, therefore, been careful to notice the
very great extent to which Augustine's notion of *caritas*-love has
undergone Christianization. Still it remains true that ingredients

[24]*On Grace and Free Will*, ch. xxxiv (*Basic Writings*, I, 751). (Italics mine.)
[25]*On the Spirit and the Letter*, ch. lvi (*Basic Writings*, I, 508). (Italics mine.)

of Platonism may be observed in Augustine's doctrine of love much more than in the case of other aspects of his thought—for example, his doctrines of man, sin, and grace.

As an indication of his fundamental difference from St. Augustine, St. Paul maintained unity in the orientation of Christian love in a fashion which at first glance appears in no wise different from some secular humanitarian reduction of love for God to love for neighbor. Instead of treating love for neighbor as but a special case of man's love for God, as was Augustine's tendency, St. Paul also "puts one for both": he twice summarizes the *entire* law in terms of the *second* love commandment. "The commandments, 'You shall not commit adultery, You shall not kill, You shall not steal, You shall not covet,' *and any other commandment,* are summed up in this sentence, 'You shall love your neighbor as yourself' " (Rom. 13:9). "For the *whole* law is fulfilled in *one* word, 'You shall love your neighbor as yourself' " (Gal. 5:14). The words "any other commandment" refer also to the verse in Deuteronomy, quoted or approved by Jesus, commanding love for God. Paul's selection of the second love commandment only, his including the first within the meaning of neighbor-love, must have been entirely deliberate in one who as a Jew had repeated the *Shema* several times daily and as a Christian knew how to distinguish between his own words and the words of the Lord (I Cor. 7:6).

Of course, Paul was no mere humanitarian who believed a man becomes a "Christian" simply by loving his neighbor, as if that were a simple matter. To the contrary, he will need to become a Christian ever to be able to love his neighbor *with Christian love.* Man's relation to God was for Paul quite prerequisite to having neighborly relationships with his fellow-man. Paul simply used another word, "faith," to designate man's response to "the love of God" for man which in Christ first establishes man's relation with God. Christian love for neighbor he believed to be unquestionably more than love for neighbor in the humanitarian sense of this expression. It is "the fulfillment of the law," *i.e.,* it is perfect obedience out of gratitude to God whose whole require-

ment may be summed up: You shall love your neighbor as yourself.

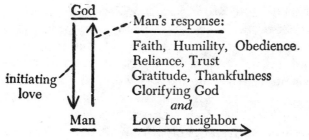

Whatever definition be given to the word "love," it is difficult,
if not impossible, to employ precisely the same meaning, clearly
and without variation, in speaking of man's attitude toward God
and toward his fellow-men. The word "love" does not speak with
one voice. It is used equivocally rather than univocally. One has
to go in heavily for analogy, or even commute back and forth
from one meaning to another, ever to suppose that "love," *or any
other single term*, can adequately convey the meaning of a Christian's response to God and also his love for neighbor. The words
"faith," "obedience," "humility," and—to indicate greater intimacy
and warmth—the words "gratitude" and "thankfulness," and—to
keep the distance between God and man—the expression "to
glorify" are preferable, singly or as a cluster, for describing how
Christians think of themselves standing in relation to God. These
are the Reformation categories. They were also central in Paul's
theology and in his description of Jesus Christ in his "humility"
being "obedient" unto death, even the death of the cross. For
them may also be claimed greater verisimilitude to Jesus and the
ethics of the Synoptic Gospels than for Neo-Platonic notions of
love for God and union with him in some final mystic vision.
Jesus did not act like a would-be mystic yearning to attain a religious experience or some otherworldly union with God, but like
a man who had already seen his heavenly vision and was obedient
to it in *this* world. In any case, Augustine himself confirms the
main point that needs to be made: If the word "love" is used to

describe man's way of relating himself to God, this general no-tion must then be broken down into two different species, such as "enjoyment" and "use," to apply, respectively, to God and man. C. A. Anderson Scott makes an effort to use only a single word in both these connections. "We should guard ourselves against serious misunderstanding," he writes, "if in many passages of the New Testament we rendered the word *Agape* by 'care.' 'Thou shalt care for the Lord thy God with all thy heart.' 'Thou shalt care for thy neighbor as thyself.' "[26] But the word "care" seems appropriate for both cases only because it is a rather neutral word. Like "consideration" or "response," what "care" means becomes clear only when Scott describes what this response means in re-lation to God and in relation to man; and then he finds it neces-sary to employ different terms.

A mere term, of course, has no importance. Logical and ter-minological considerations may therefore be dismissed and the word "love" freely used of man's attitude toward God—provided only that care is taken not to lose sight of the *purely responsive* character of this love. God's love for man is "first love," man's for God "second love." On account of the strength and direction gained from God's love, man's love for neighbor is again, in rela-tion to him, "first love." "First love" takes the lead; it gives what is needed, it does not first seek what the agent himself needs or desires. Christian, responsive love stands in no need of seeking, desires nothing but out of gratitude obediently loves the neigh-bor. "In this is love, not that we loved God but that he loved us. . . . We love, because he first loved us" (I John 4:10, 19). No man ought to "use" himself or his neighbor even for the sake of some supremely desirable end or for the sake of union with God; yet every man ought to "treat humanity" in himself as a means used in his neighbor's service. Underneath these termino-logical considerations lies an exceedingly important issue, an issue arising from the fact that "on the whole, God's love for us is

[26]*New Testament Ethics*, Macmillan, 1930, p. 23. At one point Karl Barth de-fines "faith" in terms of "love" and takes fully into account the special meaning "love" has when directed toward God. "Faith is," he says, "the love of God that is aware of the qualitative distinction between God and man and God and the world" (*The Epistle to the Romans*, transl. by Edwyn C. Hoskyns, Oxford Uni-versity Press, 1933, p. 39).

a much safer subject to think about than our love for Him."[27]

Whatever he may have learned from the Platonists, a Christian's love for God St. Augustine knew to be always a responsive love. This was true, he believed, because of a defect in the will which prevents it from naturally willing anything "resolutely and thoroughly."[28] Man loves God, but not entirely. He loves certain creaturely goods, but not entirely. His will does not command anything entirely, because it always countermands or has aversion for the good which at the same time he desires.

> I it was who willed, I who was unwilling. It was I, even I myself. I neither willed entirely, nor was entirely unwilling. There-fore I was at war with myself, and destroyed myself.[29]

This war within the will, or *Mensch im Widerspruch,* man in self-contradiction, is perhaps better expressed in poorer English: "It was I who willed, I who nilled, I, I myself. I neither willed entirely, nor nilled entirely. Therefore was I at strife with myself, and rent asunder by myself."[30] The defect in the will, Augustine believed, came not from deficient willing, or from being *unwilling,* but from positive, contradictory willing, willing and nilling the same thing at the same time. This applied both to his love for God and his love for his "ancient mistresses." He willed them both, but not entirely. As a consequence, from the account of the spiritual life given by the Platonists, two things were missing: an understanding that, even though the human heart be restless until it rests in union with God, no man living can succeed in loving God with such integrity of desire as is required to reach him, and, secondly, "the Word made flesh" for the relief of this condition. Christian love for God, then, depends altogether on God's love for man in the Word made flesh in Christ—him we love in loving God, through him alone we love God—and upon God's grace reintegrating the individual will so that for the first time a man may resolutely and thoroughly love God.

No different meaning was ever assigned by scripture to man's love for God than *purely responsive* love. Where the Old Testa-

---

[27]C. S. Lewis, *op. cit.,* p. 53.
[28]*The Confessions,* Bk. VIII, ch. viii (*Basic Writings,* I, 121).
[29]*Ibid.,* ch. x (*Basic Writings,* I, 123).   [30]Everyman edition, p. 166.

ment enjoins, Thou shalt love the Lord thy God with all thy heart, no other god was meant than the living God who had already shown his love for Israel in the events of deliverance and in his covenant with Abraham and Moses. No man has seen his face at any time or communed with his essence; even Moses caught only a glimpse of God's backsides; why should any one else aspire for more? Thou shalt love and follow after and obey the Lord thy God, whose "righteousness" has been made manifest toward his people: this was the *Shema* repeated seven times daily by devout Jews. Jesus' approval of the first formulation of the love commandment could have had no other meaning. So far then was he from making man's chief end mystic union with God, the soul's beatific vision of God gained by desiring to be filled with the divine. To the contrary, man's whole duty was summed up in obedient, responsive love.

Most of all, Christians who live from the righteousness of God in Jesus Christ and in memory of God's new covenant with man-kind love God because he first loved them. This is "the love of God," "God's love" which "has been poured into our hearts through the Holy Spirit which has been given us" (Rom. 5:5). Strictly speaking, the Christian church is not a community of prayer, but a community of memory. When Christians pray they pray "in Christ's name"; prayer thus is set decisively within the context of grateful remembrance of the God who put forward Christ. Strictly speaking, Christians are not lovers of God; they are *theodidacti*, "taught of God." Various forms of mysticism, from Plato's *Symposium* to the present, speak of various ladders of ascent, steep and hard steps whereby one finally attains a rela-tionship of the soul with God which tends to swallow up all other relations. In contrast, "Christ-mysticism" (if this expression in-deed is not a contradiction in terms) from St. Paul to the present finds its center well within this world. Christian morality stems therefore from a this-worldly, not an other-worldly, supernatu-ralism. And it is the incarnational element in all "Christ-mys-ticism," the controlling love of Christ, which turns a man's face toward his neighbor in all concreteness.

IV

FAITH'S EFFECTIVENESS

"Faith which dwells in the heart . . . is the head and substance of all our righteousness."
—Martin Luther, Works, II, 322.

B UT what of "salvation"? Is not "salvation" the end for which Christians quest? What of rewards in the kingdom of heaven? What of man's everlasting and supernatural good, the soul's life with God *in the hereafter;* man's "chief end," glorifying God and enjoying him *forever?* Is not "salvation" itself a supreme value which Christians seek with earnest passion, each first of all for himself?

It is significant that rewards and punishments spoken of in the New Testament are always separated by an eschatological gulf from action in this present age to which by promise they are added. What is right action in the present age is determined wholly on this side of that gulf, according to the nature of what is done in the present in response to present demands. Man lives, of course, from faith in God's faithfulness, but he ought not to try himself to overleap the abyss between the ages by aiming at his own future welfare. Promise of reward may be the *condition* of action, the *ground* or premise of strength, but reward is never action's *goal.* Reward is always *added to* the nature of the act, not a direct result of it such as might become a part of the agent's own prudential calculation. If he were calculating, the nature of his act would change, it would not be the kind of action for which reward is promised. If he acts *for the sake of* the reward, he has not yet done what God requires of him in readiness for the kingdom, he has not yet become entirely trusting and obedient, not yet single-minded in obedient love.

"Truly, I say to you, there is no one who has left house or brothers or sisters or mother or father or children or lands, *for my sake and for the gospel,* who will not receive a hundredfold now in this time, houses and brothers and sisters and mothers and children and lands, with persecutions, and in the age to come eternal life" (Mark 10:29, 30). Perhaps Jesus here caricatures all reward-hunting by blowing up the promise to inconceivable proportions: in return for one mother forsaken, a hundred mothers! But supposing a man to have houses, etc., and in the age to come eternal life, none of these is what he *intends* here and now. His present act is perfectly obedient and thoroughly sacrificial, not intent on recompense. He acts "for my sake and for the gospel," not for the sake of his own title to heavenly mansions or for the sake of eternal life. He does not have to aim at these things, the promise guarantees them, thus providing the conditions upon which a man may have nothing more to do but go about the business of obedient love, and may have the strength to do so. Just as "for my sake and the gospel's" interrupts any prudentially dependable connection between "losing life" and "finding" it, so here "for my sake and for the gospel" indicates what monopolizes the disciple's orientation, engrossing his whole subjective intention. Living *from* faith in eternal life and *for* Christ's sake as a motive is far removed from the motive of living to gain possession of eternal life, as far removed as gratitude and obedient love are from religious shrewdness.

Martin Luther contended mightily against the belief that those who do good, do it from "a servile and mercenary principle in order to obtain eternal life."[1] He severely condemned such anticipations of reward:

> Nay, if they should work good in order to obtain the Kingdom, they would never obtain it, but would be numbered rather with the wicked, who, with an evil and mercenary eye, seek the things of self even in God. Whereas, the sons of God do good with a

[1]*The Bondage of the Will,* tr. by H. Cole (Atherton, London, 1931), p. 192 (quoted by Philip S. Watson, *Let God Be God.* London: Epworth Press, 1947, p. 45).

free-will, seeking no reward, but the glory and will of God only; ready to do good, even if (which is impossible) there were neither a Kingdom nor a hell. . . .[2] Those who are not pleasure-seekers serve God for His own sake alone and not for the sake of heaven or of any temporal thing. And even though they knew that there were no heaven, nor hell, nor any reward, they would nevertheless serve God for His own sake.[3]

Luther argues also that action which aims at reward is precisely the opposite of the sort of action for which reward is promised:

> Be not thou concerned about the reward; that thou shalt have in due time, even if thou be not so eager after it. For although it is impossible that the reward should not come to them who worship God . . . without any consideration of gain or wages; yet, certain it is that God hates those mercenary characters, who seek themselves and not God, and will never give them any reward at all.[4]

Therefore, he counsels, "if you wish to pray, fast, or establish some foundation in the Church, take heed not to do it in order to obtain some benefit, *whether temporal or eternal.*"[5]

"Salvation" cannot be the goal or aim of Christian endeavor, the highest good among all goods upon which the Christian draws his sights. This would be to "seek the things of self even in God." Whether from misinterpretation or not, incalculable damage has been done Christian ethics by the passage near the beginning of *The Pilgrim's Progress* where Christian, fleeing from the City of Destruction, "had not run far from his own door, but his wife and children perceiving it, began to cry after him to return; but the man put his fingers in his ears, and ran on, crying, Life! Life! eternal Life!"[6] Properly understood, Christian love "counts not equality with God a thing to be grasped" (Phil. 2:6), nor fellowship with God in heaven a thing to be sought simply by using the neighbor as only a proximate or apparent object of

2*Ibid.*, p. 190 (quoted by Philip S. Watson, *op. cit.*, p. 45).
3*Sämmtliche Werke,* 67 vols. (Erlangen, 1826–1857), xxii, 133 f. (quoted by Philip S. Watson, *op. cit.*, p. 67 notes).
4*Selected Works of Martin Luther,* tr. by H. Cole, 4 vols. (London, 1826), I, 426 (quoted by Philip S. Watson, *op. cit.*, p. 67 notes).
5*Works,* Muhlenberg Press, II, 342 (italics mine).
6John Bunyan, *The Pilgrim's Progress,* Everyman edition, p. 10.

love. Hereby the very nature of neighbor-love would be destroyed, and this by consequence of a quite religious desire—an indefensibly self-centered desire—for salvation. "Salvation by faith alone" was designed precisely to avoid this outcome, as can plainly be seen in both Paul and Luther.

It is the genius of Christian ethics to understand that the possibilities are not exhausted in the two alternatives presented by the author of the Epistle of James: faith without works *or* faith consciously demonstrating itself by works, salvation without good deeds *or* good deeds performed for their value as evidence of salvation, itself the supreme end. Christian faith doubtless does not exist without leading on to ethical action, but Christian faith does not claim to be demonstrated by its works. Between these two alternatives stands a third: Paul's conception of faith working through love. This is obviously not the sort of faith James opposes. It is not an inner religious feeling that is content to be unrelated to deeds. A gulf equally wide, however, separates faith active in love from the faith James commends. Christian faith of which Paul spoke was concerned only with what it could effect, not with displaying *itself* by means of its works. Faith working through love is concerned only to show what *love* is and to discover the neighbor's needs, not to demonstrate that it itself is faithful. While Christian faith is related to deeds and cannot exist without being related to deeds, it is not self-centeredly related to them, not even in the apparently very religious declaration, "I by my works will show you my faith" (Jas. 2:18). Christian love does not *claim* good works; it *gives* them. Christian faith does not seek its own salvation, even salvation by faith, for *faith is effective in love which seeks only the neighbor's good.*

The Reformation, it is well known, abolished the distinction between sacred and secular areas of life, between special duties owed to God and ethical duties toward man, between specially meritorious religious vocations and the tasks of ordinary Christians in the world. All useful vocations, the Reformers said, are sacred and have religious merit. Duties to one's neighbors *are* duties to God. There is no special class of religious obligations;

all obligations are religious. For Protestantism, there can be no
going back to a Catholic distinction of *area* between things secular
and things religious.

Nevertheless, whether the word "faith" or the word "love" be
used to designate man's responding relationship to God, there is
danger of a similar distinction with respect to the amount of
inner devotion, energy, or trust which properly ought to be given
to God and to man. There need be no division of the ground into
separate secular and religious areas for the view still to prevail
that a Christian ought to hold in proper proportion the energy
he devotes to God in faith or love and that directed toward man
in loving works. The latter may be kept under severe ration controls lest, by undue devotion to man or trust in some humanitarian
program, a Christian commit the sin of idolatry and subtract too
much from the trust he owes to God alone. The resulting description of a Christian at work in collective social action is that of a
man who is not very enthusiastic. He sees "pagan" comrades falling over their heels to get things done, believing unreservedly
in their common project, and trusting its outcome as beneficial.
The Christian, however, is too worldly-wise to believe much in
anything in the world. Whether he calls himself a man of great
faith in God or a man of great love for the beatific vision of
God, only a certain modicum of spiritual energy remains over
for his task on earth. Having ultimate trust in some other world
or infinite love and longing for his true homeland, ethical action on his neighbor's behalf cannot really engage him, or at
least *ought* not. He cooperates, of course, in all worthwhile
community endeavors here below, even joining hands with humanists who believe in them, but he looks with religious cynicism
upon any one who thinks something significant can in time be
accomplished. At all cost, he must not have great faith in any
finite objective or great love for anything human. This tragic
device of moving away from humanism in the direction of
religious orthodoxy, or of moving away from orthodoxy in the
direction of humanitarian social action, by a division of spiritual energy and enthusiasm rests upon a grave misunderstand-

ing of the notion "faith" or "trust" in Reformation teaching.

Luther's *Treatise on Christian Liberty* is the classic formulation of the doctrine of justification by faith alone as it relates
to the freedom of a Christian from all requirements of work-
righteousness. Yet this treatise gives absolutely no support for
the view that distrust or lack of faith in the beneficent results
of neighbor-regarding action should be the attitude of a Christian man. In rejecting "good works," Luther carefully distinguishes between the "impious addition" of trust in them and
good works themselves. Moreover, when Luther rejects *"trust
in good works,"* his every sentence insists that Christians should
not trust their good works to pile up benefits *for themselves*. But
he enjoins *all possible trust that good works will benefit our
neighbors.* To seek salvation by good works means to seek one's
personal salvation by attributing merit to oneself flowing from
one's own good works. Luther rightly rejects such religious
egoism, yet he makes his positive position equally clear: A Christian ought, and will, seek the salvation *of others* by good works
(insofar as they are ordered thereto) and will attribute merit
to works as *benefiting his neighbor*.

In Luther's view, then, a Christian need not put a halter on
his spiritual energies in order to make sure of not trusting anything finite. His real need is to curb his ego, or rather to have
his self-concern suspended, in order ever to have as much devotion as he ought to human activity for the benefit of his
neighbor. The distinction is between trust in works out of concern for one's own eternal welfare and trust in works out of
concern for the needs of another. This is the *pons asinorum* of
Christian ethics, and one not crossed by the comparatively easy
device of moderating one's trust in all things human. Luther in
fact makes the somewhat surprising judgment that concern for
others directed toward the finite and the this-worldly is preferable to a high spirituality or other-worldliness which remains
a primarily self-concerned yearning for one's eternal welfare or
salvation.

Read with a mind that does not preclude the foregoing inter-

pretation, and one determined not to be mystified by religious
terminology but to ask of all terms their meaning, passages in
the *Christian Liberty* spring to life. Consider, for example:

> If works are sought after as a means to righteousness . . . and
> are *done under the false impression that through them you are
> justified,* they are made necessary and freedom and faith are
> destroyed, and *this addition to them* makes them no longer good,
> but truly damnable works. . . . What the works have no power
> to do, they yet, *by a godless presumption,* through this folly of
> ours, *pretend* to do, and thus violently force themselves into the
> office and the glory of grace. We do not, therefore, reject good
> works, on the contrary, *we cherish and teach them as much as
> possible.* We do not condemn them for their own sake, but be-
> cause of this *godless addition* to them and *the perverse idea* that
> righteousness is to be sought through them. . . . Our faith in
> Christ does not free us from works, but from false opinions con-
> cerning good works, that is, from the foolish presumption that
> [our own] justification is acquired by works.[7]

A story recounted by Grushenka in Dostoevsky's *The Brothers
Karamazov* puts Luther's religious and ethical analysis, and that
of St. Paul as well, into dramatic form:

> Once upon a time there was a peasant woman and a very wicked
> woman she was. And she died and did not leave a single good
> deed behind. The devils caught her and plunged her into the
> lake of fire. So her guardian angel stood and wondered what
> good deed of hers he could remember to tell to God; "she once
> pulled up an onion in her garden," said he, "and gave it to a
> beggar woman." And God answered: "You take that onion then,
> hold it out to her in the lake, and let her take hold and be pulled
> out. And if you can pull her out of the lake, let her come to
> Paradise, but if the onion breaks, then the woman must stay
> where she is." The angel ran to the woman and held out the
> onion to her; "Come," said he, "catch hold and I'll pull you out."
> And he began cautiously pulling her out. He had just pulled her
> right out, when the other sinners in the lake, seeing how she
> was being drawn out, began catching hold of her so as to be
> pulled out with her. But she was a very wicked woman and she
> began kicking them. "I'm to be pulled out, not you. It's my

[7] *Works,* II, 333, 344 (italics mine).

onion, not yours." As soon as she said that, the onion broke. And the woman fell into the lake and she is burning there to this day.[8]

The moral is clear: a good deed claimed is not a Christian deed. Yet even a casual deed may have value for others: the onion did not break under the load of its service to others. Deeds of service to others may be trusted, even trusted to be of ultimate worth: until she said that her deed was of worth only as merit to her own salvation, the woman was actually righteous before God and was being pulled out.

One major point remains for understanding Luther's view of the relation of Christian faith in God to loving works, namely, his answer to the question, How does a person come to have such disinterestedness as to be able to plunge wholeheartedly into action on his neighbor's behalf? The comment has been made that here Luther gives ethical teaching and displays psychological insight that are "worthy of profound admiration."[9] What is the "ethical quality of such teaching" as Luther's? What is the "psychological insight displayed"? The ethical teaching, of course, is the view that a so-called good deed is *not even good* unless motivated by disinterested love. "Goodness" here receives its essential definition in terms of Christian love, which we have seen to be the primary notion in Christian ethics. This was not new with Luther, since Paul said the same in I Corinthians 13. Such goodness will always remain objectionable to moralists who can think of no way to recommend an action except by pointing out some benefit to accrue to the agent if he performs it. In this connection, the Protestant rejection of "salvation by works" has frequently been greatly misunderstood. It has often been stated so as to accent the *inability* of man's *puny* good works to save him, and by contrast God's power to save. Properly understood, however, what is called in question by this doctrine is not so much the *saving power* of good works, as the *goodness* of all

---

[8]Fyodor Dostoyevsky, *The Brothers Karamazov* (Modern Library Giant edition), pp. 369–370.

[9]A. C. McGiffert, *Protestant Thought Before Kant*, Scribners, 1911, pp. 39–40.

so-called "good" works done without faith. Let it for the moment be granted that *if* really good works were done apart from salvation by faith, they would indeed have power to save. But according to Luther, this is an hypothesis contrary to fact. Faith first gives "works" the ability *to be good;* it does not simply add some supplementary saving power to good works. Faith saves the goodness of "good works"; it enters into the very constitution of goodness; it does not simply save the agent who otherwise or without faith performs good works. Works done, even martyrdom suffered, for the purpose of saving one's own soul are not even *good* works, much less saving works. "But this . . . perverse notion concerning works is *insuperable* where sincere faith is wanting. Those work-saints cannot get rid of it unless faith, its destroyer, come and rule in their hearts. Nature of itself cannot drive it out, nor even recognize it, but rather regards it as a mark of the most holy will."[10]

It is even more difficult for a modern man to understand, much less sense, the profundity of Luther's psychological insight, since the modern mind has so far ceased to be concerned in an agonizing personal way with the problem of sin and forgiveness. What Luther says is simply that, unless and until a man knows himself already to be saved *behind* or prior to his good works, then "he cannot do otherwise, as a serious minded and religious man, than give time and thought to his own state"[11] and seek to save himself rather than to help his neighbor by his good works. On the other hand, "when you know that you have through Christ, a good and gracious God who will forgive your sins and remember them no more, and are now a child of eternal blessedness, a lord over heaven and earth with Christ, *then you have nothing more to do than to go about your business and serve your neighbor.*"[12] Faith in God's gracious forgiveness *causes* liberality in us and produces other disinterested good works,

[10]Martin Luther, *Works,* II, 334 (italics mine). Luther's criticism of the goodness of so-called good works may be compared with Augustine's criticism of the virtue of the so-called pagan virtues. These have the form but not the substance of righteousness. See below, Ch. six, sections I and II(a).

[11]A. C. McGiffert, *op. cit.,* p. 37.

[12]Luther, quoted by McGiffert, *op. cit.,* p. 38 (italics mine).

142   *Faith's Effectiveness*

while distrust *causes* covetousness and other selfish attitudes. Far from faith or trust in this sense cutting down on the energy one can then half-trustingly give to good works, to the contrary: Faith and trust in God's graciousness are prerequisite to having utmost commitment to and passion for whatever may be of benefit to our neighbors. Otherwise, like the old woman we keep a firm, selfish grasp on the onions we give away. "Our own self-assumed good-works lead us *to and into ourselves,* that we seek only our own benefit and salvation; but God's command *drives us to our neighbor.*"[13]

There can be no stronger statement than that given by Luther of the whole response of a Christian to his neighbor's needs in any action:

> Therefore, in all his works he should be guided by this thought and look to this one thing alone, that he may serve and benefit others in all that he does, having regard to nothing except the need and advantage of his neighbor. Thus the Apostle commands us to work with our hands that we may give to him who is in need, although he might have said that we should work to support ourselves; he says, however, "that he may have to give to him that needeth." And this is what makes it a Christian work to care for the body, that through its health and comfort we may be able to work to acquire and lay by funds with which to aid those who are in need. . . . Lo, this is a truly Christian life, here faith is truly effectual through love; that is, it issues in works of the freest service cheerfully and lovingly done, with which a man willingly serves another without hope of reward, and for himself is satisfied with the fullness and wealth of his faith. . . .
>
> I will therefore give myself as a Christ to my neighbor, just as Christ offered himself to me; I will do nothing in life except what I see is necessary, profitable and salutary to my neighbor. . . .[14]

Whatever may be said for Augustine's largely Platonic "love for God" as a way of characterizing man's relationship to God, "salvation by faith," far from subtracting anything at all from the energy or changing the direction of neighbor-regarding love, alone

[13]*Works,* II (italics mine).
[14]*Works.* II, 335–336, 337–338.

gives abundance to the phenomenon of love; it alone is premise to "the strength of the individual who can give."

The "fall of Christianity" did not occur when, changing its economic action, the early church abandoned the experiment in communism at Jerusalem, nor when, changing its political action, the church came to terms with Constantine's empire, nor when in any age there has taken place a radical change of tactics. Christianity "fell" from the purity of its original ethical motivation, and repeatedly falls, when love which "seeks not its own" begins earnestly to seek its own eternal reward. Commenting on a passage from the *Didaché*, Harnack writes,

> It is beyond question, therefore, that a Christian brother could demand work from the church, and that the church had to furnish him with work. What bound the members together, then, was not merely the duty of supporting one another . . .; it was the fact that they formed a guild of workers, in the sense that the churches had to provide work for a brother whenever he required it. . . . We must attach a very high degree of value to a union which provided work for those who were able to work, and at the same time kept hunger from those who were unfit for labour.[15]

Very high value, indeed, is to be accorded an ancient community which could sustain the needy without pauperizing them and could administer charity so well without knowledge of modern sociology or the techniques of social case work. Though early Christians were economically naïve, their love which had regard only for what might benefit the neighbor made them wiser than serpents. Look now at Europe from two to ten centuries later during the Catholic middle ages, teeming with thousands of paupers considered as pitiable objects for Christians to exercise their charity on for the sake of earning merit in heaven. The orientation of Christian love curved inward under the guise of being

[15]Adolf von Harnack, *The History of Dogma*, Williams and Norgate, 1896–1905, I, 175–176. The passage he is commenting on reads: "If any brother has a trade let him follow that trade and earn the bread he eats. If he has no trade, exercise your discretion in arranging for him to live among you as a Christian, *but not in idleness*. If he will not do this [*i.e.*, engage in the work you furnish him], he is trafficking with Christ. Beware of men like that." *Didaché*, XII:3 ff., *cf.* Paul, II Thess. 3:6–12.

turned heavenward. Conversely, there takes place a revival of Christian ethical motivation whenever love ceases to seek its own and through faith seeks only to see and serve the neighbor's need.

It is, of course, another question whether any man can measure up to this test. This ethic is "scandalous" to sinful human nature. It is "other-worldly" and "super-natural," *i.e.*, beyond what is natural to man. It draws a man out of the citadel of the self into the world of another's needs. This is the only sort of otherworldliness there is in Christian ethics. In contrast to Greek, mystical other-worldliness which, imported by St. Augustine, lay at the root of the Catholic middle ages, true Christian this-worldly supernaturalism weans a person away from the city of the self and requires that he act outside the gate of self-concern. "So Jesus also suffered *outside the gate* in order to consecrate the people through his own blood. *Therefore let us go forth to him outside the camp,* bearing abuse for him. For here we have no lasting city, but we seek the city which is to come" (Heb. 13:12–14). This Christian supernaturalism (oriented toward a kingdom which is *to come,* not one which is *above*) does not subtract from the energies men may devote to practical "causes" in the present age. Rather it directs human energies fully toward the world of other people's interests, which for natural man is indeed another world requiring that he rise above his own nature and go outside his own camp.

We have seen that Christian ethics does not draw its standard for man from man himself, and, moreover, that this standard goes far beyond what is natural to sinful men. Nevertheless, on condition of faith, Christian love is not impossible for man. Frequently it is argued that all men are always selfish, since no man does anything or continues to do those things out of which he gets no satisfaction. But gaining satisfaction out of some activity is one thing, *intending* only to gain selfish satisfaction quite another. If selfishness be defined so as to include all actions from which the agent actually gets satisfaction, then doubtless all men are selfish *by definition,* and the classification of "unselfish acts" becomes a class without any members. But this is not a very significant use of language. The only important distinction among people is between those who gain satisfaction only from living with their own interests alone in view and those who (whether naturally or by faith or by practice) take pleasure in living with the interests of others in view. In no significant sense can men be proved selfish simply from the psychological fact that satisfaction doubtless accompanies all human activity which continues to be practiced.

No more can ethical hedonism be established merely from the fact that psychological pleasure must accompany any plan of action. Perhaps all action springs from "pleasant ideas," but not every "pleasant idea" must be the idea of some pleasure to be gained. J. S. Mill confused these two things:

> And now to decide . . . whether mankind do desire nothing for itself but that which is a pleasure to them. . . . Desiring a thing and finding it pleasant, aversion to it and thinking of it as painful, are phenomena entirely inseparable, or rather two parts of the same phenomenon; in strictness of language, two different modes of naming the same psychological fact: that to think of an object as desirable . . . and to think of it as pleasant are one and the same thing; and that to desire anything, except in proportion as *the idea of it is pleasant*, is a physical and metaphysical impossibility.[16]

Granting that nothing is desired except in proportion as the idea of it is pleasant, this does not prove that only pleasure is ethically desirable. For there are other ideas, ideas of other goods or values, *e.g.*, truth, beauty, or goodness, which men hold in mind with pleasure. From these pleasant ideas they may act for the sake of truth, beauty, or goodness, which may be proportionately more pleasant to them than the idea of some pleasure to be pursued.

In the same way, granting for the moment what seems obvious, that no man does anything except in proportion as the idea of it is pleasant and satisfactory to him, this proves nothing of any consequence concerning man's selfishness or unselfishness. For some

[16]*Utilitarianism*, ch. iv (Modern Library edition, *The English Philosophers from Bacon to Mill*, ed. by E. A. Burtt, p. 926). (Italics mine.)

men only the idea of deliberately *intending* and *aiming* at some good for themselves is a satisfactory plan of action or pleasant policy by which to live. For others, at least on some occasions, the idea of deliberately *intending* and devoting themselves to securing good for another person proves quite satisfactory. Of course, satisfaction which is the unintended by-product of intending the neighbor's good easily turns into seeking satisfaction primarily for the self and the neighbor's good only as an unintended consequence. Christianity is quite aware of this danger; indeed under the name of sin it declares such incurving of the self on itself to be universal. Still, as regards choosing between the self's satisfaction in serving the needs of others and the self's satisfaction in serving only the needs of self (including its need for satisfaction through sociability), why, out of the heart are the issues of life! And the main point here may be taken as established: Christian love is not inherently impossible for man.[17]

We can penetrate more into the heart of this matter by considering for a moment the relationship between *amor Dei* (love for God) and *amor sui* (love for self) in the thought of St. Augustine. On the one hand, Augustine understands love for God and love for self to be mutually exclusive. He declares that "two cities have been formed by two loves: the earthly by the love of self, even to the contempt of God; the heavenly by the love of God, even to the contempt of self," and the opposition between these two loves was the theme of his monumental work *The City of God*.[18] Yet as we have seen, in other aspects of his thought these two loves are said to be ultimately identical. He who loves

[17]Jonathan Edwards sometimes bordered on saying that "true virtue" is impossible simply because man's nature is what it is by nature. Nevertheless, he sees clearly the foregoing distinction regarding self-love: "Which comes only to this, that self-love is a man's liking, and being suited and pleased in that which he likes and which pleases him; or that it is a man's loving what he loves. For whatever a man loves, that thing is grateful and pleasing to him, *whether that be his own peculiar happiness, or the happiness of others. And if this be all that they mean by self-love, no wonder they suppose that all love may be resolved into self-love. For it is undoubtedly true, that whatever a man loves, his love may be resolved into his loving what he does—if that be proper speaking.*" (*Representative Selections*, ed. by C. H. Faust and T. H. Johnson, American Book Co., 1935, p. 358.) (Italics mine.)

[18]Bk. XIV, ch. xxviii (*Basic Writings of St. Augustine*, ed. by Whitney J. Oates, Random House, 1948, II, 274).

God must needs love himself properly and he who truly loves his own good loves God. Love for God and love for self are therefore entirely compatible.

Pointing out this apparent contradiction in St. Augustine's views, Anders Nygren attempts to resolve it.[19] He suggests that *amor sui* (love of self) is used in two different senses, first, to indicate the *nature* of love, and then to indicate its *object*. When St. Augustine was thinking of the nature of love which always acquisitively seeks its own, he held that obviously such love is entirely compatible with love for man's supreme good, God. Understood in this sense, without doubt *amor sui* finds its completion in love for God, and in any case may be directed toward many other objects besides the self itself.

On the other hand, "the love of self," *amor sui*, may be taken to indicate the object of love or that in which love seeks some good. On this reading, *amor sui* and *amor Dei* refer to two rival objects of love. If we seek our *bonum* in one, we cannot seek it in the other. Understood as pointing out *whom* we should love, love for God and love for self prove mutually quite exclusive. Understood as expressing the assumption that all love by nature consists of desire for some good, the love of self (or written more exactly, the self's love) for some *bonum* needs only to be directed toward God for its object. Nygren's analysis of Augustine's viewpoint may be diagrammed as follows:

The Nature of Love:	*The Object of Love:*
Amor sui, or	in oneself (*amor sui*)
Seeking one's own *bonum*	in God

In the preceding chapter it was suggested that more of the Neo-Platonic ingredients ought to be jettisoned from Augustine's doctrine of love by submitting it again to the judgment of the New Testament norm of disinterested *agape*-love for neighbor. It is tempting at this point to insist upon the possibility of such

[19]*Op. cit.*, Pt. II, vol. II, pp. 315–331.

neighbor-love simply by making use of the analysis Nygren has made of Augustine's position. With necessary changes, this could be done; and indeed there is a close comparison between the foregoing account of the harmony between *amor sui* and *amor Dei* and what has been said so far in this chapter to refute the charge that disinterested love for neighbor is *un*natural in the sense of *going against* human nature. We have spoken of the self's satisfaction in serving only the needs of self and the self's satisfaction in serving the needs of others. It cannot be denied that even on the basis of a love which by nature seeks some *bonum* there is significant difference between the self seeking its good only in itself and a self which seeks its good sometimes also in the neighbor. The diagram used above might be repeated in the case of love for neighbor.

The Nature of Love:　　　*The Object of Love:*

Amor sui, or
Seeking one's own *bonum* $\left\{ \begin{array}{l} \text{in oneself} \\[1em] \text{in the neighbor} \end{array} \right.$

In similar fashion, the objection was made against J. S. Mill that "pleasant ideas" may sometimes be ideas of other objects or values besides pleasure. Frequently it proves to be quite a pleasant and satisfactory experience for a person to do some good for another.

However, such a delineation of the nature and the possibility of Christian neighbor-regarding love would not be thoroughgoing enough. Christian love has to do with the very *nature* of love itself, it does not simply provide love with another object—the neighbor—in whom one's *bonum* should still be sought. Christian love in its nature *gives* some good, it is not primarily concerned to seek good. It is deontologically, as a matter of obedience, related to the neighbor as such; it is not teleologically, as a matter of desire, related to some *bonum*.

Along with distinguishing between the nature and the object of love we need also to speak of the *subject* of love. Of course, the self is the subject of every love of whatever kind. The self is therefore the subject of Christian love; hence we can speak of *the self's love* just as we can speak of Christ's love. But if there is any hope of an understanding here, it should never be allowed that the nature of Christ's love was to seek his own *bonum* nor that ideally the nature of a Christian's love is to seek his own. Allowing that obviously no one else than the self is ever the *subject* engaged in loving, still it is the nature of Christian love, as has been said, to invert self-love. This then is the alternative with which we are confronted:

$$\text{The self's love} \begin{cases} \text{for self} \\ \text{for the neighbor} \end{cases}$$

Only a diagram such as the above takes fully into account the fact that the self may not only direct its natural desire for good toward other objects than itself, but also may become the subject of a love whose nature is not to seek its own whether on earth or in heaven. The self's *bonum,* if it follows upon an act of Christian love, follows as a quite unintended consequence.

Indeed, it may legitimately be suspected that in seeking its own *bonum* the quality or nature of love always in some measure enters into determining the intended object or aim of love. Thus the nature of love influences the selection of objects for love. God, the self, neighbors and every other creature easily become objects for such love only insofar as in them one's own *bonum* may also be held in view. Perhaps not inevitably but also not illogically did Roman Catholicism during the centuries after St. Augustine become more and more open to Luther's stricture against it—"seeking the things of self even in God." In this connection it is noteworthy that in Latin the expression *amor sui* is not like *amor Dei* an instance of the ambiguity of the genitive case. Therefore it cannot be argued that, just as on one reading "the love of God" or *amor Dei* means "God's love," so likewise *amor sui* means "the self's love" as well as "love for the self."

There is another expression in the Latin, *suus amor,* which means *his love* or *the self's love,* which Augustine might have used. The fact that he does not do so but speaks instead of *amor sui* shows that the self together with some *bonum,* or some *bonum* which the self aims to share in, comprise the composite object love always holds in view even in the enjoyment of God. It is true that the English expression, "the self's love for God," brings together the subjective and objective aspects of love, and indicates them to be entirely harmonious, indeed necessary to each other. However, the Latin equivalent for this is *suus amor Dei,* in which simply by adding one word, *Dei,* the object of the self's love (*suus amor*) may be pointed out. By speaking so frequently of *amor sui* Augustine plainly means to say more about the nature of love than that obviously the self as subject engages in it. Moreover, we have said that the neighbor becomes for the Christian the object of *suus amor;* "the self's love for neighbor" indicates both the subject and the object of Christian love, whose nature is determined by the love of Christ.

Having now so sharpened the issue, it remains for us to point out that men of flesh and blood may actually manifest Christian love. This requires no *unearthly* transformation of human consciousness; Christians are not joints on some heavenly pipe-line. On the part of the agent or subject who engages in love for neighbor, what is demanded and all that is demanded is the complete exclusion of any intention (conscious or subconscious) of himself profiting (immediately or in the future, on earth or in heaven, singly or mutually) from the benefit done for another. Among subjective factors that remain there may very well accrue to the agent a great many accompanying satisfactions as quite unintended by-products of intending not his own but his neighbor's good. Undoubtedly, his neighbor's good proves "grateful and pleasing" to the Christian. "And if this be all that they mean by self-love, no wonder" some people "suppose that all love may be resolved into self-love." For even with regard to quite disinterested benevolence "it is undoubtedly true, that whatever a man loves, his love may be resolved into his loving what he does."[20] But this is no proper manner of speaking, since a significant moral distinction can be drawn between finding one's own peculiar happiness or the happiness of others (with no intention focused on one's own) suitable, "grateful and pleasing" to oneself. The thesis of this chapter has been that "salvation by faith" is that in the self which enables man to become the subject of this *giving* sort of love. Christian love is the work of faith.

To sum up the matter of faith's effectiveness, or what the Christian does with "salvation": Faith makes what is not unnatural for man spontaneous; provides the condition by which what is not against nature becomes true. Christian ethics is a prolongation of the incarnation, incarnation among those in need, not a prolongation of human aspiration even for religious salvation, nor, as Augustine too often supposed, a rebound from incarnation in this world back into the ways of otherworldly ascent. Christian salvation, salvation by faith, no doubt provides indispensable propelling motivation *from behind,* but it is never motivation *from in front,* never an ultimate goal pursued in everything the Christian does. The old Calvinistic test for candidates for the ministry, "Are you willing to be damned for the glory of God?" is, of course, totally unacceptable, even a repulsive, "horrible decree," for what it says about God. But it would be difficult to frame a more succinct statement of the bearing of "salvation" on Christian ethics. Whoever is willing to be damned for the glory of God is truly saved—for his neighbor. Whoever willingly lets go his own supreme interest in eternity presumably among lesser values in this life seeks not his own but acts always for the glory of God, for Christ's sake and for the gospel, and obediently in love for his neighbor. Whether we say with Luther "complete, *prior* assurance of salvation" or with the old Calvinists "willingness to be damned for the glory of God," *ethically* the consequence is the same: Christianity is the negation of the general religious desire for salvation as the supreme personal value *to be gained;* "What do *I* get out of religion?" another of those preferential questions which Jesus radically reformulates and turns upon the questioner

[20]Jonathan Edwards, *ibid.* (note 17 above).

with the words, "Go thou and do . . ." Properly understood,
Christian faith "enables us to go about our business and serve our
neighbor"; trust in God thrusts us completely into "love in action . . . which is labor and fortitude, and for some people, too,
perhaps, a complete science," active love which does not, like a
"hired servant expect payment at once—that is, praise, and the
repayment of love with love."[21]

21Fyodor Dostoyevsky, *op. cit.*, pp. 56, 57.

V

CHRISTIAN VOCATION

"'And the shepherds returned, glorifying and praising God for all the things that they had heard and seen, as it was told unto them.'

"This is wrong. We should correct this passage to read, 'They went and shaved their heads, fasted, told their rosaries, and put on cowls.' Instead we read, 'The shepherds returned.' Where to? To their sheep. Oh, that can't be right! Did they not leave everything and follow Christ? Must not one forsake father and mother, wife and child, to be saved? But the Scripture says plainly that they returned and did exactly the same work as before. They did not despise their service, but took it up again where they left off with all fidelity, and I tell you that no bishop on earth ever had so fine a crook as those shepherds."

—The Martin Luther Christmas Book (ed. by Roland H. Bainton), p. 50.

I. THE PROBLEM OF CHRISTOCENTRIC VOCATION

THE Protestant Reformation abolished the medieval Catholic distinction between special religious merit and dignity attached to the role of the clergy and the inferior, though altogether necessary, function of ordinary lay Christians in the world. All vocations, said the Reformers, rank the same with God, none more sacred, none more secular than others, no matter how they are ranked by men. Of course, some callings are socially more pivotal than others, in that the vocation of many other individuals are subsumed under them; but the difference between monk or magistrate and gardener or garbage collector is an "official" distinction only, implying no real difference in merit or dignity before God. Therefore no individual, whatever his

153

work may be, has any necessity for forsaking the responsibilities
of his calling to go off on a crusade or to enter a monastery out
of bad conscience about what he is now doing and under the
illusion that he can be more perfect somewhere else.

> . . . The Lord commands every one of us, in all the actions of
> life to regard his vocation. . . . He has appointed to all their
> particular duties in different spheres of life. . . . Every individ-
> ual's line of life . . . is, as it were, a post assigned him by the
> Lord, that he may not wander about in uncertainty all his days.
> . . . Our life, therefore, will then be best regulated, when it is
> directed to this mark; since no one will be impelled by his own
> temerity to attempt more than is compatible with his calling, be
> cause he will know that it is unlawful to transgress the bounds
> assigned him. He that is in obscurity will lead a private life
> without discontent, so as not to desert the station in which God
> has placed him. It will also be no small alleviation of his cares,
> labours, troubles, and other burdens, when a man knows that in
> all these things he has God for his guide. The magistrate will
> execute his office with greater pleasure, the father of a family
> will confine himself to his duty with more satisfaction, and all,
> in their respective spheres of life, will bear and surmount the
> inconveniences, cares, disappointments, and anxieties which be-
> fall them, when they shall be persuaded that every individual
> has his burden laid upon him by God. Hence also will arise
> peculiar consolation, since there will be no employment so mean
> and sordid (provided we follow our vocation) as not to appear
> truly respectable, and be deemed highly important in the sight
> of God. . . .[1]

Martin Luther likewise wanted everybody to be somebody in
the eyes of God even though this meant that no one would be
anybody by comparison with each other.

> What you do in your house is worth as much as if you did it
> up in heaven for our Lord God. For what we do in our calling
> here on earth in accordance with His word and command He
> counts as if it were done in heaven for Him. . . . Therefore we
> should accustom ourselves to think of our position and work as

[1]John Calvin, *Institutes of the Christian Religion*, III, x, 6. (*A Compend of
the Institutes of the Christian Religion*, edited by H. T. Kerr, Jr., Westminster
Press, 1939, p. 107.)

sacred and well-pleasing to God, not on account of the position and the work, but on account of the word and the faith from which the obedience and the work flow. No Christian should despise his position and life if he is living in accordance with the word of God, but should say, "I believe in Jesus Christ, and do as the ten commandments teach, and pray that our dear Lord may help me thus to do." That is a right holy life, and cannot be made holier even if one fast himself to death. . . . It looks like a great thing when a monk renounces everything and goes into a cloister, carries on a life of asceticism, fasts, watches, prays, etc. . . . On the other hand, it looks like a small thing when a maid cooks and cleans and does other housework. But because God's command is there, even such a small work must be praised as a service to God far surpassing the holiness and asceticism of all monks and nuns. For here there is no command of God. But there God's command is fulfilled, that one should honour father and mother and help in the care of the home. . . .[2]

All this is familiar. Less has been said so clearly of how a Christian's duty in some secular calling stands in relation to Christian love which should be normative for everything he does. Granted that a theocentric or a law- or decalogue-centered theory of vocation may very well be formulated, how can there be a *Christocentric* vocation without withdrawing an individual quite completely from actual tasks in the world?

Count Leo Tolstoy, Russian novelist, Christian idealist, and opponent of all government, understood to the full the essential meaning of non-resisting Christian love in the respect that such love has absolutely no *selfish* reason for preferring one person to another. He defined Christian love as "a preference for others over oneself," with the immediate implication that before a man can love he must "cease from preferring some people to others *for his own personal welfare*."[3] For a Christian the activity of love does not

> proceed in any definite order with the demands of his strongest love presenting themselves first, those of a feebler love next, and

[2]*Works,* V, 102; IV, 341; V, 100. (Quoted by A. C. McGiffert, *Protestant Thought Before Kant,* Scribners, 1911, p. 33.)

[3]Leo Tolstoy, *On Life,* xxiv, translated by Aylmer Maude (World's Classics edition, Oxford University Press, pp. 102, 103). (Italics mine.)

so on. The demands of love present themselves *constantly* and *simultaneously* and *without any order*. Here is a hungry old man for whom I have a little love and who has come to ask for food which I am keeping for the supper of my much-loved children: how am I to weigh the present demand of a feebler love against the future demand of a stronger?[4]

Tolstoy not only seems to comprehend clearly the essential nature of unclaiming, non-resisting, non-preferential love for neighbor, but also his deep suspicion of introducing any other sort of preferences into the activity of love sprang from considerations which Christian ethics must judge quite correct. Any sort of preference among neighbors so easily turns again into care for them only in the sequence and degree called for by self-love.

If I admit that a freezing child may remain unclothed because my children may some day need the clothes I am asked to give, then I may also resist other demands of love out of consideration for my future children. . . .

If a man may reject the present demands of a feebler love for the sake of the future demands of a greater love, is it not evident that such a man, even if he wished it with all his might, will never be able to judge to what extent he may reject present demands in favour of future demands; and therefore, not being able to decide that question, *will always choose the manifestations of love which please him best*—that is, he will yield not to the demands of love but to the demands of his personality. If a man decides that it is better for him to resist the demands of a present very feeble love for the sake of a future greater love *he deceives himself and others and loves no one but himself*.

Future love does not exist. Love is a present activity only.[5]

Tolstoy's views are at many points actually a paraphrase of the Sermon on the Mount and other of Jesus' strenuous teachings which we have seen are an eschatological stimulus making us well acquainted with the pure and perfect will of God. Jesus said, "If any one comes to me and does not *hate* his own father and mother and wife and children and brothers and sisters, yes, and even his own life, he cannot be my disciple" (Luke 14:26);

[4]*Ibid.*, xxiii, p. 97 (italics mine).
[5]*Ibid.*, pp. 97–98 (italics mine).

and to a would-be disciple who wanted first to wait until his father was dead and buried, he laid down the condition, "Follow me, and leave the dead to bury their own dead" (Matt. 8:22). What then becomes of vocational obligation to one's own family? How can non-preferential love *prefer* some persons to others so far as must be the case within the actual lines of any vocation? How can non-resisting love take upon itself any responsibility for public protection or in support of just social reform through the vocation of legislator, judge, sheriff, hangman or soldier? How can the strenuous teachings of Jesus come into actual practice? How can the ferment of ideal perfectionism in Christian ethics provide foundation for any actual calling except by outright or thinly disguised compromise? These questions have now to be answered.

II. NON–PREFERENTIAL LOVE AND DUTIES TO ONESELF

Tolstoy's position may be described as an "unenlightened unselfishness" in that he determines the activity of love simply by blind chance. Whoever happens to be in need and *near* was for him the *only* neighbor to be taken into account. The beginning of a more enlightened unselfishness is to be found in St. Augustine's answer to the question, "How Are We to Decide Whom to Aid?" He too makes reference to "a sort of lot," but the chance determining which neighbor should be served was for him *not entirely* random or accidental.

> Further, all men are to be loved equally. But since you cannot do good to all, you are to pay special regard to those who, by the accidents of time, or place, or circumstance, are brought into closer connection with you. For, suppose that you had a great deal of some commodity, and felt bound to give it away to somebody who had none, and that it could not be given to more than one person; if two persons presented themselves, neither of whom had *either from need or relationship* a greater claim upon you than the other, you could do nothing fairer than choose by lot to which you would give what could not be given to both. Just

so among men, since you cannot consult for the good of them all, *you must take the matter as decided for you by a sort of lot*, according as each man happens for the time being to be *more closely connected* with you.[1]

It is not only some need momentarily confronting the Christian which defines his duty. The permanent relationships he has established with other persons within the limits of his particular calling have also to be taken into account. This calls for decision and preference among the needs to be served.

In Tolstoy's interpretation a fundamental mistake has been made in passing from a description of what a Christian man (or group) should do in relation to a single neighbor, other claims disregarded and the agent alone involved in the consequences, to what he should do in relation to more than one neighbor. Christian love, itself absolutely non-resistant in one-one neighbor relationships, may be required to change its tactic to resistance when concerned for the fate of more than one neighbor. Itself non-preferential so far as concerns only the agent's own "personal welfare," Christian love *for the neighbors' sake* may actually prefer certain persons to others. Itself not at all self-defensive, Christian love may nevertheless devise an ethic of protection for third parties; itself unclaiming, may yet be obliged to fulfill the claims of neighbor by first or at the same time performing certain duties to the self. These are the vocational duties of Christian love.

When right relation to the neighbor has been established, then and then only, we have said, does Christian love need to become as enlightened as possible about what is truly good—for the neighbor. Then and then only, as a secondary though quite essential concern, does it enter into a Christian's head for his neighbor's sake to ascend whatever scale of values he may find reasonably creditable. This has already been pointed out; Christian ethics means "neighbor-centered concern for value." Among the values between which the Christian must make some sort of settlement are the goods to be given this or that neighbor at the

---

[1] *On Christian Doctrine*, I, ch. xxviii (*Nicene and Post-Nicene Fathers*, Scribners, 1908, First Series, vol. II). (Italics mine.)

moment in which their claims conflict or when the demands of present and future love prove incompatible. This judgment he will make only in great peril of deceiving himself and others and loving no one but himself, but under no necessity of doing so. When making preferences he may, of course, choose only the manifestation of love which only pleases him best, but he may also make the choice actually required for maximum service to his neighbors. In short, there may be a "neighbor-centered preferential love" replacing "self-centered preferential loves."

Among actual instances of regard for others it has been necessary to distinguish "neighbor-centered regard for others" from the "self-centered regard for others" recommended by enlightened selfishness. A crucial test for this was provided by love for enemy. Of equal importance is the distinction among actual instances of deeds which, externally viewed, seem to be primarily self-regarding between "self-centered regard for the self" (which Christian ethics rejects) and a "neighbor-regarding care for the self" which may be of vital importance for Christian vocation. Self-love or duties to the self, it is true, are not to be found on the ground floor of Christian ethics, nor is there any primary appeal to treating humanity as such as an end, which would imply as part of the agent's duty making his own good also the intentional object of action. Self-love is only an unflattering presupposition about men which Christian love immediately reverses. Nevertheless, some definition of legitimate concern for the self must be given, even if only as a secondary and derivative part of Christian ethics. For certainly as a part of vocational service grounded in Christian love for neighbor, an individual has great responsibility for the development and use of all his natural capacities, or else he takes responsibility for rashly throwing them away.

"Enlightened selfishness" defines duties to others in terms of duty to self. Mutual love, on the other hand, and self-realization ethics generally, adjust the "claims and counter-claims" of individuals, their duties and rights, in terms of an enlightened pursuit of some common good. Critics of an ethic which sets out to accomplish a radical leap to the neighbor's side often imply that only self-love or love for some mutual good could possibly be "enlightened." Thus H. J. Paton says,

> The flabbiness of much that passes for modern thought is never shown more clearly than in an attempt to identify goodness with altruism. The very word "altruism" is an offense. To satisfy the whim of a second or other is in no way better than to satisfy the whim of myself. I satisfy the whim of another only because I myself have a whim to do so, and altruism is merely a particular case of egotism. It may be either good or bad, and to identify it with morality is simply ludicrous. If Joseph had acceded to the desires of Potiphar's wife, his action would have been altruistic, but it would not therefore have been moral. Nor does an action become moral, because we satisfy the whim of many or even of a whole nation, as for example when Pilate freed Barabbas and condemned Christ. A good act satisfies, not the whims of others, but rather their will so far as it is good. That is to say it satisfies them, not as mere others or mere individuals or even as a mob, which is just a conglomeration of mere individuals, but as members of a good society and organs of a coherent cooperation. An act is not good because it satisfies others than myself, but because it satisfies a social will which is manifested not only in others but equally in myself.[2]

But Christian love feels no such impulse to act whimsically; on the contrary it needs to become as enlightened as possible—for the neighbor. "And would that it were as easy to seek the good of our neighbor, or to avoid hurting him," exclaims St. Augustine, "as it is for one well trained and kind-hearted to love his neighbor! These things require more than mere good-will, and can be done only by a high degree of thoughtfulness and prudence."[3]

In contrast both to an enlightened selfish system of ethics and to the mutual love of self-realization ethics, Christian ethics is based on a radically unselfish love, but it is an "*enlightened* unselfishness." And the ethics of "enlightened unselfishness" defines duties to the self vocationally in terms of duty to others. In this

---

[2]*The Good Will*, copyright by The Macmillan Company, 1927, p. 310.
[3]*On the Morals of the Catholic Church*, xxvi (*Basic Writings of St. Augustine*, ed. by Whitney J. Oates, Random House, 1948, I, 343).

way neighbor-love corrects "a man's selfishly loving himself" and yet at the same time, overcomes "the fact that he selfishly does not wish to love himself in the right way."[4] While the positive will to be one's self does not contest the ground with neighbor-love, nevertheless, an individual existing with gratitude and faith "before" God and out of love "for" another has abundant reason to be "willing" to be himself and to develop his own capacities to their maximum. After the leap to the neighbor's side has been effected, on the basis of self-acceptance there may be (indeed, there must be) a derivation of duties to one's self.

> "Somebody said [concerning love]," Alice whispered, "that it's done by everybody minding their own business!"
> "Ah, well! It means much the same thing," said the Duchess.[5]

But this must be understood in a Christian way.

"Each man will have to bear his own load" (Gal. 6:5) is one way men have of obeying the commandment, "Bear one another's burdens, and so fulfill the law of Christ" (Gal. 6:2); taking care of themselves and not being a burden upon others is one of the duties they owe to their neighbors. As Kierkegaard writes:

> When the "as thyself" of the commandment has taken from you the selfishness which Christianity, sad to say, must presuppose as existing in every human being, then you have rightly learned to love yourself. Hence the law is: "You shall love yourself as you love your neighbor when you love him as yourself." Whoever has some knowledge of men will certainly admit that as he has often wished to be able to influence men to give up their self-love, so he has also often wished that it were possible to teach them to love themselves.[6]

The Chinese hold human life in low esteem, one observer has written, because of a deficiency of vocational self-love rather than a breakdown of Confucian humanism. "In being careless of us," their allies on the field of battle, "they love us just as they love

[4]Soren Kierkegaard, *Works of Love*, Princeton University Press, 1946, p. 20.
[5]*Alice in Wonderland*, ch. ix.
[6]*Op cit.*, p. 19.

themselves. They strike us as not loving us enough, because they love themselves too little."[7]

Nevertheless, the statement given above of the sort of "self-love" which may be commanded as a Christian duty, "You shall love yourself as you love your neighbor when you love him as yourself," only thinly conceals behind somewhat tortuous, brain-twisting wording the supernatural standard in Christian ethics: Not anything in the neighbor, not anything in the agent himself nor any treaty of peace between them but the controlling love of Christ reverses natural self-love into neighbor-love and, at the same time, requires of a person infinite willingness to be himself, not fleeing his post under any circumstances, but with complete self-acceptance developing whatever abilities in himself his vocation requires. In short, he *ought* to love himself for the purpose of loving his neighbor as he naturally loves himself.

Christian love transcends self-love in the same way it leaves the law behind: Everything is now permitted, everything may now be thrown away in an heroic act of self-sacrifice without a single limiting exception made on account of the remaining legitimacy of self-love or autonomous duties to the self or the inherent claims of "humanity" wherever it may be found. Yet, everything may still be required, the performance of every duty to the self without a single exception, so that a Christian goes about his business like any other man, deriving his diligence, however, from inward intention fixed elsewhere than on himself or on the objects of purely personal ambition. Precisely that which frees him altogether from calculating obligation in terms of self-interest also absolutely binds him to whatever concern for himself he sees most needful from the point of view of his neighbors.

In a selfish system of ethics, duty only appears to be done toward others, duties to others are forms of self-love, they are really duties to the self performed upon another. If love be not selfish but mutual love for some value, then, duty only appears to be done either to the self or to another person, duties to the self or (indifferently) to another person are in reality forms of

[7]Paul Geren, *Burma Diary,* Harpers, 1943, p. 21.

mutual love for value, they are duties to the "greatest good altogether" performed upon whichever person can at the moment gain most. In place of either of these alternatives, in a theory of Christian vocation duty has only the appearance of being done toward the self or toward value, duties to the self are forms of neighbor-love, they are really duties to the neighbor performed first upon the self.

Indeed, Christian love may require a person on occasion to take more overt care of himself than of other people. Once the main part of Sidgwick's maxim of rational benevolence has been altered in a more Christian direction, "Each man is morally bound to regard the good of any other individual *as more than his own*," the appended qualification still holds true: ". . . except when he judges it to be equal or less when impartially viewed *from the standpoint of vocational service*, or less certainly knowable or attainable by him."[8] Often an individual can more certainly and effectively care for himself than he can do anything of real, immediate worth for his neighbor. Christianity does not advise that men brush one another's teeth. In this and many other instances, what is good for a person may be more certainly knowable and attainable by an individual's action on his own behalf than by deeds done externally for another or by their both acting upon one another. But Christianity does advise men to care for their bodily health for the sake of effectiveness in their vocation. "Thus, the Apostle commands us to work with our hands that we may give to him who is in need, although he might have said that we should work to support ourselves; he says, however, 'that he may have to give to him that needeth.' And this is what makes it a Christian work to care for the body, that through its health and comfort we may be able to work to acquire and lay by funds with which to aid those who are in need. . . ."[9]

Moreover, it may also happen that a given individual's life and well-being are actually, when impartially viewed from the point of view of potential benefit to his neighbors, of greater value than

[8]Henry Sidgwick, *The Methods of Ethics*, Macmillan, 1893, III, xiii, 382.
[9]Martin Luther, *Works*, Muhlenberg Press, II, 335.

that of another individual. A man in the office of President of
the United States ought to be more careful of his life than an
ordinary citizen. Precisely by taking special care of himself he is
specially careful of his responsibilities. And lest he privately be
unwilling to perform for the citizens of his country the extraordinary duties which he can perform only by protecting himself, the
President is surrounded by secret service regulations which any
ordinary citizen would consider an unwarranted invasion of his
personal right to do as he pleases. The President should be cautious to a degree which would be considered illegitimate self-
concern on the part of any individual whose office is of less importance to the welfare of others.

Selfish and self-realization ethics seek to distinguish between
reasonable and rash self-sacrifice in terms of either wise self-love
or mutual love. The need for such a distinction, of course, is
obvious. But must it be presumed that self-denial is reasonable
only as a form of self-realization? That only a "selfish system" or
an idealistic system of self-realization ethics can make this distinction between prudent and imprudent sacrifice of life? A neighbor-centered ethic need be no less enlightened than a value-
centered ethic. To determine from the point of view of "sharable
goods" just when and in what manner one's own life should be
preserved or sacrificed is no less difficult than to decide the same
from the viewpoint of the multiple needs of neighbors and pri-
orities that exist among the claims they make upon us. Indeed, is
not constant and clear-headed concern to insure that self-sacrifice
actually serve some purpose more likely present where selfish
partiality has been dethroned by the leap to the neighbor's side?
A young American, as he outstripped hobbling, heavily laden, and
famished refugees trekking out of Burma,

> fell to thinking of St. Francis and my lost saints. Perhaps God's
> Troubadour would have flung his share of food and strength suf-
> ficient to carry only himself across the mountains into a pool of
> food and strength whose other contributors were so wretchedly
> poor that the whole would be meager—meager. Perhaps such a
> sharing would provide only a moment's betterment. But there

was always the possibility that his little would multiply with his courage and hope until it was swollen enough to get both him and his brethren across. I have decided that the gamble asks too much of hope, pays too little heed to the realities of bread and distance. One should save his life for a better accounting even if it means only a more promising opportunity for sacrifice. Almost certainly this is right. But St. Francis walks at my side to trouble me.[10]

It is a fatuous assumption that a person cannot perform an en-lightened action without abandoning his position of existing in grateful obedience "before" God and "for" the neighbor.

Equally false is the assumption that other necessary aspects of every actual vocation cannot constitute some part of the recom-mendations of Christian love. Love, which by its nature would be non-resistant where only the agent's own rights and the per-haps unjust claims of a single neighbor are involved, may change its action to resistance by the most effective possible means, judi-cial or military, violent or non-violent, when the needs of more than one neighbor come into view. Love which by its nature has ceased altogether from preferring some people to others for one's own personal welfare may yet for other reasons exercise prefer-ence in a forced decision among them. Love not itself self-de-fensive, which would rather suffer any deprivation than go to law against a brother, nevertheless will impel men to develop an ethics of protection lest injustice be done to innocent third parties.

Of course, witnessing such radical change of tactics taking place within the vocation of Christians in the world, it is possible for an observer to suspect cynically that some basic alteration of strategy has taken place. Has not Christian love itself suffered alteration before ever these things are done? Undoubtedly this may be so; undoubtedly also it may not. But one thing must in all cases be understood: No external test can ever show decisively when an action manifests selfish partiality or when it is the fruit of truly obedient love. Saving money in preparation for some vocation is no more evidence of the absence of Christian love than giving all one's money to feed the poor or even one's body to be

[10]Paul Geren, *op. cit.,* p. 37.

burned is evidence of the presence of Christian love in the heart. It is no more difficult for a man with humility to spend years training himself for some career than for him deliberately to renounce the advantages of an education (which may indeed happen to be his vocation) without becoming prideful about what he has done. It is at least as easy to lose one's life without charity as with charity to save it for better accounting; no more difficult to resist injustice with love than to suffer injustice without grievance; no more difficult out of compassion to prefer some persons to others than to suffer injustice to be done without some cloture on compassion for its victims.

III.   A PREFERENTIAL ETHICS OF PROTECTION AND THE TEACHINGS OF JESUS

Unless the instance in which Jesus fled from the territory of Herod Antipas in order to avoid arrest (Luke 13:33) was a case of his saving his life for a better accounting and a more promising opportunity for sacrifice in Jerusalem, an explicit manifestation of "duties to himself" can hardly be expected within the short closing period of Jesus' lifetime to which our knowledge of him is largely limited. Nevertheless, neighbor-centered preferential love and a Christian ethic of protection do have their beginning in him, in spite of the effect of apocalypticism in expelling concern for the permanent organization of justice and making men well acquainted with the pure will of God in the case of a single neighbor.

To see this, we need not bandy proof-texts back and forth or engage in St. Augustine's hair-splitting exegesis on the saying, "If any one strikes you on the right cheek, turn to him the other also" (Matt. 5:39). This teaching, Augustine reasoned, involved only a case of insult, not of assault; for, assuming a greater number of right-handed assailants in the world, their blows would normally be delivered to an opponent's left cheek. A blow upon the *right* cheek, which Jesus talked about, would most likely be struck by the *back* of the hand; this is as if a glove were thrown in the face; we need only conclude, then, that in case a Christian is *insulted* he turns the other cheek and avoids *unnecessary* conflict. This interpretation, or any other which seeks to moderate the extremity of Jesus' requirement, cannot be correct, because Jesus spoke this saying merely as an illustration of his strenuous teaching, "Do not resist one who is evil," than which nothing could be more severe. In case of attack *or* insult from "one who is evil" turning the other cheek can be the only possible meaning of non-resisting love.

Nevertheless—and this is to understand, not to lessen the requirement—Jesus deals only with the simplest moral situation in which blows may be struck, the case of one person in relation to but one other. He does not here undertake to say how men, who themselves ought not to resist at all or by any means whatever when they themselves alone receive the blows, ought to act in more complex cases where non-resistance would in practice mean turning another person's face to the blows of an oppressor. We are not at all uncertain what Jesus' ethic was in bilateral, two-party situations. When his life alone was concerned Jesus turned the other cheek, when smitten he smote not again, and he died quite without defending himself.

Yet without distorting the text, the beginnings of a multilateral ethics of protection, certainly a multilateral neighbor-centered preferential love, may be found in Jesus' own attitudes and example. On occasion he showed indignation, even wrath, over injustice, using vitriolic words as weapons against the devourers of widows' houses (Luke 20:47). He was unsparing in his condemnation of the complacency of Israel's religious leaders. Indeed, a great Jewish scholar, while attributing real originality to the teachings of Jesus, raises serious objection against the consistency of Jesus' practice:

> I would not cavil with the view that Jesus is to be regarded as the first great Jewish teacher to frame such a sentence as: "Love your enemies, do good to them who hate you, bless them that curse you, and pray for them who ill-treat you" (Luke 6:27, 28). Yet how much more telling his injunction would have been if

we had had *a single story* about his doing good to, and praying for, a single Rabbi or Pharisee! One grain of practice is worth a pound of theory. . . . But no such deed is ascribed to Jesus in the Gospels. Towards his enemies, towards those who did not believe in him, whether individuals, groups, or cities (Matthew 11:20–24), only denunciation and bitter words! The injunctions are beautiful, but how much more beautiful would have been a *fulfillment* of those injunctions by Jesus himself. . . .[1]

Jesus' prayer on the cross that God forgive his executioners (Luke 23:24) might be cited in reply, and here and there a friendly conversation with an inquiring scribe, or the act of healing the daughter of Jairus, a ruler of the synagogue. Moreover, some responsibility for anti-Jewish sentiment in the gospels must be laid at the door of later controversy between Christians and Jews. Still, in the last analysis, the only answer to the charge that Jesus did not always display an attitude toward his opponents consonant with the main body of his own teachings must grant the fact yet deny the interpretation given. When it was a question of injustice done to persons other than himself, especially when he confronted the huge burden of fossilized religion fastened upon the people of the land, Jesus did not remain at his ease lifting up their faces to additional blows or supporting by silence their compulsion to go a second mile. Although his words were, "Do not resist *one who is evil*," Jesus did not even draw out very explicitly the distinction between resisting *evil* yet not resisting the evil-*doer*, between condemning "the system" and denouncing people who support it, which Christians often insist was his meaning. The evil and the one who does it are in any actual situation bound so closely together that a person who, in one-one relationship to an enemy-neighbor, wishes not to resist the evil-doer can find no way of resisting evil; and a person in multilateral relationships with more than one neighbor who wishes for their sakes to resist evil will be unable to avoid resisting the evil-doer as well. With prophetic indignation, therefore, Jesus denounced those who were

[1] C. G. Montefiore, *Rabbinic Literature and Gospel Teachings*, pp. 103 f. (Quoted by Major, Manson, and Wright: *The Mission and Message of Jesus*, Dutton, 1938, p. 344.)

evil as well as impersonal forms of evil itself. This he did from neighbor-centered preferential love, although so far as his life alone was concerned he showed no preference for his own personal welfare and did not resist evildoers when evil fell upon him.

When the two perspectives, Jesus' personal ethic of non-resistance and the beginning in him of a preferential ethic of protection, are not kept quite separate the resulting blend is some form of non-violent or passive *resistance*. This permits more concern for the self in relation to the single neighbor than by its nature *non-resisting* Christian love allows, and at the same time limits what such love may find needs to be done when weighing the claims of more neighbors than one and the actual ways they may be served. Whether the whip Jesus used in driving the money-changers out of the Temple was plaited of straw or of leather, whether he applied it to animals or to men, whether the decisive factor that day was the force of his own powerful personality justifiably indignant on behalf of a righteous cause or the threatening multitude of people gathered in Jerusalem who forestalled the immediate use of the Temple police, in any case some form of resistance was raised that day not only against perverse practices but also against the men who engaged in them. Force does not become any less resistant because of its "spirituality," or resistance wrong to a greater degree because it takes material form. Circumstances similar to those which warranted a change from Jesus' announced ethic of non-resistance to any manner of resistance he may have used in cleansing the Temple may not only permit but even on occasion require Christian love to adopt physical methods of resistance.

A recent study of Christian attitudes toward war and peace puts the issue of a preferential ethic of protection in terms of Jesus' story of the Good Samaritan: "And now arises one of the unanswerable 'ifs' of literary history. What would Jesus have made the Samaritan do while the robbers were still at their fell work?" In answering this question, the author, apparently without any hesitation, substitutes Jesus' personal ethic in relation to a single neighbor, and all his apocalyptically derived strenuous teachings having to do with this simple situation, for what might have been his ethic in multilateral relation to two or more neighbors. He writes, "The protection of one life would have seemed to Jesus no excuse at all for taking the life of another, even a robber." Surely the most that can be said is that quite plainly the protection of *his own* life did not seem to Jesus any excuse for ceasing to express non-resisting love for another. It may be "there is no evidence for the suggestion that Jesus would have had him wield his traveler's sword."[2] Still, in the rudiments of preferential ethics to be found in Jesus' attitude toward the perpetrators of injustice there is some suggestion that he *might*, at least no decisive evidence that he would *not*, have approved such action. We perhaps should not go to the other extreme so far as to say, "When I try to imagine what would have happened had Jesus come upon the scene a little earlier than the Good Samaritan, I find it more natural to suppose that he would have helped the traveler in his struggle with the thieves than that he would have waited until the man was injured and the thieves departed before coming to his aid."[3] To say the least this would have been a different ethical situation from the one pictured in the story or from an attack by thieves upon Jesus himself. The difference is precisely that non-resisting, unself-defensive love must determine its responsibility in the one case toward more than one neighbor, in the other simply toward the neighbor or "the enemy" when injurious consequences of the decision will fall upon the agent himself alone.

> To express love at all in some situations one must seem to deny it. Jesus said: "If any man smite you on one cheek turn the other also"; here the situation is relatively simple—you and your enemy. But Jesus did not say: "If any man smite one of your friends, lead him to another friend that he may smite *him* also." Not only is it clear that Jesus could have made no such statement, but also that he would have felt that the involvement of the interests of others (that is, others besides one's self and one's

[2]T. S. K. Scott-Craig, *Christian Attitudes to War and Peace*, Scribners, 1938, p. 43.
[3]L. A. Garrard, *Duty and the Will of God*, Oxford: Basil Blackwell, 1938, p. 78.

enemy) transformed the whole moral situation and placed our obligations with respect to it in a radically different light.[4]

Jesus once told the parable of a servant whom a merciful king released from debt to the fantastic amount of ten million dollars who nevertheless insisted that a fellow servant pay in full a debt of twenty dollars. "Then his lord summoned him and said to him, 'You wicked servant! I forgave you all that debt because you besought me; and should not you have had mercy on your fellow servant, as I had mercy on you?' And in anger his lord delivered him to the jailers, till he should pay all his debt" (Matt. 18:32, 33). From this story it is evident that love which for itself claims nothing may yet for the sake of another claim everything, that any one who unhesitatingly and times without number renounces "what is due" when he himself alone bears the brunt of such a decision may nevertheless turn full circle and insist with utter severity upon full payment of what is due to others; and what is due to others is never simply just payment but full forgiveness "as I had mercy on you," never exact justice alone but Christian love. This may be called neighbor-centered rather than self-centered severity, forgiving love which pronounces judgment on all that is not love, an attitude which gives up judging men in terms of their conformity to some legal or moral code and yet insists that men are judged in terms of the demands of unconditional self-giving. "So also my heavenly Father will do to every one of you, if you do not forgive your brother from your heart" (Matt. 18:35).

IV. A CHRISTIAN ETHIC OF RESISTANCE

Whether or not so much preferential ethics of protection may be seen in Jesus himself, beyond question Christian ethics soon developed such a view, the primitive pacifism generally practiced by early Christians so long as they were in a minority giving way to what were judged more effective means for assum-

---

[4]John Knox's essay in the symposium, *The Christian Answer* (ed. by H. P. Van Dusen, Scribners, 1945), p. 173.

ing responsibility for the whole of organized society. Although decades before their time individual Christians had begun to accept service in the Roman legions, often with the explicit approval of church authorities, St. Ambrose (340–396 A.D.) and his great convert St. Augustine (354–430 A.D.) were the first to give fully elaborated theoretical defense of Christian participation in armed conflict. Since Christian ethics is not a legalism concerned with external deeds only or even mainly, it would be a great mistake to regard Christianity's accommodation to Constantine's empire as necessarily a compromise of its genius or a "fall" from the pristine purity of its ethic. As a matter of fact, careful examination of the first literary defense of Christian participation in war gives striking evidence that underneath the obvious reversal of tactic, the general strategy of Christian love continued without abatement and without any alteration in its fundamental nature.

While first formulating for Christian thought a theory of *justum bellum,* both St. Ambrose and St. Augustine continued to teach that when a man himself alone is concerned he ought never to resist "one who is evil." Both combine their justification of war because of a Christian's responsibility for public protection with an utter denial that under *any* circumstances he ever has any right of private self-defense. No Christian, they said, should save his own life at the expense of another; yet when other persons than himself are involved in the decision, no Christian ought to fail to resist evil by effective means which the state alone makes available to him. This combination of ideas, which seems strange to men today, is clear proof that non-resisting love was still the groundwork of all reasoning about Christian participation in conflict of arms; and indeed this continued to be true down to the "holy war" enthusiasm of the crusades, as can be seen in the requirement that a private soldier do penance for the evil he may have done or thought while participating even in just wars he *should* have joined.

Commenting on a passage from Cicero, St. Ambrose asked the question, Should a wise man in case of shipwreck take away

a plank from an ignorant sailor? Leaving aside the consideration that an emaciated philosopher probably would not prove
victor in struggle with an ignorant sailor, *ought* he try to save
his own life at the expense of another? Ambrose answered this
question in the negative, and likewise for all one-one neighbor
situations.

> Some ask whether a wise man ought in case of a shipwreck
> to take away a plank from an ignorant sailor? Although it seems
> better for the common good that a wise man rather than a fool
> should escape from shipwreck, yet I do not think that a Chris-
> tian, a just and wise man, ought to save his own life by the death
> of another; just as when he meets with an armed robber he
> cannot return his blows, *lest in defending his life he should stain
> his love toward his neighbor.* The verdict on this is plain and
> clear in the books of the Gospel. . . . What robber is more hate-
> ful than the persecutor who came to kill Christ? But Christ
> would not be defended by the wounds of the persecutor, for He
> willed to heal all by His wounds.[1]

A Christian ought never to value his own possessions so highly as
to be willing, for his own sake, to take the life of another person,
though from identically the same sort of neighbor-love he will
value the possessions of another enough to resist, for his sake,
a criminal attempt against them. This he will do not only occasionally but in the vocation of police or judge as well. When
he alone is imperiled he will not presume to estimate the comparative worth of his own wisdom or righteousness and another
man's lack of these qualities, though in the vocation of prince
or soldier such judgments about relative justice must be made
by a comparison of the righteousness of one conflicting side or
party with another.

In the views of St. Augustine we can penetrate more deeply
the reason for this strange combination of doctrines, why for
Christian ethics generally *self-defense is the worst of all possible excuses for war or for any other form of resistance or any
sort of preference among other people.* Augustine makes this

[1] *The Duties of the Clergy*, III, iv, 27 (*Nicene and Post-Nicene Fathers*, Scribners, 1908, Second Series, vol. X). (Italics mine.)

distinction between public and private protection when considering the more general question "whether *Libido* dominates also in those things which we see too often done."

> For me the point to be considered first is whether an onrushing enemy, or an assassin lying in wait may be killed with no wrong-headed desire (for the saving) of one's life, or for liberty or for purity. . . . How can I think that they act with no inordinate desire who fight for that (*i.e.*, some creaturely good), which they can lose without desiring to lose it? . . . Therefore the law is not just which grants the power to a wayfarer to kill a highway robber, so that he may not be killed (by the robber); or which grants to any one, man or woman, to slay an assailant attacking, if he can, before he or she is harmed. The soldier also is commanded by law to slay the enemy, for which slaying, if he objects, he will pay the penalty by imperial order. Shall we then dare to say that these laws are unjust, or more, that they are not laws? For to me a law that is not just appears to be no law. . . . For that he be slain who lays plans to take the life of another is less hard (to bear) than the death of him who is defending his own life (against the plotter). And acting against the chaste life of a man in opposition to his own will is much more evidently wrong than the taking of the life of him who so does violence by that one against whom the violence is done. Then again the soldier in slaying the enemy is the agent of the law (in war), wherefore he does his duty easily with no wrong aim or purpose. . . . That law therefore, which for the protection of citizens orders foreign force to be repulsed by the same force, can be obeyed without a wrong desire: and this same can be said of all officials who by right and by order are subject to any powers. But I see not how these men (who defend themselves privately), while not held guilty by law, can be without fault: for the law does not force them to kill, but leaves it in their power. It is free therefore for them to kill no one for those things (life or possessions) which they can lose against their own will, which things therefore they ought not to love. . . . Wherefore again I do not blame the law which permits such aggressors to be slain: but by what reason I can defend those who slay them I do not find. . . . How indeed are they free of sin before Providence, who for those things which ought to be held of less worth are defiled by the killing of a man?[2]

[2]*De Libero Arbitrio*, Bk. I, ch. v (trans. by F. E. Tourscher, Peter Reilly Co., 1937), pp. 25–29. *Cf. Ep.* XLVII, 6.

When a judge on the bench renders decision between two parties other than himself, it is universally agreed, he will likely be more impartial and clear-headed about justice than when he judges in his own case. Now, Augustine believed that the decision of a prince or a man acting in some public capacity might well be of this same sort. In multilateral relationships a man can weigh what is just and unjust without undue influence on account of his selfish partiality. In this way he may express decided preference, but from neighbor-regarding considerations, not simply on account of what pleases him best from the point of view of his own personal welfare. The contrary is true, he believed, in all cases of private self-defense, even instances which a third party would call entirely just. Every man is so centrally interested in his own preservation that, Augustine believed, private self-defense could only arouse or proceed from some degree of inordinate self-love or "wrong-headed desire." In defending himself a man's egoism either manifests or gains control over his action, and the passion of selfishness, *concupiscence* or libido warps his moral judgment so far as to render him totally incapable of deciding rightly between himself and his neighbor. If he should happen to defend the right person in defending himself, if he should actually save the life of the person a third party would assist or protect, this would be only by chance; it would be because of egotism, not because of justice or love.

Now, Ambrose and Augustine doubtless need to be criticized for their rather unqualified acceptance of public protection and also for their complete rejection of private self-defense. They tend to understate the danger that in conflict between nations collective egotism will be so aroused that the judgment of any individual member of the group will come rather fully under the sway of self-interest. Even in his vocation, where multilateral neighbor-relationships intersect, an individual finds himself drawn not by neighbor-love alone or by considerations of justice alone but by selfish preference or personal affinity for *these* persons rather than *those*. In actual conflict situations he is already inextricably bound to one side or the other by geography or language or existing mutual interest. In short, he *always* judges his own case; and, though he is sinfully incompetent ever to judge in such a situation, he cannot, like a judge of some court, disqualify himself and let some one else decide the issue. Love for neighbor must necessarily be exercised from points of view which are never quite those of an impartial observer. Beyond question there takes place grave exaggeration of the claims to righteousness made on behalf of the relatively innocent individual or nation even by those who more or less "unselfishly" champion them.

On the other hand, Ambrose and Augustine were perhaps too extreme in excluding private self-defense as in every case unjustified for the Christian. Luther disagreed with them on this point, but he did so only after surrounding the exercise of any right of personal self-defense with extreme conditions:

> You ask, Why may I not use the sword for myself and for my own cause, with the intention by so doing not of seeking my own interest, but the punishment of evil? I answer, Such a miracle is not impossible, but quite unusual and hazardous. Where there is such affluence of the Spirit it may be done. . . . No one but a real Christian and one who is full of the Spirit will follow this example. If reason also should follow this example, it would indeed pretend not to be seeking its own, but this would be untrue. It cannot be done without grace. Therefore, first become like Samson, and then you can also do as Samson did.[3]

We must ask, What moral conditions will be effected by being full of the Spirit? The answer to this question should be given in light of the fact that Christian ethics always recognizes the holy Spirit as the spirit of Christ. If from the motivating strategy of Christian love there can be vocational resistance and Christian vocations in society using protective coercion, may there not also be such a thing as vocational self-protection? A Christian does whatever love requires, and the possibility cannot be ruled out that on occasion defending himself may be a duty he owes to

[3]*Secular Authority: To What Extent It Should Be Obeyed, Works,* Muhlenberg Press, III, 249–250.

others. Whenever sacrificing himself, or in any degree failing to protect himself and his own, actually would involve greater burdens or injury to others, surely then a Christian should stick to his post whether he wants to or not. In such circumstances self-protection becomes a duty, a form of neighbor-regarding love, the protection of others performed first and most effectively upon oneself. Making use of the distinction between "self-defensive self-protection" and "neighbor-regarding self-protection," self-defense may be but an extreme instance of those "duties to the self" which are a part of Christian vocational obligation. This we can conclude without in any way ignoring the fact that Christian ethics from Ambrose to Tolstoy has always, quite correctly, looked upon self-defensiveness and any other form of selfish preferential love with profound suspicion. The Christian point of view, we should always remember, also surrounds an act of giving one's body to be burned with just as grave doubt.

During the height of the submarine warfare in the North Atlantic, four chaplains gave over their lifebelts to four "ignorant sailors" and went down with the ship. This was, so far as men may judge, a Christian act of self-sacrifice. Suppose the captain of the vessel, himself not involved in the case, had presumed to choose among these men, by his command saying whose life should be saved, whose lost. In order to make such a decision, the captain would have to take many factors into account; on the side of the sailors, their greater service to immediate military ends; against one of them, the fact that he had broken ship's rule by going to sleep without his lifebelt on, that he was unmarried and had few fixed responsibilities to others, that he was not so wise or well-trained or likely to serve humanity in more than ordinary ways; on the side of one of the chaplains, that he was married and the father of several children, moreover a "wise man" and a man of rare character and capacity for unusual service. Now arises the crucial question: In the absence of a third, impartial party responsible for the decision, should a wise man ever refuse to give up his lifebelt to an ignorant sailor? Ought ever an individual act in favor of himself, making the same choice between two lives, his own and his neighbor's, which every one would regard as entirely just, even obligatory, when such a decision is rendered by some third person not himself involved in the issue?

Men, being evil, may nevertheless know how to give good gifts to their children (Matt. 7:11). Just as selfish partiality is never completely absent from decisions about public protection, so also partiality for the interests of one's neighbors need not be completely excluded from decisions and actions which actually undertake to protect the self. Enlightened weighing of a person's responsibilities to others may not only permit saving one's life "for better accounting even if it means only a more promising opportunity for sacrifice" by the merely *negative* act of keeping possession of a lifebelt or failing to pause and help countless other refugees trekking out of Burma. Care for others for whom a person is vocationally responsible, closely and obviously bound in with protecting himself, may also require more *positive* action, actually taking away the lives of others, as can be seen in the following modern version of "taking away a plank from an ignorant sailor":

> Today Tom, one of our ambulance drivers of whom I have spoken, went to China. He wanted to go, and yet he did not want to go. The reason he did not want to go was that he found India pleasant, and besides this, he was attached to us as we were to him.
>
> The reason he wanted to go was this: When we were coming out of Burma, before we had to abandon our trucks and start walking, we came across a company of wounded Chinese soldiers near Katha. There must have been two hundred of them. My guess is that they had been evacuated from the battlefield to the south and had progressed to Katha. Here the railroad was hopelessly blocked with the tangle of fleeing traffic and the soldiers were thrown on their own to get away from the Japanese who were closing in on all of us. In the staggering heat of that day they saw our convoy of trucks rolling toward them on the dusty road. They must have said to themselves, "Here is perhaps a way of escape. We are desperate men." When our trucks, which had to proceed haltingly for all the traffic, dust, and crowds of evacuees thronging the road, drew opposite them, they hobbled out and swarmed all over the trucks, stopping us.

I cannot find it in me to say a word of blame for what Tom did. I was spared this fearful problem by losing my truck in the muddy bottom of the last river we tried to cross by fording. We were under strict orders not to take on anybody else. To take anybody else would prejudice the hopes we held of getting our already large, weary, half-sick crowd through safely. We had been without enough to eat, without much sleep for forty-eight hours, and the dust was a distressing coat on our eyelids.

With all these things, elemental, physiological, and spiritual in the setting, *Tom got out and pushed the wounded Chinese soldiers off his truck* as the only means of being able to carry on.—More than one night on the walk out and later in Assam he told me, "I owe the Chinese a debt." When he left today he went to pay it.[4]

The foregoing analysis, it should at once be granted, comes dangerously close to one of Raskolnikov's justifications for his "right to crime" in Dostoyevsky's *Crime and Punishment*.

I simply hinted that an "extraordinary" man has the . . . inner right to decide in his own conscience to overstep . . . certain obstacles, and only in case it is essential for the practical fulfill- ment of his idea (something, perhaps, of benefit to the whole of humanity). . . . I maintain that if the discoveries of Kepler and Newton could not have been made known except by sacrificing the lives of one, a dozen, a hundred or more men, Newton would have had the right, would indeed have been duty bound . . . to *eliminate* the dozen or the hundred for the sake of making his discoveries known to the whole of humanity. . . . But if such a one is forced for the sake of his idea to step over a corpse or wade through blood, he can, I maintain, find within himself, in his conscience, a sanction for wading through blood—that de- pends on the idea and its dimensions, of course.[5]

What, if anything, is the difference between this line of reasoning and a justifiably Christian ethic of protection? For one thing, the Christian does not suppose that *he* is "extraordinary," but that *his duty* is extraordinary, or in another sense ordinary, all too ordinary, human, all too human. For another, the Christian acts not for the sake of "the idea and its dimensions" or primarily for

[4]Paul Geren, *op. cit.*, pp. 55–56 (italics mine).
[5]Pt. III, ch. v, Modern Library, pp. 247, 248.

the sake of some abstract truth. He acts on behalf of his neighbors and their concrete needs which may have to be served on occasion by the employment of unpleasant means. Christian morality does not permit him even to disguise his private self-assertion under the rubric of abstract concern for "benefit to the whole of humanity." This Raskolnikov finally confesses was the true analysis of the nature of his crime. As for wanting to be an extraordinary man who really has the right to step over corpses, he says later:

> Of course that's all nonsense, its almost all talk! . . . I wanted *to have the daring* . . . I wanted to murder without casuistry, to murder for my own sake, for myself alone . . . I didn't do the murder to gain wealth and power and to become a benefactor of mankind. Nonsense! I simply did it; I did the murder for myself, for myself alone . . . I wanted to find then and quickly . . . whether I can step over barriers or not. . . .[6]

Purified of such perverse self-concern, the Christian nevertheless must adjudicate and decide one way or another among the claims and needs of neighbors he is to serve. In doing so, he at least omits to serve some, and in this sense he wades through blood and suffering. If such a one is forced for the sake of his neighbors visibly to step over a corpse, he can, I maintain, find within himself, in his Christian conscience, a sanction which depends on a proper reading of his actual situation, and the needs of neighbors determining his vocation. The only way of avoiding this conclusion is by recourse to "intuition" as the basis of obligation. This would be a form of "unenlightened unselfishness" which surely requires for justification more than the fact of man's proneness to sin in using his intelligence.

No doubt a man stands always in grave peril of choosing only the manifestation of love which pleases him best. He faces this same peril of deceiving himself and others and loving no one but himself even when he sacrifices himself and others. This, we saw near the end of Chapter One, gives special relevance and validity to Christian love as a requirement in every action. Men who are

[6]*Op. cit.*, Pt. V, ch. iv, pp. 392, 395.

always surrounded on every side by complex relationships delineating their vocational obligations, and whose moral decisions can never escape from these bonds, for this very reason have special need of a sense that they still "owe the Chinese a debt," they need some St. Francis to walk by their side troubling them. Since *there is always more than one neighbor,* men have special need of an ethic which defines with utter clarity and rigor their full duty toward any and every one of them. Whether Jesus intentionally or from his sense of apocalypse pictured the simplest possible moral situation, the result is undeniable: men may see in his strenuous teachings how they ought conscientiously to act toward every neighbor. Walking beside this unqualified disclosure of the pure will of God, measuring their lives in this mirror, Christians find repeated stimulus for remembering all their obligation, even though they are always surrounded by a vast network of neighbor-claims which converge and create for each of them some specific vocation. The essential meaning of Christian vocation, therefore, is not simply some worldly position interpreted in general religious fashion as *God-given.* Christian vocation means the secular occupation, the "station" and its full, often obnoxious duties, to which an individual feels himself assigned by Christian love or by the love of Christ controlling him.

The fundamental meaning of Christian ethics may be thrown into bolder relief by comparing the entire expulsion of legitimate private self-defense by Ambrose and Augustine with what has happened in much modern pacifism. Modern pacifists frequently revealed their non-Christian rootage by making quite the reverse combination of ideas from that which prevailed for centuries in Christian ethics. Early Christian thought, we have seen, was concerned to deny any analogy between private and public defense in order to say that a Christian, who might participate in armed and bloody conflict for the sake of public protection, would *of course* not resist even by mild or passive means any neighbor who might assault him when his own goods and life alone were threatened. In direct contrast, much modern pacifism also attempts to break down all analogy between private and public defense, but for purpose of establishing almost the reverse conclusion, namely, that *of course* individuals ought to resist by going to law if some one wishes to take away their coat and with possibly bloodless methods in case they individually (and certainly when their grandmothers) are violently attacked. We need have no great sympathy for the "grandmother argument" often presented by draft boards to "conscientious objectors" to military service. Nevertheless, it is clear that modern pacifists, in withdrawing completely from resistance on behalf of national defense, frequently make greater accommodation to the supposed natural necessity of self-defense (or some sort of multilateral ethic of defense limited to the private area where extreme violence need not be used) than ever occurred to the great thinkers who first forged a Christian theory of *justum bellum*.

Searching for an explanation, we may be driven to reflect that both the pacifism of early Christians and their shift over to resistance in the light of increasing responsibility were basically grounded in Christian love, while in contrast a good deal of contemporary pacifism is grounded in horror and revulsion at the sight of violence or bloodshed and in an ethic which values life above everything else. Violence and bloodshed are no doubt horrifying, especially in destructive, total war, but the word "unlovely" has in Christian ethics a mainly spiritual not a mainly physical meaning. A selfish act is the most unlovely thing, and an unselfish motive may lead the Christian to perform necessary responsibilities which prove not so "nice" in terms of physical contamination. For a Christian outlook, sin came first into the world, death followed; sin, or the contrary of love, is the greatest evil from which men need to be delivered, death is only the last enemy of mankind which shall be destroyed, and the sting of death is in fact sin (I Cor. 15:26, 56). For many pacifists, however, bloodshed and death are the worst evils, life a conditional or even the highest value which ought never to be violated. And as a consequence they are willing to approve resistance in those forms and under circumstances, in court or at fisticuffs or by aiming low, when a man may hope to stop short of bringing death to an opponent.

Such a view has more in common with dualistic pacifism in the ancient world or with otherworldly Indian religious ethics than with early Christian pacifism. As we have seen, Christian ethics first of all approved public protection and the defense of organized justice as the only means of loving the neighbor with all his concrete physical and social needs in *this* world, and judged that such action might be unselfish even if hopelessly bloody. Centuries later Christian ethics approved private self-defense, which doubtless is nicer but almost always more selfish.

Moreover, it is still true that emotional horror over physical evils may indicate stronger love for ourselves than love for neighbor.

> Today we had to move the evacuee patients out of one hospital building into another. It was a filthy job because so many patients had dysentery. The man whom this foul disease clutches soon becomes unable to move or do anything for himself. He fouls his clothing, the bedding, the stretcher on which we have put him. There is no fresh clothing and bedding to change him. Piles of it lie all about the place all the day unwashed.
>
> It rains every day and no one has the resolution to start the cleansing job since he could never get the things dry. Patients, soiled bedding, soiled clothing all join to send up a reeking stench like a burnt offering to some perverse devil.
>
> Three of us stood surveying the preparations for moving: an American boy who had joined the British Army before we got into the war, his British soldier comrade and I. We saw that the patients had to be moved and that the sweepers who had been assigned to the task were not getting along very quickly with it. If the others were feeling what I felt, we were all dreading to get on any more intimate terms with the stench and handle it. The American turned to his British comrade and said, "I am very glad at this moment that I am agnostic."
>
> I do not know how seriously he intended this. However that is, the conclusion which he implied certainly held: Since he did not believe in the love of Christ he could leave the handling of these dysentery victims to the sweepers. Since his friend did believe in it, he was not free to stand by and watch. Nor was I. Get down in it! Pick the patients up! Soil yourself with this disease! St. Francis kissed the beggars' sores. However this ended in him, it must have begun as the practice of the only medicine

he knew. There is no need to call this filthiness sweet, or to start enjoying it through a strange inversion. Only one thing is necessary: for love's sake it must be done.[7]

Participation in regrettable conflict falls among distasteful tasks which sometimes become imperative for Christian vocation. Only one thing is necessary: for love's sake it must be done. All things now are lawful, all things are now permitted, yet everything is required which Christian love requires, everything without a single exception.

V. A THEORY OF VOCATION ACCORDING TO THE CHRISTOCENTRIC PRINCIPLES OF THE REFORMATION

So long as Christian love is given primacy, Christian ethics can draw enlightenment from any source whatever, from "natural law" or from some theory of value or, lacking these, from some purely pragmatic sociological or psychological approach. Nothing else than love, however, can occupy the ground floor if Christian ethics is not to suffer fundamental alteration. This happened in medieval scholasticism when a theory of natural law and the ethics of Aristotle were assigned the fundamental, Christian faith and love only the second-story, position. With the Protestant Reformation there came a revival of salvation by faith alone, replacing salvation by both faith and works following the directions of Aristotle or other philosophical moralists. There came, too, a revival in understanding the essential nature of Christian love and of the realization that Christian ethics revolves around this alone as center.

As a consequence we find in Luther clear and forthright analysis of the nature of Christian vocation in terms of doing whatever love requires without the limiting necessity of first consulting another, equally primary ethical standard. Luther saw quite

[7]Paul Geren, *op. cit.*, pp. 51–52.

plainly that resistance by any means whatever, holding office in government, going to law for self-protection, claiming "rights" for the self, or turning away from any borrower, were all alike and to equal degree apparent violations of the gospel ethic, and he set himself the task of justifying every one of these actions as a part of Christocentric vocation. To lay claim to rights is a violation of the Sermon on the Mount just as much as taking the sword; a Christian does either for one reason only: for the service of God in devotion to the good of his neighbor, which is a fulfillment of the Sermon on the Mount. Luther's treatise on *Secular Authority* is often interpreted as teaching that the spirit of self-abandonment which the Sermon on the Mount requires of a Christian is his obligation only as a matter of inner disposition but that in outward action he may, and should, bear the sword and hold public office as magistrate or hangman. To distinguish between inward disposition and outward action, however, is to pay attention to Luther's terminology and not to his thought. This has led to extraordinarily unfair criticisms of the Lutheran position. His real distinction is between what is right for the Christian when only he himself is involved and what is right when responsibility to others plays a part. What Luther terms "God's kingdom inwardly" and "the kingdom of the world outwardly" amounts precisely to the distinction already drawn between what a Christian should do when he and his cause alone are likely to suffer and what the same sort of love requires him to do when many more persons have claim upon his action. Both of these alternatives combine inner disposition with some form of external action.

> As concerns yourself, you would abide by the Gospel and govern yourself according to Christ's word, gladly turning the other cheek and letting the mantle go with the coat, when the matter concerned you and your cause. . . .
> For in the one case you consider yourself and what is yours, in the other you consider your neighbor and what is his. In what concerns you and yours, you govern yourself by the Gospel and suffer injustice for yourself as a true Christian; in what con-

cerns others and belongs to them, you govern yourself according to love, and suffer no injustice for your neighbor's sake.[1]

The same inner disposition which, so far as one's self is concerned, leads to a practice of the absolute demands of the Sermon on the Mount may, so far as others must be served, lead to the reverse action: in both, "you govern yourself according to love."

Now a Christian theory of vocation and a Christian account of political rights occupy the same place in Christian ethics as does the Christian's service of the neighbor through the state or in any other capacity. The same inner disposition which, so far as one's self is concerned, leads to a renunciation of rights may, so far as others must be served, lead to utter insistence upon them: in both, "you govern yourself according to love." Luther wrote: "No Christian shall wield or invoke the sword for himself and for his cause; but for another he can and ought to wield and invoke it, so that wickedness may be hindered and godliness defended."[2] Paraphrasing this statement: No Christian shall claim to possess or invoke rights for himself and for his cause; but for another he can and ought to claim and invoke them. As for milder forms of resistance through courts of law, the Christian "uses the forbidden oath to serve another, just as he uses the forbidden sword in another's service."

The rights invoked need not simply be his neighbor's rights for his neighbor's sake but may also be *his own rights for his neighbor's sake.* In invoking his own rights simply for his neighbor's sake he is willing to suffer a deprivation of purely personal rights just as much as when, himself alone concerned, he does not insist on his rights but suffers an actual deprivation of rights

---

[1]Martin Luther, *Secular Authority: To What Extent It Should Be Obeyed* (*Works*, III, 241, 242). In the *Christian Liberty* Luther argues the necessity for good works by advancing two considerations: For one thing, the soul (which by itself might live wholly by faith alone) needs to work to "keep under" the body. For another, the Christian should freely perform works of love wholly for the neighbor's sake. In the second of these considerations, the metaphysical dualism of body and soul is replaced by the more Christian problem of dualism between self and another, which for Luther was obviously the most important reason for good works. This confirms the interpretation given above of the inner-outer distinction made in the *Secular Authority* as involving no metaphysical or psychological dualism.
[2]*Ibid.*, pp. 248–249.

for love of his (enemy) neighbor. Personal rights as well as the rights of others are thus derived from Christian love, but it must always be remembered that these personal rights are concretely determined by the obligations which the needs of the neighbor place upon their bearer. They are conditions of life which a person must possess and exercise in order effectively to love his neighbor. They are "derived backward" from consideration of the neighbor; or "elicited" as forms of neighbor-love. A claim to possess them is a claim that my neighbor possesses them in me. If my neighbor possesses them in me, these rights are my duties, duties to myself which also, if they are Christian duties, I owe to my neighbor for Christ's sake. "If, as a good Christian," an industrial worker "is willing to endure the injustice of his position —so far as he is concerned—for the sake of others he ought not to do so."[3] If, as a good Christian, a person is willing to suffer his rights to lapse—so far as he is concerned—for the sake of others he ought not to do so: this, too, is a Christian's vocational duty.

A Christian derivation of personal rights as forms of neighbor-regarding love is not far different from the idealistic social derivation given by self-realization ethics. A right, said T. H. Green, is a socially recognized claim to exercise some power or capacity for the common good.[4] This definition agrees with the Christian analysis on the negative point that the individual is not in himself privately a possessor of rights. In both traditions rights devolve upon the individual on account of their relation to some service to be performed, without which he may not legitimately lay claim to rights for himself. In idealistic, self-realization ethics, rights for the self are forms of service to the *common* good. In Christian ethics, rights for the self are forms of service to the neighbor, and ideally a Christian agent gives no express consideration to whether he participates in, or is a mutual recipient of the good he does. In the one case, mutual self-realization in the common good is the ideal, and in the other, self-sacrifice to the good of the neighbor.

[3]Emil Brunner, *The Divine Imperative*, Macmillan, 1937, p. 431.
[4]*Lectures on the Principles of Political Obligation*, Longmans, 1937, pp. 41, 44 *et passim.*

Far from wishing to tone down the demands upon a Christian in his secular vocation, Luther actually opposed the Catholic view that the strenuous teachings of the gospel ethic were only "counsels of perfection," advisory opinions as to what a comparatively few individuals might do to gain more than ordinary perfection, not commanded of every one under every circumstance. Every Christian everywhere, no matter what his function in society, is obliged, according to Luther, to measure his life by non-resisting love, and not only his inner disposition but his outward action as well. Luther believed that from Christian love would follow not only "good conscience" in the doing of ordinary or even menial tasks, but good conscience also in doing necessary evil if for love's sake it must be done. "Therefore," he wrote, "should you see that there is a lack of hangmen, beadles, judges, lords or princes, and find that you are qualified, you should offer your services and seek the place, that necessary government may by no means be despised and become inefficient or perish."[5] If a Christian does not actually "run for" these offices like an American politician, he will "stand for" them like the British. And "standing for" vocational responsibilities means a good deal more than simply to "stomach the dirty business," of soldiering, for example, for the Christian always has positive reason for doing whatever his vocation requires. He may pray God to be delivered of his necessities, but he does not irresponsibly deliver himself from them. The "mournful Christian warrior" does not blubber over his gunpowder, no more than the Christian who resists non-violently over his passive resistance, or the Christian judge over delivering sentence, or the Christian parent over the necessity of turning away from the need of some neighbor in order to have money for paying the next premium on his life insurance.

The Reformation doctrine of vocation recognizes a large area of relativity in ethics, disclaiming any hard-and-fast absolute principles or rigid laws. If philosophy fails him and no suggested scale of values seems really persuasive, a Protestant Christian knows how to proceed pragmatically without any other guide

[5] *Op. cit.*, p. 241.

than consulting moment by moment his neighbor's need and reading up on social case studies. On the other hand, the Reformation
doctrine of vocation requires that Christian love penetrate everything a man does, absolutely everything without the slightest
exception. This means that he has every possible stimulus for
carrying on the philosophical quest for determining the universal
needs of human beings, for ascending the scale of values as far
as possible, for finding out about the highest good, for becoming
as enlightened and effective in the attainment of these ends as
his capacity allows. For his enlightenment also the Christian is
"servant of all" the sources of information employed by the human
mind and "subject to every one" of the ways his neighbors' true
needs may be adequately found out and best served.

Why, it may be asked, is it that Christianity, which thinks so
little of man, expects so much of him in his vocation, no less than
self-abandoning love even in his political participation in common effort to make human rights secure? In part, it may be replied, this is a radical remedy for a radical disease, by which
Christianity knows that only when governed by the intentional
orientation of self-sacrificial love toward the welfare of another
can mutual love be prevented from degenerating into divisive
self-interest. In part the reply is that only in the light of the glory
of God which has shone forth in the face of Jesus Christ does
Christianity assess man; and, consequently, *from knowing that so
much is, in fact, expected of man* comes to think so little of him
as he actually is. The answer also is that Christianity expects man
to be in every moment "converted" from himself to concern for
others, redeemed, radically transformed in his nature.

Let it not be said that an ethic which in ideal renounces the
claim to private resistance and the private possession of rights
is quietistic. This seems true only to one antecedently convinced
of some selfish or mutualist system. A Christian man has reason
for all possible self-improvement, for resistance by all effective
means and ceaseless political action on behalf of human rights
in Christ's name and for his neighbor's sake. He cooperates to
the fullest extent with men whose action is grounded in consid-

erations as to the dignity of man as man and whose adoption
of natural-law theory, inalienable rights, the inherent sacredness
of human personality, or even the doctrine of *imago Dei* as a
pious political principle allows the agent to claim more for himself than is countenanced by the Sermon on the Mount. Inwardly, also, a Christian man finds himself joined by the "natural man," who from self-interest pursues success in a career or
engages in the struggle for human liberty. But in Christ's name
and for his neighbor's sake a Christian man finds himself compelled to return again and again to the battle—long after the
"natural man" within himself would grow tired and accept expedient compromises with tyranny. Christian love will not permit him to live out his own lifetime with a modicum of rights,
content simply with a degree of protection for himself within
the dugout of some vocation useful mainly as a tool for oppression and for his own advantage. Truly, "the magistrate will execute his office with greater pleasure, the father of a family will
confine himself to his duty with more satisfaction, and all, in
their respective spheres of life, will bear and surmount the in-
conveniences, cares, disappointments, and anxieties which befall
them, when they shall be persuaded that every individual has
his burden laid upon him by God," when they shall be persuaded
that every individual has his burden of vocational obligation
laid upon him by the God who put forward Christ, by what for
love's sake must be done.

VI

CHRISTIAN VIRTUE

". . . Your pious English habit of regarding the world as a moral gymnasium built expressly to strengthen your character in, occasionally leads you to think about your own confounded principles when you should be thinking about other people's necessities. . . . Bend your energies on that; and you will see your way clearly enough." —George Bernard Shaw, *Man and Superman.*

"It beseemed him . . . to erect himself into an example of virtue and show the gun deck what virtue was. But alas! when virtue sits aloft on a frigate's poop, when virtue is crowned in the cabin of a commodore, when virtue rules by compulsion, and domineers over vice as a slave, then virtue, though her mandates be outwardly observed, bears little interior sway. To be efficacious, virtue must come down from aloft even as our blessed Redeemer came down to redeem our whole man-of-war world; to that end mixing with its sailors and sinners as equals." —Herman Melville, *White Jacket,* ch. liv.

THROUGH Christian ethics generally there runs a deep undercurrent of opposition to every peril of Pharisaism. Every doer is likely to love the deed, as Nietzsche said, himself and his virtues more than they ought to be loved. Can a man know, should he even be concerned to know, that he is good? Highly critical of all self-conscious goodness, Christian ethics seems often not to care for goodness itself. This is especially true of moral theory according to the principles of the Reformation. Luther's well-known disparagement of Aristotle, the greatest moral analyst in the ancient world, and his apparent rejection of consciously cultivated righteousness, put in jeopardy the theory and practice of virtue in Reformation Christian ethics.

Nevertheless, the enterprise of analyzing virtues of moral character constitutes a large part of general ethical theory. And effort to attain virtue is no less a part of moral practice. There is need, therefore, for an account of Christian virtue controlled by the distinctive perspectives of Christian faith and love, and primarily by these alone. It must be confessed that this has not been true of those Christian moralists who have written most on the subject of virtues of moral character. Too often analysis of moral goodness springs from some form of coalition ethics in which Christian themes prove the sleeping partner. In St. Augustine, Neo-Platonism; in St. Thomas Aquinas, Aristotelianism; and in more recent times, self-realization ethics provide, to less or greater degree, the dominant motivation for the development of character and for analyzing its constituent elements.

Nevertheless, in these instances Christian themes are by no means altogether dormant. Whatever understanding of the meaning of moral goodness be drawn from one or another non-Christian philosophical source, there always takes place, to less or greater degree, a Christianization of these elements in the mind of the person who sponsors them for admission into Christian ethics. It is instructive, therefore, to watch the Christianization of virtue which results from the meeting of Christian themes with Platonic and Stoic ones in the mind of St. Augustine and with Aristotelianism in the mind of St. Thomas Aquinas. What happens when a theory of virtue becomes Christian may be abstracted from the discussion of virtues given by these men. The distinctive Christian elements thus isolated provide an understanding of the role of character in Christian ethics. In the discernible impact of Christianity upon the Græco-Roman philosophical heritage of Augustine and Aquinas we can see "writ large" the persistent and universal influence of Christianity upon personal character. Distinctively Christian elements in the theories of virtue given by St. Augustine and St. Thomas, when corrected from within and by reference again to the New Testament, display surprising similarity to the insights of the Reformation. This similarity in turn suggests the possibility and desirability of developing a theory of virtue within Protestant theological ethics.

I. THE MEASURE AND UNITY OF VIRTUE

How to measure moral character has been declared to be the most important question in the world, infinitely superior to concern for knowledge and twice infinitely superior to concern for happiness. There can be no doubt that the Christian answer to this question, the Christian ideal for human character, is summed up in the person of Jesus Christ. Jesus may not have been the happiest man or even the wisest man, but he was a man perfect in moral goodness and in obedience to God's will for his life.

How men need to measure themselves by "the stature of the fullness of Christ" can best be seen by acknowledging what narrow specialists in virtue we all are. Moral goodness seems to travel in sections which never arrive at the same destination at the same time. The wise are not ordinarily humble, and humble folk too frequently have only small capacities of which they might be proud. The courageous are not always temperate, or the temperate fearless. College students maintain an honor system in one department of conduct, too little honor in others. Standards for professional ethics rarely go far enough in designing moral controls for professional practice. James Thurber tells the fable of a bear who frequently went on sprees of drunkenness, and would come home at night in this condition, throw his weight around the house, break the furniture, frighten his children, and drive his wife to tears. Then one day he decided never to touch a drop again; and ever thereafter he would come home and demonstrate how fresh he still was at the end of the day and how vigorous his new manner of life had made him by doing gymnastic exercises in the living room, throwing his arms akimbo, thus again breaking the furniture, frightening his children, and driving his wife to tears. The moral of this tale is: It's Better to Fall Flat on Your Face than to Lean Over too

Far Backward. How often have you heard it said that some one's
greatest strength is his greatest weakness? We commonly pull
one trait of character up snugly round our necks only to discover
our feet are showing, our goodness not full length enough to
cover us.

Yet the Christian ideal of character is not the same as the
Greek, "In nothing too much, and something of everything";
Aristotle's ethic of the "mean" not the same as Jesus' "ethic of
the extreme." The classic and Renaissance ideal of moderate and
well-rounded human activity, and the Romantic ideal, so well
exemplified by Goethe, of never fixing upon any single moment
in experience as if it were enough without something of all the
other possibilities going to make up a full life—these must be
subjected to radical revision before being baptized Christian.
This can be seen in the single instance of Albert Schweitzer:
Which as Christians do we admire more, the world of learning,
music and art he carries on his shoulders, or the triumph in him
of Jesus' ethic of the extreme? Which makes him more mature,
more truly a man, moderation or immoderation? While undoubtedly he comes close to being admirable in every respect, the
question may still be raised whether the distinctively Christian
thing about this man Schweitzer consists in what he has been
able to include or what, without having to, he has been able
to exclude. And we may search for the organizing principle or
main theme of his many virtues, re-examining our conception
of ideal human character, and the bearing Christianity has upon
it. The prcblem of giving unity and fullness to moral charactei
Christian ethics answers, not by encouraging a moderate or well-
rounded development of all human capacities, but by pointing
man to a standard of excellence altogether outside himself. We
need to "grow up in every way into him who is the head, into
Christ," into the stature of his fullness (Eph. 4:15).

In its ideal for character, the Christian religion does not begin
with man's natural capacities, suggesting merely how these may
best be balanced and developed. It begins wholly outside of
ordinary human nature itself and from beyond our general ex-

perience of moments of self-realization, and suggests that these be made to conform to the Christ-standard. It aims to cut man to fit the pattern, not the pattern to fit man. It organizes our notions of maturity around him as center. St. Paul's hymn in praise of Christian love he did not so much think up as copy down. Insofar as we are in process of growing into maturity of Christian living, it is because we too look away from ourselves toward such love as was seen in the flesh only in Jesus Christ, and from this allow to be transcribed into our lives what St. Paul for the first time in the thirteenth chapter of I Corinthians transcribed into language as the definition of perfect maturity for the Christian. For we may be sure that when he goes on in the fourteenth chapter to elaborate a sort of scale of values which Christians will endorse and strive to include in their lives, St. Paul is still not so much thinking them up as copying them down.

In more than one place St. Paul specifically points up this conception of Christian maturity. "Brethren, do not be children in your thinking," he writes; "be babes in evil, but in thinking be *mature*" (I Cor. 14:20). And we know of what this maturity consisted. It consisted of concern for "edification," for the building up of others. "I will pray with the spirit and I will pray with the mind also, I will sing with the spirit and I will sing with the mind also, in church I would rather speak five words with my mind, in order to instruct others, than ten thousand words in a tongue" (14:15, 19). Why is this? Unmistakably not because intelligence is the supreme value. There is in fact no way of telling what St. Paul thought about inspiration and intelligence, special revelation and reason, when these are simply compared with one another with no reference beyond their own inherent worth. He sets above them both concern for edification; and only in terms of the supreme value of love or by reference to the needs of others to be served, does he distinguish between speaking from inspiration and speaking more deliberately with concern for the intelligible meaning of words. Intelligence does not sit in judgment upon love, determining when and how and in what manner and how long and up to what point another person is to be loved. Instead it is love which judges intelligence. From this we know that praying and singing with the mind, and waiting for the translation of tongues to be given, are right and proper for our brother's sake. Putting away childish things means putting away unedifying things, such as prolonged ecstasy, not because this is not inspired but rather because it is not very helpful. The fact that everything is permitted does not prove everything edifying; the fact that something has been privately revealed does not prove it to be edifying; the fact that something has been reasonably thought out does not prove it helpful; and this is what must be proved of either special revelation or reason.

Again in Ephesians (4:13) the apostle points out the Christian conception of maturity and makes his meaning even more explicit when he speaks of our attaining unto "the unity of the faith and of the knowledge of the Son of God, to *mature manhood,* to the measure of the stature of the fullness of Christ." Here plainly the standard for perfect maturity is not drawn from a consideration of human capacities in general or from general human experience of realized values or values to be realized. Beyond any doubt, the standard for man is not drawn *from man;* what is expected *of us* is not taken *from us.* Here plainly what maturity means Paul links decisively with the measure of the stature of the fullness of Christ. Jesus Christ was for him mature manhood, and the ultimate standard for measuring maturity among men. Jesus Christ was God's idea of what man ought to be, not a Platonic idea of manhood laid up in heaven, but God's Word irradiating earth. He was "the image of the invisible God" in which man was originally created. He was "mature manhood," the second Adam by whom the measure of what it means to be a true man may again be taken, and taken with entire accuracy. Undoubtedly much may be gained from comparing ourselves with, say, St. Francis or Schweitzer, much of humility over our achievements and incitement to diligence in our tasks; but lest there arise some mistake let us not fail to imitate in them their imitation of Christ. For in him we find most plainly placarded the organizing and reorganizing principle of Christian character. In speaking, then, of ideal human character we are speaking of one main aspect of the fullness of Christian faith, one main element in the fullness of Christ, and one of the main Christian doctrines, the person of Christ. Christianity does not compose its own conception of maturity out of available cultural values; it points maturity out, defining righteousness by indication, by citing the man Christ Jesus.

"Some ancient writings one reads to understand antiquity," Friedrich Nietzsche once said; "others, however, are such that one studies antiquity in order to be able to read them." This is true of great men as well as great books. The lives of some men we study in order to understand their times; others, however, are such that we study their times in order to be able to understand them. Christians believe Jesus was at least such a man. We do not study him in order to understand his period; his times we study in order to be able to comprehend him. That "fullness" or crater from which Christianity first burst forth must be understood as a fullness that was in Jesus Christ himself, not simply in his times.

How, physically, the world was ready for the spread of the Christian message by preachers traveling along Roman roads; how, culturally, that world was held together by Roman power and Roman law and the Greek language; how, spiritually, people in the Hellenistic age were all "very religious"; how not only the mysteries but schools of philosophy as well were seeking yet failing to answer the great felt-need for personal salvation—all this may be cited to show that time had reached a certain fullness when Jesus was born. But all this did not comprise the fullness of the Christian message itself. St. Paul who spoke of the fullness of time was among the first missionaries to push out along the Roman roads; *he* knew nothing of the readiness of Rome to lend itself to the final triumph of Christianity. The fullness of which he spoke so confidently was, he believed, a certain fullness in God's dealing with men. This fullness had only just come into time; before this event it was not to be found there. Indeed, the fullness of which the New Testament everywhere speaks was *in Christ,* not in Rome, for Roman civilization, her philosophies and religions, were only full of deficiency and growing emptiness. When Jesus came, for all time, time became full. To speak now of only one aspect of the matter, in him for all time history became full of God's Word irradiating earth with the meaning of human maturity. Though cultures perish, and whenever it may be that the human story will end around the last flickering embers of the universe, we have now had in the measure of the stature of the fullness of Christ God's Word as to the nature of mature manhood in the form of an actual man—*The man,* as the Hebrew, *Adam,* has it, manhood as it must have come straight from the hands of the Creator.

In the theological era just ending men found it difficult to retain a doctrine of the so-called divinity of Christ. It is frequently not noticed that to the same degree they often omitted any real sense, not of the humanity of Jesus (that was known well enough), but of his *perfect* humanity. This will seem a strange assertion, for we commonly suppose that if a humanist religion is expert at any one thing it is in encouraging the imitation of this man Jesus. Yet these two belong inseparably together: very God of very God and very man of very man, whether we believe them both or reject or modify them both. The one gives intensity and meaning to the other. When one lapses, so does the other also. Having no Absolute in time has also meant having no "perfect" or "mature manhood" in time. Jesus Christ as one revealer and mediator among many others means also one human hero for imitation among many others; and he has been a hero for *possible* imitation and not One commanding unconditional discipleship. As one among other clues to knowledge of God Jesus Christ means also one among other clues to a right estimate of human character, however supreme he may be in both these respects, as source of our penetration into the nature of God and into the nature of mature manhood. It begins to appear that the new theology will make the same error in an opposite direction. By performing a surgical operation on the humanity of Christ it is apt to gain through him no really available knowledge of God; humanity mutilated, divinity hidden, a question mark was made flesh and dwelt among us!

He who loses hold on the full manhood of Christ will never make a straight start toward understanding the doctrine of his divinity. He who loses all hold on the divinity of Christ will never confront the commanding presence of Jesus the man. How often do we imagine that the issue as to the divinity of Christ turns upon some extraordinary statement about his mixed-up manhood; and then with some half-and-half, faunlike creature on our hands, we skirt the fact that the so-called divinity of Christ actually means a most astounding assertion about the true nature of divinity. All along, this phrase "the divinity of Christ" was a most unfortunately misleading manner of expression, tempting us to sever him from humanity or split him asunder, holding him half a hostage for both worlds. This we saw in Chapter One when considering Jesus Christ as "the righteousness of God." Likewise by losing hold on the conviction that it was *God* who put forward Christ, that God was in some final sense active in him, or that he was God's act, we then qualify in some degree the absolutely unconditional imperativeness of his full stature as the perfect measure of mature manhood. When we cease to hold him prototypal of what it means to be divine, we also cease to hold him prototypal of the meaning of mature moral character. That he was one picture of what it means to be a man, this we easily grant, balancing it with other types of character that have been placarded before us. Thus we judge Christ by our composite notions of maturity, and fail to compose our ideas of maturity by decisive reference to him. That we should grow up in *some* ways into his stature, in emulating his blessing little children, his kindness and other attributes universally recognized as elements of human greatness in him—this we say as easily as we allow that doubtless *in some ways something* of divinity shone through him, his marvelous works for example. But that we should grow up *in every way* into his stature, into his great denial of self; and that here, precisely in his concern for the poor of earth, was all the fullness and essence of God without anything essentially altered or left out—this St. Paul called "the folly we preach" (I Cor. 1:21).

What happens, we may ask, when men encounter in Jesus Christ perfect God and perfect manhood, the essential nature of the divine and the essence of human moral maturity? By this indeed we may know that we have personally confronted Jesus Christ as the Lord of life and the Sermon on the Mount as the perfect will of God:—there begins to be brought about in us a combination of increasing humility and increasing achievement. This has been the hall-mark of Christian character in all ages. Repeatedly moment by moment we discover from comparing ourselves with Jesus Christ and his teachings how to have humility increased in us without sabotaging effort and how to make every effort without provoking pride. Hence we have whereof to glory, but are not tempted to glory save in the Lord. Hence arises that "autobiography" of the sinner which accompanies the biography of every Christian saint. *Vis à vis* Christ, *at least every one* who is going on to perfection remains always sinful. As Pascal put the matter:

> The Christian religion . . . teaches men these two truths; that there is a God whom men can know, and that there is a corruption in their nature which renders them unworthy of Him. It is equally important to men to know both these points; and it is equally dangerous for man to know God without knowing his own wretchedness, and to know his own wretchedness without knowing the Redeemer who can free him from it. The knowledge of only one of these points gives rise either to the pride of philosophers, who have known God, and not their own wretchedness, or to the despair of atheists, who know their own wretchedness, but not the Redeemer. . . . We can have an excellent knowledge of God without that of our own wretchedness and of our own wretchedness without that of God. But we cannot know Jesus Christ without knowing at the same time both God and our own wretchedness.[1]

This truth still holds, even if we find some way to avoid using Pascal's terms "wretchedness" and "corruption." The distinctive

[1] *Pensées*, 555.

reorganization of character which relation to Christ brings about is that at the same time we are humiliated and brought down to nothing in our own eyes and lifted up from despair to renewal of life and effort. We are allowed no ground for becoming self-complacent authorities on good and evil; but by the authority of Christ we cannot quit our efforts either. Thus the better we become the less we think we are, and the less we think we are the better we become. This is not brought about by walking some tight rope between extremes in an attempt to become only moderately prideful and only moderately modest; but by correlating our lives with his who was the master of life, articulating the teachings we practice with the extreme spirit of the teachings he gave. By thus viewing ourselves in "the mirror of the Word," in the course of every achievement of our moral purposes, however noble, there is reflected back upon us a picture of how we still look in comparison with Jesus Christ, together with the requirement that we become not so much good as good *for edification.* Thus we already know what would be entire maturity in our thinking and in our acting, and at the same time we are forced to acknowledge how much of childishness we have not yet put away, until we grow up *in every way* and attain to "the unity of the faith and of the knowledge of the Son of God, to *mature manhood,* to the measure of the stature of the fullness of Christ." No doubt, men in this culture or that, in this or another age, will want to include many more of the things valued by their day and generation, and all this will be to the larger good; but here we find our principle of inclusion or exclusion, an ethic of the extreme which overcomes triviality without seeking that "universality" to which Goethe aspired. Christian ethics demands the well-balanced inclusion of everything—everything that is helpful. This was the organizing principle for selecting and unifying the moral virtues of which St. Paul spoke: Everything is permitted which edification allows. Everything is required which edification demands. "Be babes in evil, but in thinking be *mature.*" Be *this* mature.

The Christocentric principle for the reorganization of our notions of ideal moral character shows itself in operation in the thought of St. Augustine, and, with somewhat less penetration, St. Thomas Aquinas. Augustine speaks of a "fourfold division of virtue"[2] instead of four cardinal virtues, thus emphasizing the unity of virtue in all its aspects. With similar purport recent translations of Galatians 5:22 refer to Paul's list of various qualities of Christian character not as many different "fruits" but as a single "harvest" or "fruit" of the Spirit.[3] The principle of unity in a Christian account of moral goodness does not consist in a neat balancing of virtues one against another but in referring to some end beyond itself which all virtue explicitly serves. "The fourfold division of virtue," Augustine writes, is "taken from four *forms* of love."[4] And he would doubtless consider the same thing true if on analysis a ten- or hundredfold division of virtue were discovered, these divisions of cardinal and subordinate classifications of virtue being all of them forms of love for some object or end other than character itself.

Thus, according to Augustine, pursuit of pleasure takes the form of certain virtues insofar as the policy of seeking pleasure is practiced with deliberation and enlightenment. A hedonist, because of his love for pleasure and his desire to secure a steadier flow of pleasurable states of consciousness, refuses many pleasures, and concerning them all he exercises moderation. He has courage to undergo remedial pain to restore possibility of continued enjoyment. The hedonist's cardinal virtues are four forms of his love for pleasure, the love of pleasure being enough to drive a man to temperance. Indeed, the love of pleasure is likely to go further and, as in the case of Epicurus, bring about a rigorous asceticism toward most pleasures. Disciplined participation in the joys of human living may become even more extreme on the part of a hedonist than in the case of another man who unites the same virtues in the service of some other end than pleasure itself. He whose virtue is informed by some other love than the love of

[2]*On the Morals of the Catholic Church,* xv (*Basic Writings of St. Augustine,* ed. by Whitney J. Oates, Random House, 1948, I, 331).
[3]Moffatt and Revised Standard versions.
[4]*Op. cit.* (italics mine).

pleasure is likely to live more pleasurably than the hedonist, since, as G. B. Shaw once said, "The secret of being miserable is to have the leisure to bother about whether you are happy or not." Whether love for pleasure is an adequate principle of unity among virtues may be doubted; in any case a *good* hedonist needs to be both virtuous and wise.

At one point in his discussion of the virtues of the hedonist, Augustine draws

> . . . a kind of word picture, in which *Pleasure sits like a luxurious queen on a royal seat,* and all the virtues are subjected to her as slaves, watching her nod, that they may do whatever she shall command. She commands *Prudence* to be ever on the watch to discover how Pleasure may rule, and be safe. *Justice* she orders to grant what benefits she can, in order to secure those friendships which are necessary for bodily pleasure; to do wrong to no one, lest, on account of the breaking of the laws, Pleasure be not able to live in security. *Fortitude* she orders to keep her mistress, that is, Pleasure, bravely in mind, if any affliction befall her body which does not occasion death, in order that by remembrance of former delights she may mitigate the poignancy of present pain. *Temperance* she commands to take only a certain quantity even of the most favorite food, lest, through immoderate use, anything prove hurtful by disturbing the health of the body, and thus Pleasure . . . be grievously offended. Thus the virtues, with the whole dignity of their glory, will be the slaves of Pleasure, as of some imperious and disreputable woman.[5]

Virtues typical of Roman character, which Augustine admired so much, were, he said, forms of love for honor, prestige, glory, and power rather than love for pleasure. In a somewhat similar vein Nietzsche later remarked of the nation of shopkeepers he despised, "Not all men desire pleasure; only Englishmen do that." The love of honor and glory forming the civic virtue of the Romans made them "less base," more splendidly vicious, than a virtuous love for less worthy ends, pleasure or wealth. Augustine's criticism of character organized and unified by love of honor is, however, overstated by the chapter title in *The City of God,* "That It Is

[5]*The City of God,* V, 20 (*Basic Writings of St. Augustine,* ed. by Whitney J. Oates, Random House, 1948, II, 85). (Italics mine.)

as Shameful for the Virtues to Serve Human Glory as Bodily Pleasure."[6] His point is simply that "he has the soundest perception who recognizes that even the love of praise is a vice"[7] and the virtues which are its forms vicious, "for, though that glory be not a luxurious woman, it is nevertheless *puffed up, and has much vanity in it.*"[8] Not much is gained by turning moral excellence from the service of a strumpet, pleasure, to the service of the trumpets of the Roman legions and their triumphal processions.

It must be remembered that St. Paul and St. Augustine were not the first to affirm the unity of virtue. Before them, Socrates taught the fundamental unity of all the virtues as "forms" of knowledge. Particular virtues such as courage and temperance are not essentially different from one another, since all are reducible to knowledge of the good. Diversity disappears in the unity of Socratic ethical insight. Aristotle restored diversity to the theory of virtue by saying that virtues were not simply forms of knowledge but habits in the passions acquired as a result of the exercise of practical reason. Knowledge is necessary to virtue, according to Aristotle, but a virtue itself is a skill consequent upon knowledge and practice. This account left the virtues resident in the passions more or less separate from one another. Stoicism returned to an emphasis upon unity of character, but this was accomplished only by making virtue largely internal to the will and by regarding imperturbability as the main, if not the only, virtue in comparison with which all other aspects of moral goodness are unimportant, if not actually harmful. These views all agree in drawing the standard for man from man himself; they know nothing of any way of measuring human excellence and preserving its unity by reference to a source and an end altogether outside man himself.

The notion in Aristotelianism and Stoicism that virtue is its own reward, that moral excellence is to be sought for its own sake alone, gives an account of virtues, and perhaps of their unity, which seems not to require love for anything else as their integrating force. Nevertheless, Augustine detects underneath the

[6]*Loc. cit.* (italics mine).
[7]*Ibid.*, V, 13 (*Basic Writings*, II, 74).
[8]*Ibid.*, V, 20 (*Basic Writings*, II, 85). (Italics mine.)

virtues of the Stoic sage a thoroughgoing love for himself. All virtues which appear to be valued for their own inherent worth are really forms of the love their possessor has for himself. "For although some suppose that virtues which have reference only to themselves, and are desired only on their own account, are yet true and genuine virtue," he writes, "the fact is even then they are *inflated with pride*, and are therefore to be reckoned vices rather than virtues."[9] Virtues never really have reference only to themselves, nor are they ever desired simply on their own account. As an exercise in ethical analysis, moral character may be abstracted from the spirit of the man who consciously possesses it, just as we may consider knowledge and art in abstraction from the actual persons who pursue them. But the fact that this abstraction has been made should not then be ignored. Every one would grant that such abstracted virtues and values are doubtless in themselves things of worth, but they are never experienced merely in themselves. Every experience of them is also a self-conscious experience of ourselves as possessing them. Since value judgments are always the judgments of men who are also sinful, no virtue-centered or value-centered ethic can ever be complete. According to Augustine it is better forthrightly to face the fact that virtues and values never have reference only to themselves but always also a prideful reference to their possessor. Thus, love of self, as well as love of virtue, gives unity to the Aristotelian and Stoic table of virtues.

In summary, then, virtues are the forms of some love, whether love of pleasure, love of glory, or love of self masquerading as love of virtue for its own sake. These *ends* Augustine criticizes as finite, mortal, and therefore unsatisfactory ends for character to serve. These *loves* he criticizes as vain and selfish. Both insufficiency and sin beset these ways of securing unity in goodness. ". . . Where there is no true religion" relating man to an infinite, enduring good in the love of which inordinate love for the self is overcome, "there are no true virtues."[10] Upright pagans have the empty form but not the substance of virtue.

[9] *Ibid.*, XIX, 25 (*Basic Writings*, II, 504). (Italics mine.)   [10] *Loc. cit.*

Augustine's own constructive theory of virtues follows logically from his general definition of virtue as forms of love for whatever is loved. He then defines virtues of Christian character as forms of Christian love, which he understands as man's love for God. "I hold virtue to be nothing else than perfect love of God."[11]

> . . . Temperance [in general] is love giving itself entirely to that which is loved . . . so we may express the definition thus: that [Christianized] temperance is love keeping itself entire and incorrupt for the sake of God.[12] [Christian] temperance . . . promises us a kind of integrity and incorruption in the love by which we are united to God. The office of [Christian] temperance is in restraining and quieting the passions which make us pant for those things which turn us away from the laws of God and from the enjoyment of His goodness, that is, in a word, from the happy life.[13] The love, then, of which we speak, which ought with all sanctity to burn in desire for God, is called temperance in not seeking for earthly things.[14] . . . That this love must be preserved entire and incorrupt . . . is the part of temperance.[15]
>
> [In general] fortitude [or courage] is love readily bearing all things for the loved object [whatever it may be] . . . so we may express the definition thus: that . . . [Christianized] fortitude is love bearing everything readily for the sake of God.[16] The love, then, of which we speak, which ought with all sanctity to burn in desire for God, is called . . . [Christian] fortitude, in bearing the loss[17] [of earthly things for the sake of this love. That this love] give way before no troubles . . . is the part of fortitude.[18]
>
> Justice [generally] is love serving only the beloved object [whatever it may be], and therefore ruling rightly . . . so we may express the definition thus: that . . . [Christian] justice is love serving God only, and therefore ruling well all else, as subject to man.[19] The lover, then, whom we are describing, will get from justice this rule of life, that he must with perfect readiness serve the God whom he loves, the highest good, the highest wisdom, the highest peace; and as regards all other things, must either rule them as subject to himself, or treat them with a view

[11]*On the Morals of the Catholic Church*, xv (*Basic Writings*, I, 331).
[12]*Loc. cit.*
[13]*Ibid.*, xix (*Basic Writings*, I, 336).
[14]*Ibid.*, xxii (*Basic Writings*, I, 339).
[15]*Ibid.*, xxv (*Basic Writings*, I, 342).
[16]*Ibid.*, xv (*Basic Writings*, I, 331–332).
[17]*Ibid.*, xxii (*Basic Writings*, I, 339).
[18]*Ibid.*, xxv (*Basic Writings*, I, 342).
[19]*Ibid.*, xv (*Basic Writings*, I, 331–332).

to their subjection.[20] [That this love] serve no other . . . is the part of justice.[21]

[In general] prudence [or practical wisdom] is love distinguishing with sagacity between what hinders it and what helps it. The object of this love [for Christians] is not anything; but only God, the chief good, the highest wisdom, the perfect harmony. So we may express the definition thus: that . . . [Christian] prudence is love making a right distinction between what helps it towards God and what might hinder it.[22] [To Christian prudence] it belongs to discern between what is to be desired and what to be shunned. . . . It is the part of prudence to keep watch with most anxious vigilance, lest any evil influence should stealthily creep upon us.[23] [That man's love of God] be watchful in its inspection of things lest craft or fraud steal in . . . is the part of prudence.[24]

In contrast to Augustinian insistence upon the unity of virtue, Thomas Aquinas notably divides Christian character into a lower level of natural virtues and a superstructure of theological virtues. In spite of the apparently greater independence and worth which he gives to acquired or Aristotelian virtues, Aquinas nevertheless stands in essential agreement with the view that Christian faith and love affect moral character to the bottom by disconnecting the natural virtues from the service of sinful or mundane ends and relating them at least to some extent to the supernatural end which they naturally ("con-naturally"—or naturally within us when given to us supernaturally) ought to have. A prudent man as such is better than an imprudent one, and, if a man be a navigator, of course he ought to be a prudent navigator. In contrast to a prudent and courageous navigator, a prudent and courageous thief harnesses his qualities of character to an evil end, so that the better he becomes in these particular respects, the worse he is in the total unity of his character. Preferable either to prudent theft or prudent navigation, however, is the prudent service of God. Through loving devotion to God prudence and other acquired virtues are Christianized. Thus, more than is commonly

[20]*Ibid.*, xxiv (*Basic Writings*, I, 341).
[21]*Ibid.*, xxv (*Basic Writings*, I, 342).
[22]*Ibid.*, xv (*Basic Writings*, I, 331–332).
[23]*Ibid.*, xxiv (*Basic Writings*, I, 341).
[24]*Ibid.*, xxv (*Basic Writings*, I, 342).

recognized, Aquinas agrees with Augustine's view that virtues may become forms of the love of God, whatever sort of love originally informed them. Aquinas' view of perfectly Christianized character is that "All the moral virtues are infused together with charity. . . . It is therefore clear that the moral virtues are connected, not only through prudence, but also because of charity."[25]

Nevertheless, unity of personal character is incomplete because of the distinction St. Thomas makes between the natural and the supernatural virtues. It is true that natural virtue is unified within itself since, according to Aquinas, prudence is the leading or guiding moral virtue without which all other virtues are impossible to acquire, from which all other virtues will follow, and whose perfection perfects all the rest.[26] The virtues given by divine grace are themselves also joined together by their leading virtue, charity.[27] These two, prudence and charity, unify virtue at each of its levels; but prudence remains, to a degree, independent of charity's leadership, and character is sundered between them.

The conflict between Aristotelian and Christian themes in Aquinas' analysis of virtue, however, is of less consequence for destroying the unity of virtue in Christian ethics generally than the primacy both he and Augustine assign to "love for God" and the opposition which immediately arises between two formulations of the love commandment, love for God and love for neighbor. Assuming that Christian ethics finds in love its principle of unity among all the virtues, disunity nevertheless results among them if Christian love itself is divided into two sorts of love or love for two different objects. One set of virtues will appear as forms of man's love for God, another as forms of his love for neighbor. Thus, Christian character, as we have seen of duties in general, would imitate Don Quixote dashing off at once in at least two directions.

In the third part of Chapter Three on the nature and mean-

[25]*Summa Theologica*, I–II, Q. 65, art. 3 (*Basic Writings of Saint Thomas Aquinas*, ed. Anton C. Pegis, Random House, 1945, II, 500); cf. *Summa Theologica*, II–II, Q. 23, art. 7.
[26]*Ibid.*, Q. 65, art. 1.
[27]*Ibid.*, Q. 65, arts. 4 and 5.

ing of Christian love, St. Augustine's Neo-Platonic notion of love was revised and corrected by reference again to the New Testament; and in a moment we shall see that hereby his views on the moral life gain consistency and strength. Every expression of medievalism in Christian ethics must be subjected to similar amendment. For example, St. Bernard's four degrees of love, according to which a man first loves himself, then loves God because he is good to him, then loves God because he is good, and finally loves himself only *"propter Deum."*[28] Four corresponding approximations to Christian love for neighbor, inverting self-love, are: A man first loves himself (crude selfishness), then loves his neighbor because he is good to him (enlightened selfishness), then loves his neighbor because he is good (love for value, Aristotle's friendship for the sake of the good), and finally loves himself only *"propter"* his neighbor. He loves himself, takes care of himself, performs duties to himself, and endeavors to acquire strength of character in himself, all as a part of Christian vocation bending his energies to other people's necessities.

II.   THE SOURCE OF VIRTUE

In its genesis virtue may be traced to (a) evocation or elicitation, as in the view of Augustine, (b) infused grace, as in Thomas Aquinas, (c) acquirement, as in Aristotle, or (d) justifying grace, according to the principles of the Reformation. Each of these views will be found, on examination, to possess a certain aspect of the truth.

(a) *The Evocation or Elicitation of Virtue: A Revision of Augustine*

Augustine's analytical account of the structure and unity of character describes virtues as forms of Christian love. His genetic account of the origin of virtues is that they are not so much made as born. They "arise from" Christian love consciously intent upon God with all the heart, soul, and mind, little or no

[28]*De deligendo Deo,* chs. 8–10.

consideration being given to self-development for its own sake.

The virtues of the hedonist, the Roman citizen and soldier, and the Stoic sage all alike have their origin in some love. They "arise from" the love of pleasure, love of glory, love of self; they are "forms of" love "arising from" each of these several sorts of love. Similarly, virtues of Christian character are "forms of" and "arise from" man's love for God.[1]

A simple paraphrase of Augustine may now be used to indicate the theory of virtue which results from transposing his account, in both its analytic and genetic aspects, from the context of *caritas*-love for God to that of *agape*-love for neighbor:

> Virtue is nothing else than the perfect love of the neighbor, and love of neighbor calls for virtues of character. The traditional fourfold division of virtue is taken from four forms of this love. The virtues, the forms any love assumes, are Christian virtues or forms of Christian love when and insofar as the beloved object which has evoked their formation is the neighbor and not the self or any "value." However, Christian virtues arise from this love. Insofar as a Christian loves his neighbor well and wisely, it will be discovered that his character takes on various kinds of reliability which we call virtues. He does not love his neighbor merely for the sake of cultivating in himself a good moral character; nor does he value character for its own sake, lest he be separated from his neighbor by reason of pride in his own goodness. Good moral character, Christian moral character, is rather the unintended result or by-product of loving one's neighbor with the full and undivided view that the neighbor's welfare be served as wisely as possible; or else, insofar as intended, it is intended *vocationally* for the sake of the neighbor. Whether virtue be fourfold or manifold, the traditional doctrine of four cardinal virtues indicates traits of character which sincere love, and most of all Christian love, calls forth. A neighbor-ward oriented life will come to have at least these four fundamental qualities, lest the neighbor suffer loss.
>
> In general, temperance is love giving itself entirely to that which is loved, so that we may express the definition of temperance in the Christian sense as love keeping itself entire and incorrupt for the sake of others. Temperance is the ability to

[1] The expression "forms of" occurs in *On the Morals of the Catholic Church*, xv; "arising from" in chap. xxv of the same work (*Basic Writings*, I, 331, 342).

promise a kind of integrity and incorruption in the love by which we serve our neighbors. The love, then, of which we speak, which ought with all sanctity to burn in desire for the good of others, is called temperance in not being turned aside or seeking after any selfish thing.

In general, fortitude or courage is love readily bearing all things for the object loved, whatever it be; so that we may express the definition of courage in the Christian sense thus: Christian fortitude is love bearing everything readily for the sake of the neighbor. The love, then, of which we speak, which ought in all sanctity to burn in concern for others, is called fortitude, in bearing the loss of selfish things in order to persevere in Christian service. To insure that this love gives way before no troubles, no matter how grievous, is the part of Christian courage.

Justice generally is love securing only the loved object, whatever it be, and therefore ruling all else rightly; so that we may express the definition of justice as a personal Christian attitude thus: It is love so intent on securing the true welfare of the neighbor that a man rules himself and assesses with an impartial judgment uncorrupted by self-interest the claims and counterclaims that come before him.

In general, prudence or practical wisdom in making everyday decisions is love distinguishing with sagacity between what hinders it and what helps it; so that we may express the definition thus: Christian prudence is love making a right distinction between what is to be desired and what to be shunned with a view to this end. To be ever watchful lest crafty self-interest steal in and defraud the neighbor is the part of prudence. Christian prudence or practical wisdom is "the mind of love"; the neighbor is its "heart."[2]

In this way a more thorough Christianization of elements of pagan philosophy, left unreformed in the mind of St. Augustine, may be secured. Moreover, greater lucidity and strength are given Augustine's own ethical analysis by this correction of his view of Christian love, suggesting the validity of the proposed shift of emphasis from the first to the second love-commandment in his interpretation of the unity and source of virtue.

St. Augustine's criticism of all virtues other than those of a

[2]The words in quotation marks are taken from the title of Father M. C. D'Arcy's recent book, *The Mind and Heart of Love*, Holt, 1947.

Christian as only "splendid vices" and his statement "that where there is no true religion there are no true virtues," as they stand, have uncertain meaning and doubtful truth. The ethical judgment that the virtues of natural men at their best are "rather vices than virtues so long as there is no reference to God in the matter"[3] is an obscure verdict made in a dim religious light, if, indeed, it be not sheer authoritarian exaggeration. In Augustine's view, of course, these judgments follow from certain perfectly clear metaphysical distinctions: Human desire or love should conform to the gradations in being. It is better to love a creature higher in the scale of being than one which is lower; and love is most truly virtuous when it has for object God who is himself perfect being. Augustine's criticism of the pagan virtues would be strengthened if made first of all on ethical and not on metaphysical grounds.

In the suggested revision of this position and its reorientation around love for neighbor, the statement that virtues are rather vices than virtues so long as there is no reference to the *neighbor* in the matter has definite ethical meaning and may be defended, without reference to metaphysics, as an entirely accurate account of moral experience. In this sense, only a Christian virtue is a virtue; the rest are "splendid vices." Not alone are the cardinal and other natural virtues subject to deterioration in all their splendor the more concern for self supplants concern for neighbor as the central reason for self-discipline, but the same applies also to qualities of character often supposed to be distinctly Christian—humility and the so-called theological virtues.

The early Christians were not charitable out of prudence. They were prudent or practically wise out of charity. Love for neighbor made these otherwise socially and economically naïve people exceedingly shrewd in the administration of charity, caring for the needy without pauperizing them. Soon, however, Christians let their eyes waver from their neighbors' benefit; their gaze turned inward by way of turning toward merit in heaven; they continued to be charitable for prudence's sake. Both prudence and charity then became "splendid vices," still splendid on ac-

[3]*City of God*, XIX, 25 (*Basic Writings*, II, 504).

count of the discipline and liberality they induced, vicious on account of the neighbor whose welfare they ignored so successfully. As selfish calculation, prudence was no longer Christian; at the same time it was no longer really virtuous. Charity became the "splendid vice" of alms-giving. The "use" of the neighbor for the sake of the enjoyment of God here attains a denouement which clearly reveals the Neo-Platonic (and the universally human) rather than the Christian parentage of any attempt to ground the unity and origin of virtue in man's love for God. Thus, in order to establish on *ethical* grounds the validity of Augustine's severe criticism of non-Christian virtues, his conception of Christian love must be revised. Unqualified agreement may then be given to the view that such love evokes virtue. From love virtue "arises." Bend your energies on other people's necessities and you will see your way clearly enough. To be Christian, to be really virtuous, virtue must concern itself more with other people's necessities than with the strengthening of one's own character or with one's own "confounded principles."

(b) *The Infusion of Virtue*

Aquinas held that the distinctly Christian virtues—faith, hope, and charity—were not to be acquired by any kind or amount of human effort, but have their origin in an infusion of character by God's grace. An incidental objection to this position, and to the general theory and practice of the Roman Catholic church, is that the operation of infusing grace is confined to the seven sacraments as the sole channels or means of grace. A more fundamental objection is to the whole notion of infusing grace and to the idea that human character is perfected miraculously. Ethical phenomena should be explained in ethical terms; and if divine grace is thought to be relevant to matters of morality, its operation *upon us* cannot be mechanical but must be, quite explicitly, an operation *with us* as cooperating moral agents.[4] This

---

[4]Aquinas, of course, denies this: ". . . Virtue which directs man to good as defined by divine law, and not by human reason, cannot be caused by human acts, whose principle is reason, but is produced in us by the divine operation alone. Hence Augustine, in giving the definition of this virtue, inserts the words, *which God works in us without us*" (*Summa Theologica*, I–II, Q. 63, art. 2, *Basic Writings of St. Thomas Aquinas*, ed. Anton C. Pegis, Random House, 1945, II, 484).

suggests a reinterpretation of the infusion of virtue as meaning rather the *elicitation* of virtue or virtue arising from love.

The grace which infuses faith, hope, and charity into a Christian's character may go further, according to Aquinas, and infuse moral virtues as well. There is an infused temperance taking the place of and supplementing any deficiency in the acquired virtue of temperance. Likewise, infused fortitude, infused justice, and infused prudence are available to the Christian to the degree that there is defect in his acquired fortitude, justice, or prudence. So also for the remaining moral virtues subordinate to the cardinal ones. Thus, there is a table of infused moral virtues exactly identical with St. Thomas' table of acquired moral virtue, each bearing the same name and referring to almost the same essential quality of character. These duplicate sets of virtues differ mainly in that their source is different. One is acquired by following Aristotle's recommendations; failing this or in addition to this, the other is available through infused grace in the sacraments.[5]

The experience behind this theory of infused moral virtue is described much better as a process of the elicitation of virtue by Christian love, love grounded, of course, in Christian faith. St. Thomas gives an illustration of a simple old Christian lady whose entire life has been spent in circumstances not calling for special courage and who therefore did not have a very highly developed habit of courage in the structure of her character. Nevertheless, she might suddenly and without practice *prove* courageous even to the point of martyrdom. The early Christian martyrs were not, in the main, persons habituated to courage in the Aristotelian sense; they were *made* courageous by their response to God through loyalty and obedient love. The theory explaining these manifestations of strength of character by reference to infusing grace is more questionable than the data themselves.

Augustine's account of virtue arising from love is both a more ethical and a more plausible interpretation of the facts. It is true he thought this love itself was directly infused by grace becoming a quality or attribute of human moral goodness, while we have

[5]*Summa Theologica*, I–II, Q. 63, art. 3; Q. 65, arts. 2 and 3.

suggested that Christian love be regarded as the work of faith in the heart—faith in the graciousness and the faithfulness of God. Nevertheless, in expressing the connection between love and the virtues Augustine always sticks close to concrete moral experience. All the virtues may be regarded as aspects of moral goodness "infused," so to speak, from the cherished *end* "backward" into character; they are Christian moral virtues if they have been produced by reverberation from man's love for God. The expression "elicited" or "evoked virtue," unlike "infused virtue," rightly suggests an operation in us of our own love or devotion to something other than our own character calling for habits of strength in us.

The Reformers also believed in the infusion of moral goodness by Divine grace, operating "preveniently" and beyond sacramental limitation. Thus, Calvin accounted for much of man's observable goodness by reference to supernatural "restraining grace":

> For in all ages there have been some persons, who, from the mere dictates of nature, have devoted their whole lives to the pursuit of virtue. And though many errors might perhaps be discovered in their conduct, yet by their pursuit of virtue they afforded proof, that there was some degree of purity in their nature. . . . These examples . . . seem to teach us that we should not consider human nature to be totally corrupted; since, from its instinctive bias, some men have not only been eminent for noble actions, but have uniformly conducted themselves in a most virtuous manner through the whole course of their lives. But here we ought to remember, that amidst this corruption of nature there is some room for Divine grace, not to purify it, but internally to restrain its operations. For should the Lord permit the minds of all men to give up the reins to every lawless passion, there certainly would not be an individual in the world, whose actions would not evince all the crimes, for which Paul condemns human nature in general, to be most truly applicable to him. . . . Thus God by his providence restrains the perverseness of our nature from breaking out into external acts, but does not purify it within. . . .[6]

Surely this is absurd. Instead of taking man's observable good-

[6]John Calvin: *The Institutes of the Christian Religion,* II, iii, 3 (*A Compend of the Institutes of the Christian Religion,* edited by Hugh Thomson Kerr, Jr., The Westminster Press, 1939, pp. 48–49).

ness into account by revising his original hypothesis concerning total depravity, Calvin bolsters it by adopting a second hypothesis, tracing home the goodness he plainly sees in men to an operation, not of human nature, but of supernatural grace. As a consequence of this queer reasoning, the ground is cut from under any man's taking personal goodness as an occasion for pride in his own powers. This is of importance for ethics, especially for Christian ethics which regards Pharisaism as man's gravest peril. Nevertheless, commending humility in this manner not only is logically suspect but also, as we shall soon see, it does not plumb the depth and nature of true humility. Instead of reviving Catholic notions of grace as a substance actually infused into human character, the same ethical interest in putting down pride and inducing humility might better have been served by sticking to insights more distinctive of the Reformation: grace as God's graciousness toward us, and the Gospel ethic as the mirror of the Word in which all men, viewing themselves, are brought down to nothing in their own eyes.

(c) *The Acquirement of Virtue*

Accepting the foregoing interpretation of the ethical truth behind the theory of infusion, it is possible both to make greater room in Christian ethics for semi-Aristotelian effort to attain virtue and at the same time to extend the Christianization of character further than Aquinas found possible. Aristotle had spoken only of the deliberate acquirement of virtue. Augustine had spoken only of the elicitation of virtue by love based on faith. Aquinas attempts a synthesis of the two, but in such fashion as to break the backs of both, attributing virtue to its source in intentional acquirement for only part of the way and then turning to infusion, or what we now may call "unintended elicitation," for the rest. An explanation of the genesis of character is needed which recognizes that both intentional acquirement and unintended elicitation may each, separately or together, cover the entire ground in originating moral goodness.

Such a view is indeed suggested by Aquinas' two sets of moral virtues entirely duplicating each other. This is not, as may appear, a violation of the principle of parsimony: there are not two different virtues in us, each named temperance. Yet there really are two sources of the single virtue of temperance. We may build up in ourselves virtuous habits by concentrating on their cultivation. At the same time or in addition to this, virtuous habits are elicited or built up in us as quite unintended consequences whenever we control our various impulses and sublimate them for the sake of something else altogether other than ourselves and our own goodness. Moral character is very often "infused backward" from the ends we care about, although none can deny that deliberate effort can often do much to acquire it. These two sources converge upon each other in almost all character development. Virtue arises from these two sources not simply as two habits deserving the same name because of similarity but as identically the same habit capable of bearing only one name. There is a single habit of temperance, acquired by direct action upon ourselves or indirectly elicited in us or, more probably, both. Courage also is a single habit, acquired by direct action upon ourselves or indirectly elicited or both. And so on throughout the manifold of character.

When Paul says that "love is patient and kind; love is not jealous or boastful; it is not arrogant or rude. Love does not insist on its own way; it is not irritable or resentful; it does not rejoice at wrong, but rejoices in the right. Love bears all things, believes all things, hopes all things, endures all things" (I Cor. 13:4–7), he is listing some of the qualities which love elicits. On the other hand, if a man has already acquired in some degree such control of himself as to be patient and kind, not jealous, boastful, arrogant, rude, irritable, or resentful and in a measure is one who can believe, hope, and endure, he is likely to be a better servant of the ends of Christian love than he would be without these abilities.

There may need to be, of course, a Christianization of virtues already acquired in the service of the self or some end other than the neighbor; but this does not mean that a Christian cannot also be consciously concerned about acquiring virtue. In addition to deriving virtue indirectly as an unintended by-product of love for neighbor, a Christian needs also a conscious intention to improve himself vocationally for his neighbor's sake.

To have integrity of character evoked, is nevertheless more important than to cultivate character, even though the two processes are in constant reciprocity. Men do not first dress themselves up and then wonder where to go. Ordinarily they dress because they know where they are going. More Christian virtue arises from the elicitations of love supervening as unintended results, than from a neighbor-regarding, vocational pursuit of self-development. In either case, however, the righteousness of the Pharisees is exceeded and the Narcissus taken out of man's awareness of the beauty of holiness.

This view of the place which effort to acquire virtue has in Christian ethics meets an objection often raised by Protestant theologians.

> The Bible ethic remains throughout an *ethic of present decision.* . . . Obedience is too concrete to be reduced to a qualitative attribute. Man does not obey by learning the *art* or developing the *habit* of obedience. Obedience to God cannot be absorbed into a stable character pattern so that each subsequent decision becomes easier and more assured. . . . However many times repeated, it does not become a fixed personality trait. Every present moment presents a new occasion for disobedience as well as a new need for divine help. When one objectifies obedience as a virtue to be cultivated, his choices become determined by his relation *to that virtue* rather than by relation to God. And obedience to one's own virtue is far removed from obedience to God. When transferred from the area of contemporaneous demand to the area of character development, obedience may easily be turned into its opposite.[7]

This passage illustrates excellently the difficulty of ever developing a theory of virtue within Protestant theological ethics. However, the idea that moral goodness has its source partly in an intentional although vocational cultivation of virtue does not

[7]Paul Minear, *Eyes of Faith,* Westminster Press, 1946, p. 48.

fall into these errors. Love of neighbor, which is a Christian's obedience to God and the source of his virtue, is never *itself* a "habit," "stable character pattern," or "fixed personality trait." It is always a "present decision." However many times repeated, it does not become easier or more assured. Such obedient love is not a virtue; it *has* virtues. Love is a relation by which one man exists for another. Every present moment presents a new occasion for using virtuous habit either self-centeredly or vocationally. This decision is not easier but must be made again, no matter how far character has developed or whether virtue has previously been gained intentionally by acquirement or unintentionally by evocation. The choices of a man who seeks virtue vocationally are not determined by his relation to character for *its* or *his* own sake but by his relation to virtue as *among his duties to his neighbor*. Obedience to one's own virtue *with the neighbor's benefit in view* is always a present decision not far removed from obedience to God.

(d) *Virtue and Forgiveness, According to the Principles of the Reformation*

The foregoing analysis of the origin of virtue leads to the conclusion that virtues are elicited, not infused, and elicited by Christian love for neighbor, not by love for God. How is this position distinguishable from a simple humanitarianism? One difference is that ethical humanism is grounded on the infinite inherent value of *human* personality in general, while the view here suggested proceeds on the inherently more Christian principle of infinite preference for the *neighbor's* welfare. But still it may be asked: Does not a Christian's relation to God have decisive influence upon his character? Is not virtue derived from relation to God as well as from duty to neighbor? This seems altogether excluded by the rejection of *caritas*-love for God and infused grace. Are not faith, humility, obedience, and gratitude—which have been retained in place of "love" to characterize, from the human side, man's relation to God—themselves qualities essential to Christian character?

The answer is, first, that these qualities are each a response of the human spirit to the forgiving graciousness of God disclosed in Christ and have their source in the constraint of this love of God for man. And, secondly, they are not virtues alongside other virtues, Christian virtue added, as Aquinas believed, to Aristotle's list; they are characteristics of man's God-relationship which, along with *agape*-love for neighbor, unify and Christianize all his virtues. Faith, humility, obedience, and gratitude are relations of the *whole* character to its source in God's forgiving graciousness in Christ, just as love is a relation by which the self *with all its virtues* exists for another. The sources of virtue are by no means complete without making the most of the important shift made by the Reformation from the Catholic understanding of God's grace as infusing power to an understanding of grace as grace for justification manifesting itself as God's attitude of gracious forgiveness toward men. Humility may be taken as an illustration of a quality of Christian life which cannot be fully understood except in relation to divine forgiveness.

Humility as a virtue among other cultivated virtues can, along with charity and the virtues of the Romans, become a "splendid vice." Considered simply as an additional virtue, humility may be merely another way in which the self stands in relation only to itself and not to any other being, God or his neighbor. Thus, Anders Nygren writes, ". . . In reckoning his own humility as a way of fellowship with God, as entitling him to an imperishable value in God's sight, [a person] is in truth not humble at all."[8] And Nietzsche said, "He who despises himself feels at the same time a certain respect for himself as being the despiser of himself."[9] Humility as a separate virtue may be employed by pride as a way of attracting more attention.

Humility can *neither* be cultivated *nor* elicited by Christian love. Like love itself, humility springs always from present decision; it cannot be grown. Since every new deed in the moment it is done stands under the same danger, moral goodness cannot

[8]*Agape and Eros*, Macmillan, 1941, Part I, p. 89.
[9]*Beyond Good and Evil*, 78.

be saved from peril of pharisaism by some additional "work." No more can humility be thought of as elicited by Christian love for neighbor, because, without faith and humility as its precondition, Christian love itself would never come into existence. Christian humility arises when all virtues together "come down from aloft," and this has decisive relation to "our blessed Redeemer" who "came down to redeem our whole man-of-war world; to that end mixing with its sailors and sinners as equals."

> Our conception is framed according to this notion, when we believe that God was made man for us, as an example of humility, and to show the love of God toward us. For this it is which it is good for us to believe, and to retain firmly and unshakenly in our heart, that the humility by which God was born of a woman, and was led to death through contumelies so great by mortal men, is the chiefest remedy by which the swelling of our pride may be cured, and the profound mystery by which the bond of sin may be loosed.[10]

God as gracious to us in Christ evokes humility in its ultimate degree, for these are in fact the same: Christian humility and the acknowledgment that we live wholly from Divine forgiveness.

Moreover, the fact that humility is a relation of all the virtues to divine forgiveness is also suggested by the paradoxical relationship between Christian humility and a great man's estimate of himself, between Christian humility and an Aristotelian estimate of personal merit. "A story is current that when some one expressed amazement over the size of the fortune which Mr. Churchill demanded for the journalistic exploitation of his memoirs he justified the price with the assertion that since Cæsar no one but him had mastered the three arts of political strategy, military tactics, and their recording for posterity. This possibly apocryphal dictum represents a rare instance of uninhibited self-esteem corresponding with the truth."[11] Now, Winston Churchill may actually not be a paragon of Christian humility, but noth-

[10]St. Augustine, *On the Trinity,* vii, 5 (*Basic Writings of St. Augustine,* ed. by Whitney J. Oates, Random House, 1948, II, 778).
[11]Reinhold Niebuhr, "Churchill's Hour," a review of *The Gathering Storm* by Winston Churchill, *The Nation,* June 26, 1948, p. 720.

ing in the nature of Christian humility requires a great man to make a mistake about himself and think less highly of himself than he ought to think, or pretend to do so.

Aristotle calls a man modest "who estimates himself lowly and at the same time justly" or correctly "as a man of average ability." His "greatminded" man is one who "values himself highly and at the same time justly" because in fact he *is* a great man. Each of these has as much humility as he reasonably ought to have. The vain man is one who "values himself highly without just ground."[12] Not every one who repeats the criticism that Aristotle has no place for humility really disagrees with his statement, "He that values himself below his real worth is smallminded." No definition of humility as a virtue can be in frontal opposition to Aristotle's notion of reasonable modesty and reasonable pride.

As a Christian, however, Gilbert Keith Chesterton had a different view of humility:

> . . . Every generous person [will] agree that the one kind of pride which is wholly damnable is the pride of the man who has something to be proud of. The pride which, proportionately speaking, does not hurt the character is the pride in the things which reflect no credit on the person at all. Thus it does a man no harm to be proud of his country, and comparatively little harm to be proud of his remote ancestors. It does him more harm to be proud of having made money, because in that he has a little more reason for pride. It does him more harm still to be proud of what is nobler than money—intellect. And it does him most harm of all to value himself for the most valuable thing on earth—goodness. The man who is proud of what is really creditable to him is the Pharisee, the man whom Christ himself could not forbear to strike.[13]

Christian humility does not contest the ground with a reasonable estimate of merit or a sense of moral achievement. At the same time, the greater the virtue, the more Christian humility reduces all realized qualities of character by setting them in relation to

12*Nicomachean Ethics*, 1123b.
13*Heretics*, John Lane Co., 1905, p. 169.

a divine perfection which transcends them—a relation whose nature is most clearly specified by St. Paul and Martin Luther in their conviction concerning God's surprising condescension toward man.

There can be no true humility without some sense, implicit or explicit, of one's relation to God, an acknowledgment that man lives out his existence under a power and a goodness which are above him. The ethics of Confucianism, having no place for the God-relationship, has no place for humility. In the humanistic ethics of Confucianism one man is always measured against another; never does man measure himself against the ultimate. As a consequence, the highest virtue for Confucianism is the Good-for-man-in-relation-to-another, represented by the Chinese character depicting one two-legged creature in horizontal connection with a possible second such creature: $\overbrace{}$=[14]. Then follow the virtues of Rightness, Ritual or Decorum, Wisdom, and Sincerity or Good faith. But no humility.

Taoism, in contrast, begins to measure man against the ultimate, the *Tao* above him and according to this view within him. And as a consequence Taoism finds room for humility among the virtues. The religious ethic here in question, a form of pantheism, stresses, along with humility, the virtue of Naturalness or Effortlessness, Purity, Simplicity or Weakness, Gentleness, etc. Moreover, humility is defined largely by reference to man in his condition of greatest dependence (infancy) and by reference to that which is lowest in nature (the ravine, water seeking the lowest level, etc.). Contrasting with this, Christian humility has decisive orientation, not toward God in general or God in everything or God gravitating downward, but toward God in Christ freely seeking the lowliest by an act of love. Nevertheless, the presence of humility among the Taoist virtues shows the primary difference between religious and humanistic ethics. Whatever may be the defects in the actual lives of nominally religious people, the God-relationship even in the religious ethics of pan-

[14]The Chinese character *jen*. For a discussion of *human-heartedness*, see Fêng Yu-lan, *A History of Chinese Philosophy: Period of the Philosophers*. Peiping, H. Vetch, 1937, pp. 69–73, 120–121.

theism, conceived as being vitally important for man, tends to produce an ideal of humility as one of the chief qualities human beings should possess. No doubt in forms of *theistic* ethic humility has ground for a higher degree of intensity, on account of man's measuring himself in the light of an infinite qualitative distinction between Creator and creature. In any case, there is always some reference to God in the matter of humility.

Among types of Christian ethical outlook, the meaning of humility varies with how men are convinced God deals with them. Is he the one on whom men absolutely depend? Is he the source of an infusion by grace of a new substance into moral character? Is he at once the fullness of the stature of Christ and the one who forgives? The meaning of humility changes significantly, if ever so slightly, according to *which* of these references to God primarily enters into the heart of the matter.

Christian humility cannot be sufficiently constituted by a man's lively sense of his dependence on God for everything he is and has. Recognizing that frequently it is more exhilarating to give than to receive, St. Francis wanted his friars to be willing to receive alms, to have the humility of recipients of favor. He had a profound sense of man's general dependence upon God. ". . . The greater the gifts and graces God bestows upon us, the greater ought our humility to be; for without humility no virtue is acceptable to God."[15] Yet such an acknowledgment of dependence is possible within the perspective of any religion (*e.g.*, Taoism) or else, more specifically, it may have reference only to God's grace understood as infusing power. This is not enough. The man who went up to the temple to pray was not only a man of great righteousness (thus qualifying as Aristotle's greatminded man), but also he was willing to *thank God* that he was not as other men are. A good man can thank God continuously for his goodness, he can be wholly possessed by what Schleiermacher called a sense of his absolute dependence, he can recognize himself as the recipient of infused grace, and still be a Pharisee.

[15] *The Little Flowers of St. Francis*, chap. xii (Everyman ed., p. 22).

Reasonable judgment upon ourselves becomes humble only from comparing ourselves with the perfection of divine love in Jesus Christ. From questioning ourselves in relation to others, there is no man living who cannot worm himself around so as to feel flattered. From questioning ourselves in relation to Jesus, however, and seeing ourselves in "the mirror of the Word," none of us can come off justified. Only by ceasing to compare ourselves exclusively with one another will the pride be taken out of even our just estimates of ourselves and our pious thanksgiving to God for these merits. Comparing ourselves with Christ produces in us a lively sense of sin, and for the first time a sense of humble equality with all men before God. "This is the edification there is in the thought that before God we are always in the wrong."[16] For "all have sinned," said Paul, "and come short of the glory of God"—the glory of God as it has shone forth in the face of Jesus Christ. With this Word and not one another as the standard by which we measure ourselves, humility is assured no matter how far we progress in the moral life or how virtuous we become.

Confession of sin requires deeper humility than acknowledgment of dependence. Yet:

> How much more crushing than the most pitiless conviction of our present sinful state is even the feeblest conviction that there will be eternal justification for our temporal existence. Only our strength in supporting this second conviction, which in its purity completely subsumes the first, is the measure of faith.[17]

Even more pitiless than conviction of ever-present sin is the pitiless hound-of-heavenly love. To be willing to receive favors, to be willing to acknowledge sin, and to be willing to be forgiven represent increasing degrees of self-renunciation. To acknowledge dependence means willingness not to play the agent; to confess sin means willingness to have acted otherwise and confession is itself another act; to receive forgiveness means willingness to have

[16]Soren Kierkegaard, *Either-Or,* Princeton University Press, 1944, Vol. II, p. 287.
[17]Franz Kafka, "Reflections on Sin, Pain, Hope, and the True Way," 95, in *The Great Wall of China* (Schocken Books, 1946), p. 303.

the past entirely annulled and our lives begun on a new basis, and that not by any action of our own, not even the act of confession. Christian humility flows also from the edification there is in the thought that before God we are always, by his gracious forgiveness alone, in the right. Dostoyevsky described such a humble relation to God in words that might well have been a comment on Jesus' parable of the Last Judgment: "Thy sins which are many are forgiven thee for thou hast loved much. . . . This is why I receive them, oh ye wise, this is why I receive them, oh ye of understanding, *that not one of them believed himself to be worthy of this.*"[18] True humility must always have some reference to justifying grace in the matter. A humble man lives with his entire being simultaneously sinful, penitent, and justified; and this last, his forgiveness, subsumes the rest. The so-called "virtues," humility and faith, then, are responses decisively oriented toward the infinite graciousness of God who put forward Christ.

III. THE IMMODERATE LIFE

Augustine described temperance not as restraining all impulses but as restraining all competing impulses except one, so that love might give itself entirely and *without restraint* to that which is loved. On this view, the Greek ideal of moderation is set aside. Jesus' "ethic of the extreme" gains supremacy over Aristotle's "doctrine of the mean" and over the curbing of all passions in the Stoic ideal. According to Augustine, temperance and the other virtues are, so to speak, forms of an *intemperate* love for God. There can never be too much love for God, nor too little of the impulses which impede it.

Plato had pointed out that the virtues with which seekers after pleasure serve their "chief end" are simply forms of an intemperate love for pleasure. In the hedonist, moderate enjoyment of immediate pleasure and courage in the face of present peril are disciplines flowing from his fundamental intemperance. Thus,

[18] *The Brothers Karamazov*, Pt. I, ch. ii.

Plato describes ordinary men as temperate because they are immoderate:

> For there are pleasures, which they are afraid of losing; and in their desire to keep them, they abstain from some pleasures, because they are overcome by others; and although to be conquered by pleasure is called by men intemperance, to them the conquest of pleasure consists in being conquered by pleasure. And that is what I mean by saying that, in a sense, they are made temperate through intemperance.[1]

However, this seeming contradiction does not disprove the value of virtues derived from the love of pleasure, since it holds true with regard to any virtues whatever relative to their end. The temperance and courage of the Romans were forms arising from their intemperate love for personal prestige and honor or for the glory and power of the empire. The so-called "bourgeois" virtues—thrift, sobriety, and industry—the admirable self-discipline of the business and professional man two generations ago, arose from an intemperate ambition for success in a secular "calling."

The same is true of a theory of moral virtue for its own sake which ostensibly extends moderation throughout the whole analysis of moral goodness. One thing Aristotle is immoderate about: the pursuit of moderation. One thing he is intemperate about: the love of wisdom. The Stoics were tremendously concerned about withdrawing from all concern. The one thing over which they could be vitally perturbed was their own imperturbability, as that Stoic evidenced who committed suicide because he scratched his little finger.

Similarly, Augustine spoke of virtues subordinate to a quite intemperate love for God. For the sake of an enthusiastic love, impulses which are potential hindrances thereto will be sublimated and habitually restrained.

In spite of the influence of Aristotle upon him, Thomas Aquinas likewise Christianizes character by shifting from the moderate to an immoderate life as an ultimate ideal. According to Aquinas, infusing grace, which penetrates to the ground floor of character

[1] *Phaedo*, 69 (Jowett).

to add infused moral virtues, continues operative at this same level by the successive addition of "gifts," "fruits," and "beatitudes." These stages of infused moral perfection, from infused virtues to the beatitudes, accomplish the transition from Aristotelian moderation to Christian immoderation and asceticism.

It has been previously said that acquired and infused moral virtues differ only in their source and not in their essential nature. This is not quite true. Infused moral virtues begin to draw the Christian away just a little from the Greek ideal of moderation. Aristotle advises the curbing of too ardent desire for the sake of more continuous health of body and more serene operation of man's intellectual faculties. Through infused temperance, however, a Christian moderates his bodily appetites, not simply for the sake of these finite goods or for more perfect "activity of the soul" in accordance with reason, virtue, and degrees of human excellence, but for the sake of his unqualifiedly enthusiastic love for God. To the degree that the human soul is loyally subject to God and perfectly obedient, a proportionately greater emphasis will, as a consequence, be placed upon subjecting the body to the soul. Thus, by infusion of moral virtue, a Christian is shifted slightly to the ascetic extreme, though he still engages in the moderate satisfaction of desire. "The theological virtues are indeed beyond the range of natural ethic and must be infused by divine grace," Wicksteed comments, "but when so infused they can raise the Aristotelian virtues to a higher degree of intensity and carry them beyond their sober limitations into a region of more aggressive and enthusiastic activity, for they take down into the very springs of action and the inmost sense of values a transforming spirit of charity."[2]

The remaining three waves of influence, "gifts," "fruits," "beatitudes," complete this process of altering the very definition of virtue. These words refer to passages in the New Testament which classify traits of Christian character. While the virtues (acquired or infused) moderate a man's desire for wealth and honor, the "gifts" and "fruits" lead him to despise these things and the "beati-

[2]Philip H. Wicksteed, *The Reactions Between Dogma and Philosophy*, London: Williams and Norgate, 1920, p. 493.

tudes" crown him with poverty of spirit. The several Aristotelian virtues under the name-virtue, courage, moderate the hopes, fears, and angers of the "irascible appetites" (passions irritated by difficulty), but a Christian is finally set free from them by blessed meekness. The virtues grouped under temperance moderate the "concupiscible appetites," while "gifts," "fruits," and "beatitudes" find these satisfactions unnecessary and finally call it a greater blessing to be mournful.[3]

Indeed, contrary to his recommendations for men in the thirteenth century, Aquinas declares that no man can be an Aristotelian in heaven. Need for personal moral virtues will have ceased with the cessation of recalcitrant impulses in the body. Of social moral virtues only justice, or rendering to another his due, will remain, and that chiefly in its subspecies, religion, or rendering to God his due. Of intellectual virtues only the most formal ones shall remain, those by which we grasp truth intuitively. Indeed, faith will disappear in sight, hope will be supplanted by realization, love or union with God alone remaining of the theological virtues.[4]

Thus, when we are through with the Christianization of the virtues, or rather when the infusing grace of God is through with us, or rather when the eliciting power of great love for God is through with us, the Aristotelian way of moderation is left entirely behind, and inserted in its place is a Christian ascetic ideal. Moderation in everything becomes in principle asceticism in almost everything. This results simply from being from the beginning explicitly and unlimitedly immoderate about *one* thing, love for God. From this acknowledged intemperance, all other satisfactions fall under more severe restriction. To a great extent, as we have seen, Aquinas agrees with Augustine that, while splendid, a virtue such as prudence in the service of some earthly or evil end is not really virtuous; without charity and a reference to true religion in the matter, there are no true virtues. The foregoing analysis makes clear that, *with* charity and true religion at the heart of the matter, the virtues will become utterly dif-

---

[3]*Summa Theologica*, I–II, Qq. 68–70, esp. Q. 69, art. 3.
[4]*Ibid.* Q. 67: "On the Duration of the Virtues after this Life."

ferent from what otherwise they are supposed to be. With charity and all the other supernatural renovations of human character which follow, the ideal of the "golden mean" is reformed away. Aquinas' account of Christian character in its most perfect expression shifts, through these stages of infused Christianization, so far to the side of ascetic self-denial that one wonders why, if he was pointing toward this position, he ever took the trouble to begin with Aristotelian moderation.

The value of immoderation in the moral life is indubitable. When the end a person has in view is clearly apprehended, when the object of his love is powerfully attractive, then the virtues or forms in which this love springs into effectiveness are not likely to be the moderate type, nor ought they to be. Instead of stopping short with just so much restraint of diverting impulses, a good man will expel them altogether. The measure of his asceticism about other tempting goals will be set only by the degree of hindrance these things put in the way of the good chiefly desired. Martyrdom may even be the final form his goodness takes. Christian ethics is emancipated from all preconceived rules and laws by Christian love for neighbor *permitting* everything to be done which the neighbor needs, absolutely everything without a single exception. Christian love *requiring* everything the neighbor needs, absolutely everything without a single exception, also delivers Christian ethics from a predecision that the nature of virtue is Aristotelian moderation.

In contrast to the virtues of reasonable, temperate living stand the intemperate religious attitudes, faith venturing beyond the limits of what is neatly demonstrable, hope remaining expectant when the conditions do not warrant it, love forgiving the unpardonable. These are the exuberant, jubilant virtues; and Christians know that without such enthusiasm there can be no religion —no, nor much living either. Hope is the typical "theological virtue" when these are considered as characteristics of immoderate Christian living.

Hope springs in part, like faith and humility, from man's relation to God. St. Paul wrote of Abraham that "when all hope was gone, he hoped on in faith." This means that Abraham continued to expect a manifestation of divine power through miracle; his virtue, therefore, was not unlike the Catholic conception of hope gained from infused grace. Protestant ethics would contend, however, and correctly, that Christian hope is more firmly grounded in the new beginning made possible again and again by forgiveness and by the possibility it brings of life on a new basis. When all love and hope are gone, a Christian lives on, hopeful and loving, by faith—a faith convinced that God's gracious forgiveness and renewal are "for me and for thee." No doubt such trust in God provides always the primary, creative source of hope. God mixing with this world's sailors and sinners as equals, God as gracious to us in Christ, enables hopefulness to be renewed in face of the ultimate degree of despair. For these two are actually the same: Christian hope and the acknowledgment that we live again wholly from forgiveness come down from aloft.

However, Paul traces hope to another source when he writes that "love hopeth all things." Here too the essential intemperance of Christian ethics becomes wholly explicit. Ordinary teachers of wisdom, such as Aristotle, treat hope as an emotion which needs curbing, so that we habituate ourselves to expect only a little —the little we prudently have a right to expect. Christian ethics finds that love for neighbor, measured by the controlling love of Christ, stretches hope far beyond prudent moderation. Christian love goes to the extreme of hoping all things, and this only an everlasting love, or a love perpetually renewed, can accomplish.

Hence the Apostle does not say that youth or temperament but love "hopeth all things." No moment even of highest enthusiasm can succeed in hoping all things at once. For then comes the next moment or the next day or year, and if a man does not continue to live in anticipation, then is it disclosed that formerly he did not hope all things. Hope must be given reality anew in every moment of our conscious existence; we can now have hope for the future, but we cannot now have our future hopes. Paul's description of Christian love hoping all things sets for such love the task of *"always hoping."*[5] Neither can one learn such hope

[5]Soren Kierkegaard, *Works of Love,* Princeton University Press, 1943, pp. 199–213 *passim.*

from age and experience, since obedience to God and the love by which a man exists for another are always present decisions and, no matter how many other virtues they elicit and accumulate, cannot themselves be stock-piled into a habit.

Nor can external conditions ever give sufficient warrant for always hoping. As Chesterton says, hope means expectancy when things are otherwise hopeless or it is no virtue. "For practical purposes it is at the hopeless moment that we require the hopeful man, and the virtue either does not exist at all or begins to exist at that moment. Exactly when hope ceases to be reasonable, it begins to be useful."[6] Confidence grounded in external conditions is not Christian hope; it is merely calculating common sense. What Paul means by hope, always hoping so as eventually to hope all things, springs from within; it is an enthusiasm perpetually renewed out of the fires of Christian love, issuing out of the spirits of men with transforming power upon the otherwise hopeless conditions which surround them.

There is not much difference whether we say that Christian hope springs from Christ's self-emptying love for man (the love of Christ controlling us) or from love of neighbor as one's self, since both these statements mean love directed toward man *altogether for his own sake*. Lest mutual love or an exchange of self-interest be taken as the norm, the words "as thyself" and also the golden rule should be interpreted in terms of Christ's love. But provided this understanding is secure, it will then be seen that "to be a Christ to one's neighbor" (Luther) and to love one's neighbor as one's self mean the same thing. Both attitudes unite especially in "always hoping." Yet if there is anything lacking of self-acceptance and perennial hopefulness in natural self-love (inverted) as a provisional measure for what ought always be given in Christian love to the neighbor, the deficiency had better be made up by reference, no longer to inverted self-love, but to the controlling love of Christ. Love according to this measure always proves hopeful even when self-love may not. Love according to this measure proves hopeful even when a person

6*Op. cit.,* p. 159.

has not the love and hope for himself which is required if he is to love himself as he loves his neighbor when he loves his neighbor *rightly, i.e.*, when he loves his neighbor as Christ loves him —unconditionally under every circumstance.

Still, every man ordinarily loves himself; consequently every man usually has hope for himself. We love ourselves more than we desire any kind of self-improvement for ourselves. We, therefore, do not cease to love ourselves when we fail of a certain degree of self-development; and hence love for ourselves is always *hopeful:* it always lays hold expectantly on *another* possibility for good. Christianity desires simply to reverse all this and requires us to love our neighbor as unswervingly as we love ourselves. If we love our neighbors as we love ourselves, we will love them more than we desire their improvement. Therefore, we will not cease to love them on account of any kind of setback in their improvement. And hence love for neighbor is *always* hopeful; it always lays hold expectantly on *another* possibility for good. Love always hopes something; this is how it manages without sentimentality to hope all things. We love ourselves even when we fail of being civilized. Christianity desires simply to reverse all this and requires that we love our *existing* neighbors more than we desire them to be cultured. However troubled Christians may be, they do not join the hue and cry that our civilization is perishing or that all will be lost if this be so. The death of a civilization is no final destruction of Christian hope. While love for certain values would be driven to despair in the face of the destruction of all the values men hold dear, both self-love and love for neighbor *as one's self* (especially since the latter is the response of faith), possess a sense that the end of *a* world is not the end of *the* world (Maritain), the end of a civilization is not the end of the human story, nor the end of the human story the end of everything. While under any historical circumstances love for certain values is soon driven to moderation, love for self and for neighbor as one's self always remains hopeful; and *a fortiori* love for neighbor according to the controlling love of Christ immoderately hopes all things.

VII

THE WORK OF CHRISTIAN LOVE

> The foundations of that code were not love and mercy,
> faith and sacrifice, but honesty and duty, truth and jus-
> tice, justice exact and inclusive, justice that never for an
> instant overlooked his own interests.
> —Douglas S. Freeman, *George Washington*.

FREQUENTLY Christian ethics is represented by an image which makes clear, it is supposed, the foolishness of the whole idea. Two men alone on a desert island made their living by taking in each other's washing. Does not the notion of two or more people having disinterested regard for one another amount to just this, each doing for the other what he might better have been left to do for himself, the inverted self-love of each living in the other's interest? Are not ordinary honesty and exact justice which never for an instant overlook one's own interest better principles on which to found society?

The prevalence of objections of this sort and their apparent reasonableness make necessary a word about the special function of Christian love in maintaining human life in community. Too much should not be claimed for Christian love, even if that little be the salt of the earth. Its role may be a limited one. Nevertheless, the image of men taking in each other's washing happens to be an exceedingly apt account of how existing societies carry on exchange and preserve community of economic services. In order to preserve life in economic community, one man's good must serve another. If this be true in forms of external interdependence where only the surfaces of selves touch one another, why should it be considered so passing strange in the realm of personal, spiritual community where each self must more fully enter if it is ever to meet with another?

For the ego is a dream
Till a neighbor's need by name create it.[1]

In order to create and maintain community of persons, or to evoke and sustain personality in community, much more (and more intentionally) than in economic exchange it is necessary that each seek not his own good, but the good of his neighbor (I Cor. 10:24). There is nothing illogical about this idea, however unusual such an attitude may be in practice.

For bridging the gulf separating man from man, two types of solution besides Christian love have in general been suggested for which much can be said. One is self-centered, the other value-centered. Either because he is greatly concerned for himself or because he is greatly concerned for certain values, an individual may be led to take upon himself certain duties to others. The traffic safety slogan, "Be careful. The life you save may be your own" or the injunction, "Hire the handicapped: it's good business" (enlightened selfishness), and the slogan of the sanitation department, "This is *our* city, let's keep it *clean*" (mutual love for value), have each their work to perform. A self-centered derivation of regard for others finds illustration in Aristotle's two inferior types of friendship, friendship for profit and friendship for other sorts of utility; value-centered regard for others in his highest type of friendship, friendship for the sake of the good.

I. THE WORK OF LOVE IN CREATING COMMUNITY

The utilitarian social philosophers of the nineteenth century also chose between one or the other of these alternatives. Jeremy Bentham gave self-centered reason for performing duties to others or standing in some sort of community with them; John Stuart Mill, value-centered reason. In his "selfish system" Bentham, unlike Spinoza before him, did not rely merely upon the theoretical judgment that there is nothing more useful to man than man. Instead Bentham presupposed the existence of an organized

[1]W. H. Auden, *The Age of Anxiety*, Random House, 1947, p. 8.

society in which informal social disapproval and the formal political "sanction" meted out by law, courts, and penalties for crime served to keep the individual in line with the general interest. Under these conditions, and only under these conditions, would an essentially selfish individual calculating his own greatest good in terms of the quantity, duration, intensity, purity, and fecundity of pleasurable experience discover any reason at all for being concerned about the "extent" or just distribution of such happiness. His only reason for not infringing the pleasure of others lies in prudent calculation of the pains which will inevitably follow from the operation of moral and legal sanctions; his only reason for contributing positively to the good of others, the expectation of a returning increase in his own pleasure, which surely is more personal and less extensive motivation than that given negative duty to others by the fact of legal sanction. An individual who lives under the law, however, may be granted to have sufficient reason for not being very bad.

But what of the legislator, who was indeed chiefly in the mind of this school of liberal social reform? What possible reason can any one engaged in making law have for being really concerned about more equitable distribution of goods? Since *his own* pleasure and pain alone point out what he ought to do as well as determine what he will do, ought not a wise legislator, and will he not, use legal and political sanctions for his own arbitrary and selfish ends *if he can?* Plainly, the "greatest happiness of the greatest number" and "each to count for one and none for more than one" were for Bentham words without any real foundation, or rather whose real foundation in the already established community of the English nation was quite disguised. Evidently individual and social interests agree with one another only in well-established communities of mutual interest and only to the extent that the machinery for enforcing social cohesion operates smoothly and by common consent and practice already applies justly to every one. Where such community of interest does not already exist, or when in the twentieth century community has broken down and ties of power persist without supporting mutuality, enlightened selfishness alone can by no means be trusted as far as Bentham in his day found plausible.

No more can a value-centered derivation of duties be trusted, not even supposing values themselves to be more commonly agreed upon than they are likely ever to be. ". . . The utilitarian standard," wrote J. S. Mill, "is not the agent's own greatest happiness, but the greatest amount of happiness altogether," "not the agent's own happiness, but that of all concerned."[2] But the crux of the matter lies in Mill's simple supposition that any one concerned to secure the "greatest amount of happiness altogether" necessarily desires "the greatest happiness *of the greatest number.*" Now no very weighty argument is needed to prove that "each person's happiness is a good to that person, and the general happiness, therefore a good to the aggregate of all persons";[3] the only issue is whether the good of the aggregate of all persons is *each* person's good, and for what reason. Mill's only suggestion on this point is his short and easy passage from "greatest happiness altogether" to "greatest number." In a footnote Mill argues that "equal amounts of happiness are equally desirable, whether felt by the same or by different persons."[4]

In whatever way "the good" be defined, this is the viewpoint of every value-centered derivation of duties to others and of every notion of community grounded in mutual love for the good: equal amounts of value are equally desirable, whether experienced by the same or by different persons. Any one whose attention really focuses on "the greatest value altogether" takes no notice, or should take no notice, of the quite incidental difference between *mine* and *thine.* In a given moment in which he can secure more total experience of value by seeking it for another, for the sake of value (and not for the sake of the other person) he will readily do so. When, on the other hand, he can attain greater experience of value by seeking some good for himself, again for the sake of value (and not for his own sake) he will do so.

[2] *Utilitarianism* (Modern Library Giant edition of *The English Philosophers from Bacon to Mill,* ed. by E. A. Burtt), pp. 903, 908.
[3] *Ibid.,* p. 923.   [4] *Ibid.,* p. 946.

Questions raised concerning the naïveté of the view of human nature contained in Mill's viewpoint need not be pressed. Men who demand interest-payment before they are willing to give up present good for the sake of *their own* future good are not apt to be more open to the persuasion that their own present and future good ought to be given up whenever the "greatest value altogether" or "good to the aggregate of all persons" requires it. They are not likely to believe the good equally desirable no matter whose. Keeping clear, however, as Mill did not, the distinction between what is desirable and what may actually be desired, here serious consideration should be given only to the question, not what men will actually do, but whether simply on the grounds put forward by Mill, *i.e.*, from value considerations alone, men may even know that they *ought* to desire the greatest possible extension of happiness.

Real community with the good of others cannot be traced home to concern for value alone, as Mill believed, any more than to concern for self alone. Only an element of concern for the other person *for his own sake* creates community among men. Mill's line of reasoning, as we have seen, leads to the conclusion that the "greatest happiness of the greatest number" *simply means* the "greatest happiness altogether," *whoever* or *how many* happen to experience it. Then the last four words of the utilitarian slogan, "of the greatest number" are quite redundant; they add nothing meaningful not already fully contained in the first two, "greatest happiness." Reference to "number," extent, more equitable distribution flows simply from concern for the value of happiness wherever it may be found. The slogan "greatest happiness of the greatest number" unfortunately misleads many into supposing that the value of happiness and the extent of its distribution were equally primary for Mill. This cannot be true, for pleasure is primary, duty to others entirely derived.

Yet utilitarianism as a liberal British reform movement actually gave greater primacy to the persons participating in the common good than ever was justified theoretically by either the self-centered approach of Bentham or the value-centered views of Mill.

This praiseworthy inconsistency was still an inconsistency, containing some fundamental dependence on the Christian heritage of regard for others for their own sakes whatever the value and even if great uncertainty continues always to surround the question, *What* is the good? Suppose Mill had been confronted with a situation, certainly a conceivable one, in which justly extending happiness would actually decrease the total amount of happiness in present society. Suppose the amount of happiness of which privileged people would have to be deprived *exceeds* the quantity (or the quantity of a special quality) of happiness that can possibly be added to the experience of the larger number among the so-called lower classes. In this case Mill would have had no *reason* for sharing social goods among a greater number at the expense of "greatest happiness altogether." Or take the more problematic case of a situation in which the amount of happiness social reform would take from certain people *exactly equals* the quantity (or the quantity of a special quality) of happiness made available to others, the "greatest happiness altogether" thus remaining precisely the same. Would not the utilitarian, or any one else who derives duty to others entirely from consideration of increased value, have to remain in perpetual indecision, with no reason at all for judging either the *status quo* or the proposed social change better or more just than the other? Whatever may have been Mill's reply to these dilemmas, from them we may conclude that just community among men contains some reference to the neighbor *for his own sake* in the matter, and that the creation of such community never results entirely, or even mainly, from love of self or from love of value. Only the fact that he was a member of a well-established community of value, moreover a national community living largely off the Christian heritage, could have disguised from Mill that merely from concern for value he could not derive as much concern for justice and participation in the common good as he actually championed.

An answer which can be given to the foregoing ethical dilemmas should not be ignored. It may be said that more equitable distribution of goods or extent of pleasure in each of the instances given is ultimately justified only because of the reasonable expectation that, after a temporary period of adjustment following reform, in the long run a society in which happiness is shared by the greatest number will prove to be altogether the happiest society, any temporary loss or equivalence in the total soon repairing itself as every man, and his children, come more fully into their own. Granting that this may often be true, does the motive of justice wait for thought to trammel up all the innumerable consequences of a proposed social action? Is present duty to others inclined by no more than the weight of obligation remaining over after realistic estimates of the probabilities of increase or decrease or sameness in experienced value cancel out one another? Have not even those champions of justice, like the utilitarians, who believed that increased just extent and increased total happiness invariably go together, have they not actually been men bound to other men by a good deal more than this value-centered regard? Alongside concern for the "greatest happiness altogether" there was for Mill some reference to the neighbor in his concern for "greatest number."

The force of neighbor-centered attention supporting justice and creating community perhaps needs to be more completely isolated from attention to values before any final answer can be given concerning the effect of each alone. Perhaps this separation can be accomplished by considering what should justly be done if by subjecting a single individual to indefinite torture all the rest of humanity would promptly become unimaginably happy. Suppose that by this device and only by this device a vast increase of total happiness could be gained, and gained permanently for as long as the victim continued to be tormented. Concern for "greatest happiness altogether" here shows itself totally incapable of including within ethics any duty to *this* neighbor, yet is there any one who does not feel that in this instance justice may require real sacrifice of potential value?

Of course under such circumstances Christian ethics gives a person strong leading to elect *himself* to the position of victim, but this would proceed from a "neighbor-centered concern for value," the very opposite of "value-centered concern indifferently for self or for others," which calculates that a person has no duties to others whenever no real increase of values may reasonably be expected as a consequence. Jesus and Caiaphas before whom he stood trial acted from utterly different ethical principles even though they both might have spoken the same words: "It is expedient that one man should die for the people" (John 18:14). But Caiaphas applied this principle to the other person, while Jesus applied it to himself. Caiaphas was concerned to maintain an existing order of relatively just institutions, Jesus to bring reconciliation and community where before there was none.

Provisionally then, in our quest for the special function of Christian love, a distinction may be made between *preserving* community that already exists among men and *creating* community where none is. Wherever there already exists community of mutual interest, such community needs always to be preserved and strengthened by all manner of appeals to enlightened self-interest and calling to mind advantages shared mutually in the "commonwealth." Always unenlightened selfishness tends to tear asunder such existing communities as family, neighborhood, school, church, or nation. The individual needs to be shown the interest he himself actually has in the continuation of these human groupings. His selfishness needs educating. It needs to be extended as far as possible to include within *his own* good the good of all the men to whom he is actually bound whether he recognizes it or not. Appeals should constantly be made to considerations of justice in distributing the goods and services for mutual love of which these communities exist. Examination of the utilitarians shows how far the self-centered and the value-centered approach can actually go in supporting duty to others within existing communities and in preserving these communities against waves of faction and party-spirit.

However, the creation of community where none exists is altogether another problem. For the purpose of *increasing* real community among men, by its very nature even the most enlightened self-interest can do nothing. No more can exchange of benefits by mutual love according to distributive justice. Some community of interest must already exist for self-interest or mutual interest to provide ground for the conviction that it is good for a man or nation to act justly. Of course, appeal may be made to implicit and as yet largely unrecognized common interest which, for example, the nations of the world today have in an order of international justice. *Insofar as* international community actually exists already, insofar as economic ties and fear of reciprocal military destruction actually bind nations together, then the self-interest of each nation when fully enlightened and the mutual interest of all in the commonwealth of nations operate to preserve this community, even making it more explicit. But *insofar* as community among the nations does not yet actually exist at all, insofar as national interests actually diverge from one another in spite of their partial agreement, then obviously to appeal to the common interest or to self-interest spins on the spot where it stands. Pointing out to self-interest the partial reality of certain common interests gets no further than this existing area of common interest; it perhaps keeps human community from breaking down altogether into smaller and still smaller competitive ingroups; herein the work of justice finds support in already established societies. Self-love and mutual love for common values are admittedly invaluable motives for preserving community, or for bringing about greater recognition of the interdependence which now exists among men. Yet no matter how enlightened these motives become they can never move across the border where community still needs to be created if it is to exist at all. This is the work of Christian love, the work of reconciliation. Only Christian love enters the "no man's land" where dwell the desperate and the despised outcastes from every human community, and brings community with them into existence.

Christian ethics differs from utilitarianism in the primacy each assigns and the answers given to the problem *Whose* good? This question utilitarianism answers in fashion derivative from a prior question, *What* is the good? while for Christian ethics there can be no more fundamental question than, *Whose?* This contrast again appears in the case of Henry Sidgwick, last of the utili-

tarians. No longer deriving duty to others from considerations of
value but from basic rational "intuition," Sidgwick nevertheless
defined "justice" as "treating similar cases similarly." "Benevolence" or love was but a sub-case of justice: for him the rational
intuition of benevolence meant, "Each man is morally bound to
regard the good of any other individual *as much as his own*,"
i.e., similar to his own.[5] Nothing could be clearer than that Christian ethics must judge quite insufficient such fifty-fifty division
of the ground between a man and his neighbor, whether duties
to others are derived from self-love, from love of value, or from
rational intuition. The meaning of Christian love may be stated
in sharp opposition to Sidgwick: It means "treating similar cases
*dis*similarly," "regarding the good of any other individual as *more*
than your own," when he and you alone are involved. Moreover,
instead of benevolence being a sub-case of justice, for Christian
ethics the reverse is true—love is always the primary notion, justice derivative, since justice may be defined as what Christian love
does when confronted by two or more neighbors. Justice perhaps
means treating similar cases similarly (Aristotle's corrective justice) when a Christian judges, not between himself and his neighbor, but between two or more neighbors, or it may even mean
treating them dissimilarly, taking into account essential inequalities between them, as Aristotle's distributive justice requires.[6]
Without entering further into the idea of justice so important for
social ethics, it should be clear that just as any who are "but men"
are apt to exercise partiality when judging their *own* cause, so
Christian love (which is self-love inverted) judges with partiality
the *neighbor's* cause, treats his case as exceedingly dissimilar
from one's own. The extremity of this contrast between the Christian and a typical philosophical perspective in ethics is to be
understood first of all in terms of the suggested distinction between preserving and creating community, the latter being the
special role Christian love assumes.

The importance of keeping community intact can hardly be
overestimated. Nevertheless, creating community among men

[5]*Methods of Ethics*, London: Macmillan, 1913, p. 382.
[6]See Emil Brunner, *Justice and the Social Order*, Harpers, 1945, ch. 5.

where none now is, the task of reconciling man with man, is a still more important problem. As regards it, "if you love those who love you . . . And if you salute only your brethren, what more are you doing than others? Do not even the Gentiles the same?" (Matt. 5:46, 47). If you love only within societies held together by mutual self-interest, what more are you doing than others? Does not even Bentham the same? If you love only for the sake of some increment in value, loving yourself and others alike, what more are you doing than others? Does not even Mill the same? If you follow natural rational intuition, uninstructed by Christ, in considering yourself and others each as similar "cases" to whom distribution of goods should be given, what more are you doing than others? Does not even Sidgwick the same? These all alike assist perhaps in conserving life in community, but they can hardly bring an isolated or hostile man into community with you or you with him. "But I say to you, Love your enemies and pray for those who persecute you" (Matt. 5:44). Let love penetrate the barriers between man and man at which, by definition, all mutual self-interest halts, all concern for one another *over* concern for some good is bound somewhat to fail. Any advance beyond where men are at any given moment in their relationships with one another takes place not fundamentally by increasing enlightenment about their own interest or by concern for value which pretends there is no real clash, but by that motive alone which can reconcile real differences and bring community into being where, *man against man,* it must be acknowledged there is no basis for it. This uniquely is the work of loving regard for another for his own sake. Paraphrasing Plato's confidence in the philosopher-king, we may affirm, without fear of successful refutation, that "until preserving and creating community somehow meet in one, and those common natures who pursue either to the exclusion of the other are compelled to stand aside, cities will never rest from their evils—no, nor the human race—and then only will God's kingdom have a possibility of life and behold the light of day."[7]

[7]Cf. *The Republic,* V, 473.

II. THE WORK OF LOVE IN PRESERVING COMMUNITY

In the last analysis, however, the distinction between preserving and creating community proves to be only a quite provisional one. The work of love is also the primary, though not the only, ingredient preserving community among human beings. An attitude which brings a person over to his neighbor's side, originally making community of need and interest possible between them, serves also to keep him there throughout every time of trouble. No one ever enters *permanent* marriage merely from enlightened love for self or from love of mutual value. Even if these motives may in a given instance last a lifetime, marriage that is *essentially* permanent depends on some regard for the other person for his or her own sake. And at least every one within the family-community has some time or other been the recipient of love that did not first count the cost to self or estimate whether the recipient would gain as much value as value was willingly sacrificed. For all self-interest and mutual regard may do in occasionally healing some breach, love for another for his own sake really holds the family together. An orator in the public forum may play upon self-interest in his audience or may invoke mutuality, perhaps quoting Booker T. Washington to the effect that "you can't keep a man down in the ditch without staying there with him." Still he himself would not always speak out on behalf of greater justice for the Negro or other people discriminated against in our society, nor would he stand up as long under adverse circumstances, if these were *his* only motivation, if *he* had no regard for oppressed people for their own sakes, if *he* had no more sense of justice than may logically be drawn from consideration of the "greatest happiness altogether." Thus justice in community lives off love both for its creation and also in large measure for its preservation.

Friendship grounded either in selfish considerations of utility or in mutual love of "the good" must change, as Aristotle saw so clearly, whenever the friend changes. Perhaps a person will not break with a former friend instantly, but he will delay doing so only if there is a chance of his friend's amendment; and if friendship promptly ends, then, according to Aristotle, "he who should break off the connection is not to be judged to act wrongly, for he never was a friend to such a character as the other now is."[1] This is an excellent example of what

> we may say about all merely human love, even when it is most beautiful, that there is a little thievishness in it, that it still steals the perfections of the beloved, while the Christian love grants the beloved all his imperfections and weaknesses, and *in all his changes abides with him,* loving the man it sees.[2]

Instead of talking about how the object of love ought to be in order to be worthy of love, Christian ethics talks about how love ought to be in order to be love.[3] For this reason, Christian love bears all things, believes all things, hopes all things, endures all things, never ends (I Cor. 13:7, 8), while other love changes. For this reason, Christian love also *preserves* community where otherwise it would cease to be. This is the reason it is said of Jesus Christ that in him is reconciliation, that "all things were made through him" (John 1:3), and also that "in him all things *hold together*" (Col. 1:17).

III. THE WORK OF LOVE IN VALUING HUMAN PERSONALITY

It can also be said that Christian love is the source from which men learn to *attribute* value to human persons. From Christian love, men "have life, and have it abundantly" (John 10:10). The creation and preservation of community among men, as this has been understood above, is in fact the same thing as persistent attribution of worth to another human being. As a matter of historical fact, there can be no doubt that Christianity trained western European man in his high regard for human personality. Even the most cautious historian must make some reference, along

---

[1]*Nicomachean Ethics,* 1165b.
[2]Soren Kierkegaard. *Works of Love,* Princeton University Press, 1946, p. 140 (italics mine).
[3]*Ibid.,* p. 128.

with other factors, to the working of Christian love in order ever
to give adequate explanation of the technological advancement
made during the middle ages. Men during this period first thought
of putting sails on their vessels, thus releasing the galley slaves;
and water-wheels appeared on every waterfall in Europe. In these
and in other respects the technological revolution accomplished
by the medieval period had a cultural significance far greater
than the more obvious, large-scale application of the machine in
the modern period. And the reason was not that men suddenly
became inventive—the Greeks, after all, had a word for the steam
engine!—but that men suddenly gained a most unnatural concern for saving human labor. The dignity of labor and the dignity
of human beings who labor was not the consequence of reasoning
about human nature, much less was it a consequence of empirically observing man's needs and finding in general human
experience foundation for the rights of man. Men were first
"taught by God to love one another" (I Thess. 4:9). From loving
neighbor as themselves men first attributed worth without first
finding it in those to whom they were duty-bound by Christ.
There took place what Nietzsche referred to as the "awe-inspiring
catastrophe of two thousand years' training in truth,"[1] the awe-
inspiring spectacle of two thousand years' training in *valuing*
human persons. A long period of Christian nurture made it possible for men in the modern period, such as John Locke, to speak
of the "natural rights" of man. But one thing is certain: these
so-called natural rights have been measured out historically to
men in the west by the supernatural measure given the meaning
of obligation by Christian ethics. By its very nature Christian
love *counts* men to be things of value, ends to be served in spite
of everything. As T. S. Eliot has said, "If you remove from the
word 'human' all that belief in the supernatural has given to man,
you can view him finally as no more than an extremely clever,
adaptable and mischievous little animal."[2] By its increasing absence from human relationships, men in the twentieth century

[1]*The Genealogy of Morals*, Third essay, 27.
[2]"Second Thoughts about Humanism," *Selected Essays*, Harcourt, Brace, 1932,
p. 397.

are in a better position than Nietzsche to observe the awe-inspiring spectacle of two thousand years' training in acknowledging the value of truth, in according value to other human beings and in living in enduring community with them.

VIII

THIS HUMAN NATURE

"Better even a little teeth-chattering than idol-adoration!"
—Friedrich Nietzsche, *Thus Spake Zarathustra*, III, 1.

> For plainly it is not
> To the Cross or to Clarté or to Common Sense
> Our passions pray to but to primitive totems
> As absurd as they are savage; science or no science,
> It is Bacchus or The Great Boyg or Baal-Peor,
> Fortune's Ferris-wheel or *the physical sound*
> *Of our own names* which they actually adore as their
> Ground and goal. *Yet the grossest of our dreams is*
> *No worse than our worship which for the most part*
> *Is so much galimatias to get out of*
> *Knowing our neighbor . . ."*
> —W. H. Auden, *The Age of Anxiety*, p. 136.*

I. THE IMAGE OF GOD

SOME ONE will ask, Do not Christians believe that man was created in the image of God? Is not the doctrine of the image of God one of the basic principles of Christian morality? Certainly this must be affirmed, and cannot be denied. Unfortunately, however, there is a widespread opinion that the notion of the *imago Dei* has been simply a peculiar religious manner of expression or archaic way of saying what other interpretations of human nature manage to say more clearly, by speaking, for example, of the inherent dignity or worth of man on account of his freedom or his reason. We must now inquire: How much more (and how much less) do Christians mean by this expression "the image of God" than a simple confession of

*Published by Random House, 1947.

belief in the inherent value or sacredness of human personality as such?

(a)

Two types of theory regarding the image of God may first be distinguished, two ways of thinking about man according to which may be classified most of the traditional discussions about human nature. One view singles out something *within* the *substantial form* of human nature, some faculty or capacity man possesses, and identifies this as the thing which distinguishes man from physical nature and from other animals. It may be the glance of the eye which only man possesses and no animal has. It may be the size of man's brain, or his upright stature which has freed man's hands for tool-making and the creation of art, and whose connection with man's capacity for thought we acknowledge whenever we speak of "grasping" an idea. Or man may be defined as *Homo faber*, a fabricating or tool-making animal, and much then may be made of the significant difference between man's thumb and a gorilla's grip. All civilization may be viewed simply as an extension of man's thumb.

More frequently, however, some inner capacity of mind, or soul, or will is identified as the image of God *within* man. The ancient Stoics spoke of a "divine spark" within man, by which man shares in the "eternal fire" pervading all Nature. This viewpoint, strongly revived during the eighteenth-century Enlightenment, decisively influenced modern rationalism and modern secular democratic thought. The idea that there is a spark of the divine in every man (the Stoic notion) gave rise to our modern conceptions of the inherent natural sacredness of human personality as much as or more than did Christianity. Just so, most current formulations of the universal brotherhood of mankind have to be traced home to the cosmopolitan outlook of Stoicism.

Aristotle's definition of man as a rational animal may be cited as the outstanding example of ways of thinking about man which specify some capacity, some substantial part of human nature, as the essence of what it means to be in the image of God. Christians who follow in Aristotle's train simply make use of the religious label, the *imago Dei,* for everything he intended to say. The *imago Dei* in man is his reason. This is the view often held also by the common man: what sets man apart from the beasts is his mind. Man is "that living nature which possesses reason in its own right."[1] Man is a rational animal. Man is a rational animal endowed with the capacity of speech. Man is a rational animal endowed with the capacity of laughter. In each of these Aristotelian definitions of man, according to the logical structure of definition *per genus proximum et differentiam,* the adjective "rational" indicates man's unique essence in contrast to the substantive "animal," which he shares with other species of the biological kingdom. Rationality also goes to the root of his distinctive powers more than do the "universal properties" of speech and laughter which (*pace* all parrots and jackals) accompany the possession and exercise of intellect. To be a rational animal is man's essential definition while to be a "lingual" or a "risible" animal does not go to the heart of the matter. To use the theological term, the *imago Dei* in man consists of the fact that he is set apart from other "living nature" by the possession of powers of reason in his own right.

Instead of reason other aspects of human nature, themselves not so cool or dispassionate in their functioning, may be defined as the image of God. Influenced by romanticism we may incline toward the belief that the capacity most commanding respect is man's faculty for imagination and artistic creativity. Influenced by Kant's dictum that "nothing in the whole world, or even outside the world, can possibly be regarded as good without limitation except a good will,"[2] we may be greatly impressed with man's moral capacity, his moral will or moral freedom, and call these the image of God in him. This, in general, is the viewpoint of personalistic idealism.[3] All these views have in common the definition of the image of God as some capacity native to man or some part of the substantial form of his nature.

[1] Aristotle, *De anima,* ii, 1 and 2.
[2] *Fundamental Principles of the Metaphysics of Morals,* sect. I.
[3] *E.g.,* A. C. Knudson, *The Principles of Christian Ethics,* Abingdon-Cokesbury Press, 1943, ch. iii.

This first type of theory concerning the *imago Dei* may be criticized for its proneness to blur the distinction between man and God. Seeking to provide a barrier against a naturalistic reduction of man to the dead level of physical or animal nature, these views fall into the error of exalting man to the level of the divine. They assert discontinuity between man and nature in such fashion as to overlook or understate the discontinuity between man and God. In order not to homogenize man with physical nature, they homogenize human with the divine nature. To the degree that man and biological nature are said to be heterogeneous, man and divinity tend to become by nature homogeneous. Man is, no doubt, smaller than God, but quintessentially they are the same. Thus, man is thought to be *consubstantial* with God; whereas, according to the biblical view, man was made of the same substance as the dust of the earth, consubstantial with all other *living beings* (*nephesh*) whose breath is in their nostrils (Gen. 7:22–23; Isa. 2:22). "Now the Egyptians are men, and not God; and their horses flesh and not spirit" (Isa. 31:3).

The clearest illustration of this defect is to be found in the Stoic doctrine of the divine spark in man. "You are a being of primary importance," announces Epictetus, the Stoic slave-philosopher; and gives as his reason for so saying:

> You are a fragment of God; you have within you a part of Him. Why, then, are you ignorant of your kinship? . . . Will you not bear in mind, whenever you eat, who you are that eat, and whom you are nourishing? Whenever you indulge in intercourse with women, who you are that do this? Whenever you mix in society, whenever you take physical exercise, whenever you converse, do you not know that you are nourishing God, exercising God? . . . In the presence of even an image of God you would not dare to do anything of the things you are now doing. But when God Himself is present within you, seeing and hearing everything, are you not ashamed to be thinking and doing such things as these, O insensible of your own nature, and object of God's wrath![4]

No such idea of the inherent importance of human personality

[4]*Discourses*, Bk. II, ch 8 (Loeb Classical Library, Vol. I, p. 263).

should be identified with the idea of *imago Dei* in Christian ethics. It is true that St. Paul in a familiar passage also teaches that the body is the temple of the Holy Spirit, and also uses this consideration as motivation for purity of conduct. But the Holy Spirit is in no one by nature; the body is "a temple of the Holy Spirit within you, *which you have from God*" (I Cor. 6:19); this is a vastly different conception from the view that there is something of the divine in every one by nature.

Perhaps a more refined way of blurring the distinction between God and man was that of Aristotle, who considered the essence of man to be his reason. Reason he believed was a point of identity between God and man and among individual men so far as they reason correctly. Suppose, for example, a number of people in the same room agree to think at the same time of the idea of a perfect circle or triangle. Insofar as this idea is present in the mind of one person, he becomes in reality one with all the other minds thinking this thought, and in this respect one with the mind of God. If human minds were wholly occupied with perfect thoughts or thoughts of real essences, there would remain no significant distinction among them, or between them and God who is perfect reason eternally contemplating perfect thoughts. Reason thus serves as a principle of identity running through all thinking beings; only *matter* composing their bodies keeps them apart as separate individuals. Matter is the principle of individuation; Reason, the divine in us. Individual men may die, but Reason as their "substantial form" endures forever. The measure of how far such a view is from the biblical understanding of man may be seen from the words of Isaiah:

"For my thoughts are not your thoughts,
Nor are your ways my ways" is the oracle of the Lord;
"But as the heavens are higher than the earth,
So are my ways higher than your ways,
And my thoughts than your thoughts" (55:8, 9).

Such an egregious error personalistic idealism does not make because of its emphasis on man's individual moral freedom. Never-

theless, while personalism keeps persons *metaphysically* separate
from one another and from God, *ethically* the reverse is true: it
is significant that Knudson tends to interchange "God" and the
value of human personality. He motivates moral conduct by identifying the Augustinian notion of "the love *of God*" with the love
of value, worth or perfection *in* oneself or *in* one's neighbor.

> The object of true love must have personal worth. . . . This was
> the reason why Augustine interpreted true self-love and true
> love of neighbor as a love of God. It was God in men, in oneself
> and in others that gave to them their moral worth and made
> them proper objects of Christian love.[5]

Knudson's view calls to mind the Stoic doctrine of the divinity
within man: not the neighbor but "God" or "perfection" in the
neighbor should be loved.

In short, definitions of the image of God as some faculty or
capacity or perfection within man's possession tempt him to
abandon his proper place as *creature* and encourage his preten-
sions of being sufficient unto himself, in fact himself his own God
in microcosm. Therefore the chief danger in employing this sort
of definition of the image of God is that man thereby *ceases to
be in the image of God* in the second meaning of the expression,
which is the crucial one for Christian thought.

The first type of theory regarding the *imago Dei* uses an analogy
with the plastic or pictorial arts, such as sculpture or painting.
In these arts, a model has the "form" or image of that after which
it has been fashioned; a sketch is in the image of the object of
which it is a drawing; just so, something within the make-up of
man himself may be said to be modeled or made in the image
of God. On the other hand, there is a second type of approach
to this problem. There are views which may be described as *relational*, and which make use of the analogy of a mirror reflecting
the image of some object. Nothing *within* the make-up of man,
considered by himself apart from a present responsive relationship to God, has the form or power of being in the image of God.

[5]A. C. Knudson, *op. cit.*, pp. 130–131.

The image of God is rather to be understood as a relationship *within which* man sometimes stands, whenever like a mirror he obediently reflects God's will in his life and actions. Man is a theological animal to the root of his essential being. However significant from other points of view may be man's capacity as a culture-producing, history-bearing animal, or however important the fact that man is "a living nature which possesses reason," nothing about man not presently involved in response to God can be called God's image. The *mirror* in itself is not the image; the mirror images; God's image is *in* the mirror. The image of God, according to this view, consists of man's *position* before God, or rather, the image of God is reflected in man because of his position before him.

In the course of Christian thought, most of the decisive and distinctive Christian interpretations of man have been of this sort. Those of St. Augustine, Soren Kierkegaard and Karl Barth may be cited as examples; and, back of them, that of St. Paul. St. Augustine was taught by the Platonists how to conceive spiritual substance. Since God and the self are not just rarefied matter but both of them truly spiritual in nature, nothing would have been easier than for Augustine to have concluded that *on this account* the human spirit in itself is the image of the Divine spirit. At one point he writes of man as "created after Thy image and likeness, in that very image and likeness of Thee (that is, the power of reason and understanding) on account of which he was set over all irrational creatures."[6] But if such an account of the mental powers man possesses were all that needed to be said concerning him, then the scriptures would simply assert that God made him "after his kind," no doubt endowed as a species with distinctive capacities which no other species has to the same degree. "Therefore Thou sayest not . . . 'after his kind,' but, after 'our image' and 'likeness.' Because, being renewed in his mind, and beholding and apprehending Thy truth, man needeth not man as his director that he may imitate his kind; but by Thy

---

[6]*The Confessions,* Bk. XIII, ch. xxxii (*Basic Writings of St. Augustine,* ed. by Whitney J. Oates, Random House, 1948, I, 253).

direction proveth what is that good, and acceptable and perfect will of Thine."[7] For Augustine, therefore, being in the image of God requires not only unique intellectual powers but correct posture; likeness to God involves more than "spirit," it consists of the spirit of obedience. Thus Augustine writes:

> . . . There was danger lest the human mind, from being reckoned among invisible and immaterial things, should be thought to be of the same nature with Him who created it, and should fall away by pride from Him to whom it should be united by love. For the mind *becomes like God,* to the extent vouchsafed by its subjection of itself to Him for information. And if *it obtains the greatest nearness by that subjection which produces likeness,* it must be far removed from Him by that presumption which would make the likeness greater.

> . . . The slippery motion of falling away [from what is good] takes possession of the negligent only gradually, and beginning from a perverse desire for the likeness of God, arrives in the end at the likeness of beasts. . . . For the true honor of man is the image and likeness of God, *which is not preserved except it be in relation to Him by whom it is impressed.*[8]

It is true that in his work *On the Trinity* St. Augustine declares that "the mind must be first considered as it is in itself, before it becomes partaker of God; and His image must be found in it." Worn out and defaced "the image of God still remains. For it is His image in this very point, that it is capable of Him, and can be partaker of Him; which so great good is only made possible by its being His image."[9] This emphasis arises from Augustine's endeavor, in this work, to find the Trinity prefigured in the very structure of the human mind itself. He notices that the plural pronoun is used in Genesis 1:26: "Let us make man in *our* image, after *our* likeness," and concludes from this that "man was made after the image of the Trinity, because it is not said, After

---

[7]*Ibid.,* Bk. XIII, ch. xxii (*Basic Writings,* I, 244).
[8]*On the Morals of the Catholic Church,* 12, and *On the Trinity,* XII, 11 (*Basic Writings of St. Augustine,* ed. by Whitney J. Oates, Random House, 1948, I, 329–330, and II, 818). (Italics mine.)
[9]*On the Trinity,* Bk. XIV, ch. 8, par. 11 (*Nicene and Post-Nicene Fathers,* Scribners, 1908, First Series, Vol. III).

my image, or After thy image."[10] The image of the Trinity in the mind consists of the three faculties, memory, intellect, and will. "Well, then, the mind remembers, understands, loves itself; if we discern this we discern a trinity, not yet indeed God, but now at last an image of God."[11] Considered as it is in itself apart from God the mind remains in a certain sense in the image of God, because it is "so constituted that at no time does it not remember, and understand, and love itself."[12] Nevertheless, Augustine speaks of the renewal and "forming again" of the mind after the image of God.[13] In this connection, he says in so many words that the image of God consists of man's relation to God and expressly denies that the mind images God simply by remembering, understanding and loving itself.

> This trinity, then, of the mind is not therefore the image of God, because the mind remembers itself, and understands and loves itself; but because it can also remember, understand and love Him by whom it was made. And in so doing it is made wise itself. But if it does not do so, even when it remembers, understands, and loves itself, then it is foolish. Let it remember its God, after whose image it is made, and let it understand and love Him.[14]

According to Kierkegaard, the image of God does not exist *in man;* man only exists *in the image* of God whenever he consents "to be nothing through the act of worship." Man is spirit, spirit is man's "invisible glory," and "the fact of being able in truth to worship, is the superiority of the invisible glory above all creation." But this means that properly understood the *imago Dei*

> *is in truth only within the infinite difference,* and therefore the act of worshipping is the resemblance with God, as it is the superiority over all creation. *Man and God do not resemble each other directly, but conversely:* only when God has infinitely be-

---

[10]*Ibid.,* ch. 19, par. 25.
[11]*Ibid.,* ch. 8, par. 11.
[12]*Ibid.,* ch. 14, par. 18.
[13]*Ibid.,* ch. 16, par. 22. Augustine sometimes speaks of the "forming again" of the mind as a renewal of man's "likeness" with God. This significantly influenced the later Catholic distinction between "image" and "likeness."
[14]*Ibid.,* ch. 12, par. 15.

come the eternal and omnipresent object of worship, and man always a worshipper, do they resemble one another.[15]

Karl Barth also interprets the *imago Dei* as man's appointed position *vis à vis* God and his response to God. "The text speaks not of a quality" inhering in man, he writes,

> but of that for which man's "nature" is *appointed* in his existence, life and action. . . . He is appointed to *recognize* God's glory and so to *act* as to give God the glory. . . . We cannot know if this recognition and this action, for which man is appointed, is more pleasing to God than the roaring of the sea, or the gentle falling of snowflakes. Once again we are not asked this.
> The sea and the snowflakes owe Him gratitude too, but *our* gratitude can take only the form of the knowledge of God and the service of God; for we are not snowflakes or drops of water.[16]

In other words, the image of God does not consist of man's being man and not snowflakes or the sea, however humanly important this may be, but in his being in the relationship of acknowledging and serving God with all these human powers, for this he was appointed to do and in the image of giving God glory was he created.

Doing this involves a decisively Christocentric orientation; the viewpoint of St. Paul makes this fact sun-clear. Jesus Christ was for him "the image of the invisible God" (Col. 1:15), which is the same thing as to say that Jesus Christ was for him "perfect man" and that the fullness of his stature recreates that image in which man was originally created (Ephes. 4:13). Understanding this was central in our analysis of virtues of Christian character in a previous chapter. Jesus Christ must be equally central for understanding the image of God in any Christian account of human nature. "For it is the God who said 'Let light shine out of darkness,' who has shone in our hearts to give the light of the

---

[15]*The Gospel of Suffering and The Lilies of the Field,* Augsburg Pub. House, 1948, pp. 211, 212 (italics mine).

[16]*The Knowledge of God and the Service of God According to the Principles of the Reformation,* Scribners, 1939, pp. 42–43. ". . . Where God acts, man has to be present without considering his own importance" (*No!* in *Natural Theology,* Geoffrey Bles, 1946, p. 104).

knowledge of the glory of God in the face of Christ. . . . And we all, with unveiled face, beholding [marginal reading: *reflecting*] the glory of the Lord, are being changed *into his likeness* from one degree of glory to another; for this comes from the Lord who is the Spirit" (II Cor. 4:6; 3:18).

The conclusion of every discussion of the "image of God" among Christians should then be this: This term cannot be defined by probing deep into the nature of man or by employing some sub-Christian sources of insight into what it means to be man. This term, like all the other "Christian categories" whose meaning we have explored in this book, can be defined only *derivatively* by decisive reference to the basic "primitive idea" in Christian ethics, *i.e.*, the idea of Christian love which itself in turn can be adequately defined only by indicating Christ Jesus. Jesus' pure humility and prompt obedience to God and his actions expressing pure and instant love for neighbor: these were in fact the same thing, the same image, the very image of God. Standing wholly within the relationship of imaging God's will, "with unveiled face, *reflecting as a mirror* the glory of God,"[17] and fully obedient love: these are in reality the same. There is no obedience, no response to God, there are no religious duties beyond this: Thou *shalt* love; and love fulfills every legitimate obedience. Existence within the image of God is the same thing as existence for another. Hence he who wrote that "only when God has infinitely become the eternal and omnipresent object of worship, and man always a worshipper, do they resemble one another," also said with equal appropriateness that "we can resemble God only in loving."[18] "*Think* this in you which also in Christ Jesus . . .,"[19] being changed into his likeness from one degree of glory to another.

[17]Goodspeed translation of II Cor. 3:18.

[18]Soren Kierkegaard, *Works of Love*, Princeton University Press, 1946, p. 52.

[19]Millar Burrows' translation of "Have this mind in you which was also in Christ Jesus . . ." (Phil. 2:5). *An Outline of Biblical Theology*, The Westminster Press, 1946, p. 139. Barth summarizes the idea of the Christ-like image of God: "On the one hand the *imago Dei* points across to christology, since Christ is the original of that likeness, the human *imago*. But it points even more certainly to soteriology since the full content of the *imago Dei* can only be known from the *reparatio*, from the *regeneratio* through Christ and the Holy Spirit" (*No!* in *Natural Theology*, p. 407).

The Catholic tradition has attempted to harmonize substantial
and relational conceptions of the *imago Dei* (and at the same
time to harmonize Aristotelian with biblical notions) by distinguishing between the "image" of God and his "likeness." The
imago Dei, they say, is natural human reason. It is man's native
power of "synderesis" or the immediate apprehension of "practical first principles" on the basis of which a reasonable and
universally valid code of ethics may be constructed and action
directed to accord with these principles. The "similitude" or "likeness" of God, on the other hand, is man's relation to the supernatural and his responsive obedience to and reflection of God's
revealed will. Only the "likeness" was lost by Adam's fall, and
a human nature thus disabled has since been handed on by propagation to the rest of the human race. God's grace alone can restore
the relationship for which man at creation was originally intended;
and this takes place through the sacraments. If any one, therefore,
desires to know more about that lost "likeness" of God which
Adam had in the beginning let him look to the infusion of theological virtues and other infused gifts and graces. The infused
moral nature, "connatural" or natural to man once given to him,
was man's created nature before sin came into the world. This
part of man's original nature Catholic thought designates by the
phrase *donum superadditum,* indicating that these supernaturally
added gifts are not, like reason, of the unalterable substance of
human nature. But here, as in any other *theonomous* conception
of human nature, man's relation to God enters into the very
essence of the meaning of manhood; man is what he is only in
relation to God, indeed he *is* this relationship. These gifts or "likeness," therefore, have residence "between" man and God: man
stands *within* his "likeness" to God, while the "image" of God
has residence within that structure of human nature which continues to be what it is quite apart from any continuing relation
to God. As a penal consequence of sin, the relational "likeness"
has been totally wiped out, while the "image" of God or man's
rational capacity for grasping the first principles of practical morality remains unimpaired, and needs no restoration. Catholic

interpretation fails to note the fact that in Hebrew parallelism "image" and "likeness" are synonyms, one line and term repeating the identical meaning of the other (Gen. 1:27). This Luther noticed; and he also believed that man's God-relationship does not stop short of penetrating to the root and embracing every human capacity within (or without) the image of God. The latter was a correction of Catholic error in biblical theology, an error occasioned by homage to Aristotle; the former was merely to correct their misunderstanding of literary form.

Mention in passing should be made of the most serious attempt in our own time to effect a new synthesis of a substantial with a relational understanding of the *imago Dei*. Emil Brunner distinguishes in human nature between the "formal" and the "material" *imago Dei*.[20] The "formal" *imago Dei* he identifies as the *humanum* in man, *i.e.*, all those capacities of the human spirit which make man a marvelous culture-producing animal: reason, imagination, will, sensitivity to values, etc. This is equivalent to what we have been calling the *imago Dei* as some distinctive part of the "substantial form" of human nature. Nevertheless, with all these marvelous powers, Brunner says, man may be totally—*i.e.*, pervasively—sinful; he is then not "materially" in the image of God; there is no health in him, no Archimedean point within his *humanum* (or in the civilizations he erects by means of this merely formal *imago Dei*) on which man may stand and where he will be competent to save himself and his civilizations from ruin. In the dimension of salvation, that is to say, in the dimension of the "material" *imago Dei*, a saving relationship with God can be established by God's grace and by faith *alone*. Brunner's "material" *imago Dei* is, then, the equivalent of what we have been calling the "image" as a relationship *within which* man stands and not something simply "formally" or structurally true of his nature apart from this relationship. In the dimension of salvation by faith alone and in the dimension of what comprises man's

[20]See *The Divine Imperative*, Macmillan, 1937, chap. v, and Appendix I where Brunner renounces the terms "formal—material" (employed in his essay *Nature and Grace*, 1934, now published in *Natural Theology*, Geoffrey Bles, 1946, pp. 22–35) but restates the viewpoint summarized above.

"material" or authentic being in the image of God, it is difficult to see what Barth and Brunner disagree about except what they disagree about.

In paying tribute to human reason or any other unique capacity of man, we should take care not to let this take the place of understanding man as wholly within (or without) his relationship imaging God. Nevertheless, without doing violence to Genesis or giving a semi-rationalistic interpretation of human nature after the fashion of Catholic thought, it is possible to recognize a certain degree of truth in philosophical anthropology of the Greek persuasion. Indeed, a proper understanding of the *mythological* meaning of the Genesis story requires this admission. A distinction may be made between the image of God in which man was created and the image of God which he acquired by virtue of the Fall:

> Formerly, man lived a life of happiness in the garden of God, but only possessed the intelligence of a child; now, however, that he had become "as an *elohim*" in intelligence, it was necessary that he should be deprived of happiness, . . . [and] that he should be shut off from the tree of life: since, if he had acquired immortality in addition to intelligence, he would have become wholly an *elohim*.[21]

"See, the man has become like one of us, in knowing good from evil; and now suppose he were to reach out his hand and take the fruit of the tree of life, and eating it, live forever!" (Gen. 3.22). Lest this happen, the angel with the flaming sword was placed at the Garden gate. Here are indicated three attributes or images of God: happiness, which as a creature man can have only in innocent obedience; rational intelligence; and immortal life. Man has happiness by God's gift of creation and retains it so long as he obeys. By sinning, he creates himself in another divine image, gaining full rational powers and knowledge as, now by acquirement, his nature. Herein was the Serpent justified. Man secures this acquired image of God, only at the expense of losing the created image of God. This was the point the Serpent

[21]Adolphe Lods, *Israel*, Knopf, 1932, p. 484.

shrewdly failed to mention. And the third image of God, immortality, man possesses neither by creation nor by acquirement. Man is not inherently immortal, as he is now inherently rational and as he was completely happy as long as he remained obedient. Immortality comes as an eschatological gift, always more God's possession than man's even when it is given him, lest it become true, as was said by God when at Babel he viewed another of man's efforts to assault the battlements of divinity, that "if this is what they can do as a beginning, then nothing that they resolve to do will be impossible for them" (Gen. 11:6).

In the Genesis story, reason and intelligence are far from being *the imago Dei;* at least in coming to full flower in the "knowledge of good and evil," these are capacities gained only through sin and the Fall. God told Adam what fruit of the Garden to eat and what not to eat. Adam did not discover this by the light of natural reason, and ever since then the sons of Adam have had difficulty seeing any reason in it. Thus, in Genesis, far from being *the imago Dei,* reason comes to its full height only through an act of sin. Man's created nature was originally in the image of God, in the sense that he stood within a relation of responsive obedience to his Creator and had the blissful happiness of innocently reflecting the will of God in all his actions and attitudes. By rebellion and disobedience he ate of the tree of knowledge. Reason and intelligence as we know them empirically in man came into existence only as a consequence of the Fall. And the temptation to which man succumbed was the suggestion that, through disobedience, he might become more like God than he was and learn to know good from evil. Thereby was lost *the imago Dei* in which he was created and which sustained him as a theonomous creature. Man's nature and his response to God were originally one and the same: the obedient reflection of God's will and "image." Only by denying his original likeness to God does man "know good and evil."

Along with the distinction between the image of God in which man was created and the image of God acquired by virtue of the Fall, there is a distinction to be noted between penal consequences of the Fall and certain other results that are not punitive in character. Knowledge is, if one may say so, a good result of the Fall. It is not a penal result. It is not one of the evil things that the narrator is explaining. Adam is punished by the interposition of toil between himself and the fruit of the ground; Eve, by the addition of pain to childbirth. Later on, the confusion of tongues and man's inability to understand his fellows are the penalty for the spirit that inspired the building operations at Babel. These things are presumed to be inherently evil. But rationality as a result of the Fall does not belong in the same classification. It is a good consequence of the Fall, so good, indeed, as to warrant God's associating evil penalties with it to remind Man the Reasoner that he still is a creature whose more fundamental nature requires him, if he would be himself, to be himself before God and to place all his attitudes and actions within the will and activity of God.

The relevant truth of this *mythological* analysis is its teaching that rationality is, as the Greeks say, of supreme worth, an essential part of man's dignity and definition, nay even *an imago Dei* in him; but that, as the Greeks generally do not say, human rationality is rebellious and evil unless set within the context of responsive obedience by the creature to his Creator. However superior its value, rationality is an instrument either of pride or of obedience. Nothing will ever alter the intellect's instrumental function. Man is a creature whose nature is always to be in some God-relationship; whichever way man faces in that relation, reason is always in service to his spiritual orientation. In the transaction recounted in Genesis, there was some loss and some gain of the image of God in man.[22] The fundamental religious teaching remains the same: man's deepest spiritual reality is attained when reason is in the service of recognized theocentric obligation. In contrast, the Greeks of all ages are satisfied if only man increases in understanding.

[22]Richard Kroner interprets man as in a measure "creating himself" and attaining "new likeness" to God by the Fall (*The Primacy of Faith*, Macmillan, 1943, chap. ix).

(b)

Although it should not enter into the theological definition of *the* image of God relationship, a philosophical understanding of man "after his kind" is necessary to complete one's total account of man's nature. What a modern man may believe on the basis of reasoning about this human nature of ours does not comprise the essence of man's relationship to God, but rather may be substantiated by reason without any particular reference to Christianity. It is true that Christians may persist in using the term *imago Dei* as a religious label for these same beliefs when they hold them. This manner of speaking effects no real gains in strengthening the case for philosophical humanism; and indeed considerable confusion results from using such an expression to refer to what may, and should, be believed about man apart from any immediate connection with Christian thought. It is important, however, for every man (Christian or non-Christian) to say for himself what "kind" of creature man inherently is—man whom Christians believe was also made for life within the image of God. Let us therefore next ask: What in the light of present knowledge and sound reflection may be believed to be incontrovertible about the nature of man, about his particular "kind" of being?

The interpretation of the nature of man most commonly accepted in our day is that given by naturalism in its various forms. Naturalism sees no essential discontinuity between man and physical nature or between an individual human being and his social environment. "I am not much more than an animal taught to dance by blows and scanty fare."[23] This statement of Nietzsche's sums up the naturalistic reduction of the stature of man to the level of nature, although his words "not much more" allow some slight room for special human dignity. "Imperial Cæsar dead and turned to clay might stop a hole and keep the wind away": Naturalism is the view that alive or dead Cæsar was no more than this. Reality, including human beings, consists of matter in motion, stimulus and automatic response; all the rest is moon-

[23]Frederick Nietzsche, *Thus Spake Zarathustra*, Prologue 6.

shine. Man the poet Mansfield described as "wet and saltness held together / To tread the earth and stand the weather."

The philosophy of naturalism varies according to what ultimately the nature of "nature" is conceived to be. Does "nature" consist of tiny atoms of matter? Some vital biological life-force? Electro-magnetic charges in a field? The totalitarian influence of the environment? The blood and soil of a people: Whatever be the nature of "nature," in one way or another naturalism always *homogenizes* man with nature. Man and physical nature are both cut from the same cloth, it matters little what the cloth is made of. The middle ground of a truly "humanistic" interpretation of man, which used to be presented as an alternative to religious ethics, has in recent years been largely captured from two sides by the naturalists and the supernaturalists, mainly by the former. As a consequence, the word "humanism," which used to imply essential discontinuity between man and nature, nowadays has only the negative meaning of "non-theism." Intellectuals who continue to call themselves humanists more often than not are actually naturalists; in one way or another they *homogenize* man with the physical or social context to which undoubtedly in large measure he belongs.

The influence of modern science was beyond question the main factor making for the spread of naturalism, though it is not difficult to show that such a conclusion was thoughtlessly drawn. The great genius of modern psychology, Sigmund Freud, spoke of three *offenses* against man's conception of himself. Copernicus gave the *cosmic offense*, Darwin the *biological offense* and Freud himself the *psychological offense* to man's traditional high regard for the powers of man. It might be added that in the reduction of man Karl Marx provided the *cultural offense*.

Astronomy frequently gets the blame for the first and the severest blow to the religious, or even to a humanistic, estimate of man. One historian of ideas writes:

> The Copernican revolution in reality swept man out of his proud position as the central figure and end of the universe, and made him a tiny speck on a third-rate planet revolving about a tenth-

rate sun drifting in an endless cosmic ocean. The absolute in-significance of man before the mighty and relentless will of Calvin's stern deity seems pomp and glory indeed compared with the place to which he has been relegated by modern as-stronomy.[24]

Still, decades after Copernicus, the philosopher Descartes, one of those "tiny specks," was able to think his way again to the center of the universe. Astronomically speaking, man may be a sick fly clinging dizzily to a whirling planet; but at the same time, speaking astronomically, man is *the astronomer.* He may be a reed, but a thinking reed. The Copernican revolution, while threatening man's physical position and making his fate exceed-ingly problematic, was itself a manifest tribute to man's spiritual stature as a thinking being. The reaches of the mind expanded to precisely the degree man's physical height became infinitesi-mally small. For this reason, Descartes, Pascal or Kant, or any one else who thought much about it, felt no less respect for man as man because of these findings of science.

By far the most impressive blow to a religious or a humanistic view of human nature was delivered by evolutionary naturalism in the nineteenth century. Toward the end of that century in a book which went through over a dozen editions and reprintings, Ernst Haeckel, no mean scientist and a popular writer, drew the blunt conclusion made necessary, he believed, by the science of biology, particularly by the theory of evolution:

> Our own "human nature," which exalted itself into an image of God in its anthropistic illusions, sinks to the level of a placental mammal, which has no more value for the universe at large than the ant, the fly of a summer's day, the microscopic infusorium, or the smallest bacillus.[25]

Unable as a naturalist to conceive of essentially different natures or of "spiritual substance" within the world of substance, Haeckel referred to God as a "gaseous vertebrate" and spoke quite seri-ously of experiments that might be performed on the human "soul," if only man had a soul.

[24]J. H. Randall, *The Making of the Modern Mind,* Houghton, 1926, p. 226.
[25]Ernest Haeckel, *The Riddle of the Universe,* Harpers, 1899, p. 244.

If, then, the substance of the soul were really gaseous, it should be possible to liquefy it by application of a high pressure at a low temperature. We could then catch the soul as it is "breathed out" at the moment of death, condense it, and exhibit it in a bottle as "immortal fluid." By a further lowering of the temperature and increase of pressure it might be possible to solidify it —to produce "soul-snow." The experiment has not yet succeeded.[26]

Human nature could not be more completely homogenized with everything else in nature! While, astronomically speaking, man still was the astronomer, it looks as if, biologically speaking, man, including the highest elements of his consciousness, his noblest capacities of intellect, appreciation or character, now is only a high-grade placental mammal. Not only facing "backworldsmen" who seek in God the original cause of life but facing as well the humanists who seek to find some special nature or worth in man, "the grinning ape stands in the way."

Instrumentalism has been in fact the most influential conclusion drawn from Darwinism. The human mind, according to this viewpoint, is only an instrument of survival developed in process of survival. Man, poor animal, must live by his wits! As an instrument for bringing the organism and its environment into better adjustment with one another, no doubt nothing has yet appeared so effective as the human brain, but this tribute to man's powers is in no way essentially different from what may be said of the human thumb in comparison with a gorilla's grip. What is the chief end of man? The theist answers this question, "To glorify God and enjoy him forever." The humanist answers, "To enjoy truth, beauty, goodness and to pursue and create them forever." If he is an instrumentalist, the naturalist replies, "To live in the world and adjust it forever." To this end ideals and gods alike are instrumental.

Other life-sciences, economics, sociology, psychology, only change the nature of that "nature" with which man is mixed and it is frequently affirmed that with the findings of these sciences the naturalistic interpretation of man now stands complete. Meth-

[26]*Ibid.*, p. 201.

odologically predisposed to the task of erecting a "physical" science of man, psychological and social sciences frequently speak as if, once their systems have been completed and a few more discoveries laid end to end, a complete account of human thought and human behavior can be given in terms of a closed system of natural laws which men are bound to observe like stars in their courses. The economic determination of history and culture, the social derivation of behavior, the reduction of morals to *mores*, behaviorism and Freudianism (at least in popular forms most significant for the prevailing understanding of man) all alike decapitate man in order to hold him more easily within the grasp of scientific reason.

Yet this is the quandary of every possible form of naturalism: If any viewpoint is ever *known* to be *true*, then nothing can be more certain than that man transcends nature in apprehending the truth about nature. If the proponent of naturalism asserts that his theory is *true* and that he *knows* it to be true, then, no matter what the theory itself says about man taken as an object for scientific investigation, the man who as subject holds this theory and puts forward this claim to truth is himself manifestly a truth-apprehending animal, and this constitutes his distinction from all other animals (no matter what his theory says). If ever the *truth* of some form of naturalism were established, precisely then nothing could be more certain than that naturalism is false.

Is all human thought merely the product of matter in motion, as the Epicureans believed, the rubbing of one smooth brain atom against another? If so, then, this theory, atomism, itself likewise reduces to atoms. And a thousand years later, quadrillions downward in the void, if the same two immortal atoms rub together and produce in another man's mind the thought that all human ideas come from God whispering in the ear, then this second theory on the face of it has truth equal with the first, because neither is true nor can ever be known as true *if atomism or naturalism is true*. On the other hand, if a single exception be made and the known truth of this one human thought, the theory of atomism, be granted, then *not all* human thought can be reduced to matter in motion (but only all thoughts except this one) and we find after all that the theory of naturalism is not altogether true.

Are ideas only weapons? Does truth consist only of an idea's operational effectiveness? If so, then this applies also to the theory of operationalism or instrumentalism itself, and should some other mind prove able to operate better with the idea that truth is supernaturally revealed, then "truth" would abide with him. Or rather truth can rest with neither viewpoint, there can be no truth *if* practical operation be the only test and if the human mind be nothing but an instrument for survival produced in course of survival.

Is man no more than an animal who has been taught to dance by blows and scanty fare? If so, then this theory likewise reduces itself to a certain number of blows and some form of scant fare. Whenever in another mind blows and scant fare happen to result in grandiose, compensatory dreams about the nature of man, then this second theory has truth equal to the first, because neither is true nor can ever be known as true *if* such naturalism be really true. On the other hand, if a single exception be made and the known truth of this one human thought, the theory of blows, be granted, then *not all* human thought can be reduced to blows and scant fare (but only all thoughts except this one) and we find again that the naturalist refutes himself by claiming truth for his views.

Is all human thinking and culture mere "ideology," the epiphenomonal consequence of factors in economic production, shadows of the class struggle thrown upon the screen of the mind? If so, then the theory of economic determinism itself likewise reduces to economic determinism, and who can judge truth between shadows or between ejaculations? Are all human thoughts and behavior determined by environmental influence? Then, environmentalism and behaviorism, supposing them true, have been similarly produced and cannot be truer than any other, even a contrary, theory which in fact may exist also because of some conditions or other.

Is the mind only an instrument in the struggle for existence? Do ideas evidence their truth by the survival of the fittest? Was Darwin simply engaging in the biological struggle for survival when he himself formulated the theory of natural selection? If no more than this, then other people have the right to survive by any other, even a contrary, idea if they can; there would be no truth obliging them to accept one belief rather than another concerning evolution.

If men think and act the way they do only because of wish-fulfillment in dreams, or as an outcome of sex frustrations, then the theories of Freud himself or of any other psychologist are themselves only manifestations of the same drives and compensations in the psychologist himself. Any man is then at liberty to dream and compensate for frustrations in his own way, for example, by preferring some theory of psychology other than such naturalism.

The same quandary will beset any possible future form of naturalism. Does electro-magnetic theory seem on the verge of explaining human consciousness in fashion that homogenizes the mind with rarefied and lively natural phenomena? All human thought except the electro-magnetic theory itself may perhaps be subject to such an interpretation; but if ever science succeeds in explaining itself and its own explanations as simply the product of physical factors, at that moment science destroys itself and all ground for knowing truth of any sort. The humanistic value of truth cannot be called in question by reducing truth getting to some natural reaction or interplay of physical forces. Of any such theory it can still be asked, Is it true? to which question only a distinctly human answer can be given. A naturalism like that of A. N. Whitehead perhaps avoids this quandary. Whitehead, it is true, cuts man and nature from the same cloth. Yet he avoids *reducing* man to that with which he is continuous by first conceiving the nature of "nature" to be *panpsychic, i.e.,* made of the same stuff the *self* is made of. Moreover, there are other evidences of Idealism and Platonism in Whitehead's metaphysics.

On second thought, therefore, biologically speaking, man is also the biologist with capacity to tell truth from error and this sets the biologist qualitatively away and above the biological kingdom he studies. Speaking in Marxian terms, all the higher reaches of human thought and culture seem the natural consequence of economic modes of production; but, still speaking in Marxian terms, man is the being who discovers this, who knows what is here asserted, who puts forward claims for its truth, who acts decisively on behalf of justice, and who can reflect that, since he does so, the theory cannot be altogether true. Speaking in Freudian terms, man's mind is a tissue of sex-frustration and dream-fulfillment, but at the same time man is he who knows this; and this knowledge can itself be no dream-fulfillment or else the whole theory is not true and need trouble us no longer. In short, it is not within the power of any naturalistic viewpoint to destroy the humanistic ground for the special dignity of man, for the simple reason that any such theory, if true, is a manifest tribute to man's spiritual stature as a thinking being. By every such theory known to be true the reaches of the mind expand no matter what the theory itself says about man, and this fact ought not to be thoughtlessly overlooked by the theory itself.

Beyond question there is an "ideological" factor in all thinking; "pure reason" is not really so pure as was once supposed. A person thinks the way he does largely on account of biological impulse, his class position and economic interests, and the submerged subconscious eight-ninths of his mental iceberg. With its penetration into reason's involvement in sin, Christian thought has much in common with the discoveries of Marx and Freud and their criticism of human reason and culture. Nevertheless, not *everything* in the conscious content of the one-ninth of our minds which glisten in the sun above dark waters can be due simply to what is below, or else this truth itself has no place on which to rest.

The quandary of naturalism is, of course, a "thought that wounds from behind," a "stab in the back" argument. Careful notice, however, should be taken of the fact that it is the naturalist who wounds *himself*—by claiming truth for naturalism. "It might be said paradoxically, that the worst fate that could befall this hypothesis [naturalism] would be to be proved, for then it would be most certainly refuted."[27] This dialectical quandary simply calls the naturalist's attention to the fact that he ought not to forget himself as a truth-seeking, purposive, conscious being in all his thinking about man as an impersonal object of scientific investigation. This has the form of an *argumentum ad hominem,* but not in the objectionable sense of bringing as evidence against the truth of a man's ideas some merely contingent factor about his personal life. What is cited here is entirely general and invariable, namely, the fact that only a mind transcending nature can know truth about nature—a fact which the naturalist forgets when, in a somnambulant state or condition of absentmindedness about himself and his own claim to possess truth, he concludes that naturalism explains everything. If this be the *argumentum ad hominem,* then it is the argument basic to all reasonable discussion of any subject of vital interest to man.[28]

Reason, or that in man which rises above physical nature, should not be thought of too narrowly. Many of the functions of reason can be regarded as simple extensions of sense perception by virtue of man's more complex nervous system. Human reason means more than awareness of the world which as animals we gain exclusively through the senses. There is something more in man than awareness; and this is *self-awareness.*

> We not only know, but we know that we know, and we can ponder in thought over the very fact that we are able thus to reflect in thought. . . . Even if it were possible that the mental content was gained through mere experience, that comparisons, syntheses, and abstractions were formed according to the laws of association, and that these were sublimed and refined to general ideas, and could grow into axioms of logic and of geometry, or crystallise into necessary and axiomatic principles—none of which can happen—yet it would always be a knowledge of *something.* But how this something could be given to itself remains

27Rudolph Otto, *Naturalism and Religion,* Putnam, 1907, p. 155.
28W. M. Urban, *The Intelligible World,* George Allen & Unwin, Ltd., 1929, pp. 45, 92–93, 96–98 and *passim.* Mr. Lowes Dickinson calls this "the only argument possible and, indeed, the only one in which any one much believes."

undiscoverable. The mind is a *tabula rasa* and a mere mirror, says this theory. But it would still require to show how the silver layer behind the mirror began to see itself in the mirror.[29]

What stands out in man above nature is his rational *self*-consciousness or awareness *of self*. Many philosophers who have described man's uniqueness as his capacity for "thought" have really meant his capacity for being aware of himself as a personal being and knowing the world in relation to himself or his place in the world. Pascal, for example, called man a "thinking reed" and spoke of "thought" as man's "whole dignity." Nevertheless, the full context makes plain that in these celebrated words Pascal paid tribute not to man's knowledge of this or that thing in the world but to his knowledge of himself or his self-awareness.

> Man is but a reed, the feeblest in nature, but he is a thinking reed. It is not necessary for the whole universe to arm itself to crush him. A vapour, a drop of water, is sufficient to slay him. But were the universe to crush him, man would still be nobler than that which kills him, for *he knows that he dies*, while the universe knows nothing of the advantage it has over him. Thus our whole dignity consists in thought.[30]

The meaning of rational self-consciousness or self-awareness we know better than anything else in the world. We may have more, and more exact, information *about* other objects, but we know the meaning and nature of self-awareness in ourselves more immediately and more intimately than we can ever know anything else. In fact, it is only in connection with or even by means of self-awareness that we become at all aware of other objects. To try to explain self-consciousness in terms of atoms, cells, physical impulses, physical energy, stimulus-response mechanism, or electrical charges amounts to an attempt to explain the more well-known by things that are considerably less well-known to us.[31] The meaning of selfhood every man understands by himself alone. If he would learn it from another, or from studying some-

[29]Rudolph Otto, *op. cit.*, p. 314.
[30]*Pensées*, 347 (italics mine).
[31]Tolstoy's essay *On Life* makes this point in vivid and unforgettable fashion.

thing else in the world, he does not know in the least what self-hood means and cannot possibly learn to know it. This has been a great part of what has been meant by calling man a "spirit." St. Augustine learned from the Platonists how to conceive of "spiritual substance" when thinking of the Divine or the human spirit. In speaking of the "substantiality" of man's consciousness of selfhood, St. Augustine

> means that it is not rendered in the slightest degree more in-telligible by being translated into terms other than itself, espe-cially into terms of physiology; to do this indeed is merely to add one mystery to another.[32]

Man never feels the stirring of impulse or observes that he has a body or thinks about some idea or pursues some good without being at the same time aware of *himself* as possessing impulses, employing a body, or identifying himself with ideas in their origin or with the realization of the good. He never experiences pure animal impulse, pure thought or pure value-judgment. Al-ways is he conscious of himself feeling, thinking, or desiring. This understanding of the spiritual nature of man derives in large measure from Platonism and it was a crucial point in St. Augus-tine's "order of natures." In the modern period, idealism became the bearer of this truth that man is a spirit and that personal spiritual existence plays the primary role in all knowledge and in all human activity—a truth which in the present day "existen-tialism" has rediscovered in its own special way.

Now it should be plain enough that there is nothing specially Christian, or even religious, in viewing man as unique because of his reason or his self-awareness. That man is this special "kind" of being should be apparent on grounds other than those of re-ligion. Moreover, as Augustine said, there is danger in designat-ing rational self-consciousness as the image of God in man. There is danger lest the human mind, being reckoned among invisible and immaterial things, should be thought *on this account* to be in the image of God and of the same nature with him who cre-

[32]Charles N. Cochrane, *Christianity and Classical Culture*, Oxford: Clarendon Press, 1940, p. 404.

ated it. Hereby the human spirit would fall away by pride from him to whom it should be united by obedience. To avoid this peril, it must be emphasized that rational self-consciousness becomes like God only by its relation of humble obedience to him. The mind can resemble God only by loving. And if it obtains the greatest nearness by humble obedience which produces within human consciousness the *imago Dei,* it must be far removed from him by that presumption which would make the likeness greater. In calling attention to rational self-consciousness as the distinctive capacity of human nature, we have simply elaborated what man's created nature is "after his kind." Beyond question this gives man "dominion" over all living things and the obligation and ability to "fill the earth and subdue it" (Gen. 1:28); but man's special glory is to acknowledge and serve God.

Persons who themselves agree with the present writer in accepting some form of a rapprochement between a Christian and an idealistic interpretation of human nature cannot exclude the possibility that other Christians likely will remain convinced of some form of naturalism. This may be held by some to be both philosophically more defensible and more suggestive for drawing up the principles of a social ethic than humanism, which, it must be admitted, always tends toward an unchristian dualism. Today naturalism and behaviorism have indeed carried through a "defense in depth," and contemporary exponents of these positions contend with some justification that they have made room for all the higher aspects of the human spirit formerly supposed to be ground for asserting man's discontinuity with nature. In addition to the philosophy of Whitehead, the so-called "higher naturalism" or "humanistic naturalism" of John Dewey is a case in point; his contextualism with its stress on "creative intelligence" differs very greatly from the reductive or mechanistic naturalism of an earlier day.

The foregoing "quandary of naturalism" may be used, if not to refute naturalism, at least to force the naturalist to use the term "nature" when applied to man with such broad meaning as no longer to have much significance. Nevertheless, the specifically religious or Christian meaning of the image of God may become a vital or governing element in an interpretation of the nature of man drawn from various philosophical sources, including naturalism. It must be acknowledged that there is about as much reason for describing the biblical point of view itself as a "theocentric naturalism" as for finding in the Bible the roots of theocentric or Christian humanism. In any case there is enough freeplay between a Christian view of man reflecting the image of God and insights concerning man's inherent nature drawn from various schools of philosophy or social science for "Christian naturalism" to remain permanently a possible position for Christians in the present day. Any one who happens to be convinced of this presumably has responsibility for showing how pragmatism or naturalism serves as basis for the image of "obedient love" or the Christ-like image of God in man without the latter becoming altered in its own essential nature. The Christian humanist or idealist has to do no less.

(c)

Certain implications follow from a thoroughgoing attempt to view man in the light of God, and these may now be briefly indicated in concluding this section. In the first place, from viewing man as a theological animal we are driven to regard all truly human worth as derivative, not inherent. Christian interpretations of man's dignity affirm something about man in relation to God, not just something about man *per se*. The Platonic doctrine of the inherent, substantial immortality of the soul endowed the soul with such power of outwearing bodies as to amount to divinity, and the early Christians quite properly regarded this viewpoint as a species of robbery of God. The same is true of many of our notions of the inherent sacredness of human personality. For the Christian both "the immortality of a mortal" and his personal worth are derivative, derivative from God's appointment. The human ethical situation in respect to the *way* in which value should be assigned to the human "spirit" differs only slightly, if at all, from other creatures God made and said that they were good: the sea, the snowflake and the lily of the field Kierkegaard speaks of:

> God takes pleasure in arraying the lily in a garb more glorious
> than that of Solomon; but if there could be any thought of an
> understanding here, would it not be a sorry delusion of the lily's,
> if when it looked upon its fine raiment it thought that it was
> on account of the raiment that God loved it?[33]

If there could be any thought of an understanding here, would
it not be a sorry delusion on man's part, if when he looks upon
his fine qualities and distinguished powers he thought that it was
on account of this raiment that God loves him? The creature has
no metaphysical business turning the image of God into a claim
upon God's or his neighbor's love for him, when in fact due only
to God's love is he *within* the image of God; nor any business
first asking about the image of God *within his neighbor* as a way
of *first* justifying his own love for neighbor, when in truth he
himself can resemble God only by loving.

A second implication to be drawn from conceiving the image
of God as a relation of response to God in which man may, and
should, live out his appointed length of days is that the image
of God in him may be entirely lost. Hereby man does not cease
to be a man in the substantial form of his human nature (undoubtedly an important consideration for philosophical humanism and for any man), but sinful man no longer images the will
of God. He images rather his own will or the will of some idol
(and this surely is the significant issue for Christian thought).

". . . Whatever sins they commit," declares St. Augustine,

> do not eliminate his manhood from man; nay, God's work con-
> tinues still good, however evil be the deeds of the impious. For
> although "man being placed in honor abideth not; and being
> without understanding, is compared with the beasts, and is like
> them" (Ps. 49:12), yet the resemblance is not so absolute that
> he becomes a beast. There is a comparison, no doubt, between
> the two; but it is not by reason of nature, but through vice—not
> vice in the beast, but in [human] nature. For so excellent is a
> man in comparison with a beast, that man's vice is beast's nature;
> still man's nature is never on this account changed into beast's
> nature. God, therefore, condemns man because of the fault where-

[33]Soren Kierkegaard, *Philosophical Fragments*, Princeton University Press, 1944,
p. 23.

withal his nature is disgraced, and not because of his nature which is not destroyed in consequence of its fault.[34]

In writing this, St. Augustine makes use of his doctrine interpreting reality as an hierarchical order of superior and inferior "natures," which he derived from Neo-Platonism. As he says,

> corrupt gold is assuredly better than incorrupt silver, and corrupt silver than incorrupt lead; so also in more powerful spiritual natures a rational spirit even corrupted through an evil will is better than an irrational though incorrupt, and better is any spirit whatever even corrupt than any body whatever though incorrupt.[35]

The human mind "obtains the greatest nearness by that subjection which produces likeness," and consequently "it must be far removed from Him by that presumption which would make the likeness greater."[36] Nevertheless, loss of the image of God *in this sense* does not entail loss of manhood. "For by turning itself from the chief good, the mind loses the being a good mind; but it does not lose the being a mind."[37]

If we do actually know that corrupt gold is better than incorrupt silver, this significant information must be taken into account by Christian thought, especially since the supposed inherent worth of corrupt gold may not be quite apparent in every market. If some philosophic doctrine of the "order of natures" proves rationally persuasive, this will be all to the good for man, and also for Christian thought and practice. For this reason we have suggested an interpretation of man's nature "after his kind" which draws upon the idealistic conception of man's supremacy over physical nature, and in the following chapter we shall have occasion to suggest how Christian thought makes use of such conviction in formulating social policy. This amounts to adopting an "order of natures" not unlike that St. Augustine took over from Platonism and employed as a Christian. Nevertheless, if reason-

[34]*On the Grace of Christ and Original Sin*, Bk. II, ch. xlvi (*Basic Writings of St. Augustine*, ed. by Whitney J. Oates, Random House, Vol. I, p. 652–653).
[35]*Concerning the Nature of the Good*, ch. v (*Basic Writings*, Vol. I, p. 433).
[36]*On the Morals of the Catholic Church*, ch. xii (*Basic Writings*, Vol. I, pp. 329–330).
[37]*On the Trinity*, Bk. VIII, ch. iii (*Basic Writings*, Vol. II, p. 776).

able judgment to this effect should not be forthcoming, then Christian thought would have to get along without the assistance of the Platonic or any other comparative ordering of "natures" after their kind. This calls attention to the fact that the distinctive perspective of Christian ethics has to do with standing within, or without, the image of God. This either/or allows, of course, that man's nature is never on account of sin changed into another nature. Yet *sinful human nature* may actually, for all we know, be worse than another sort of nature from the point of view of the glory of God which all his creatures declare after their kind, and worse precisely by virtue of the human nature which, remaining unaltered, has fallen under the control of sin. It is significant that St. Augustine did not always evaluate stones, mice, men, and angels in exact ascending order. "These are the gradations according to the order of nature; but according to the utility each man finds in a thing there are various standards of value." There is also a "scale of justice," which, like judgment of utility, pays no absolute regard to comparative position in the order of being.

> Who, *e.g.*, would not rather have bread in his house than mice, gold than fleas? . . . Thus the reason of one contemplating nature prompts very different judgments from those dictated by the necessity of the needy . . . for the former considers what value a thing in itself has in the scale of creation, while necessity considers how it meets its need. . . . But *of such consequence in rational natures is the weight, so to speak, of will and of love, that though in the order of nature angels rank above men, yet, by the scale of justice, good men are of greater value than bad angels.*[38]

Augustine himself nowhere suggests that a good rainfall is better than an evil man. In fact, he frequently argues that we justly blame the fault of sin in man because it mars so praiseworthy a nature; creatures lower in the scale than man are not better simply because they cannot be miserable. "And this its sin is itself proof that its nature was originally good. For had it not

[38]*The City of God*, Bk. XI, ch. xvi (*Basic Writings*, Vol. II, p. 158). (Italics mine.)

been very good, though not equal to its Creator, the desertion of God as its light could not have been evil to it. . . . So the nature which once enjoyed God teaches, even by its very vice, that it was created the best of all, since it is now miserable because it does not enjoy God."[39] Yet whenever Augustine speaks in this manner he is thinking of the "order of natures" and as a Platonist speaking of the worth *inherent* in different beings. It would therefore introduce no inconsistency into his thought for us to speak also of the *relational* worth of everything. Some one may question whether, in the scale of righteousness and of usefulness to God and to men, a good harvest is not better than a bad man. In rational natures the weight of will and of love is of such consequence!

John Donne expressed the equivocation within which a Christian man's confession and his understanding of himself must necessarily twist and turn:

> . . . Man, of whom David has said (as the lowest diminution that he could put upon him), *I am a worm and no man,* he might have gone lower and said, I am a man, and not a worm; for man is so much less than a worm, as that worms of his own production shall feed upon his dead body in the grave, and an immortal worm gnaw his conscience in the torments of hell. . . . Man that is infinitely less than nothing.[40]

Certainly without being accused of misanthropy we may reflect that to call human sensuality and dissension "bestial" insults the beasts. Man distends his lusts and falls upon creatures of his own species with a fury of which no animal nature is capable. ". . . These mortals . . . run to such enormities in sin, that even the beasts devoid of rational will, and who were created in numbers from the waters and the earth, would live more securely and peaceably with their own kind than men, who were propagated from one individual for the very purpose of commending concord. For not even lions or dragons have ever waged with their kind such wars as men have waged with one another."[41]

[39]*Ibid.,* Bk. XXII, ch. i (*Basic Writings,* Vol. II, p. 610).
[40]*Sermons* (London, 1640), No. viii, pp. 64–65.
[41]Augustine, *The City of God,* Bk. XII, ch. xxii (*Basic Writings,* Vol. II, p. 204).

Precisely because sensuality and hatred are *human* desires and attitudes they are so evil. To lose "the being a good mind" yet not lose "the being a mind," thus to remain men and not one of the good creatures of God who do praise their Creator after their kind, this but adds to the evil we may accomplish.

The Reformers taught that the image of God may be utterly lost from sinful human nature. Their dreaded and dreadful doctrine of "total depravity" (so-called) should be understood first of all as teaching the total loss of man's proper orientation toward God or his relationship reflecting the image of God. In addition to this relational interpretation of the image of God, and of sinful man standing *without* this image, there is another way of understanding the Reformation notion of depravity, one which approaches the matter from the point of view of the unity of human personality in all its aspects and powers.

Catholic doctrine, we have seen, distinguishes between "likeness" and "image"; and from this beginning Catholic analysis goes on to designate a multitude of other compartments or "faculties" within the psychological nature of man. There has taken place a total loss of man's original "likeness" with God; *in this respect* man is as totally depraved as ever Calvin conceived him to be. Nevertheless, according to Catholic teaching, the "image" of God in human reason remains unimpaired. Because Catholic theologians conceive of man as made up of separate compartments or faculties, they allow the effects of sin to be exceedingly grave in one respect or upon one aspect of human nature, utterly destroying man's supernatural relation to God; yet at the same time they deny that sin seriously affects man's grasp and exercise of the first principles of natural reason.

Luther and Calvin opposed this limitation of the injurious effect of sin upon man's nature. They asserted the unity and wholeness of human personality—in comparison with "faculty psychology," a more modern and a more acceptable view of man. Whatever happens to damage one part of human nature happens throughout the whole and runs through all the notes in the scale. If the influence of sin has been felt at any point, this reverberates, without diminution and without any exception, among all the "faculties" man possesses. The expression "total depravity" unfortunately suggests a *quantitative* totality of sin and an absolute *destruction* of human nature, which, however, even he who runs while he reads should know the Reformers never intended to affirm. They really meant to say (and this indeed is what they said) that sinfulness spiritually pervades the whole self with all its human capacities fully intact yet all alike under the sway of sin.

Sometimes Luther and Calvin wrote as if they too thought in terms of the *amount* of damage sin had done: a "relic," they said, but only a "relic," of the image of God remains.

> . . . The natural talents in man have been corrupted by sin, but . . . of the supernatural ones he has been wholly deprived. . . . Reason, therefore, by which man distinguishes between good and evil, by which he understands and judges, being a natural talent, could not be totally destroyed, but is partly debilitated, partly vitiated, so that it exhibits nothing but deformity and ruin. . . . Some sparks continue to shine in the nature of man, even in its corrupt and degenerate state, which prove him to be a rational creature, and different from the brutes, because he is endued with understanding; and yet . . . this light is smothered by so much ignorance, that it cannot act with any degree of efficacy. So the will, being inseparable from the nature of man, is not annihilated; but it is fettered by depraved and inordinate desires, so that it cannot aspire after anything that is good. . . .[42]

The Reformers' doctrine that underneath the quite extensive corruption of man's natural powers there remains only a "relic" of the image of God was simply a way of saying that more territory had been taken by the enemy than according to Catholic reports. These said: the "image" as a whole has escaped corruption, while it is true the "likeness" has been completely wiped out. Interminable would be the debate between these two, and any number of other, divisions of the ground between sin and the image of God, so long as the problem is stated in terms of a "faculty" or

[42]John Calvin, *The Institutes of the Christian Religion,* II, ii, 12 (*A Compend of the Institutes of the Christian Religion,* ed. by H. T. Kerr, Jr., Westminster Press, 1939, pp. 47–48).

a part or remnant of a faculty, here or there, more or less. To suppose, from the preceding quotation that Calvin believed reason still competent in some *portion* of its powers, yet fettered by corrupt desires, would be a gross mistake. Calvin's true meaning entails the unity of human personality and a consequent pervasiveness of sinfulness, sin penetrating the whole human spirit.

> Original sin, therefore, appears to be an hereditary pravity and corruption of our nature, *diffused through all the parts of the soul. . . . Sin has possessed all the powers of the soul. . . .* Man has not only been ensnared by the inferior appetites, but abominable impiety has *seized the very citadel of his mind,* and pride has *penetrated into the inmost recesses of his heart.*[43]

As a consequence of conceiving of man as being-in-relation-to-God to the very bottom of his being, Christian thinkers strongly influenced by the Bible ordinarily avoid all body-soul or *imago-similitudo* dualisms; and taking this same approach the Reformers overcame a faulty faculty-psychology long before modern thought taught us to regard man as a unity. If the unity of human personality be taken seriously, then the only way to avoid a notion of "total" sinfulness is to have no notion of sin at all.

II. SIN

The first assertion Christian ethics makes about man is that he was created for personal existence within the image of God, and that Jesus Christ most perfectly reveals this image. The second assertion is that man is sinful. So fundamental is this doctrine in Christian thought that it cannot be overlooked. Indeed, many theologians regard it as basic equally with the first for any full understanding of man in the light of God. This has been the view not only of more "pessimistic" thinkers; it was the view also of John Wesley, whose emphasis upon "going on to perfection" is well known.

> This, therefore, is the first grand distinguishing point between Heathenism and Christianity. The one acknowledges that many

[43]*Ibid.,* II, i, 8–9 (pp. 43, 44). (Italics mine.)

men are infected with many vices and even born with a proneness to them; but supposes withal that in some the natural good
much overbalances the evil: the other declares that all men are
"conceived in sin" and "shapen in wickedness"—that hence there
is in every man a "carnal mind" which is enmity against God,
which is not, cannot be subject to His law. . . . Hence we may
secondly learn that *all who deny this, call it original sin, or by any
other title, are but heathens still in the fundamental point which
differences Heathenism from Christianity.* They may, indeed,
allow that men have many vices; that some are born with us; and
that consequently we are not born altogether so wise or so
virtuous as we should be; there being few that will roundly
affirm, "We are born with as much propensity to good as to evil,
and that every man is, by nature, as virtuous and wise as Adam
was at his creation." But *here is the shibboleth:* Is man by nature
filled with all manner of evil? Is he void of all good? Is he
wholly false? Is his soul totally corrupt? Or, to come back to the
text, is "every imagination of the thought of his heart evil con-
tinually"? *Allow this and you are so far a Christian. Deny it,
and you are but a Heathen still.*[1]

These words, which may have to be modified to a great extent
before they become acceptable to us today, are at least a striking reminder that the doctrine of sin cannot simply be dismissed
as "strict Calvinism" or as a conclusion hastily drawn from the
cultural crisis of our time.

Sin, it must be pointed out first of all, is something a man *does,*
not something he *suffers.* Its locus is within the *will* of man, within
the *human spirit* itself. Sin is a man's *own* act, not the effect of
some influence upon him. This must be kept clear even when we
learn to regard sin as a deeply inward spiritual act or pattern of
activity, and no longer simply as some particular infraction of
a known moral law or series of such infractions. Christian ethics
dissociates itself from those points of view which explain moral
evil in terms of something outside of man or on the surface of
his nature. It is not sinful to make a mistake or to do some evil
deed purely because of ignorance, however unfortunate these
may be. It is not sinful to have been born in a poor environment

[1] *Sermon* xxxviii (*Wesley's Standard Sermons,* ed. by Edward H. Sugden, Nash-
ville: Methodist Publishing House, Vol. II, pp. 222–223). (Italics mine.)

or to have a strong set of natural appetites or to be behind the times. Social evil may result in large measure from the "social lag"; but not sin, though sin may partly explain why we are so laggard. To be unreasonable may not be sinful. All these explanations succeed only in explaining sin away. In contrast to every interpretation of moral evil which regards it as the effect of environmental conditions or some incidental aberration in human nature, Albert Camus' symbol of "the plague" probes deeply into the question where sin has its residence.

> In this respect our townsfolk were like everybody else, wrapped up in themselves; in other words *they were humanists: they disbelieved in pestilences.* A pestilence isn't a thing made to man's measure; therefore, we tell ourselves that pestilence is a mere bogy of the mind, a bad dream that will pass away. But it doesn't always pass away and, from one bad dream to another, it is men who pass away, and the humanists first of all, because they haven't taken their precautions. Our townsfolk were not more to blame than others; they forgot to be modest, that was all, and thought that everything still was possible for them; which presupposes that pestilences were impossible.
>
> I know positively . . . that *each of us has the plague within him;* no one, no one on earth is free from it. And I know, too, that we must keep endless watch on ourselves lest in a careless moment we breathe in somebody's face and fasten the infection on him. What's natural is the microbe. All the rest—health, integrity, purity (if you like)—is a product of the human will, of a vigilance that must never falter.[2]

A religion such as Christianity whose God is Creator must dissociate itself from the belief that "the plague" is entirely natural; and as a religion of redemption it must dissociate itself from Camus' confidence that by itself the human will must resolutely produce whatever good there is. Nevertheless, in tracing sinfulness home to its source in the heart or will of man and not stopping at some point on the rim of the self, in this there is entire agreement. The word "sinfulness" designates some structure or pattern of man's own spiritual activity.

[2]Albert Camus, *The Plague,* Knopf, 1948, pp. 35, 229 (italics mine).

This truth A. C. Knudson does not sufficiently acknowledge in his "personalistic" account of man's moral goodness and sin. He distinguishes between man's "moral nature" or "moral freedom" and his "acquired moral nature." Reserving the word "sin" to refer to specific actions in which man willfully breaks known moral law, he allows that there is an "evil tendency" present in man's "acquired moral nature." This tendency toward evil has come to be present because in infancy and early childhood every person was trained to avoid pain and desire pleasure. Habituated in this way, when a person comes to the age of free moral choice he inevitably finds himself drawn in the direction of animal pleasure and often away from doing right. This constitutes his acquired evil tendency, and if he agrees to it he sins.[3]

Knudson's moralistic definition of sin has the merit of regarding sin as man's own act. However, the word "sin" becomes merely a class name, a way of grouping particular actions, and the words "sinful" and "sinfulness" have no referent at all in human nature. Only the words "evil tendency" have anything corresponding to them in human nature, and this only on the periphery of the self in its acquired moral nature. Tendency toward evil is never man's own act, but something he has suffered. Knudson's position might be described as a nominalistic interpretation of sin: "sin" he regards as a label useful for the purpose of classifying immoral acts. These actions themselves alone are real, while the class-name "sinful" itself has no reality corresponding to it in human nature. Undoubtedly the traditional doctrine that sin is a *status* man has suffered and inherited fails to regard sin as man's own act, but it at least used the word "Sin" or "sinful" meaningfully. By criticizing both the moralistic and traditional definitions of the meaning of sin, Christian ethics in the present day should try to understand sin both as man's own doing and as a dynamic structure or pattern or orientation within man's activity which goes to the root of his existence as spirit or person. To speak of sin as "original" means that it originates in man himself by his own will, and cannot be traced away from man to find its origin in some-

[3]A. C. Knudson, *op. cit.*, pp. 84–85.

thing man suffers or in some superficial aspect of his person. There is a sense in which the doctrine of "original" sin is the most significant thing you can say about man, because it makes him responsible for the origination of sin.

The second thing that should be said concerning the Christian understanding of sin is that this is no *ad hoc* judgment upon man rendered in some moment of gloom by theologians who should be psychoanalyzed instead of being believed. The idea of sin is not a conclusion reached simply from analyzing the capacities and propensities within human nature as such, temperament and mood of the observer having decisive effect in the matter. It is rather a conclusion to which Christian thought is forced from viewing man in the light of God as Christians know him, *i.e.*, in Jesus Christ. At the deepest level the doctrine of sin has least to do with mankind in general and most to do with one's self in particular; it amounts to confession prompted by viewing one's self in the mirror of the Word. Once again, in this notion "sin" we confront a term to which Christian ethics gives Christocentric definition, or perhaps we ought to say "Christofugal" (compare "centrifugal") definition.

How shall the Christian doctrine that "man is a sinner" be Christianly taught? This truth grasped by personal appropriation would require a confession of one's own sinfulness and, as Luther said, a mantle of charity thrown over the failures of other men. How shall the doctrine of sin be taught, when teaching requires demonstration of general human sinfulness and this, in turn, requires cynical peering into the sins of other men? Plainly, the Christian doctrine of human sin, in being taught, is in grave danger of being taught un-Christianly and thus of not being taught at all. If from an "inquisitive experimentation which treats sin as a curiosity" a man "would magnanimously forget himself he with his zeal to explain humanity,"[4] it is evident that the Christian view of sin is not being taught. This dilemma was Kierkegaard's meaning:

[4]Soren Kierkegaard, *The Concept of Dread*, Princeton University Press, 1944, pp. 46, 51.

When the individual then is foolish enough to inquire about sin as about something irrelevant to him, he speaks as a fool; for either he does not know in the least what the question is about and cannot possibly learn to know it, or else he knows it and understands it, and knows too that no science can explain it. . . . How sin came into the world every man understands by himself alone; if he would learn it from another, he *eo ipso* misunderstands.[5]

And if he would apply the doctrine first of all to another, he *eo ipso* misunderstands. No one has yet come to the Christian doctrine of sin without being driven to it, not by theology or the present crisis of our civilization, but by the crisis created by personally confronting Christ.

Nevertheless, from this acknowledged, personal point of standing in relation to Christ, Christians have gone on to elaborate general statements to the effect that "all have sinned." This doctrine must still be understood, not as a consequence of a dispassionate anthropological or psychological analysis of man, but in a Christocentric, or "Christofugal," sense. Clearly this was St. Paul's ultimate ground for supposing all mankind was in bondage to sin. It is too often not noticed that St. Paul paid great tribute to man's natural powers. In two respects he praises the goodness and competence of man. Man has a native capacity for natural morality: "When Gentiles who have not the law do by nature what the law requires, . . . they show that what the law requires is written on their hearts" (Rom. 2:14, 15). In the second place, man is naturally religious:

For what can be known about God is plain to them, because God has shown it to them. Ever since the creation of the world his invisible nature, namely, his eternal power and deity, has been clearly perceived in the things that have been made. So they are without excuse; for although they knew God they did not honor him as God or give thanks to him (Rom. 1:19–21a).

It is true Paul finds evidence of sinfulness even here, in that men "became futile in their thinking and their senseless minds were

[5]*Ibid.*, pp. 45, 46.

darkened. Claiming to be wise, they became fools, and exchanged the glory of the immortal God for images resembling mortal man or birds or animals or reptiles" (Rom. 1:21b–23). Nevertheless, one might question *to what extent* "their senseless minds were darkened" and *to what extent* men still retain their capacity for natural religion. For Paul what chiefly reflects upon man is not his incapacity for natural religion or natural morality. Let these for the moment be allowed to remain in him, especially man's competence for naturally being moral. And it should be remembered that optimistic eighteenth-century thought found it difficult to say more in tribute to human nature, save by drawing upon man's perfectibility at some period in the future. The decisive issue for St. Paul was not the degree of ability or inability man has for living up to his own insights in morals and religion; it was man's plain inability to attain to the *Christian* religion and the *Christian* ethic, unless God gives what he commands. "For all have sinned," he declared, "and come short of the glory of God" (Rom. 3:23). This expression "the glory of God" is a semi-technical term meaning throughout the Bible God's disclosure of himself to man. For Paul it meant, of course, God's disclosure of himself in Jesus Christ. He speaks elsewhere of God shining "in our hearts to give the light of the knowledge of the glory of God in the face of Christ" (II Cor. 4:6). This expression, then, "falling short of the glory of God," falling short of Jesus Christ as standard, may be taken as Paul's primary definition of the meaning of sin, in terms of which he states, with some logic and keenness of perception, that all have sinned.

If the reader will call to mind what has been said in earlier chapters of this book concerning the nature of Christian love, it will be possible to give in a very few words several summary definitions of what "sin" means, namely: the opposite of all that Christian love means. Any falling short of disinterested love for neighbor for his own sake, love cut to the measure of Christ's love, any falling short of the strenuous teachings of Jesus, any falling short of the full definition of obligation contained in I Corinthians 13—this is what is meant when Christians speak of man as sinful. If we ought to have "faith effective through love," then sin means "pride (or anxiety, the opposite of faith) working through selfishness." Sin means: anxious self-centeredness or self-centered anxiety.

If this be the meaning of sin, there is nothing really so astounding in the Christian judgment concerning the universality and totality of sin in the flesh. What was truly astonishing was the screwing of the standard for man up to such a sticking point. In all probability the Christian theologians who have spoken most of sin have not been altogether incompetent observers of themselves or of the men around them. In them the juices of life ran strongly, and joy over ordinary goodness and a degree of understanding for human frailty was not altogether lacking from their make-up. They would have described human behavior with its mixture of observable goodness and observable evil much as any one else would describe it. However, this has been their misfortune, their burden and their ultimate hope: no longer to compare men with one another, or one day's deeds with another, but in all things to compare themselves first and secondly mankind in general with the glory of God and the image of perfect manhood seen in Jesus Christ. Man comes off worse from this comparison than from his own. When measured by the ethical principles "nature herself teaches" undoubtedly men prove better than Christians have judged them to be, and less in need of what they declare God has done for their salvation. In terms of the two chief questions of ethics, *What* is the good? *Whose* good shall it be? every man may give competent answer to the first, while every man in fact, whatever happens to be his definition of "the good," gives sinfully incompetent answer to the second question whenever he comes actually to the task of doing the deed. "Corruption" pervades but does not destroy man's ethical reasoning or action. In every action to some degree he judges himself and his own cause: who except Christ would have expected better of him? As Reinhold Niebuhr remarks:

> The love commandment stands in juxtaposition to the fact of sin. It helps, in fact, to create the consciousness of sin. When,

as in utilitarian doctrine, the moral ideal is stated in terms of a wise egoism, able to include the interests of others in those of the self, *there is no occasion for the consciousness of sin.*[6]

The only way to avoid the corollary of sin penetrating to the heart of man yet being man's own act is to water down the teachings of Jesus or replace them with some other ethic.

Understanding the consciousness of sin in this way places the Genesis story in proper perspective. Christians read their Bibles *backward,* first the New Testament, then the Old. Although not much is said about sin in the synoptic gospels themselves, the consciousness of sin arises especially from thinking about oneself in relation to this part of the New Testament Word. The depth of sin has to be acknowledged before reading Genesis, else it would never be drawn from there alone. Jews have this same scripture, yet Jewish thought contains no notion of man's deep sinfulness. Christians do not believe man sinful because of the account of Adam's first sin in Genesis. They first have been persuaded of man's sinfulness, and then they find the Genesis account to be something of an explanation as to *why* man is what he is. Modern theories of the origin of man by the processes of evolution do not refute the Christian doctrine of human sinfulness, because the latter was never grounded primarily in Genesis but in man's understanding of himself on encountering Jesus Christ. If Genesis should prove no longer an acceptable explanation for the phenomenon of sin the phenomenon itself would remain; it would remain given some other explanation or it would remain in need of explanation, or else, as in Genesis itself, sin would remain a "primitive," basic factor in human experience in terms of which

[6]Reinhold Niebuhr, *An Interpretation of Christian Ethics,* Harpers, 1935, p. 65 (italics mine). Acknowledgment of sin must have Christ at the center. This is shown in the sequence contained in St. Paul's statement, "For the love of Christ controls us, because we are convinced that one has died for all; *therefore all have died"* (II Cor. 5:14). This was also the reason for Luther's insistence that it is a rare and a hard thing to *become* a sinner. "As the righteousness of God lives in us through *faith,"* he remarks in his *Commentary on Romans,* "so it is also with sin; that is, we must *believe* that we are sinners." "In the strict sense," says Karl Barth, "there is no knowledge of sin except in the light of Christ's cross. For he alone understands what sin is, who knows that his sin is forgiven him" (*Dogmatics in Outline,* Philosophical Library, 1949, p. 119).

other things (the pain of childbirth and the drudgery of agriculture) receive explanation, itself susceptible of none.

The traditional doctrine of "original" sin was completed by adding to the account of man's first sin a "history" of the inheritance of sin or the transmission of sin to the entire race by biological propagation. This idea could not have occurred to a man of the Bible, where the physical body and procreation are viewed as good and where sexual intercourse is by no means disparaged. The idea of the biological inheritance of sin was, in fact, a product of Greek thought which tended to regard the body as evil and sex desire as an appropriate channel for transmitting sin; or rather, it was a product of the meeting of Greek and biblical ways of thinking in the minds of men such as St. Augustine. The early Christians, who were first convinced of man's sinfulness and had in Genesis the beginnings of an explanation for it, completed their theory by making sexual propagation the vehicle for the transmission of sin, the connecting link between man's "original" sin and our own.

Contemporary Christian thought in general rejects this idea of inherited sin. The views of St. Augustine on this point are still cherished "with public applause and secret abhorrence by the Latin Church," to quote a remark of Gibbon, because the sacrament of baptism in Roman Catholicism serves the sole purpose of removing inherited guilt for sin plus all an individual's sins up to the time of baptism. Doubtless also this notion of inherited sin has currency in the circles of simple Protestant orthodoxy. However, the main line of Christian thinking which is free from rigid adherence to ecclesiatical dogma and ceremony has rejected it. Yet many who disbelieve in inherited sin affirm their belief in "original" sin. This can be understood only by grasping the fact that the Christian verdict upon man the sinner always was a contrast-effect of seeing him in the light of Christ and never depended on or resulted from the theoretical explanation of human sinfulness in terms of a combination of the Genesis story with an essentially Greek disparagement of the physical body or physical desire as the principal source of evil.

Nevertheless, those ancient legends which were the repository of the earliest Hebrew thought about man in relation to God do contain profound truth concerning the nature and meaning of human sin. Genesis gives a theocentric, or a contra-theocentric, a "theofugal," definition of sin. Sin does not consist of particular immoral acts, or infraction of specific laws. Always, of course, sin manifests itself in terms of some particular act of disobedience or breach of moral law. What made the specific act of disobedience *tempting* to Adam and Eve, however, was the promise that "the very day you eat of it, your eyes will be opened, and *you will be like gods* . . ." (Gen. 3:5). In building the tower of Babel, men said to one another, "Come, let us build ourselves a city with a tower whose top shall *reach to heaven (thus making a name for ourselves)*, so that we may not be scattered all over the earth" (Gen. 11:4). Their wish, born perhaps out of felt insecurity, to become like gods was their sin. The quality of human sinfulness can perhaps best be seen in contrast to what God must do in order to correct sin and hold it within bounds: He is a zealous and a "jealous" God who will have no other gods before *or beside* him. In the Bible, God is experienced as that which severely limits as well as that which securely upholds man. The trouble with man is not that he is too weak but that, without God, he is too strong for himself.

The contra-theocentric definition of sin which runs throughout the story of God's dealings with man in the Old Testament was perhaps best summarized by the late Archbishop William Temple:

> When we open our eyes as babies we see the world stretching out around us; we are in the middle of it; all proportions and perspectives in what we see are determined by the relation—distance, height, and so forth—of the various visible objects to ourselves. This will remain true of our bodily vision as long as we live. I am the center of the world I see; where the horizon is depends on where I stand. Now just the same thing is true at first of our mental and spiritual vision. Some things hurt us; we hope they will not happen again; we call them bad. Some things please us; we hope they will happen again; we call them good. Our standard of value is the way things affect ourselves. So each

of us takes his place in the center of his own world. But I am not the center of the world, or the standard of reference between good and bad. I am not, and God is. In other words, from the beginning I put myself in God's place. This is my original sin. I was doing it before I could speak, and every one else has been doing it from early infancy. I am not "guilty" on this account because I could not help it. But I am in a state, from birth, in which I shall bring disaster on myself and every one affected by my conduct unless I can escape from it.[7]

Such an understanding of the meaning of sin improves itself away only by merging into contra-Christocentric, or Christofugal, definitions of sin which lie at the root of the New Testament account of God's dealings with man. Simply by bringing to sharper focus "the righteousness of God," the New Testament Word brings to sharper focus the sinfulness of man.

III. IDOLATRY: THE WORK OF SELF-LOVE

According to the Bible, rebellion against God does not simply take the form of specific disobedient acts and these alone. Nor does sin ordinarily take the form of rebellion so utterly defiant or despairing as to break all connection with "the divine." Few if any men go so far in their assertions of self-sufficiency as to believe they need give themselves to *nothing* beyond themselves. Instead, sin always assumes the guise of idolatry, or adopting some other religious orientation than worship of the true God. This notion of "idolatry" is a religious and at the same time also an *ethical* category. It is in fact the exact opposite of "obedient love" which we have seen to be the positive religio-ethical category in Christian ethics. At this point an exploration of the biblical (and the Reformation) idea of "idolatry" in its relation to ethics will perhaps throw additional light on the meaning of sin.

Consider the classic description of idolatry given by Isaiah:

A man cuts down a cedar, or takes a plane or an oak, or lays hold of some other tree of the forest, which the Lord planted and the rain has nourished for man to use as fuel. He takes part

[7]William Temple, *Christianity and Social Order*, Penguin Books, 1942, pp. 37–38.

of it and warms himself, he kindles a fire and bakes bread; then
he makes a god and worships it, he molds an image and prostrates himself before it. Half of it he burns in the fire, and on its
embers he roasts flesh; he eats the roast and is satisfied; he also
warms himself and says, "Ha! ha! I am warm, I feel the glow."
And the rest of it he makes into a god—his idol!—prostrates himself before it, worships it, and prays to it, saying, "Save me, for
thou art my god!" (Isa. 44:14–17).

With this story in mind, an analysis of the inner nature and movement of idolatrous spirit leads to the statement that idolatry is
subconscious egotism. Idolatry is subconscious: At one and the
same time the man in the story (1) did not know that the object
of his worship was an idol and not God, else he would not have
worshiped it; and yet (2) he did know it was an idol, since he
had made it and warmed himself before the fire which consumed
the spare wood. Idolatry is egotism: The man (1) engaged in
flight from himself, he tried to get utterly out of himself into
union with his god; and yet (2) in fleeing from himself he was
careful, nevertheless, to pursue himself, because the god into
which he fled from himself was already identified with himself
and his own needs. Worship of the folk-nation or of any idea-
tional or cultural idol illustrates the complex weaving together of
these orientations or movements of the spirit distinguishable but
inseparable in all idolatry. This, for example, is true of the sin
of state-worship. Idolatry of the state contains a complex inter-
weaving of conscious and subconscious elements. The sin of the
Nazi, or of any extreme patriot, varies inversely (not directly)
with the consciousness that he is sinning in exalting the nation
into a false position, and yet all along such a man knows that the
nation is not god enough to bear the devotion he gives it. The
gods we worship, in devotion to whom we flee from ourselves,
are all of them either made by our own hands or include our being
in theirs, or else they are finite enough to be made certainly sub-
servient to ourselves. In devotion to them we do not really flee
from ourselves. In devotion to them we are not really devoted to
another than ourselves, because in idolatry we actually find ways

of adoring "the physical sound of our own names" as our ground and goal.

In *The Sickness unto Death* Soren Kierkegaard expresses the two movements (distinguished above) as (1) the "despair at not willing to be oneself, the despair of weakness"; and (2) "the despair of willing despairingly to be oneself—defiance." It is evident, then, that self-centeredness, as a continuing element in all idolatry, is essential to the definition of sin. In contrast, Kierkegaard defines "faith" in an existing individual as a reversal of the two movements contained in idolatry, amounting, therefore, to its complete exclusion. Faith is: (1) an infinite passion to become what we are, and at the same time, (2) willingness to be nothing before God; or, more moderately put, faith is (1) willingness simply to be ourselves (2) before God. To use his own words, "Faith is: that the self in being itself and in willing to be itself is grounded transparently in God."[1]

The "origin" of sin, certainly the nature of sin, is revealed most clearly in the fact that the human spirit, in its self-transcendence and freedom, with overwhelming probability centers itself upon itself in the guise of some idol rather than in faith living for another. This overwhelming spiritual probability must be distinguished not only from natural or circumstantial necessity but also from the overwhelming *moral* probability that a person born in deepest poverty in the slums will likely succumb to some specific form of immorality. At all times and places men worship idols, *i.e.*, themselves, and not just under certain variable conditions. It is always ideally possible for man to trust God and live outside himself; instead man anxiously trusts something which, because it is finite, seems more surely subordinate to the interests of the self and at the same time is actually subconsciously known to be an ultimately untrustworthy god. Modern man may be more especially prone to run back and forth between the two moods in idolatry. He first despairs over man's littleness, his limitation by physical necessity and death, and in despair he is unwilling to

[1]Soren Kierkegaard, *The Sickness unto Death*, Princeton University Press, 1941, pp. 78, 107, 130, 132, 216.

be himself the creature of dust he knows he is. At the same time he despairingly and defiantly wills to be himself in the guise of some god, some deified program or institution whose creatureliness he refuses to acknowledge.

> . . . The grossest of our dreams is
> No worse than our worship which for the most part
> Is so much galimatias to get out of
> Knowing our neighbor . . .

Our worship is for the most part so much galimatias to get out of knowing God and in "obedient love" serving our neighbors. We prefer idols which permit us in "knowing" them to serve ourselves; they help us avoid existence "before" God and "for" another. It is transparent that we always interpose ourselves, *i.e.*, some idol, between ourselves and God, between ourselves and our neighbor.

Idolatry is well understood in the Bible as a religious cloak for self-centeredness.

> Idolatry is well understood in the Bible as differing from the pure worship of Israel's God in the fact of its personification and objectification of the human will in contrast with the superhuman transcendence of the true God. When an idol is worshiped, man is worshiping himself, his desires, his purposes, and his will. . . . The idols are so described as to give the impression that they are devoid of a will or mind of their own. . . . The idols are the work of men's hands, and the personal qualities they are alleged to possess are really ascribed to them by human beings by a magnificent process of self-deception. These idols are the glorified projections of the will of their human followers and supporters. . . . [They] were really embodiments of human thought and desire. The chief sin was rebellion against God, the other-than-man, and the glorification of man-made images, who were gods in name only. These gods were made in the image of man —in the image of his mind, desire, and purpose. As a consequence of this type of idolatry man was outrageously guilty of giving himself the status of God and of exalting his own will as of supreme worth.[2]

[2]Otto Baab, *The Theology of the Old Testament,* Abingdon-Cokesbury, 1949, pp. 105, 110.

The two movements within "idolatry"—*i.e.*, absolutizing something finite, and in so doing seeking the interests of self—sum up "sin" in the self's attitude toward the employment of its own physical, mental and moral powers and in its external relationships to possessions and to other persons. Distending the importance of these values and incurving the self on itself may, without too much oversimplification, be diagrammed as follows, showing in the right-hand column the special type of sin which arises in each instance from idolatry or spiritual self-centeredness:

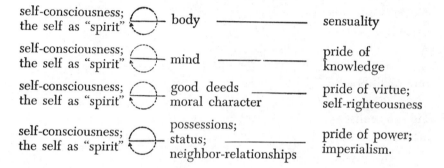

self-consciousness; body ——————————— sensuality
the self as "spirit"

self-consciousness; mind ——————————— pride of
the self as "spirit"   knowledge

self-consciousness; good deeds _____ pride of virtue;
the self as "spirit" moral character   self-righteousness

self-consciousness; possessions;
the self as "spirit" status; _____ pride of power;
                      neighbor-relationships imperialism.

Christian ethics has always regarded the more spiritual sins, pride of power, pride of knowledge and pride of virtue, as deeper and more deadly sins than sensuality; and in its analysis of "the lust of the body" sensuality as a self-conscious misuse of the body has always been distinguished from sensuous delights or the simple gratification of mere animal impulse which Christian ethics regards as good in themselves. The notion of idolatry, and self-centeredness which lies at its root, makes clear the meaning of this analysis which, in turn, is basic to an understanding of Christian ethics.

"Is sensuality . . . a form of idolatry which makes the self god," Reinhold Niebuhr asks, "or is it an alternative idolatry in which the self, conscious of the inadequacy of its self-worship, seeks escape by finding some other god?" His answer provides a perfect illustration of idolatry as an ethical category: ". . . There is a little of both in sensuality."

> . . . The instincts of sex are particularly effective tools for both the assertion of the self and the flight from self. . . . It is both a vehicle of the primal sin of self-deification and the expression of an ʾuneasy conscience, seeking to escape from self by the deification of another.[3]

There is a little of both present also in pride of knowledge, power or virtue. In each of these types of sin, a man seems, on the one hand, unconscious of the limitation of his knowledge, power or righteousness, and on the other hand such a man is driven by a darkly conscious realization of the insecurity and finitude of his achievements in these areas to making too great claims for them.

> The pride of intellect is derived on the one hand from ignorance of the finiteness of the human mind and on the other hand from an attempt to obscure the known conditioned character of human knowledge and the taint of self-interest in human truth.[4]

There is self-deception present in man's apparent ignorance that his gods are no-gods. Yet he does not know they are no-gods, else it would not be necessary for him, in devotion to them, to deceive himself.

> The self-deceiver does not believe . . . what he says or he would not be a deceiver. He does believe what he says or he would not be deceived. He both believes and does not believe . . . or he would not be *self*-deceived.[5]

The idolater does not believe what he says or he would not be able shrewdly to use physical, social, intellectual and moral goods simply as a means to his own aggrandizement. He does believe what he says or he would not worship these things so much. He both remains within the circle of self-seeking and he gets out of himself in devotion to his gods, or else he would not worship idols in place of God, for idolatry implies the suppression of egotism into subconsciousness by raising some good which serves man to the place of the divine man serves.

[3]Reinhold Niebuhr, *The Nature and Destiny of Man,* Scribners, 1942, Vol. I, pp. 233–234, 236–237.
[4]*Ibid.*, pp. 194–195.
[5]Philip Leon, *The Ethics of Power*, George Allen and Unwin Ltd., 1935, p. 258.

The reader should now be in position to grasp the difference between Christian ethics and its chief rival ethical theory in the modern period, the ethics of philosophical idealism. The ethics of idealism constitutes the *chief* rival of Christianity because so often the ethics of self-realization and Christian ethics have been identified as one and the same; and idealism is the chief *rival* of Christian ethics because what idealism calls "the good" Christian ethics calls sin or idolatry, namely, the intentional pursuit of self-realization. Of course, along with Christian ethics the idealists understand self-realization as the unintended by-product of moments of self-sacrifice or devotion to another; but then the idealists always *intend* it that way! If you find that self-realization cannot actually be achieved by direct pursuit, this simply means that self-realization ought not to be aimed at *in this fashion*. A more oblique approach proves a better course toward self-realization. Self-achievement becomes, then, not quite the unintended consequence, or not the *quite* unintended consequence, it is in the ethics of Christian love. The idea of *seeking* self-realization *through* self-giving comes to no more than covering self-centeredness under the cloak of idolatrous devotion.

Hegel made this his basic interpretation of the life of spirit. Hegel's view was that spirit always and necessarily follows the pattern of going out of itself into some other, which, however, is not truly other but really identical with self, so that in the last analysis spirit always remains at home. In every detail this describes idolatrous existence. Even Hegel's view of God and the nature of Divine Love exactly conforms to the anatomy of idolatry. It matters not that in his youth Hegel made more use of the word "love" and only later supplanted it by a more abstract analysis of the movement of spirit. Shall we say, "God is love, *i.e.*, He represents the distinction [between two beings], and the nullity of this distinction which is not to be taken seriously, and which is therefore posited as something abolished"? Or shall we say, more "spiritually," "God beholds Himself in what is differentiated; and when in His other He is united merely with Himself, He is there with no other but Himself, He is in close union only

with Himself, He beholds Himself in His Other"?[6] In either case,
Love or Spirit has the same spirit. Not since Aristotle's "contemplation of contemplation" has such narcissism been set forward
as a metaphysical principle and as the nature of divine love. In
fact, the main differences between Hegelian spirit and Aristotle's
Being eternally contemplating itself arise from the complexities
introduced when egotism maintains itself in the guise of idolatry.

Hegelianism is the last, if not the only, great school of philosophical theology concerned to formulate a Christian doctrine of
the Trinity. It is therefore tempting to regard idealism as first
setting forth the nature of Divine love and then using this as the
norm or prototype for right human spirituality. Nothing could be
farther from the truth. Hegel says nothing about the trinitarian
nature of World Spirit which might not have been uttered B.C.
His account actually arises—existentialism par excellence!—from
the trinitarian nature of idolatrous human spirit. His "voyage of
discovery" was a phenomenological analysis of the nature of
spirit; and after first studying the anatomy of spirit in the human
spirit, idealism then proceeds to show, through the whole of philosophy, that Reality itself is spiritual because everywhere there
is evidence of activity following this same dialectical pattern.

Love, or the activity of spiritual self-realization, defined in
terms of this prototype, it should have been expected, would prove
to be love patterned anthropologically after idolatrous spirit. From
this flows the decisive difference between an idealistic and a
Christian theory of ethics, for the latter cuts its pattern for man
by making reference to God's self-emptying love going out to man,
a being totally other than himself. Hegel reverses this procedure;
he makes God after man's spiritual image, and then describes all
right and proper love in a fashion apparently designed to make

---

[6]Hegel, *Philosophy of Religion* (K. Paul, Trench, Trübner & Co., 1895), III,
11, 18. This point of view was not wholly original with Hegel. Influenced by Greek
notions of love on God's part as always love for perfection, *i.e.*, for himself,
Anselm and others interpreted the love of Father for the Son as a form of self-
love which has need of an object other than self to love. It is interesting that
Barth describes this "innertrinitarian love" as a *giving* sort of love (*The Doctrine
of the Word of God*, T. & T. Clark and Scribners, 1936, p. 533 *sq.* and *cf.* E.
Brunner, *Dogmatik*, Zwingli-verlag, 1946, Bd. 1, p. 255).

the self's return to or incurving on itself explicit and fundamental. He writes:

> . . . Love implies a distinguishing between two, and yet these two are, as a matter of fact, not distinguished from one another. Love, this sense of being outside myself, is the feeling and consciousness of this identity. My self-consciousness is not in myself, but in another; but this Other in whom alone I find satisfaction and am at peace with myself . . . this Other, just because it is outside of me, has its self-consciousness only in me. Thus the two are represented simply by this consciousness of their being outside of themselves and of their identity, and of this perception, this feeling, this knowledge of the unity of love.[7]

If this be the nature of so-called "mutual love," then mutual love must be assessed as the idolatrous opposite of Christian love, as so much galimatias to get out of faith and obedience to God who stands over against the self and so much galimatias to remain always at home with self and get out of knowing our neighbor who also stands over against us in all concreteness.

Rousseau's notion of an "association . . . in which each, while uniting himself with all, may still *obey himself alone,* and remain as free as before"[8] runs like a thread of Theseus throughout all the labyrinthine expressions of modern idealistic ethics. The claim has even been made that in thus avoiding "authoritarianism," in thus relating the individual only to himself as lawgiver, idealism has given the only adequate account of the meaning of obligation. Yet from the point of view of religious existence, the primary concern of idealism to identify the self with a larger common good, supposed *because of this identity* to be the source of obligation, cultivates idolatry, invites a subtle continuation of self-interest.

Indeed, the double subjective orientation of idolatry appears in Rousseau: (1) self-alienating flight of self away from self takes form as "the total alienation of each associate, together with all his rights, to the whole community," and yet (2) the ulterior relation of the self is still only to itself: "each man in giving himself

7*Ibid.,* III, 10, 11.
8*The Social Contract,* Book I, ch. vi (Everyman edition), p. 14 (italics mine).

to all, *gives himself to nobody.*"⁹ "The voice of the people is, in fact, the voice of God";¹⁰ the voice of God is, in fact, the voice of self.

The idealistic view of the finite-infinite nature of man and of the world to which he is internally related—developed by Hegel and, somewhat more explicitly, by Bosanquet—permits emphasis to be placed, first, on the vast "difference" between finite and infinite (as in the attitude of the man who cried out to an image, "Save me, for thou art my God"), and then on the "identity" of finite and infinite (as the man in Isaiah was careful to remember, since his own hands had made the idol and the wood had already satisfied him with warmth and aided him in preparing food). The identity which absolute idealism affirms between the finite spirit and the infinite spirit functions to provide man with something to give himself to, yet in such fashion as always to remain related only to himself in all his spiritual quest.

Even idealistic logic provides no merely abstract account of the principles of reason. It is a logic of movement, the movement of spirit distinguishing in a sentence between subject and predicate yet affirming their identity. In a statement of the type "S is P," if S and P are not identical the statement is false; if they are not different the statement is not very illuminating. The word "is" means both "is" and "is not," just as the idol both is and is not god, both is and is not the self. S must be the same as P yet different from P, just as the idol must be the same as self yet, as a projection of the self, different from it. The logical principle of "identity in difference" epitomizes or illustrates the dual structure of idolatrous spirit, spirit which will not let go of self or go over to the side of another who is truly different from self.

Stress first on difference, then on identity, which by design the doctrine of the finite-infinite nature of man makes possible, is particularly evident in idealistic social philosophy. This was Bosanquet's solution of the "paradox" of ethical and political obli-

⁹*Ibid.,* p. 15 (italics mine).
¹⁰"A Discourse on Political Economy" (Everyman edition of *The Social Contract,* p. 254).

gation.[11] For obligation to be meaningful, it must come from a
source other than man as he is; and yet for obligation to be justly
imposed its source must be none other than man himself, so that
he "obey himself alone," "remain as free as before," and "give
himself to nobody." In order to provide a significant account of
obligation, idealistic social philosophy speaks of man's obligation
to respond to a general will set over against his own; then, when
the question is the justification of political coercion, it speaks of
man's free identity with this general will. The radical nature of
the requirement that a man obey the general will depends upon
the "difference" between it and his actual, momentary will; rightful obligation to obey the general will, however, arises only from
its "identity" with the "real" individual will. Thus, in order to
avoid authoritarianism and at the same time to secure that political obligation may be coercive and require the radical transformation of the individual "wie er geht und steht," Bosanquet
maintains that the general will which compels and obligates is
really the will of the finite self. The general will compels because
the finite will is "different" from it; it obliges because the finite
will is the same as itself; it both compels and obliges because both
general and finite wills have finite-infinite or idolatrous identity.
Idealistic social theory in general treats the individual first as
finite, appealing to the difference between him and the standard
for him in order to render the confronting obligation significant
and imperative; then, in order to justify his coercion, stress is
shifted to the individual's real identity with the general will or
with the infinite side of finite-infinite self. "No one would bother
with a source of obligation not significantly different from self;
yet no one should be willing to conform to an obligation which
is not a projected shadow of self"—so reasoned the man in Isaiah,
chapter 44. As is well known, idealistic social theory fluctuates
between the two extremes of releasing the ego from all limitation
and subjecting the individual under some totalitarian obligation.

[11]Bernard Bosanquet, *The Philosophical Theory of the State,* London: Macmillan & Co., Ltd., 1930, ch. iii.

No better illustration can be found of the idolatrous nature of that spiritual "becoming" on which idealistic thinking is based than the justification of the good given by the idealistic theory of society.

The foregoing analysis entails no wholesale indictment of idealistic ethics. "Objective generality" or "generality of application" remains a norm for proximate political obligation and a bulwark against tyranny, exposition of which has improved very little since Rousseau. The flaw, the idolatrous flaw, lies in the connection between this and "subjective generality." Kant's categorical imperative remains a defensible account of some measure of our obligation. The flaw, the idolatrous flaw, of idealism manifests itself in the view that the phenomenal self is obligated only to the noumenal self, that man himself is a universal lawgiver, that, at most, duties are to be performed *as if* they were duties to God. The validity of the general will as a norm for law and for proper political "consent" by no means depends upon either metaphysical identity with individual wills (Bosanquet) or the act of consent itself (Rousseau); consent is itself needed only as a practical procedure for insuring the probable promulgation of laws having maximum objective generality. To an extent in the following section and in the next chapter, we shall be dealing with some of the elements of idealistic ethics which can be salvaged for Christian thought.

IV. THE "ORIGIN" OF ORIGINAL SIN

We have observed that, in the main, contemporary Christian thought has abandoned the idea of the inheritance of sin from Adam. How, then, account for the origin of sin? The only answer that can be given to this question is to say that sin does not originate from anything besides man's own will. This is the ultimate meaning of "original" sin: that every man is his own Adam, sin originates with him, he does not sin on account of anything. The evil which man does because of ignorance, bad environment, etc., may indeed be evil, but not on that account sinful. Even temptation does not compel; it only entices. Only by sin does sin come into the world.

Nevertheless, something should be said about the *occasion* for sinning. Nowadays, the situation which gives occasion for sin is ordinarily drawn in terms of an "existentialist" or Kierkegaardian analysis of individual human freedom. This view treats man as an entirely isolated individual and, while giving profound analysis of the dimension of spiritual freedom in man, it needs to be supplemented by recovering some sense of the occasion for sin in man the social animal. In this section we shall first indicate the possibility and proneness to sin which freedom gives, and then go on to add an analysis of the occasion and stimulus to sinning which comes from the processes of social cultivation.

Kierkegaard thought and wrote a good deal about the relationships between spiritual freedom and dread, and between dread and the act of sin. The concept of "dread" or "anxiety" he defined as "the reflex of freedom within itself at the thought of its possibility."[1] By virtue of his freedom, man has a "sweet feeling of apprehension."[2] Dread means the presentiment of "the next day."[3] Facing the bare possibility of this or that particular good or evil which the future may bring, man finds himself moment by moment faced with an alluring yet threatening "maybe so, maybe not." This thought haunts and taunts him. Dread arises in him over the alarming "not-yet-ness" of his future, no matter how great the chances of its being good. Looking into the future he encounters nothingness, bare possibility of being (which means he encounters nothing at all, because the future is by definition not yet). The future now present in man's consciousness awakens anxiety all the more terrible because in fact man stands in dread of nothing. Therefore, "the concept of dread . . . is different from fear and similar concepts which refer to something definite."[4] In face of evil in particular forms a man might be brave or cowardly; but in face of whatever is only possible and quite

---

[1]*The Concept of Dread,* Princeton University Press, 1944, p. 50.
[2]*Ibid.,* p. 38.
[3]*Christian Discourses,* p. 80.
[4]*The Concept of Dread,* p. 38.

hidden in the future there is no man who does not live in dread. Dread is "the alarming possibility of *being able*"[5] or of not being able, of being or not being, of only possibly being. Kierkegaard then asks the question, In contrast to the animals, how does the possibility of "anxiety about subsistence" come about in man? and answers, From the fact that the human being has self-consciousness or self-transcendence.

> In the possession of consciousness he is eternally far, far out beyond the moment; no bird flew so far away, and yet precisely thereby he becomes aware of the danger which the bird does not suspect: when eternity came into being for him, then the morrow also came into being. Through his consciousness he discovers a world which not even the most traveled bird knows: the future; and when this future through the consciousness is withdrawn in the moment, then a concern is discovered which the bird does not know; for however far it flew and from however far it returned, it never flew to the future and never returned from the future.[6]

In the moment of return from the future anxiety is born; and this situation provides the *occasion* by which, through a free act of sin, sin comes into the world. Out of insecurity or the "dizziness of freedom," man himself acts to make himself more secure. In this, there takes place some degree of sinful cloture of the self upon itself or some distention of the security expected from possessions, power, or knowledge.

The Russian novelist Dostoievsky stands essentially in this same world of thought. In the first part of his *Letters from the Underworld* he gives a theoretical statement of his view of freedom, and the source of sin in freedom, which finds expression throughout his great novels. Among all man's interests which economic welfare and "the great and the beautiful"[7] can satisfy, according to Dostoievsky, man has one interest in particular which is his "interest of interests," his greatest need, to which nothing external

[5]*Ibid.*, p. 40.
[6]From *The Gospel of Suffering and The Lilies of the Field*, by S. Kierkegaard, translated by David F. and Lillian M. Swenson, copyright 1948, Augsburg Publishing House, used by permission, p. 214.
[7]Fyodor Dostoievsky, *Letters from the Underworld* (Everyman edition), Dutton, p. 24.

corresponds. ". . . What man most needs is an *independent* will."[8] On this account he will refuse at all cost to become part of "the keyboard of a piano" or "the handle of a hurdy-gurdy" or an item in a logarithm table,[9] however these may be calculated for his benefit. In some situations "man would *purposely* become a lunatic, in order to become devoid of reason, and therefore able to insist upon himself."[10] Even the psychical injury man sometimes does to himself rather than serenely submit to circumstance bears testimony to his freedom.

Out of freedom and will upsurging within him, man sins. No amount of social improvement will alter this fact, because, Dostoievsky believed, no "crystal palace" utopia can ever lay wholly captive the entire dimension of man's freedom.

> . . . you are persuaded in your own minds that man is bound to improve as soon as ever he has dropped some old, bad customs of his, and allowed science and healthy thought alone to nourish, to act as the normal directors of, human nature. Yes, I know that you are persuaded that eventually man will cease *to err on set purpose.* . . .

❊ ❊ ❊ ❊ ❊

> Consequently, I would ask you—what are we to expect from man, seeing he is a creature endowed with such strange qualities? You may heap upon him every earthly blessing, you may submerge him in well-being until the bubbles shoot to the surface of his prosperity as though it were a pond, you may give him such economic success that nothing will be left for him to do but to sleep and to eat dainties and to prate about the continuity of the world's history; yes, you may do all this, but none the less, out of sheer ingratitude, sheer devilment, he will end by playing you some dirty trick.

❊ ❊ ❊ ❊ ❊

> Yet I tell you . . . that there is one occasion, and one occasion only, when man can willfully, consciously desiderate for himself what is foolish and harmful. This is the occasion when he yearns *to have the right* to desiderate for himself what is foolish and harmful, and to be bound to no obligation whatsoever to desid-

[8]*Ibid.,* p. 31. [9]*Ibid.,* pp. 29, 34-37, *et passim.* [10]*Ibid.,* p. 37.

erate anything that is sensible. It is his crowning folly; it is wherein we see his ineradicable waywardness.

❖   ❖   ❖   ❖   ❖

For instance, I should not be surprised if, amid all this order and regularity of the future, there should suddenly arise, from some quarter or other, some gentleman of low-born—or, rather, of retrograde and cynical—demeanour, who, setting his arms akimbo, should say to you all: "How now, gentlemen? Would it not be a good thing if, with one consent, we were to kick all this solemn wisdom to the winds, and to send all those logarithms to the devil, and to begin to live our lives again according to our own stupid whims?" Yet this would be a nothing; the really shameful part of the business would be that this gentleman would find a goodly number of adherents.[11]

Out of freedom, by sin sin comes into the world, and it is always coming into the world. This is a consequence and concomitant of man's greatness.

In describing anxiety as "the internal precondition for sin"[12] and temptation its external precondition, Reinhold Niebuhr draws extensively from Kierkegaard's concept of dread. Neither anxiety within nor temptation from without brings with it any "absolute necessity that man should be betrayed into sin by the ambiguity of his position, as standing in and yet above nature."[13] Nevertheless, the dizzy heights to which man's freedom ascends provoke anxiety; and this gives occasion, this is the situation in which, by his own free act, man sins.

Anxiety, as a permanent concomitant of freedom, is thus both the source of creativity and a temptation to sin. It is the condition of the sailor, climbing the mast (to use a simile), with the abyss of the waves beneath him and the "crow's nest" above him. He is anxious about both the end toward which he strives and the abyss of nothingness into which he may fall.[14]

When man sins it is he who does it and not anxiety which compels him. "Sin posits itself," says Niebuhr, "sin presupposes itself . . .

[11]*Ibid.*, pp. 29, 36, 34, 30–31.
[12]Reinhold Niebuhr, *The Nature and Destiny of Man*, Scribners, 1942, Vol. I, p. 182.
[13]*Ibid.*, p. 178.   [14]*Ibid.*, p. 185.

the bias toward sin from which actual sin flows is anxiety plus sin." At this point it may be recalled that one of the definitions of sin, suggested above, was "anxious self-centeredness" or "self-centered anxiety."

Man is not in an unfree *status* as sinner; he sins by his own inner spiritual action. It is true Niebuhr deals in paradox when he affirms that "Evil in man is a consequence of his *inevitable though not necessary* unwillingness to acknowledge his dependence" and live by faith overcoming sinful or self-assertive anxiety.[15] Nevertheless, better understanding of Niebuhr, and of the problem, will be gained by interpreting his viewpoint from the side of his constant stress on freedom than from putting the weight on this word "inevitable." Even present-day science has given up the notion that a "law of nature" *compels* observance; it is rather that a "law" describes what objects in nature *do*. Similarly, to say that as a *rule* men are universally sinful may be a quite accurate statistical and introspective observation of how in fact men act without there being any implication here of something not themselves forcing men to sin.

How to comprehend every man his own Adam may be further seen in Niebuhr's treatment of the relationship between "*justitia originalis*" or "perfection before the Fall" and the origin of original sin. The real locus of original righteousness, which Genesis assigns to the garden of Paradise, is rather to be found in every man "before the act." "Perfection before the Fall" means "perfection before the act"; sin or the Fall takes place *in* the act.[16] The point here may, without too much oversimplification, be diagrammed as follows:

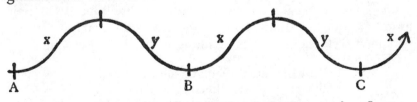

Let A, B, and C represent a series of actions. A person's reflection

[15]*Ibid.*, pp. 181, 250–252, 150 (italics mine).
[16]*Ibid.*, pp. 276–280.

upon his own activity may then be distinguished into two sorts of thinking: After the doing of any deed (points "x") he judges his previous act in terms of universal norms; he stands within the image of God or under a standard of righteousness which he acknowledges has bearing upon him. He confesses that in doing A or B or C he loved the deed too much, or himself in the deed too much. However, when he begins to orient his thinking and planning toward the doing of his next deed (points "y"), he ceases to apply universal norms to himself, or he twists them so as to make an exception of himself. He seeks himself in the deed more than, a moment ago, he knew he ought. Thus he "falls" into sin; he sins in the act and this accomplishes every man's passage from the garden of original righteousness. This illustration needs correction only at the point of remembering that man's activity, his thinking over his actions and his planning for further activity take place simultaneously and without interruption. The self in the moment of transcending itself has a memory of innocence and is able to frame universal principles of action which the self in action never fully carries out. The self as spectator of both *itself* and its world has standards in terms of which it knows the self as agent (who in acting consciously transcends only its world and not itself) always to be making undue claims for itself. Transcending history *and itself*, the self is righteous; transcending only the situation in the world upon which the self is acting, by sin sin comes into the world. In *actually* answering the question *What* is the good? man inserts himself as an end between himself as agent and the good whose nature he knows well enough when he does no more than contemplate or reflect upon it. In *actually* answering the question *Whose* good? he inserts himself as an end between himself as an agent and the neighbor whom he knows well enough when standing in the image of God.

> Behold the infant, helpless in cradle and
> Righteous still, yet already there is
> Dread in his dreams at the deed of which
> He knows nothing but knows he can do,
> The gulf before him with guilt beyond,

Whatever that is, whatever why,
Forbids his bound; till that ban tempts him;
He jumps and is judged: he joins mankind,
The fallen families, freedom lost,
Love become Law. Now he looks at grown-ups
With conscious care, and calculates on
The effect of a frown or filial smile,
Accuses with a cough, claims pity
With scratched knees, skillfully avenges
Pains and punishments on puny insects,
Grows into a grin, and gladly shares his
Small secret with the supplicating
Instant present. His emptiness finds
Its joy in a gang and is joined to others
By crimes in common. Clumsy and alarmed,
As the blind bat obeys the warnings
Of its own echoes, his inner life
Is a zig-zag, a bizarre dance of
Feelings through facts, a foiled one learning
Shyness and shame, a shadowed flier.[17]

Real insight has been gained from the analysis of spiritual free-dom and anxiety by Christian existentialism. However, this should not lead to an indiscriminate dismissal of all forms of understanding man as a social creature. Approaching man from the side of his social nature one may comprehend something of the occasion for sin yet without interpreting it simply as a necessary consequence of some variable factor in the environment. Indeed, the understanding of man in idealistic social philosophy should be sharply distinguished from the superficialities of ordinary environmentalism in this regard. To show this, Rousseau and Royce may be selected as idealists who both had penetrating understanding of sin as man's own responsible act and at the same time analyzed primarily in social terms the occasion out of which, by sin, sin arises.

In his "Discourse on the Origin of Inequality," Rousseau asks how man, essentially good as he may be supposed once to have been, could then produce corrupting and tyrannical political in-

---

[17]W. H. Auden, *The Age of Anxiety*, Random House, 1947, pp. 29–30.

314   *This Human Nature*

stitutions, whose influence in turn creates in social man such an overwhelming propensity toward evil. In order to answer this question, Rousseau gives a mythological account of the sin and fall of man. In interpreting this Discourse, altogether too much stress is usually placed upon his statement in the appendix, "That men are actually wicked, a sad and continual experience of them proves beyond doubt; but, all the same, I think I have shown that man is naturally good."[18] This is taken to be a statement of the unqualified goodness of natural man, and from this it is concluded that both the Discourse itself and all of Rousseau's thought express what is nowadays called the "institutional fallacy," or the fallacy of deriving evil (inequality) altogether from established institutions and not at all from man himself. This seductive cliché of recent criticism has come in for much popular acceptance but its sole advantage is in relieving one of the necessity of studying Rousseau to any depth. Such an interpretation Jacques Maritain adopts when, on behalf of medieval natural-law theory, he sets himself against both the Protestant and the idealistic roots of modern life. Whatever Maritain may know about Descartes, he does not understand the other two of the "three Reformers"— Luther and Rousseau—whom he criticizes. Reinhold Niebuhr and others also set themselves too severely against the philosophy of idealism on behalf of a revival of Protestant insights. The thesis of Rousseau's "Discourse on the Arts and Sciences" was, of course, that "our minds have been corrupted in proportion as the arts and sciences have improved"; but his statement that "the arts and sciences owe their birth to our vices" should have been a warning against the easy interpretation that man is simply corrupted by his culture.[19] Certainly in the "Discourse on Inequality," Rousseau describes the influence of man upon his political and economic culture (as well as these upon him) as not altogether good.

The "natural man" portrayed in the "Discourse on the Origin

[18]"What Is the Origin of Inequality among Men, and Is It Authorised by Natural Law?" *The Social Contract and Discourses* (Everyman edition), p. 239.
[19]"Has the Restoration of the Arts and Sciences Had a Purifying Effect upon Morals?" *The Social Contract and Discourses* (Everyman edition), pp. 133, 140.

of Inequality" is a being in whom the impulses of egoism and compassion are unself-consciously expressed and nicely balanced. This
was the original condition of man, and with these he possessed
also free agency and "perfectibility" (which simply means "the
faculty of self-improvement") setting him apart from the brutes.[20]
Man was then a bundle of well-integrated and equally propor-
tioned egoism and sympathy, and he made use of freedom and
his capacity for self-improvement under the ideal conditions of
"original righteousness" in a state of nature. Of this state of nature
Rousseau gives two pictures. One is that of an isolated man,
roaming the woods and entering into only the most transient relations with his fellows, bound by none of them save as his natural
needs and natural sympathy occasion. The other ideal condition
is that "first expansion of the human heart . . . which united
husbands and wives, fathers and children, under one roof" and
"soon gave rise to the finest feelings known to humanity, conjugal
love and paternal affection," in a society which was "the more
united because liberty and reciprocal attachment were the only
bonds of its union."[21] Of this picture of natural society Rousseau
says:

> Thus, though men had become less patient, and their natural
> compassion had already suffered some diminution, this period
> of expansion of the human faculties, keeping a just mean be-
> tween the indolence of the primitive state and the petulant activ-
> ity of our egoism, must have been the happiest and most stable
> of epochs. The more we reflect on it, the more we shall find that
> this state was the least subject to revolutions, and altogether the
> very best man could experience; so that he can have departed
> from it only through some fatal accident, which, for public good,
> should never have happened.[22]

The counterpoise which this ideal *social* state of nature provides
to the more Tarzanesque picture of the "noble savage" is often
forgotten.

The character of "fallen" man may be described as the predominance of egoism over compassion, a loss of the original bal-

---

[20]"Discourse on the Origin of Inequality," *ibid.*, pp. 184, 185.
[21]*Ibid.*, p. 211.   [22]*Ibid.*, p. 214.

ance between these two fundamental impulses. Rousseau gives two accounts of how this decline took place. One is an external history. By a sequence of "revolutions" in economic and political institutions, egoism within and civil inequality without came to have sway over human life. Inequality was the more established, and egoism unleashed, as successively there came into being the institutions of property, metallurgy and agriculture, and the state as an instrument for making power over others legitimate.[23] Undoubtedly, this external history of the origin of inequality and egoism commits the "institutional fallacy," as is implied by the words with which Rousseau introduces the "first revolution": "The first man who, having enclosed a piece of ground, bethought himself of saying *This is mine,* and found people simple enough to believe him, was the real founder of civil society."[24]

In addition, however, to this external history Rousseau refers to an internal moment or factor in the fall of man. From his very first social contact man began to perceive certain relations of comparative superiority between himself and other species or other individuals of his own kind: "Thus, *the first time* he looked into himself, he felt the first emotion of pride. . . ." In the first moment of self-consciousness, "*he* prepared the way for assuming pre-eminence as an individual" not only over the animals but also over fellow-members of his own species.[25] The supplanting of primitive isolation by primitive ideal society not only made possible an expansion of human affections. It also occasioned an inevitable increase of egoism, precisely because in more intimate and continuous society there is greater opportunity for comparison and for securing unwarranted, unnatural advantages by exaggerating natural superiorities.

> If this were the place to go into details, I could readily explain how, even without the intervention of government, inequality of credit and authority became unavoidable among private persons, as soon as their union in a single society made them compare themselves with one another, and take into account the differences which they found out from the continual intercourse

[23]*Ibid.,* pp. 210, 215, 222–223, 231.   [25]*Ibid.,* pp. 208–209 (italics mine).
[24]*Ibid.,* p. 207.

every man had to have with his neighbours. . . . I could explain how much this universal desire for reputation, honours and advancement, which inflames us all, exercises and holds up to comparison our faculties and powers; how it excites and multiplies our passions, and, by creating universal competition and rivalry, or rather enmity, among men, occasions numberless failures, successes and disturbances of all kinds by making so many aspirants run the same course. I could show that it is to this desire of being talked about, and this unremitting rage of distinguishing ourselves, that we owe the best and the worst things we possess, both our virtues and our vices, our science and our errors, our conquerors and our philosophers; that is to say, a great many bad things, and a very few good ones. In a word I could prove that, if we have a few rich and powerful men on the pinnacle of fortune and grandeur, while the crowd grovels in want and obscurity, it is because the former prize what they enjoy only insofar as others are destitute of it; and, because, without changing their condition, they would cease to be happy the moment the people ceased to be wretched.[26]

The fall of man from primitive domestic economy took place, therefore, not simply "through some fatal accident," which is all external history can indicate, but through an aggravation of human egoism. This expansion of egoism was occasioned, of course, and given room for expression by the increasing intricacy and permanence of social relationships. But egoism could not be aggravated in man if it were not already present in him as something more than a spontaneous natural sentiment—if, in short, his ego had not been continuously puffed up since "the first time he looked into himself." This was an inner, spiritual event. Rousseau's internal account of the fall of man explains the origin of inequality in terms of spiritual sin rather than, as in the external history, explaining spiritual sin in terms of cultural complications.

As an etiological myth this account may be compared with the Genesis story. Genesis also gives an external explanation of sin as resulting from temptation, Adam's sin from Eve's tempting him, Eve's sin from the serpent's temptation; but this only leads us back to an original angelic rebellion in heaven, where there was

[26]*Ibid.*, pp. 233–234.

no temptation. Neither Rousseau nor Genesis really explains sin by external history; they both bring sin with them into external history. Moreover, since they simply refer to sin as an internal factor in order to explain certain external realities, sin itself never is explained by either account. By sin, sin came into the world. Thus, for Rousseau, the unnatural prideful function of natural egoism in preparing its own predominance over natural sympathy was essential to a full explanation of the successive revolutions which produce vested social inequality. For the author of Genesis sin was essential to explaining why woman must bear her children in pain and why man is subject to the drudgery of agriculture. Thus, in both cases, the unquestioned reality of sin was itself the explanation of something else. "Without this mystery, the most incomprehensible of all," as Pascal said, "we are incomprehensible to ourselves . . . so that man is more inconceivable without this mystery, than this mystery is inconceivable to man."[27] Genesis understands sin as sin *before God* and therefore apprehends it with intensity as an ultimate infraction of man's God-relationship, whereas Rousseau understands sin as sin *over man* and therefore apprehends it as a less ultimate and appalling infraction which takes place somewhat less in the center of man's being. To a degree, however, it is sin which sets the problem to be solved by political thought and enactment for Rousseau, the well-spring of modern idealistic social philosophy, as well as for the Christian, especially the Reformation, tradition.

Rousseau not only comprehends something of the meaning of

[27]*Pensées,* chap. x, sec. 1. *Cf.* St. Augustine: "If the further question be asked, What was the efficient cause of their evil will? there is none. For what is it which makes the will bad, when it is will itself which makes the action bad? And consequently the bad will is the cause of the bad action, but nothing is the efficient cause of the bad will. . . . What made the *first* evil will bad? . . . That is the first which was made evil by no other will. . . . Then, why did he do so? Was it because his will was a nature, or because it was made out of nothing? We shall find that the latter is the case. . . . Now, to seek to discover the causes of these defections—causes, as I have said, not efficient, but deficient—is as if some one sought to see darkness, or hear silence. . . . Let no one, then, seek to know from me what I know that I do not know; unless he perhaps wishes to learn to be ignorant of that of which all we know is, that it cannot be known. For those things which are known not by their actuality, but by their want of it, are known, if our expression may be allowed and understood, by not knowing them, that by knowing them they may be not known. For when the eyesight surveys objects that strike the sense, it nowhere sees darkness but where it begins not to see (*The City of God,* Bk. XII, chs. vi and vii, *Basic Writings,* Vol. II, pp. 183, 185).

sin. He also understands the situation out of which sin arises. Some quite invariable factor in the human social environment, and not simply man's lonely isolation and anxious freedom, provides occasion for sin. No amount of social improvement or repairing our social institutions will alter this fundamental fact about any possible human community, namely, that men in groups are given opportunity for making comparison among themselves and securing unwarranted advantage over one another from the very fact of living together. According to the more individualistic view we first considered, anxiety was the precondition of both human creativity and sin. So also, life in community is the precondition of almost every human good and of sin as well, as soon as union into a single society makes men compare themselves with one another and take into account the differences they thus find out. Life in community does not produce sin by necessity, any more than does anxiety or the ambiguity of man's freedom standing in yet above nature. The bias toward sin from which actual sin flows is social existence plus sin. The first time man the social being looks into himself, he feels the first emotion of pride; yet it is *he* who prepares the way for assuming pre-eminence as a social individual.

Josiah Royce also undertook to plumb the depth of the original sin of man the social animal. He described himself as opposing the viewpoint of "romantic idealism" or "false liberalism" which remain "gently optimistic" and try "to cheapen religious faith by ignoring all the graver dogmas of the traditional creeds," especially by denying "the profound waywardness and wickedness of human nature," "the depravity of man and the universal condemnation of all our race in its unsaved condition."[28] In one place Royce expressed man's need for salvation by saying that "man as he now is, or as he naturally is, is in *great danger* of so missing this highest aim as to render his whole life a senseless failure by virtue of thus coming short of his true goal."[29] In *The Problem of Christianity*, however, he went further than thus saying merely

[28]*The Spirit of Modern Philosophy*, Houghton, Mifflin, 1892, pp. 441, 448; *cf.* J. Royce, *The Philosophy of Loyalty*, Macmillan, 1908, pp. 387–388.
[29]Josiah Royce, *The Sources of Religious Insight*, Scribners, 1912, p. 12 (italics mine. The entire passage is italicized in the original).

that man *may* be lost. One of the three principal Christian ideas which it was the purpose of this work to reformulate and defend was the proposition that "the individual human being is by nature subject to some overwhelming moral burden from which, if un-aided, he *cannot* escape."[30] This doctrine of "the hopeless and guilty burden of the individual when unaided by divine grace" asserts (against "lovers of mankind" in general, and in particular against Matthew Arnold's statement that "sin is not a monster to be mused on, but an impotence to be got rid of") that man's unbearable burden arises not so much from the particular sins the individual himself commits as from what has been called "original sin," not so much from any single manner in which human nature has expressed itself, or from vices acquired from a certain corrupt society, but from human nature itself and from (what is surely as natural and inevitable) the structure of *any* possible social system in its relation to the individual.[31] This view of Royce's purports not to be derived from the "legend" of Adam's fall, nor to be a mere defense of a worn-out dogma, but to depend pri-marily on "man as we empirically know him."[32]

What may be known about man Royce sums up in his con-ception of human self-consciousness as a "contrast-effect." Men-tioned earlier,[33] this notion was developed, with psychological and sociological evidence, largely in his later works. By saying that selfhood is a "contrast-effect," Royce means that, in the gen-esis of personality, a child becomes conscious of himself only by the reflections he sees of himself in the approvals and disapprovals other people exercise toward him. This psychological theory was used by Royce, in *The Philosophy of Loyalty*, to support the con-clusion that "society is constantly engaged in training up children who *may, and often do, rebel* against their mother,"[34] and in *The Problem of Christianity* to give ground for the fact that they *inevitably and always do* rebel, inwardly if not outwardly.

[30]*The Problem of Christianity*, Macmillan, 1913, Vol. I, pp. 41, 111 (italics mine).
[31]*Ibid.*, Vol. I, pp. 44, 57–58, 110, 111, 126; *cf.* 235–236.
[32]*Ibid.*, Vol. I, p. 122.
[33]Royce, *et al.*, *The Conception of God*, Macmillan, 1897, pp. 279–285.
[34]*The Philosophy of Loyalty*, pp. 34–35 (italics mine).

In order to inculcate in its members sufficient cooperativeness, society must train individuals in conformity and uniformity of conduct. This calls attention to the contrast between ourselves and our fellows and first startles us out of a natural unself-consciousness about our own conduct. Thereafter, by the combined methods of setting before us attractive models and employing coercion, society tries to develop in us a more intricate representation of itself. The social cultivation of the individual proceeds by more refined and detailed contrast-effects, a method which necessarily operates so that "the more we know of the social will, the more highly conscious of ourselves we become." When this produces in us a certain amount of opposition, the only means of forestalling rebellion which is at the disposal of society is some new form of the same thing, *i.e.*, a reapplication of social discipline which will bring us to "some higher level of general self-consciousness concerning our own doings." "Our social training thus teaches us to know ourselves through a process which *arouses our self-will;* and this tendency grows with what it feeds upon." The more skillful society is, "the more it trains its servants by a process that breeds spiritual enemies." The "very consciences" of individuals "are tainted by the *original sin* of contentiousness."[35] We are psychologically built upon trouble. Society needs individuals with consciences, but social conscience can be trained only by a process that inevitably awakens self-will. More social cultivation but inflames and increases the antagonism. It is the disease of our natural self-consciousness that we are divided and lonely creatures the more socialized we become. "Man's *fallen state* is due to his nature as a social animal."[36] Royce's theory may be credited with accomplishing what it purports to do, namely, "sound to the depths the *original sin of man the social animal,* and of the natural social order which he creates."[37] The following typical passage summarizes his profound analysis:

> The social order, in training individuals, therefore breeds conscious sinners; and sins both in them and against them. The

[35]*The Problem of Christianity,* Vol. I, pp. 134, 141, 143, 144 (italics mine).
[36]*Ibid.,* Vol. I, p. 176 (italics mine).   [37]*Ibid.,* Vol. II, p. 85 (italics mine).

natural community is, in its united collective will, a *community of sin*. Its state is made, by its vast powers, worse than that of the individual. But it trains the individual to be as great a sinner as his powers permit.[38]

It must be noticed that the rebellion to which Royce is referring may well be only an inward one. He distinguishes between the conduct of men and their consciousness about their conduct. The individual's conduct may have whatever quality, good or evil, it happens to have. Men may keep the peace, even though in spirit they are enemies of one another.[39] For this reason, it is, indeed, "unpsychological to assert that the conduct of all natural men is universally depraved"; but they all do inwardly revolt and this is their sin. Their self-consciousness about their conduct inevitably has the "form of *spiritual* self-assertion,"[40] which is both sin and loneliness.

The Problem of Christianity discusses another form of evil which is not to be identified with the original sin of our social consciousness. This is the deliberate act of treason which it is possible for the self to commit after he has found his cause, personally identified his will with it, and thus been "saved" by loyalty. His "unpardonable sin"[41] is a traitorous deed which shuts him out of what he has already defined as his own home, his own country. It is irrevocable in the sense that he can never forgive himself for such a deed,[42] and, as in the case of "original sin" itself, must be saved by an act of "grace." The connection between original sin, loyalty, and treason in Royce's exposition lends itself to chronological interpretation: First, the individual is trained up in original sin. Then, he is found by a loyalty which for the first time gains his inner commitment and overcomes the spiraling conflicts of conformity and self-will involved in all social cultivation. And, finally, he betrays this cause and cuts himself off from the community of the loyal which was his own. The last state of such a man is worse than the first. He is a traitor to a recognized cause, whereas formerly he was only a rebel against

---

38 *Ibid.*, Vol. I, p. 178 (italics mine).
39 *Ibid.*, Vol. I, pp. 127, 143.
40 *Ibid.*, Vol. I, pp. 135–136, 143 (italics mine).
41 *Ibid.*, Vol. I, pp. 245, 248.
42 *Ibid.*, Vol. I, pp. 244, 263, 266.

an unrecognized and still external order. In both cases, however, an act of grace alone can save him. Of course, the chronology of these steps should not be too much stressed. On the one hand, it is difficult to imagine a person with no commitments and no loyalties whatever, and, on the other, treason would be impossible if the grace of loyalty had fully accomplished its work of overcoming the original sin of self-will. In a single life, original sin, loyalty, treason, and particular acts of sin flowing from self-will and indicating treason but yet not considered by the self as tantamount to ultimate betrayal, these all function, if not completely simultaneously, at least so as to pervade and infect one another's character. Man's unpardonable sin is a particular act of sin when contrasted with the original sin in self-consciousness from which it derives; and, in relation to other particular sins, it is a particularly important act. The despair of the traitor, however, arises from the fact that an act, which may have been objectively traitorous before, is now recognized as such, but yet has been done.[43]

Royce gives no ordinary theory of "social sin." He does not explain sinfulness away by tracing moral evil home to variable social institutions which corrupt man's natural goodness. By tracing moral evil home to a quite invariable factor in the processes of social cultivation and in relationships among men in any possible society, he places his finger on a factor invariably present whenever, through social awakening, man becomes *man*. Since man is indeed a social animal, an individual cannot simply *wish* this were not true.

> For this social nature of man is fundamental to his being. I am not first some one on my own account who happens to be the child of my parents, a citizen of Great Britain, and so forth. If you take all these social relationships away, there is nothing left. A man is talking nonsense if he says: "Well, if I had been the son of some one else . . . etc." He *is* his parents' son; what he is supposing is not that *he* should be some one else's son, but

[43]For fuller treatment of the idealistic understanding of sin, see Paul Ramsey, "The Idealistic View of Moral Evil: Josiah Royce and Bernard Bosanquet," *Journal of Philosophy and Phenomenological Research*, VI, 4 (June, 1946), pp. 554–589.

that *he* should not exist and some one else should exist instead. By our mutual influence we actually constitute one another as what we are.[44]

Social man gains selfhood and comes to be what he is out of mutual relationship with many factors in his environment which, it is true, might conceivably be quite different from what they are at the present stage of society; but also he gains selfhood in relationship to the fundamental structures of any possible human life in community with other persons. He cannot say, "If I had been some other sort of social being . . . etc," without talking nonsense. What he would then be supposing is not that *he* should be some other creature, but that man the social animal should not exist and that some other unimaginable creature should exist instead.

Nevertheless, the self's reactions to the efforts society makes to stamp its image upon him are truly the self's own actions, his own response. Who else could be responsible for the resistance he puts forth in the course of gaining his selfhood? Kierkegaard defined anxiety as "the reflex of the freedom within itself at the thought of its possibility," over the haunting thought of the future. Conceiving the self otherwise than in such lonely isolation facing the future, must we not attribute a certain amount of resilience, "reflex" or capacity for rebound to the self in relation to its fellows and to the social environment generally? Such individual freedom or resilience under the touch of social forces provides the occasion for sin in the individual. Indeed, self-consciousness may be defined as the reflex of freedom within itself at the thought of environing social influences. When, in the course of becoming a self, any one determines to live sufficient unto himself, in estrangement and in rebellion, *he* prepares the ground —who else? By an act of sin, sin comes into the world and into the heart of man the social animal.

There is also common responsibility here. Although a child himself does whatever he does in the course of becoming a self, he also suffers. For one thing, he suffers parents. Every parent knows that he also has done what the child himself does at the

[44]William Temple, *Christianity and Social Order*, Penguin Books, 1942, pp. 47–48.

bottom of his self-conscious reactions to the family and to the world about him. Parents provide their children with most of the primary contrast-effects which comprise the material out of which they are forming themselves. No child is altogether like a wheel rolling by itself. Parents must therefore keep endless watch on themselves lest in a careless or insensitive or selfish moment they breathe in their child's face, and themselves have something to do with the degree of alienation or spiritual alarm present in this person who is coming to be. And what parent is there whose little children do not love him more than he deserves to be loved?

In the congregation Christians repeat the "general confession" in unison, each *individual* making use of the *plural* form of the personal pronoun. We do this because of common responsibility for sin socially at the root of manhood, and not simply because we are an aggregation of variously sinful and more or less perfect individuals.

> Almighty and most merciful Father; *We* have erred and strayed from thy ways like lost sheep. *We* have followed too much the devices and desires of our own hearts. *We* have offended against thy holy laws. *We* have left undone those things which *we* ought to have done; And *we* have done those things which *we* ought not to have done; And there is no health in *us*. But thou, O Lord, have mercy upon *us*, miserable offenders. Spare thou those, O God, who confess their faults. Restore thou those who are penitent; According to thy promises declared unto mankind In Christ Jesus our Lord. And grant, O most merciful Father, for his sake; That we may hereafter live a godly, righteous and sober life, To the glory of thy holy Name. *Amen*.

No man can have faith for another: repeating the creed along with an entire congregation, each person nevertheless says "I," "I believe . . ." But no man sins quite by himself. Therefore we confess concerning sin, "We . . ." While every man may be unto himself a sufficient Adam, he is also Adam to every other man. By his own act he stands within and also helps to extend the community of sin. In speaking of redemption, Christianity therefore addresses our whole humanity as social beings, and the whole of human society which gives us being.

IX

CHRISTIAN LOVE IN SEARCH OF A SOCIAL POLICY

"When I read any description of an Ideal State and think how we are to begin transforming our own society into that, I am reminded of the Englishman in Ireland who asked the way to Roscommon. 'Is it Roscommon you want to go to?' said the Irishman. 'Yes,' said the Englishman; 'that's why I asked the way.' 'Well,' said the Irishman, 'if I wanted to go to Roscommon, I wouldn't be starting from here.'"

—William Temple, *Christianity and Social Order*, p. 39.

"Christianity . . . has always been a religion seeking a metaphysic, in contrast to Buddhism which is a metaphysic generating a religion."

—A. N. Whitehead, *Religion in the Making*, p. 50.

THIS, then, is the situation: On the one hand, stands Christianity, which is a religion seeking a social policy; and, on the other, there are a multitude of social policies generating religions, or seeking to attach themselves to the Christian religion. Christian love is always in search of a social policy. Our preceding study has made clear that it is improper to speak of a Christian economic order or Christian politics, or for that matter Christian rules for personal behavior absolutely binding as laws. "The liberty of the Christian man" means that he *may* get along without any of these things and is subject to none. Nevertheless, he cannot get along without seeking to find the best possible social ethic in which Christian love may incarnate itself. Because of its very nature, Christian love must take on the flesh of some specific social order. What more can be said concerning what Christian love seeks to do in actual life? This question the present chapter undertakes to answer. We shall consider first certain basic principles for social policy already contained within Christian ethics itself, and then go on to ask what Christian love, in search of a social policy, may learn from other sources. Christian ethics already possesses certain definite implications for social policy, and an adequate social ethic can in large measure be drawn from within its own nature alone. To the extent that this is true it would be misleading for us only to speak of Christian love in search of a social policy. We should first see how far a Christian social ethic may be stated primarily in terms of Christian notions alone.

I. THE RESTRAINT OF SIN

One primary principle of Christian social ethics has been traditionally formulated as "the restraint and remedy of sin." This essential aspect of Christian social policy is no less important because it is negative. In fact, this formula sums up in large part the way Christians understand the nature of social institutions and justify their existence. The simplest social institution with its surrounding customs regulating human behavior gives illustration of the need for "restraining and remedying sin." Consider the coin box on public transportation buses: the driver checks whether the passengers put in their fares; and passengers put their own money in the box, rather than giving it to the driver, lest he be led into too great temptation. None of our markets where economic goods and services are exchanged are arranged as if only righteous men, or wholly righteous men, were engaged in them. All are arranged in part to anticipate and restrain sin. James Madison said the same thing of properly arranged political institutions.

> What is government itself, but the greatest of all reflections on human nature? If men were angels, no government would be necessary. If angels were to govern men, neither external nor internal controls on government would be necessary. In framing a government which is to be administered by men over men, the

great difficulty lies in this: you must first enable the government to control the governed; and in the next place oblige it to control itself. A dependence on the people is, no doubt, the primary control on the government; but experience has taught mankind the necessity of auxiliary precautions.[1]

No legislator since Moses has failed to allow divorce "for the hardness of men's hearts." This has been true whether the legislator was drawing up laws for some secular state, or was ruling some church community through canon law. Whether divorce legislation has been lenient or rigorous, one principle striven for in the law has always been that sin be more restrained than released from restraint by the positive law.

It may, of course, be true that some particular restraining social institution does more harm than good, and Christians have always been among those challenging the given social system as unjustifiable in major respects. Social institutions may be subject to large modification, and seem always in need of more rapid alteration. Nevertheless, restraining social institutions cannot be got rid of altogether; hereby sin would be more permitted than specific gross forms of sin or social injustice corrected; and Christians have only rarely gone as far as Tolstoy in believing in the possibility of human life in community without any restraint at all. Although specific forms of coercion may produce specific evils, not all evil is simply a consequence of restraint. In fact it works the other way round: people need restraint because of the primary fact of sin.

An illustration of this may be drawn from restrictions universally placed upon human sexual behavior. More significant than relativity among the ways mankind has devised for controlling sex is the fact that at no time and place and in no primitive stage of culture have men been able to live without *some* form of restraint in this area. A state of primitive promiscuity, anthropologists now tell us, where sex life was simply spontaneous or was allowed to take its own natural course with no pattern at all imposed upon it by the group, never existed. The question *how*

[1]*Federalist,* No. 51.

sexual behavior *should* be regulated need not be raised here. We can still see in the universal and multifarious regulations mankind has devised evidence of the significant effect human self-consciousness and human sin have upon man's physical or emotional life. "The sense of shame in relation to sex antedates the conventions of civilized society," Reinhold Niebuhr remarks, "just as the inordinate expression of sexual passion is the cause and not the consequent of the social discipline and restraints which society has set around this area of life."[2] Christians, therefore, are not so naïve as to suppose that simply by removing all the regulations society places upon sex man will at long last be free to behave entirely naturally and therefore entirely well.

> They'll tell you sex has become a mess because it was hushed up. But for the last twenty years it has *not* been hushed up. It has been chattered about all day long. Yet it is still in a mess. If hushing up had been the cause of the trouble, ventilation would have set it right. But it hasn't. I think it is the other way round. I think the human race originally hushed it up because it had become such a mess.[3]

It is really later than we think if we still imagine that the problems of sex morality can all be settled simply by disseminating certain information which hitherto has been kept under censorship.

In the marriage ceremony "before God and this congregation" a person assumes a *vow*, he promises permanence "for better or worse, for richer for poorer, in sickness or in health, till death us do part." His will to permanence constitutes his own inward acknowledgment of what society institutionalizes in the marriage laws, namely, that sin in himself should be anticipated, restrained and remedied. This vow does not gain validity simply from its conformity to some external biblical law or social custom. It works the other way round: these, with the vow, are valid if, for one thing, they take into account the fact of sin and provide appropriate control for it. In taking the vow a person acknowledges

[2]*The Nature and Destiny of Man*, Scribners, 1942, Vol. I, p. 238.
[3]C. S. Lewis, *Christian Behaviour*, copyright by The Macmillan Company, 1943, pp. 26–27. Used with their permission.

that he has not become an entirely trustworthy person, one on whom his prospective mate can truly rely, simply on account of the momentary purity of his passion or his present single-minded sentiment. He becomes trustworthy and reliable only to the degree he is able to promise. Since "I love you" may simply mean, in all sorts of subtle ways, "I love *me,* and *want* you," and since such love need not at all change its ulterior purpose in loving in order to want another in the same supposed interest of self-fulfillment, a person had better subject his love to this severe testing: see if he can promise permanence in love for another person precisely under those conditions, referred to in the expressions "for worse," "for poorer," and "in sickness," under which he will have to give rather than derive benefit from the marriage relationship. Then only will it be clear whether he loves the other person for his or her own sake, or whether in all his powerful and passionate love he actually remains only a lover of himself. There is nothing which defames human nature in this requirement, at least nothing beyond the truth. To promise permanence means, in part, to acknowledge that at his best man remains sinful and that sin may invade his very best emotions, so that a man better not trust himself to remain trustworthy, much less ask another person to rely on him, without assuming for himself commitments realistically designed to remedy the element of sin in all human love. Romantics, of course, always consider the marriage vow a quite external and superfluous arrangement, a peril to the finer feelings, and of course not made for *them.* In the marriage ceremony, Christians endeavor to acknowledge a good deal more than that wherever marriages are made there heaven is, with at least a couple of angels.

In relations among men in larger groups, political democracy may be given compelling justification only if some reference be made to the problem of restraining and remedying sin. Not only can the validity of external democratic procedures be defended because they alone put some control upon the government which in turn controls individuals and factions among the populace. But also the fundamental definition of "just law" which lies at the base of modern democratic theory quite rightly takes into account the factor of sin. Too often in the past the restraint of sin has but cloaked an uncritical defense of absolute political power whose own propensity to sin remained unchecked. Democracy does not mean going to the opposite extreme in praise of and in implementing the power of the common man in his undershirt. All are but men, apt to make exceptions of themselves if allowed to do so. Sin must be checked in every one, ruler and ruled alike. For this reason, both the external procedures of democracy and the fundamental definition of a just political order should take account of man's inclination to sin even while building upon man's capacity for doing right. What a contemporary Christian may find needful to be done in political society for the purpose of erecting safeguards against sin may perhaps best be grasped from understanding how basic this same principle is in idealistic social philosophy. This will involve, of course, the jettisoning of the "idolatry" in idealism (or the elimination of identity between the self and the source or definition of obligation).

In his *Social Contract* Rousseau developed a political theory which had as its main purpose explaining what makes coercion legitimate. According to his view, political restraint is justified, first of all, by the consent of the governed. The "general will" provides the basis for a form of association "in which each, while uniting himself with all, may still obey himself alone, and remain as free as before."[4] Disagreement may be entered at this point with the idolatrous definition of the entire extent of justifiable obligation as self-obligation; and, moreover, it may be said that the ideal of remaining "as free as before" still presupposes too much that man, when free unto himself, will remain naturally good. However, in another of its aspects the general will provides a social derivation of "rights" and a definition of just law which assume that man is not naturally altogether good. Idealistic social philosophy replaces the individual reservation of private rights in natural-law theory by affirming the reservation by civil society of an area where human rights ought to have free and

[4]Book I, chap. vi, p. 14.

unimperiled exercise. This aspect of the general will provides
realistic adjustment to the fact of human sin, which, if force be
not back of attested justice, would incline any man to take away
these rights from others. ". . . The conditions," Rousseau says,
"are the same for all; and, this being so, no one has an interest
in making them burdensome to others."[5] It is here admitted that,
if the conditions were not the same for all, every one would have
an interest in making them burdensome to others and excepting
himself. The principle of generality, thus, distinguishes legitimate
from illegitimate law among the "laws" which may be adopted
by the people precisely by asking whether the law restrains sin
or not, whether under it any one would gain greater opportunity
for manifesting his interest in making conditions unfair to others.

Rousseau's principle for determining just law, the general will,
unites subjective with objective generality, "universality of will
with universality of object." It must "come from all" and "apply
to all," thus being "general in its object as well as its essence."
The condition for lawfulness is met, therefore, only when "the
matter about which the decree is made is, like the decreeing will,
general."[6] In each of these pairs of descriptive phrases, one of
them—"objective generality," "universality of object," "apply to
all," and "the matter about which the decree is made must be
general"—has especially to do with laying down the test that the
conditions shall be the same for all. These conditions provide that
law will react upon every one so that none will imagine he can
by legislation place special burdens upon others, although admittedly every one is sinfully inclined to do so. When these normative conditions are met and individuals are still recalcitrant,
force may be marshaled on behalf of law and obedience to the
general will compelled. Individuals thus coerced are but "forced
to be free,"[7] or at least forced to be law-abiding and, in that sense,
good. Along with the people's "consent" to law this is a second
justification for political coercion which Rousseau gives, namely,
the tendency of particular wills to introduce partiality in place
of generality into law. The nature of valid law here is quite sepa-

[5]*Ibid.*, p. 15.
[6]*Ibid.*, Book II, chaps. iv and vi, pp. 27 and 33.
[7]*Ibid.*, Book I, chap. vii, p. 18.

rable from the principle of consent and, unlike the latter, is not grounded in the doctrine that justifiable obligation must always be self-imposed.

It may be that in being forced to be law-abiding and to restrain their inclination to sin, men are forced to be obedient to a norm that is more than their weak wills and less distended than their sinful wills, that thus they are obedient not merely to themselves and are both more and less themselves than they would be under conditions of freedom. Rulers legislating on behalf of generality may on occasion lawfully legislate beyond even implicit consent. Thus the second way of making political coercion legitimate does not depend on the first. Rousseau, however, identifies the two. Obligation to the principle of generality is for him the same thing as obligation to that to which the self has given implicit consent.

The truth of his position, we may provisionally concede, is that roughly the best practical machinery for assuring that the conditions be always the same for all is that every vote be counted.[8] As a practical method, consent comes in the long run as close to normative generality as those who are "but men" are likely to achieve by any other device. That full citizenship and voting privileges be given to Negro citizens and those of Japanese ancestry, in local and state as well as federal jurisdictions, is a realistic safeguard against legislation carrying particular disadvantages for them. The wisest and best "white" legislation will be prone to insinuate civil inequalities, first of all curtailing generality of application in order to prevent the rebound by which, in any proper law, the dominant race would suffer along with the rest the disadvantages in question. If it were not for the sinfulness of human nature, and therefore also of all experts at statecraft, the ignorance of the masses of any people might deter reasonable men from consulting the popular voice in political decision. "You can fool too many of the people too much of the time."[9] But because of the sinfulness of man, we must be democratic in technique, as well as in the principle that justice must

[8]*Ibid.*, Book II, chap. ii, p. 23, n. 1.
[9]James Thurber, "The Owl Who Was God," *Fables for Our Time*, Harpers, 1939, pp. 35–40.

be general in application and rights be accorded to all. The point is not that the common man in his undershirt is better than the élite any more than he is wiser but that, out of the conflict of public pressures in which all participate, "laws" may be forced to become more lawful.

Discriminatory legislation in general, however, is wrong even if the whole of the group discriminated against votes for it. It is wrong for the primary reason that law is always unjust when it does not apply generally to all. If there are in the south "darkies" or "mammies" who themselves think that the conditions, *e.g.*, of public education, ought not to be the same for all, we may say with definiteness that they ought not to think so. If their acquiring the vote would not lead to a greater equalization of the conditions, then the *vox populi* would not be a general voice; and the above judgment would in this case be wrong in expecting the exercise of the franchise even by the ignorant to force "white laws" to be more lawful. The admission of so much additional ignorance to the polls would not be counterbalanced by the only justification that can be given for democratic techniques, namely, that thereby more restraint is placed upon sin than, at the same time, expression and power is given it in other individuals or groups. Beyond question under most circumstances an effective franchise would force laws to be more just, yet we could not say this if we did not first know the meaning of just law. There may be places on the surface of the globe where this practical justification for extending the franchise does not hold true, where, indeed, there ought to be fewer rather than more votes; but everywhere the conditions of life should be the same for all.

The "right to vote" is, therefore, not so much a solution for the problem of racial tensions in this country as it is a recognition of the fact that there may be no final solution. A recent article, which criticizes Gunnar Myrdal for his reliance on the "American Creed" to find an ultimate solution to the race problem,[10] suggests that "white prejudice may not cease until evolution does away with Negro visibility" and then points out that Negro visi-

[10]Vernon H. Holloway: "Christian Faith and Race Relations," *Religion in Life,* summer, 1945, p. 345, citing Gunnar Myrdal, *An American Dilemma,* Harpers, 1944, I, 97, 109.

bility is not being eliminated.[11] If human sinfulness may be depended upon to make use, if it can, of the obvious badge of color in order to maintain unequal conditions, then the right to vote must be depended upon as the best available means of seeing to it that Negroes, with their "visibility," have a defense against such prejudice. There is no guaranty, except through the perpetual jar of contending forces, that they, in turn, will not display a tendency to make a similar unjust employment of white visibility; indeed, it should be expected that they will do so. This, however, is not democracy's present problem; and, unless democracy as a method of solution is continuously preserved, there is no solution of problems in human society which is not, at the same time, the production of problems in insoluble form.

An idealistic-Christian theory of democracy comes to close grips with this problem of justifying democratic method. Other and more abstractly idealistic political theories succeed, perhaps, in establishing general human rights or constitutionalism in government; but these views never really arrive at the proposition that every one should participate in government and make his power felt by certain established procedures. It may be said pragmatically that for the sake of the greatest total good an individual should have "rights," but why should not these rights (which, lest the question be begged, cannot yet include the right to vote or otherwise participate in political decision) simply be given him by his rulers? Why should he participate politically in securing them, unless he is in danger of not being guaranteed these more fundamental rights because of the sin of the wisest and best human ruler or rulers? As Aristotle saw, if a god came to earth as a ruler, rotation in office, which as a means for securing gloved rule was his equivalent for voting,[12] should then be suspended. The right to vote or to exercise some other established method of pressure derives directly from the reality and universality of sin and is only obliquely related to other, and more fundamental, rights of man.

Let us return, however, from considering how the democratic method of consent achieves a rough restraint of human sin to

[11]Holloway, *op. cit.*, p. 347 and note.   [12]*Politics*, 1261b and 1279a.

consider "objective generality" as itself a norm to which consent or subjective generality should conform. Mere consent does not suffice to determine the nature of political obligation. Since consent itself may be sinful, it is obliged to be right; it ought to agree only to what is just. Idealistic social philosophy does not leave objective lawfulness undefined. Two illustrations may be given of the idea that just law should apply generally to all: At one juncture in the interminable proceedings and reviews of the Harry Bridges case, a "lawmaker" arose on the floor of the Senate to announce that, if the Supreme Court did not decide against Bridges, he proposed to introduce in the Congress a law having him specified for deportation. This is a clear case of a "law" which would not be lawful even if approved unanimously by both houses of Congress and by all the state legislatures and by every voter in the United States, including Harry Bridges himself. Law can lay down conditions for deportation, conditions of a general character; and if the author of the bill himself comes later under their judgment he, too, will find himself deported. But only execution of law can deport a particular man. Objective generality as a test for just law restrains the sin of those who pass laws or who press for their enactment. At the same time, it constitutes a civil reservation of an area where the individual freely exercises rights which, however, are not individualistically justified. For legislation to become particular and single out persons for special treatment would be to encroach upon the area of individual civil rights, and, at the same time, release sinful tyranny over others from the control of the principle of generality. So-called "laws" which release the sinful tendency to grasp at tyranny present in every individual or group within the body politic from the control of the principle of general application are bound to be laws which encroach upon human rights. Where there is no equal justice, there are no civil rights; where no rights, no general rule of law.

The other illustration, taken from Paul Geren's *Burma Diary*, shows that whenever human life is reduced to its bare essentials the "general will" shows its indispensable reality:

I heard that among certain groups of Englishmen walking from Burma to India there has silently developed a solemn compact. Whoever should find himself too ill or too lame to go farther is to drop back little by little and permit his fellows to pass beyond him, perhaps forever, without notification or the indulgence of a farewell. He is to do this in such a way that his companions will not detect his absence until it is too late to turn back. Thus they insure beforehand that the safety of the larger group shall not be imperiled by the loyalties of the members for one another. Whoever arranges that the group shall not be endangered for the sake of one runs the risk that he may be that one.[13]

Human society will never so far advance that the designers of law should no longer seek to arrange it that every one who favors a measure shall run the risk of being the one disfavored by its terms. Right is secured and sin checked only if no one has an interest in making the conditions more burdensome than he himself is willing to bear. This is achieved by generality of application. The idea of the general will, thus, is framed with both justice or right and sin in mind, and it represents a way of implementing man's capacity for justice and his regard for the common good, without being unmindful of his inclination unjustly to make himself an exception. Idealistic as well as Christian democratic theory is therefore grounded in the proposition, "Man's capacity for justice makes democracy possible; but man's inclination to injustice makes democracy necessary."[14] Right policy for political society cannot be made without some basic reference to Christian realism concerning the necessity of restraining and remedying sin.

II. IS CHRISTIAN "OBEDIENT LOVE" ITSELF A SOCIAL POLICY?

The next question to be raised is this: Does the norm of Christian love in itself contain positive and definite enough social requirements for us to draw a Christian social policy directly out

[13]Harpers, 1943, p. 40.
[14]Reinhold Niebuhr, *The Children of Light and the Children of Darkness,* Scribners, 1944, p. xi.

of this norm alone without need of searching elsewhere? We have spoken of the negative policy of restraining sin. The issue raised in this section concerns a more positive Christian social ethics. Does Christian "obedient love" tell us what positively should be done in the common life? To what extent or in what way does Christian love contain a positive social policy and to what extent or in what way does such love still seek to determine a proper social ethic?

In contrast to any form of intuition-ethics, the ethics of love shows abundant content. In contrast to any form of legalism, however, the ethics of love appears to be without determinate content, always in search of a social policy yet never completely identifiable with any current program with which it happens to make common cause.

Acting from immediate feelings of right and wrong has always had large place among ordinary Christian folk. Even the most sophisticated person makes many decisions on the basis of what he would describe as intuitive moral knowledge. Pacifist Christians who have given up attempting to rationalize their position by appealing to "the *power* of non-violence" frequently defend their pacifist witness on the basis of an immediate call of duty for them. Moreover, in certain so-called Barthian circles today there is a good deal of talk about "responding moment by moment to the absolute demands of God." These "demands" from one moment of decision to another have in common only some sense of "the absolute." There is no universal truth in them, no quality characterizing what God may demand, and therefore no ground for ethics except the particular command present at one moment, quite another command at another moment in which the absolute impinges upon us. This view may be called theological intuitionism—intuitionism on stilts!

In *Fear and Trembling* Kierkegaard asks the question, "Can there be a teleological suspension of ethics?" and answers affirmatively. Abraham, he says, became the Father of Faith because he was willing to abide in his "absolute relationship to the absolute," even when this involved a religious suspension of his ethical duty toward his son, Isaac.[1] Such theological intuitionism may be objected to on two counts: In the first place, no content immediately presented through the relation of absolute faith in God can countermand human conscience or, in this instance, the dawning ethical insight that it is wrong to offer children as blood sacrifices. Religious faith proves important for the growth of natural morality, not first of all because it counters the conclusions of natural reason, but because faith speaks to the problem of saving man from the sinful employment of whatever standards moral reason leads him to accept. Faith doubtless renders more impartial and sensitive the employment of reason in actually making moral judgments, but reason itself assesses the worth of any ethical truth disclosed to it. The first mistake of such theological intuitionism lies in deriving some ethical content to supplement, if not actually to contradict, moral reason simply from an asserted immediate impression of the "absolute demands" of God.

In the second place, if Christian love defines perfect obedience to God, then no felt ethical demands should be allowed to contradict or run counter to it, no matter if these intuitions are accompanied by a high degree of felt-absoluteness. An ethic of Christian love, in contrast to an ethic of immediate moral impressions, shows abundant content for determining what should be done. This provides a principle for discriminating not only among normal ethical intuitions on the part of the common man, but also among the intuitions glorified by religion into "absolute demands" calling for "radical decision" in "the moment." We must try every spirit to see if it be of God. We must test every intuition, no matter how powerful, to see if it be a manifestation of the holy Spirit of God which is the spirit of Christ. No intuited moral demand speaking to us in this spirit can call Christ cursed; none can call Christ lord except by the spirit. Hereby we know what God demands, and can discriminate among intuitions by their specific quality and not simply respond to them as felt power or powerful feeling. "God shows his love for us in that while we were yet sinners [helpless, ungodly, unrighteous, his

[1] Soren Kierkegaard, *Fear and Trembling*, Princeton University Press, p. 49.

enemies] Christ died for us" (Rom. 5:6–10). This norm in itself carries us far in the direction of specific decisions in the problems of actual life. *Non tantus vile pro quo Christus mortus est.* Call no man vile for whom Christ died. The ethic of Christian love may fall far short of a complete social policy, yet clearly Christian love contains more positive implications for formulating a social ethic than certain forms of theological ethics which rest everything on "decision" or the momentary response of faith.

Nevertheless, Christian love takes on the aspect of a quite indeterminate norm when compared with any and all forms of legalistic social ethic. The Christian man is lord of all and subject to none of the rule-morality. Set free on account of his so great responsibility, he must therefore be constantly engaged in "building up" an adequate social ethic realistically adjusted, not to precedents in law or existing conventions of society, but to concrete and changing neighbor need. Searching for a social policy Christian love may make *use* of, say, the ethical insights summed up in the so-called "natural law," but its *base* of operations never shifts over onto the ground of the rational moral law. Precisely what the connection is between the two when there occurs a Christian *employment* of the theory of natural law or the principles of some other social policy our next section attempts to elucidate.

It is difficult to tell whether the theory of natural law should be criticized because it is a new form of legalism or because it is an ethic of intuition. On either count, natural law cannot occupy the ground floor of Christian ethics. On the one hand, Jacques Maritain remarks that the metaphor of a law written in the heart of man "has been responsible for a great deal of damage, causing natural law to be represented as a ready-made code rolled up within the conscience of each of us, which each one of us has only to unroll, and of which all men should naturally have an equal knowledge."[2] If this is not what the "first principles" of natural morality mean, then it would seem that some sort of intuition constitutes the beginning of moral reasoning. The

[2] *The Rights of Man and Natural Law*, Scribners, 1943, p. 62.

law in the heart, as Maritain says, is "hidden from us as our own heart." Interpreting "natural law" as not even a rudimentary code of law or set of first principles but as some primary intuition, it should then be said that all such intuitions need to be schooled by Christ before they become an accredited part of Christian ethics.

On the other hand, Maritain defines *jus naturale* as law which follows "in *necessary* fashion, and *from the simple fact that man is man,* nothing else being taken into account."[3] He admits, it is true, that *jus naturale* has no definite content except in the form of *jus gentium,* or law which follows "from the first principle in a *necessary* manner, but this time supposing certain conditions of fact, as for instance the state of civil society or the relationships between people."[4] This is either meaningless or self-contradictory. How can a natural law *without definite content* follow in such *necessary* fashion simply from reflecting on man as man or for that matter from anything? And how can anything else follow in such *necessary* fashion from a natural law which itself has no specific content, even supposing any number of conditions of fact? Maritain wants a natural law which both does and yet does not follow from first principles in necessary fashion. Either the natural law has specific content and may be "unrolled" according to these stages, or else by natural law is meant only a form of intuition ethics, possibly quite variable intuitions. Neither of these provides a distinctively Christian social policy. Rather such a policy follows from reflecting on man as man or on certain conditions of fact in the light of Christian love. Christian love formulates social policy by taking into account every concrete element in the situation which determines how in fact some actual good may be done for the neighbor in the state of civil society and the relationships among people existing at present. Catholic absolutism, *e.g.,* in sex ethics, would be finally corrected if once and for all it were admitted that in this area right should be determined by *Christian love* reflecting upon man as man in relation to certain conditions of fact. Instead, Catholic ethics

[3]*Ibid.,* p. 63.   [4]*Ibid.,* p. 70.

continues to say, while trying hard not to say, that "natural law" may simply be unrolled from natural moral reason alone; and consequently such ethics remains in bondage to a law which teaches a number of unlovely things.

Early in the development of the theory of natural law the extreme demands of "absolute natural law" (no war, no slavery, no property) were modified into a "relative natural law" ("just" war, justice to slaves, common "use" of private property). This accommodation was partly an adjustment to the fact that what ought to be done in specific moral decisions cannot be fully anticipated by any legal code, partly an adjustment to the fact that sin prevents man from achieving the absolute law of nature. For both of these reasons the "relative natural law" tends to lose its legalistic character. Emil Brunner points out quite correctly that the "relative Law of Nature is not a law at all, but only a *regulative principle,* from which no definite demands can be deduced," that it "simply expresses the necessity (which cannot be expressed in legal terms) of adapting the absolute Law of Nature to sinful reality," and that therefore, it really means "absence of principle."[5] No one can actually draw up a statement of the precepts of natural law for the workaday world. Social policy has to be formulated in any case in realistic adjustment to the concrete factors in any given situation; it cannot be derived through step by step deduction from a revealed or an intuitively grasped absolute natural law. "Relative natural law" may therefore be defined as intuition in search of a social policy. Moreover, there takes place no impartial apprehension of an absolute natural law (from which specific decision *might* be derived), since "in a sinful humanity" it is questionable whether "there are any 'impartial' people at all."[6]

Christian social ethics consists neither of intuition in search of a social policy nor of natural law possessed of a social policy. Christian love itself contains more definite or determinate directions for social policy than natural law interpreted as an intui-

[5] *The Divine Imperative,* Westminster Press, 1937. Note 8 to p. 269, Notes and Appendices, pp. 629–630.
[6] *Ibid.,* p. 631.

tion; in terms of these intuition should be guided. On the other hand, the ethics of love approaches the task of finding a social policy with an indefinite, indeterminate and liberating norm when this is contrasted with any legalistic understanding of the law of nature.

III. THE RELATION BETWEEN CHRISTIAN LOVE AND SOCIAL POLICIES

If Christianity may be spoken of as a religion in some measure seeking a social ethic, then what is the nature of the relationships which come to exist between Christian love and any of its adopted social policies? In attempting to answer this question it should first be pointed out that throughout this book frequent reference has been made to the connection between the ethics of love and specific types of regulation which Christian love sometimes accepts. The main point has been that, while Christian love cannot get along without seeking to find from any source the best possible social ethic, such love remains *dominant* and *free* in any partnership it enters.

For example, the distinction was made between the "strategy" of Christian love, which remains unaltered, and what such love sometimes does as a matter of "tactics." The latter may be variable and indeed should vary directly and promptly with the neighbors' needs and with the actual conditions for being of some real benefit to them. This may not be in every respect an apt analogy, but our reference to strategy and tactics suggests at least this much of truth: Christian love ought never to be identified with or permanently bound to any particular program or stipulation for action, however important. Yet no one ever did a Christian deed from Christian love alone without some reasonable, realistic decision about what specifically should be done. Very few wars have been won by those whose tactics were not subject to constant re-examination and readjustment; none have been won by strategy alone.

It has been pointed out that Christian love always occupies the "ground-floor"; no next-of-kin ethical viewpoints are allowed to move into residence there. Although much needs to be added from many sources to complete the whole edifice of Christian social ethics, no other foundation can be laid than that which has been laid. Frequently in the preceding pages criticism has also been made of "coalition" ethics. This too may be an inexact expression; but in context our meaning has been clear enough. By rejecting coalition ethics, we have rejected the idea that there need be any *necessarily permanent* coalition between Christian ethics and any other school of ethics founded on philosophical insight or the findings of social science. Of course, Christian ethics makes permanent coalition with "the truth" wherever it may be found; but as truth varies or advances, or is believed to be different from the suppositions of some other school of philosophy or science, so vary Christian ethical theory and practice. A Christian need not defend to the death either Platonism, Aristotelianism, Idealism or Naturalism; the course of Christian thought should make this quite evident.

By rejecting coalition ethics, we have also rejected the idea of allowing Christian love to become merely an equal or sleeping partner in the business of determining the full meaning of obligation. For Christian love to be the senior or controlling partner would be an entirely different sort of coalition. Perhaps the position set forth in this volume may be made clearer by saying that while Christian love makes alliance or coalition with any available sources of insight or information about what should be done, it makes *concordat* with none of these. Christian love must, indeed, enter into such alliances; it must go in search of some social policy. Yet in the relationship between Christian love and the principles of an acceptable social ethic, Christian love remains what it is, dominant and free. It does not transform itself into the coin of any realm, though it enters every realm and becomes debtor both to the Greek and to the barbarians.

It cannot be too often said or too strongly emphasized that biblical "justice," which enters into alliance with ancillary conceptions of justice formulated by Aristotle, natural-law theory,

Rousseau, or any one else, can perfectly well get along without them if such reasonably accredited notions of justice be not forthcoming. Man may be not *Homo sapiens* but *Homo faber;* human reason "technical reason." If this be so, then in making law and fabricating systems of justice man must build his little systems and establish orders of life without the guidance of "first principles" or any sort of natural justice, but not without biblical Justice; for ultimately laws are not right simply because they are spontaneous or natural or rational rather than pragmatically devised according to the positive theory of law;[1] they are just to the degree in which they accord with the justice of God made known through covenant, old and new. From this even the technical, legislating reason of *Homo faber* may know "what is good" and the meaning of "doing justice." Man, that "most religious of animals,"[2] should construct his systems of law having in mind the righteousness of God, whether he also has capacity for "first principles" or not. Then all will go well with him. This is not said in order to prompt cynicism, agnosticism or relativism regarding rational moral norms (in the author's opinion, these views are far from true). Moral relativism need not be encouraged to prepare the way for "revealed ethics." This is said simply to show that the Christian has whereon to stand even were he forced to distrust moral judgments made by reason alone. He does not cease to stand on this same ground when Christian love enters into combination with moral principles believed to be universally valid and available to all reasonable men.

Christian love must seek to find out whatever may be known concerning the just ordering of human life. It cannot be too often said or too strongly emphasized that biblical "justice," when it begins to establish some order, can make use of any of the ideas or norms for determining "worldly justice" which happen to be convincing. At the same time, it must be said with equal emphasis that a Christian, impelled by love whose nature is to incarnate itself wherever there is need, cannot remain aloof but must enter

[1] Jacques Ellul, *Le fondement théologique du droit* (Neuchâtel and Paris: Delachaux & Niestlé, 1946), chap. iii, sec. i.
[2] Plato, *Timaeus*, 41.

fully into the problem of determining right action under the particular, concrete circumstances which surround him and his neighbor. Christian love lives always in quest of a social ethic adequate to any given situation. If philosophy fails to uncover permanently valid norms, the Christian continues the search and determines or posits his action in terms of the best knowledge available to him through the social or psychological sciences. Biblical justice demands: "To each according to the measure of his real need, because this alone is the measure of God's righteousness toward him." *Non tantus vile pro quo Christus mortus est.* This in turn poses the problem: How shall the neighbor's real need be determined, and what adjustment should be made among the competing needs and claims of many neighbors? Impelled by its own concern for more than one neighbor to find *some* answer to this question, biblical justice makes coalition with various rational norms of justice or natural law, but concordats it makes with none. The fact that biblical justice never admits any other conception of justice or definition of obligation into an equal partnership appears even in Brunner; for, before changing love into the small coin of Aristotelian justice, Brunner in fact baptizes Aristotle and to a great extent Christianizes his justice.[3] We saw other examples of the independent influence Christian love exerts in making use of themes drawn from outstanding philosophical theories of ethics in the revision and reconstruction Platonism underwent in the mind of St. Augustine and Aristotelianism in the mind of St. Thomas Aquinas; and our suggestion was then that this process simply needs to be renewed and made more thoroughgoing by constant reference to New Testament ethics.

The reason Brunner has such difficulty in relating love to "the world of systems" is that in purging love of *selfish* concern for one's own rights he tends to eliminate from it also all enlightened concern for *the neighbor's* right. Like Tolstoy, he seems to think that a love which by nature has no *selfish* partiality can find no reason for ever preferring the cause of one neighbor to that of another but must serve them all at random or as they happen

[3]*Cf.* above, Chap. I, sec. I, note 21.

to come. Consequently, Brunner concludes, "Love in itself establishes no order, on the contrary when it is about its business it transcends all orders, all laws. It inquires neither into its own right *nor into those of others,* for to all it gives itself, whole and undivided and beyond all limits."[4] But love which is unselfish need not *therefore* be unreasoning or unenlightened or accept no distinctions in its vocational obligations. It is true that love which does not inquire into its rights need not wait on determining the just rights of another *against one's self.* But such love, itself whole and undivided and limitless, will need to know all that can be known about "the others," since in actual life not all of them *can* be served effectively. Love which seeks not its own may very well seek *the neighbor's own.* It must establish some order, and to do so may employ all available ways of determining what may be the neighbor's own in comparison with another. Once this is allowed, then nothing in the nature of biblical "justice" prevents it from becoming "worldly justice." Such justice may be defined as what Christian love does when confronted by two or more neighbors. Justice perhaps means treating similar cases similarly (Aristotle's corrective justice) when a Christian judges, not between himself and his neighbor, but between two or more neighbors; or it may even mean treating them dissimilarly, taking into account essential inequalities between them (Aristotle's distributive justice), preferring some to others especially on account of their manifest good will and potential neighbor-regarding service.

The present writer happens to be convinced that, more than Aristotle or natural-law theory, Rousseau's notion of the general will gives a clue to the nature of minimal justice in the ordering of human relationships. The least that justice should do is to establish orders having "objective generality" and enact laws applying equally to all, so that "the conditions are the same for all; and, this being so, no one has an interest in making them burdensome to others."[5] This is that justice of which it may be said, "Love can only do more, it can never do less, than justice

[4]Emil Brunner, *Justice and the Social Order,* Harpers, 1945, p. 50 (italics mine).
[5]J. J. Rousseau, *The Social Contract,* Book I, chap. vi, p. 15.

requires."[6] Biblical "justice," itself concerned to treat similar cases (my own and my neighbor's) *dissimilarly,* can never do less than treat a number of neighbors *similarly* when comparing their needs (not with my own but) with one another and when arranging some stable order of life in which they all may live. A will to make the burdens lighter upon those in need of help certainly excludes any selfish propensity for making the conditions more burdensome on some than on others. Willingness to give must surely first renounce special claims for the self and conquer the interest we all have in making the conditions lighter for ourselves and by comparison more burdensome for others. When this has been accomplished, biblical justice goes on to do more than Rousseau's justice; or rather, biblical justice accomplishes at least this in the course of doing more.

These two parts of justice find support in the religious man's personal existence before God. With whatever judgment you judge, you shall be judged; with what measure you mete, it shall be measured to you again! At the crucial point where selfishness tempts us to make an exception of ourselves, God stands as a threatening witness of our existence. His judgment insures that we do no less than bear our equal burden, that we at least do not make exceptions of ourselves. Since whatever measure we apply rebounds on us again, no one has an interest in making law or institutions more burdensome on others. The religious man's understanding of his own personal existence "before" God guarantees widespread and persistent acceptance of a "this-applies-to-me" attitude which must undergird every effective effort to establish justice. It has frequently been affirmed that the main individualistic elements of secular democratic theory, natural rights, the dignity of man, etc., historically may be traced to their source in the religious tradition of the west. Equally likely (and equally difficult to demonstrate) is the connection between the "objective generality" of law and a religious sense of the inescapable and universal judgment of God, between "equality of application" and equality before God, between willingness to

[6]Emil Brunner, *op. cit.,* p. 129.

be no more than equal to another before the law and acknowledgment that we are no more than equal before God. This demands minimal justice on earth, but only *minimal* justice however
far such justice exceeds our actual performance.

God's righteous judgment (*tsedeq*) places the stress elsewhere,
as in Jesus' parable of the servant whom a merciful king released
from debt to the fantastic amount of ten million dollars who
nevertheless insisted that his fellow-servant pay in full a debt of
twenty dollars. "Then his master called him in and said to him,
'You wicked slave! I canceled all that debt of yours when you
entreated me. Ought you not to have taken pity on your fellow-
slave, as I did on you?" (Matt. 18:32, 33). From this story it is
evident that righteousness which for itself claims nothing may
yet for the sake of another claim everything, that any one who
unhesitatingly and times without number renounces "what is due"
when he himself alone bears the brunt of such a decision may
nevertheless turn full circle and insist with utter severity that the
neighbor receive what is due him in terms of righteousness, in
terms of *mishpat* which pronounces judgment on men and institutions and social policies that are not slanted toward love.

The relation between Christian love and existing social institutions therefore may be summed up as the constant criticism
and reshaping of the institutions of society in the course of using
them. And the relationship between Christian love and *other
theories of social ethics* may be summed up as the constant criticism and bending of these social policies in the course of using
them.

The expression "middle axiom" has been used in recent years
to refer to elements of a social policy which a large number of
Protestant Christians judge to be imperative in the present day.
The word "axiom" is misleading, suggesting as it does the "first
principles" of a natural morality on which there can be no disagreement among reasonable people. "Middle axioms" are intended rather as attempts "to define the directions in which, in
a particular state of society, Christian faith must express itself.
They are not binding for all time, but are provisional definitions

of the type of behavior required of Christians at a given period and in given circumstances."[7] Thus, John Bennett remarks, "a 'middle axiom' is more concrete than a universal ethical principle and less specific than a program that includes legislation and political strategy."[8] Assuming that in Christian love we have the "universal ethical principle" of Christian ethics, undoubtedly there are these aspects or stages or degrees of particularity in determining the specific recommendations of Christian love. Going into action and in search of a social policy, Christian love undoubtedly passes through a number of "mid" points before arriving at concrete decision: there may be axiomatic first principles of moral reason, general but provisional and non-axiomatic directions for social practice, and concrete proposals for immediate adoption through legislation or other means. Granting all this, there was need for further analysis of the connection which holds these stages of policy determination together. What stands between a "universal ethical principle" and a "middle axiom" or between one of these and specific plans for action? Surely not another "middle axiom"! The purpose of this section has been to suggest that "the controlling love of Christ," as both standard for action and impulse toward action, in its quest for a social policy gives the unity to Christian theory and practice and itself always remains dominant and free. In finding out what to do, "middle axioms" are uncovered and appropriated, alien ground becomes adopted ground, and in fact no ground and no source of understanding are alien to love whose nature is to incarnate itself in the flesh and blood of actual life. The impact of Christian love should be felt ideally throughout the whole range of formulated social policy by its being bent in the direction such love requires. To some degree this actually happens, unless Christian love suffers fundamental alteration through bondage to the social ethics it began by using.

No matter how strongly we have insisted that Christian love cannot get along without searching for a social policy, the final

[7]W. A. Visser't Hooft and J. H. Oldham, *The Church and Its Function in Society*, Willett, Clark, 1937, p. 210.
[8]*Christian Ethics and Social Policy*, Scribners, 1946, p. 77.

word must place the accent again on freedom, freedom even from the social policies Christian love may have found in times past. The Christian criticism of life means also the Christian criticism of every known, or yet to be discovered, social policy. Christian love works as a ferment underneath every social institution and conventional code of conduct in Christendom. Whether conforming to the old or helping to create a new mode of conduct, a Christian man subjects everything to this imperial test: let every man *now* consult his neighbor's need. This may call for respecting the tried and tested ways of doing things. When however we observe how these have failed in so many ways to keep pace with the world in which we and our neighbors live, who can doubt that Christian love today requires of us willingness to take some new departure? Even the humblest Christian man must rapidly become willing to have the structures and customs of his world otherwise than they now are. These will not stand long in any case. Why not bend them more to love's desiring? Even the most unlearned (or the most schooled) must be willing to sit loose within truth as he now sees it and willingly accept the best from the words of the latest prophet or the newest discoveries of science. Nay, he must go in search of new truth, loving his previous "findings" with the moderation of an employer and not with the ardor of a lover, since only the neighbor should be loved with infinite compassion. The Christian pilgrim, therefore, should pass from one age to another with the ease and serenity of freedom, assisting the new which is always struggling to be born, because in every age he loves not the times or some abstract truth but the neighbor.

IV. MAN AND HUMAN RIGHTS: A FULL-LENGTH ILLUSTRATION

The interpretation of the nature of man set forth in the preceding chapter combined a biblical or relational notion of the image of God with the idea, drawn from the idealistic tradition in philosophy, that man has certain unique capacities consisting of the powers of rational spirit or self-consciousness by which man stands in yet above physical nature. The implications of this viewpoint for social ethics may now be taken as an illustration of the relation between Christian love and the principles of a social policy which may be reasoned out and defended as true apart from distinctly Christian themes. It should be recalled that a certain amount of free-play was allowed to exist between the view that man exists in the image of God and humanistic interpretations of the special "kind" of creature man is. A Christian who happens to be convinced of some form of naturalism presumably has responsibility for showing how Christian love can make use of social principles disclosed by pragmatism or naturalism without becoming bound or altered in its own nature by them or simply identified with them. The Christian humanist or idealist has to do no less. Without pretending to deal with the entire range of Christian social theory, we may now ask the question, What happens when Christian thought lays hold upon the truth that man is a rational spirit?

On entering an alliance with philosophical theory concerning man as a rational spirit, Christian "obedient love" must retain the dominant position in devising what should then be done in relationships with other persons and in the common life. In short, there must take place a Christian *employment* of the (I believe) incontrovertible doctrine that there is a unique dimension in human nature standing above physical nature. The fact that non-Christian use may be made of it seems clear. This happens whenever notions of "mankind in your own person as well as in the person of every other" (Kant) become the foundation for duties to the self of equal primacy with duties to the neighbor. Erich Fromm quite rightly contends that if the primary definition of obligation is "to love my neighbor as a human being, it must be a virtue—and not a vice—to love myself since I am a human being too. There is no concept of man in which I myself am not included."[1] However, in the Christian perspective on ethics the love of Christ always controls the use made of any concept of

[1] *Man for Himself*, Rinehart, 1947, p. 128.

man or any dignifying of man on account of his superior spiritual nature. Such theories may be of assistance to Christian love, in that a truly humanistic estimate of man gives ground for the performance of greater duties to the neighbor than unenlightened, or even enlightened, self-interest induces and qualitatively superior duties than naturalism easily makes room for. Unlimited egoism may be somewhat tempered and reductive naturalism forestalled by reflecting upon the worth of man as man. Tension between Christian ethics and humanistic conceptions of man arise only when, in the course of attempting to narrow theoretically the distance between self and neighbor by reference to something of inherent worth in the "substantial form" of both parties, a person actually employs these ideas for the purpose of not being driven fully over to the neighbor's side. Too frequently doctrines of the unique spiritual quality inherent in all men succeed only in justifying greater concessions to the self than, after the leap to the neighbor's side, a Christian ethic of "enlightened unselfishness" would permit. If in this matter the "least leap" is infinitely wide, then there is a chasm of difference between treating another person as a human being within a system of claims and counterclaims between you and him, and loving another person for his own sake according to the measure of Christ's love which dispenses with all claims. Nevertheless, the Christian no less than any other man will find it salutary to reflect a great deal upon man's great native potentialities, lest in actual life he sometime fall far short of treating another person as every human being should be treated. Idealistic estimations of the worth of man, when they do not become vehicles for pressing the claims of self, may very well serve to remedy sinful and calloused use of another person, and direct attention to his real qualities, even though Christian love in itself would do much more.

"The rights of man," it is to be hoped, have validity apart from the Christian understanding of being in the image of God. Human rights depend upon a proper understanding of man as a distinct "kind" of being, which may reasonably be believed apart from religion. Yet Christian ethics brings about a radical shift of em-

phasis with regard to "rights." It seeks to accomplish the shift
from rights to duties, from claiming to giving one's own, from
teleological motivation for doing good to doing good to all men
on account of motivation from behind. When a man stands most
in the image of the God whom Christians are learning to know,
he is least concerned about his own value. He does not in the
Spirit bear witness to spirit and its rights, but in the Spirit he
bears witness to God and his righteousness, which, as Christ
shows, is such self-forgetful *agape*-love as, so far as one's self alone
is concerned, not to resist the deprivation of rights. The *imago
Dei* is a relationship in which it is not we who are asking the
questions or entering the claims; and in that relationship the
question of *our* purely individual rights is not the question we
are asked. Doubtless it is true that man alone of all "living beings" has been created with capacities for his particular kind of
freely responsive, conscious obedience to God. However, to conclude from this that human personality generally is of such value
among all creatures as to have in itself independent ground for
my own private rights, would this not amount to an abandon-
ment of the very relationship to God in which man's authentic
activity consists and assume a relationship to human personality
or to the self as god in which *ipso facto* its value for imaging the
true God is lost? This is not under God the question we are asked;
and for us to ask it is to stand from under the relation in which
we were created and perhaps to answer it—negatively. When
man ceases to reflect the image of God and begins simply to
reflect upon himself and his own rights, he is no longer *in* the
image of God.

In Christian ethics, motivation for valuing human personality
is to be derived neither from the created nature of man nor
indirectly by implication from man's created capacity for responsive service of God, but centrally from within that service itself.
A Christian doctrine of rights likewise follows primarily from
man's service of God, and not from man's nature as man. Personality and its rights are in Christian ethics read, as it were,
backward from Christ into man; Christ is not vindicated because

he thought of man as highly as we otherwise know he ought to have thought. There can be no sufficient teleological motivation for the Incarnation; there need be none for love controlled by the love of Christ. Infinite value is placed upon the neighbor's personality, value is created and realized there, whenever, in the service of God, a person forgets his own claims and becomes in some measure a Christ to his neighbor. To be in the image of God means to do the work of love in valuing one's neighbor. From the supernatural measure given the meaning of obligation by Christian ethics men learn to attribute worth without *necessarily* first finding it in those to whom they are duty-bound by Christ. Without such persistent attribution of worth to the neighbor, incontrovertible rational arguments on behalf of special human dignity proved insufficient to forestall the, as yet, largely harmless naturalism of much American thought or the demonic naturalism of recent European politics.

Basis for belief in human rights may be found in the conviction that man's powers of rational self-consciousness are a dimension in his spirit raising him above nature. Of course, regarding man merely as an animal with feelings of pain should lead to a mitigation of man's cruelty to man. The Society for the Prevention of Cruelty to Animals can accomplish this much; human society founded on the same basis should be able to do the same. However, the mitigation of *cruelty* to animals does not limit by a hairsbreadth man's *dominion* over them. We still assert our right to put animals out of the way as painlessly as possible, consulting our own interests and no "rights" on their part, though within limits compassion may stay our hand. Similarly, without some notion of man as more than animal, cruelty might perhaps be kept within bounds but there would be no rightful limits to place on one man's dominion over another. Gas chambers are, after all, painless if a man has no taste for torture. Without some limitation on one man's *right* to assert dominion over another, only geography and a few more years separate us from the gas chamber.

Because he possesses reason and personal self-awareness, it

may be said, man possesses rights. Most often in the past these rights have been thought of in individualistic terms, pertaining to man as an isolated individual; and also they have been thought of as rights to be exercised with considerable indifference to their positive meaning. Man as an individual in whom rights inhere was thought to have the freedom of complete indifference as to how he uses his rights, except when he encroached on the rights of others. Freedom of speech, for example, meant freedom to speak or not to speak according to one's own private will. Freedom of religion meant the freedom to be religious if a person wanted to or the freedom not to be religious if this were his choice. On this basis, freedom *from* speaking and freedom *for* speaking were like manifestations of freedom *of* speech; freedom *from* religion and freedom *for* religion were equal manifestations of freedom *of* religion; and the negative form of freedom in each instance was thought to be on the same plane equally fundamental with its positive form.

This way of thinking about human freedom (grounded though it is in a valid humanistic conception of man) undergoes radical but subtle alteration when brought into the context of the Christian view of man as existence-in-relation-to-God and of the individual's basic community with his neighbors through Christian love.

The primary freedom of man is freedom of religion; this was in fact the first freedom, just as freedom of religious assemblage was in fact the first form of freedom of assemblage for any purpose. If man has authentic being only in relation to God, then his freedom of religion means primarily freedom *for* religion, by no means to be reduced to parity with freedom *from* religion. Men should of course also be free to be free from all religion; but this follows by derivation from the importance of freedom *for* religion, because only then would any man's positive exercise of religion be a genuine product of his freedom and not in part a result of social prestige or coercion. If a man were not free to be free from religion, in being religious he would bear testimony that he stands in relation to no reality beyond society itself, and therefore is in fact an irreligious person. However, though there is a clear right of freedom *from* religion, this comes as a secondary consequence of man's positive right to be free *for* religion since he is, by definition, a theological or religious animal. Freedom of religion in this sense has no specific reference to any particular ecclesiastical order or ceremonial practice in religion. It means only that every man should be free to establish and express his own special, personal relation to the universe, and to do so if he pleases within a community of believers. He should be free in and for himself to respond to the Word of God, and to join others of like mind. Otherwise he would not be allowed to be a man in the very essence of his manhood. In the "post-Christian" world of the present day, it appears that the first freedom may well be the last freedom, and that where men have lost effective freedom of religion, or become ineffective in religion, they have already lost every other freedom and become ineffective, uprooted men. Man should be free to acknowledge God in his life and to serve his neighbor through loving works, for this is the central meaning of human existence as such. The Word of God, and the individual person addressed, must not be bound by church or state or any other creature.

It is possible to speak of other rights also as the rights of individual men, and to draw up a list of such natural or inalienable rights. No telling objection can be made against notions of natural right on the ground that through the court's interpretation of the "due process of law" clause "inalienable rights," according to Holmes' famous remark, became "a dugout in constitutional law for the protection of private property."[2] To affirm the inalienable rights of man does not forestall their misuse; nor does gross perversion of constitutional guarantees necessarily mean that there are no rights which should be protected.

It is true, however, that drawing up lists of so-called natural rights may no longer be a very *fruitful* task. To say that man has rights because of his dignity as a person has the appearance of

[2]Quoted by Ralph Gabriel, *The Course of American Democratic Thought,* The Ronald Press, 1940, p. 242.

putting into what we understand as the requirements of personality what a moment later we draw out in the form of a system of rights. It is impossible to elaborate much on this primary point of standing; and the impression may be gained, not unreasonably, that the rights of man live by reiteration or *petitio principii* among those who already believe in them. Modern science operates on the principle that a good scientific theory is not only one which adequately covers or corresponds to known fact, but one which in addition proves productive of new insight and has greater illuminating power. Beyond question the theory of natural right corresponds with the fact that man stands in yet above physical nature. However, there may be some gain in elaborating the meaning of human rights and connecting them up in an illuminating way with concrete social circumstances if Christian love, in search of a social policy, made alliance (never a concordat) with an idealistic social derivation of rights. Remembering that here we are concerned only to say *specifically what* are the rights of man, such an account may be briefly outlined as follows:

Human rights cannot be fully analyzed as if they pertained to the individual apart from society. They are not claims which a man makes the conditions of his reluctant participation in social concerns. A person's primary relationship to the various communities of which he is a member is one of service and not first of all one of making demands upon them. Rights do not inhere in the isolated, "natural" individual. They pertain to the individual insofar as there are certain powers which he must be allowed to exercise in order that maximum general welfare may be obtained, though this welfare, being general, is his own as well as others'. Marian Anderson has a right to sing in the Metropolitan Opera, not for Marian Anderson's sake as a private self, but for the sake of a better opera association and for the sake of Marian Anderson as a contributor to the operatic art. A right is a claim on the part of the individual to use a certain ability or power he has for the public good, a claim which is *implicitly* recognized by the society in question to be for its good, even though it may unrightfully impose discriminatory legislation upon the claimant to its own injury. A man cannot claim a right for himself alone, just because he likes things that way; rather he claims it as a member of society contributing to the general welfare. Nor are his rights mere external rewards for his being cooperative. Rather, they are things that are necessary that he be allowed to do in order for him to cooperate and make his contribution to the common life. Unless it can be said that without particular individuals being protected in the doing of some particular thing the community would be less well off, a man has no right to do the thing in question. Thus, regardless of his race, color or religion, a man has a right to equal opportunity and fair treatment in the competition for participation in civic affairs, for election to offices, and for the recognitions and honors distributed by the people, because if he has and exercises such a right, he by his abilities can help make his a better community; and because by every individual having this right the community will become as active and wholesome as it is possible for it to become by the efforts of its present members. "Human" rights inhere in and arise from the fundamental conditions of good community life. Herein alone are explicit civil or enacted "social" rights validated, or, on the other hand, claims for "individual" rights justified.[3]

This view of human rights provides an adequate account of those basic powers we think it right for men to exercise. Take freedom of speech, for example. Free speech is not the right to pop off the mouth simply because one can. It is not, in short, a matter of mere personal privilege, one's private, individualistic means of self-expression which he dares anybody to take away from him, though it is his responsible means of self-expression. Nature, which, as Aristotle says, does nothing in vain, has given us the power of speech, rather than simple ejaculation, in order that we may converse about what is just and unjust and may participate in those common sentiments which form a family or a city.[4] Free speech is inseparable from responsible speaking; it

---

[3]This and succeeding paragraphs draw heavily upon T. H. Green: *Lectures on the Principles of Political Obligation*. Longmans, Green and Company, New Impression, 1937.

[4]*Politics*, 1253a.

is ours insofar as we claim to speak responsibly, because service to our community demands our responsible contribution through speaking freely.

We may translate freedom of speech, properly understood, into freedom of listening. Individuals have a right to speak freely because society has a right to hear freely from all its members. A good society needs to have all possible points of view expressed so that the people will be competent to decide what course of action is really best for them to take. If there is no free listening to all opinions, it is always possible that one of the suppressed opinions is exactly the one the people need to know about and to act upon in order to solve their problems. From this social need derives the individual's freedom of speech. The right of all the people to listen freely to all shades of opinion gives the individual his right to speak out freely.

When, therefore, a radical climbs on his soap box on the street corner or in the park of one of our cities and begins to harangue the people who gather about him, he has a right to speak freely because he is understood possibly to have something to say that might possibly be of social benefit. He does not have any such right in himself as an individual separate and apart from his fellows and with no concern for the general welfare of the group. He cannot claim freedom of speech on any other ground than this; and it would annul his right for him to claim the privilege of speaking regardless of the consequences which might follow if people did what he recommends.

On the other hand, when we scorn this man on the soap box or take no heed of him, we just as effectively deny him real freedom of speech as we do if we put him in jail. Of course, we may not listen to him because, after just a moment, we realize that we have already thoroughly investigated that point of view and already have impartially weighed the arguments he is advancing; or we may judge that to do something else is for us more necessary just now and we intend to hear him or some one of his viewpoint later. But, with these exceptions, if we positively refuse to hear either him or any one else like him with an open mind, if we deliberately refuse to give ourselves a chance to learn from one of our fellow citizens, we destroy the essence of freedom of speech almost as surely as we do if we wrench his tongue from his throat. His *right* does not consist merely in his having a tongue in his throat, though without this it would be impossible for him to exercise this right. In a very real sense, a society in which an individual has the right of free speech will be one which will always provide him a receptive audience.

It would be easy to show that the view of human rights suggested and illustrated above provides adequate ground for a more extensive system of social rights. However, it is more important to notice that by its very nature every such social right has as its obverse side an individual right, the recognition and protection of which a person, acting on behalf of the general good, and on behalf of himself as a contributor thereto, may justly claim. Moreover, at the same time that individual rights are theoretically assured, the fulfillment of obligations by the individual is required. Any right is also a duty. The right of freedom of speech, as has been indicated, is the duty to speak out boldly so far as you can hope to influence public opinion for the better; and, on the part of others, it is the duty of listening so long as there is even the barest possibility that they will thereby become better informed citizens. The right a young person has to equal opportunities within the educational facilities of his culture is the duty he has to educate himself well; and both the right and duty of education arise from society's need for educated citizens. Property rights and collective bargaining are not simply economic devices, but truly human rights in the social sense that the exercise of these powers may be said to conduce to maximum social benefit, and is therefore a duty. Thus, the right to own and use a particular piece of property is the duty the owner has to manage this property with greater care and with more resultant good for more people than society could secure by any other ownership device. The right of collective bargaining is the duty to bargain collectively: "If, as a good Christian," a worker "is willing to endure the injustice of his position—so far as *he* is con-

cerned—for the sake of others he ought not to do so."[5] The right
to vote is the duty to vote. If and when the condition no longer
exists that specific obligations devolve upon the individual from
fundamental social needs, the right to the corresponding privileges may no longer be claimed; and the social revision of recognized rights may then take place without abrogating human rights
as such.

The reason Jews have a right to different treatment from that
accorded them in Nazi Germany, and in many ways in the United
States today, is precisely because they are culturally different
(and will remain so, if the present "reconstructionist" movement,
which declares that Judaism is a "religious civilization," succeeds
in stemming the tide of secularization and individualization),
and any nation that does not recognize their right to be different
in many respects would itself be permanently impoverished. Negroes, Japanese and various brands of white people all have rights
in the community of this nation because each and all can contribute to the wealth and variety of our common cultural life; and
it is an unmitigated denial of basic human rights that during the
recent war we did not allow Japanese-American citizens to make
independent contributions to our national welfare in tasks which
we recognize as tasks that needed to be done, just as all along
we have in a more qualified fashion denied the Negro the rights
which at the same time we recognize as human rights within our
community. The rotting of the crops in California following the
en masse removal of the Japanese-Americans was a symbol of
the blight upon civil rights with which this event proceeded. The
"law" passed by the sovereign state of Arkansas providing that
no person of Japanese ancestry shall ever own property in that
commonwealth—a law which seems from the individual point of
view so discriminatory—is an inwardly contradictory social policy
in that it both does and at the same time does not recognize the
social value of the general right to own property in that state.
On the international scene, any right enforced by powerful nations beyond the point where they may justifiably claim to be

[5]Emil Brunner, *The Divine Imperative,* Westminster Press, 1937, p. 431.

exercising powers and peculiar national capacities for the common good of mankind, and any right denied to weak nations up to this point, simply disguises tyranny. Rights, thus, are the very fiber out of which peace and community are made.

Finally, a social policy comprised of human-social rights avoids the softness of much sentimental liberalism, and is not to be identified with the will of the majority possessed of the social policy that it ought to have a social policy. The people may not do anything they please; and yet on behalf of rights they may rightfully employ coercion. Those persons who think of democracy primarily as the device of voting to "construct" a social policy conclude, or should conclude, that it is a denial of democracy not to allow anti-democratic communists and fascists to vote for their candidates in our elections, even though these candidates may be advocating the nullification of the Constitution on which their candidature depends and the abolition of the democratic process of voting itself on which their hope of election rests. But no one has a right to speak freely, and in speaking to advocate the abolition of free speech. To coerce a person who is advocating the abolition of free speech is not a contradiction or inconsistency in a democracy dedicated to human liberties, because the party or person using free speech to attack free speech is himself the contradiction. Whether or not to employ coercion in such instances is, then, a question merely of expediency and not of right; and this decision should vary according to the degree of the threat and the effectiveness of available forms of coercion. There is also this further test, that sinfulness be more restrained than released or given opportunity, and this makes all questions of expediency deep-going ones. Thus, for example, from a quite justifiable fear that real rights may be encroached upon if interference with free speech becomes too prevalent, we may wait until "clear and present danger" can be shown before putting a stop to any one's words. Nevertheless, no one has the right to be asked, by the free speech of another, to vote away his rights, any more than he can be rightfully deprived of them. Rights, being the structural conditions of a good society, are "inalienable" in the sense that no one, not even their possessor, has a right to destroy them. Here we are down to absolute bedrock liberal social policy on which any political life (as distinct from tyranny) must be based.

In a broad sense, this social policy is only methodological. It does not determine the goals which a society should set before itself; these may always be relative and different as between societies. However, it does speak to the point of *how* society should do whatever it does. One group may adopt the value-aims of mechanized commercial civilization; and another, the Oriental ideal of leisure, tradition and Confucian humaneness. For one the *summum bonum* may be rapidity; for another, longevity. Within a society, one "lesser corporation" may be an opera association, and another a labor union. But, the members of each will need to exchange ideas as to how best any particular goal is to be achieved and they must work together to attain the end in view. Rights, thus, arise as the conditions by which any society may best do what it intends; by them is called forth the maximum contribution of every individual to the common end actually held. There are no absolute absolutes within the range of political ends; or, if there are, rights as the coherence of individual and social endeavor in realizing existing relative aims are also the only way by which the common goals of a hypothetical universal humanity may come into view.

What happens when Christian thought lays hold upon the truth contained in the foregoing social definition of specific human rights? Christian love remains dominant and free, for all it may find here of the social policy it seeks. As a consequence of the unqualified operation of the Christian ethical impulse, on entering an alliance with this or any other analysis the Christian does not suffer his primary definition of obligation to alter. Instead, from the illumination provided by the idealistic social definition of rights, the Christian learns more about *his neighbor's own* which he should seek. He gains greater knowledge of the nature of the concrete roles which will truly benefit his neighbor and the rights which he should give his neighbor or which he should seek for his neighbor's sake. Thus, he will seek to admit and make room for another within the community; his good will toward his neighbor will be a will toward creating or extending the boundary of the existing community so as to include this single individual, his neighbor; he will try to communicate to him a responsible share in the good society, inviting and enabling him to assume a needed role and the role he needs. Social freedom can, in a sense, be gained only by being given, not by being demanded; and this is the work Christian love performs.

The social analysis or elaboration of specific human rights will itself suffer significant alteration from its association with Christian love. Without *necessarily* breaking apart the intimate connection of the individual's contribution and desirable social functions the whole emphasis will be shifted in the direction of contributing to the individual *his own* or the realization of every capacity he has for playing a significant role in actual life. The theory of natural rights speaks of rights inhering in the individual which society should serve, while a theory of social rights speaks of goods for the society which through rights the individual should serve, and at best it encourages the individual to seek his rights and his self-realization through serving the common welfare. A Christian social policy (made up of known social rights and Christian love in a proper blending where love loses none of its catalytic power) would place upon society the responsibility for bringing every individual into full realization of his own proper selfhood (the latter being defined in large measure in terms of the social roles he plays and the social contribution he makes). It would also place upon every individual the responsibility for opening the door for his neighbor, and for doing his part in bending society in this same direction.

A Christian therefore may learn from a number of sources what rights specifically are. Only from Christian love does he learn what to do with them. With any particular theory of rights, from love he learns to engage in the reconciling task of creating community and valuing human persons *pro quo Christus mortus est.* A "Christian" society should have this same bent toward love, whatever happens to be at the moment its social aims or the roles defined as of service to these purposes. Bent by love toward "the neighbor" society will open the way for the least common individual within its system of socially defined rights, and endeavor to see that every man comes into his own. With whatever social policy, we must start from Christian love if ever we are going in the direction of Roscommon.

X

THE RELIGIOUS FOUNDATION
FOR COMMUNITY LIFE

W E have spoken of "the righteousness of God" and "the kingdom of God" as sources of Christian love. There remains one outstanding omission from the foregoing consideration of the main themes in biblical ethics, namely, the idea of "covenant." "No other aspect of Israel's faith is as conspicuous as this," declares a recent book on Old Testament theology, "and no more fruitful inquiry can be made than to search the Scriptures for light on the covenant idea. Within the scope of this idea may be found all that is relevant to the basic religious beliefs of Israel and to the faith by which she championed them."[1] Nowhere is this statement more notably true than in attempting to comprehend notions of political society in the Bible and norms for its just arrangement. In the Bible God appears as a covenant-making, covenant-restoring and covenant-fulfilling God; Israel, a people of the covenant and a covenant-breaking people.[2] In both these respects Christians conceive themselves to be heirs of the covenant. Biblical ethical ideas are all to be understood as simple corollaries of the righteousness of God, the kingdom of God and idea of covenant. The latter has specially to do with "obedience to God" as the foundation of human life in community.

The covenant, to the Hebrews, served as a kind of charter or national constitution. When the laws are thought of together with the covenant, it is referred to as "the nature of the king-

[1]Otto J. Baab, *The Theology of the Old Testament*, Abingdon-Cokesbury Press, 1949, p. 136.
[2]Paul S. Minear, *Eyes of Faith*, Westminster Press, 1946, p. 218 and *passim*.

dom" (I Sam. 10:25), "the manner of the kingdom,"[3] or, as we might say, it was the custom of the country. Nevertheless, the covenant should not be identified with law or response to the covenant with mere obedience to authority. Laws were variable; the covenant was a durable relationship, though it was also an event which might be forgotten and remembered, a successive contract which might be restored and repeated in time. The terms of the covenant might change, but the covenant itself was a living relationship with the living God that could only be adhered to or broken. "The nation is the people, constituted as such by the covenant and characterized by the social ethic 'written in' to the covenant. The covenant was, in fact, not a fixed and written code, but a living tradition which was formulated variously at different periods."[4] In philosophical terms the covenant was the "form," law codes the "content," of the religious constitution of the Israelite nation. Covenant without commandments would have been empty, laws without the covenant meaningless.

The covenant, therefore, was quite unlike an ordinary civil contract or agreement. It may be compared with a basic contract making possible all such specific agreements, a "contract of contracts" logically prior to all law. It is well known that early modern social philosophers traced out the fundamental nature of political society by analyzing a "social contract" which, they said, went underneath, if not actually before, every imaginable human community and determines the conditions for justly arranging human relations within existing states. Israel's covenant plays just such a fundamental role. Greatly increased understanding of the biblical notion of covenant, therefore, may be gained from comparing it with modern theories of social contract.

Theories of social contract took in the main two forms, according to whether two contracts were assumed or only one. By one contract, the people bracket themselves together to form a society. This is the *pacte d'association* or *Gesellschaftsvertrag*. Such

3 R. B. Y. Scott, *The Relevance of the Prophets,* Macmillan, 1944, p. 63.
4 *Ibid.,* p. 177.

single-contract theories usually affirmed that sovereignty resides always in the people (Rousseau) or that sovereignty over the people comes into existence simultaneously with their forming an effective association (Hobbes). In both types of single-contract theory, no further contract is necessary between people and ruler. However, by the other contract, people establish a government to rule over them. This is the *pacte de gouvernement* or *Herrschaftsvertrag*. In contrast to the first sort, these double-contract theories usually defined some limitation of sovereignty; they were apologies and guaranties of constitutional monarchy. Ernest Barker describes this second or "representative" theory as "the collective theory taken in two bites." "The ninety-nine first contract, by one sort of contract, with one another; and then they contract, by another sort, with a hundredth person,"[5] to whom alienable rights are given up on condition that he execute laws securing the people in the possession of certain inalienable or reserved rights. In fine, single-contract theories established absolute sovereignty; double-contract theories placed a limit on sovereignty, enthroning a king to rule on behalf of human law and the rights of man.

Millar Burrows finds elements of both types of compact in the biblical notion of covenant. He does not distinguish clearly enough between them, yet in the nature of the case any fundamental social contract must be *primarily* one or the other.

> The nation originated in the federation of tribes bound together by their common covenant with Yahweh. The covenant was not formulated by a democratic process; it was rather like a constitution voluntarily promulgated by a monarch. Yet it was ratified by the people (Exod. 24:3–8; Deut. ch. 27; Josh. 24:1–28), and it is possible that the accounts of its ratification reflect an annual ceremony in which the people solemnly renewed their commitment to the covenant. It is fair to say, therefore, that the biblical conception of law and government rests primarily on the divine will but also on popular consent.[6]

[5]Translator's Intro., Otto Gierke, *Natural Law and the Theory of Society, 1500–1800*, trans. E. Barker (Cambridge: Cambridge University Press, 1934), p. lxvi.
[6]Millar Burrows, *An Outline of Biblical Theology*, Westminster Press, 1946, p. 307.

Now which is it primarily that constitutes the covenant, the divine will or popular consent? Certainly not popular consent in any sense limiting the divine will or making God a constitutional representative of human law. Without ceasing to be fully aware of the danger of misleading analogies, it is still true to say that, of the two types of social-contract theory developed by modern political thought, Israel's covenant was more like a single covenant establishing absolute sovereignty.

This conclusion follows from considering the nature of the covenant as approximating the meaning of obedience to command and as approximating, even going beyond, the steadfastness of an order of nature. Obedience to the covenant was thought of as "commanded" on account of God's firmness, and God was firm on account of his trustworthy character and his unswerving faithfulness to the covenant. "It was because God insisted on maintaining his part of the Covenant, even when Israel had broken that Covenant, that there was any continuance of it, and any hope for even a remnant."[7] Every Jew knew that the fidelity already displayed by God in the initiative he had taken to establish it could surely be counted on to keep the covenant secure. Therefore, "the covenant idea already involves confidence in the reliability of Yahweh, his fidelity to his obligations and promises."[8] The word commonly translated "truth" and the word commonly translated "mercy" or "loving-kindness" both have this meaning. Karl Barth is correct, then, not for the Epistle to the Romans alone but for the Bible generally in saying that men shall live, as the covenanted household lived, from faith in God's faithfulness. As a consequence of "the faithful covenant-keeping character of God"[9] the covenant gains immutability. The God of truth (Isa. 65:16), God's truth and loyalty, strengthen the covenant up to and beyond the unbreakable point.

This strengthening of the covenant from God's side of the relationship may be seen whenever the meaning of the term ap-

[7]Norman H. Snaith, *The Distinctive Ideas of the Old Testament*, Westminster Press, 1946, p. 179.
[8]Millar Burrows, *op. cit.*, p. 69.
[9]Baab, *op. cit.*, p. 129.

proximates the sense of "command" and *a fortiori* when it approximates what we would call a "law of nature." Significantly, the covenant is frequently spoken of as "*My* covenant,"[10] which amounts to a contradiction in contractual language where "*our* covenant" or simply "*the* covenant" might be expected. Again, in words which oppose one another, Israel's usual share in the relationship is described as "breaking the everlasting covenant" (Isa. 24:5), breaking the unbreakable! Wherever the covenant approximates the sense of "command" (Deut. 33:9, 10; Josh. 7:11; Jer. 11:3–8), we have a contract which is primarily God's doing. It becomes a sort of decree, a *contrat d'adhésion,* or contract in which the only responsibility of one party is adherence, the other party determining all its characteristics, limits, and conditions.[11] God was thought to be faithful and able, zealous and jealous, to maintain intact the covenant he *commands:* the covenant was from man's side a covenant of "obedience."

Moreover, the covenant enacted in history has the steadfastness of an order of nature. In the time of Noah, God covenanted everlastingly with "every living creature of every sort that is on the earth" (Gen. 9:16), imposing upon the rainfall his decree, establishing its barriers and doors. Whether according to the biblical understanding "history" is interpenetrated with the dependabilities found in nature or "nature" formed of the same stuff history is made of would be difficult to determine. When the prophet Jeremiah wanted to express the inviolability of the covenant, he thought of day and night in their rounds (Jer. 33:20, 21). Yet he spoke of these natural occurrences as due to "covenant," which was also his way of comprehending the meaning of history. "These are the generations of the heavens and the earth" (Gen. 2:4a);[12] this verse concluding the first creation story would have served as a better halfway house between biblical literalism and

---

[10]This occurs, it is true, only in the priestly tradition where "covenant" becomes identified with particular codes of law. Such degeneration of Israel's living religious tradition triumphed during and after the Exile, yet it was a declension from what was there all along: God's free covenant by him freely arrived at.

[11]Jacques Ellul, *Le fondement théologique du droit* (Neuchâtel and Paris: Delachaux & Niestlé, 1946), chap. i, sec. 3.

[12]Revised version.

the theory of evolution or modern process philosophy than was found in the sequence and stages of creation itself. "These are the generations of the heavens and the earth," "These are the generations of Noah or David or Jesus," ancient authors wrote with little sense of difference between the origin or processes of "nature" and the origin or processes of "history." "In creating the world, God made a covenant with it."[13] In covenanting with Israel, he *made* her a nation. With whatever God has dealings, "nature" or "history," his glory is disclosed; and day unto day utter speech no less than do prophets. "Nature does not have a nature; it has a history. And this history is the history of creation and rebellion,"[14] which also is man's story and man's nature.

Commonly today we hear it said, and ourselves say, that the distinctive thing about the biblical point of view is its sense of history. This must not be understood as if history in itself had a clearly understood nature or as if men first learn what history means and then know better the God whose field of action history is. The Hebrews did not first know what an "event" was, a genuine and meaningful part of their history, and then learn to know God. They first knew God through the covenant and learned to sense the eventful.[15] With whatever God has dealings, history is begun, whether it be the generations of men, the generations of the heavens and the earth, or any other creature. With whatever group of men God makes a covenant, they gain a nature as a religious nation which can no more be broken than you can break his covenant with the day and his covenant with the night so that day and night no longer come at their appointed times (Jer. 33:20, 21). In the Bible neither "history" nor "nature" has a nature or an order of its own. Each has a source and an ordering. Both have meaning which stems from covenant. The idea of nature and the idea of history may neither of them be derived

[13]Minear, *op. cit.,* p. 244.
[14]*Ibid.,* p. 61.
[15]The events beginning the Exodus do not disprove this statement, for these events were eventful only to those who proleptically responded to and obeyed their covenant with God (who at that time declared only, "I will be what I will be"). They were not significant events, not parts of meaningful history, to those who, "knowing" not God, desired to remain in Egypt serving other gods or who later longed to go back to the fleshpots of Egypt.

from the other; rightly grasped, they may both be reduced to simple corollaries of the idea of covenant without which the Hebrew mind would have known little of either.

Indeed, the reliability of God's covenant far exceeds that of the natural order:

> Though the mountains should be removed
> And the hills should waver,
> My kindness shall not depart from you,
> And my covenant of peace shall not waver (Isa. 54:10).

Similarly, the faithfulness of God far exceeds the faithfulness of the most reliable relationships among human kind:

> Can a woman forget her sucking child,
> So as not to have pity upon the son of her womb?
> Even should these forget,
> Yet I will not forget you (Isa. 49:15).

> If my father and mother forsake me,
> Then the Lord will take me up (Ps. 27:10).

Both the steadfast orderliness of nature and the fidelity of parental affection are measured against God's covenanted faithfulness, not *vice versa*. Consequently, two things filled the Hebrew mind with awe: the starry heavens above declaring the glory of God and the moral law within historical covenants! The moral law within the people themselves only awakened consternation: Why are we so evil? Why do we suffer so much? Nevertheless, any one who doubts the faithfulness of God may find in nature some suggestion of his dependability. He may know from the covenant commanding nature that covenants with God made in times past also abide forever, resembling only in name agreements made among men.

The fact that Israel's covenant was more like a single contract establishing absolute or free sovereignty also finds support from a careful study of what Rousseau and Hobbes say in the course of their descriptions of the origin of society in a single contract. Thomas Hobbes's main endeavor was to establish the absolute simultaneity of the moments in which society and sovereignty, association and government, come into existence. It is vain, he contended, to grant limited sovereignty by way of some precedent covenant. Sovereignty cannot have its source in preceding contract for two reasons: First, because this would presuppose some sovereignty already existing and powerful enough to enforce contracts. Second, and a more essential reason, because the people have no unity or community before sovereign government comes into existence; they are not yet capable of moving as a body or of acting as a whole or as one person. The social contract made this possible: in one and the same moment contending individuals and factions became a single society, gaining one voice through some form of government. In Hobbes's words, they

> confer all their power and strength upon one man, or upon one assembly of men, that may reduce all their wills by plurality of voices, unto one will: which is as much as to say, to appoint one man or assembly of men to bear their person . . . and therein to submit their wills, every one to his will, and their judgments, to his judgment. This is more than consent, or concord; it is a real unity of them all, in one and the same person, made by covenant of every man with every man.[16]

This contract is based partly on inclination toward social peace and partly on the rules reason devises for finding such peace by coming out of the state of nature; and there is, of course, a sense in which the contracting act is voluntary, but not in such fashion as to lessen the obligation assumed: "When a covenant is made, then to break it is *unjust* and the definition of injustice is no other than the *not performance of covenant*. . . . For as it is there [in scholarly disputations] called an absurdity to contradict what one maintained in the beginning; so in the world, it is called injustice or injury, voluntarily to undo that which from the beginning he had voluntarily done."[17] Only one law is above the sovereign: the welfare of the people, the *salus populi;* but no one can force his compliance or decide for him how the good of the commonwealth may best be obtained.

[16]*Leviathan,* Part II, chap. xvii, in *The English Philosophers from Bacon to Mill* (Modern Library Giants), ed. E. A. Burtt, pp. 176–177.
[17]*Ibid.,* Part I, chaps. xv and xiv, pp. 168 and 164.

The differences between this contract and Israel's covenant arise mainly from the fact that Hobbes describes the *artificial* creation of earthly sovereignty, the *fabrication* and "generation of that great Leviathan, or rather, to speak more reverently, of that *mortal god,* to which we owe . . . our peace and defense."[18] Hobbes's ruler comes into existence as ruler when individuals all at once pledge one another to submit themselves to him; he himself takes no part in making the contract; whereas Israel's ruler himself initiates the making of the covenant, setting people in a juridical situation, placing them in a contracting position before him. Moreover, in fabricating political sovereignty Hobbes is forced to assume a prior sovereign autonomy of the individual which has nothing in common with the biblical view. Hobbes, Gierke remarks,

> extended the idea of Natural Right until it meant the right of all to everything, and he had done so in order that it might perish, as a right of all, from the very abundance of its own strength. He had made the individual omnipotent, with the object of forcing him to destroy himself instantly in virtue of his own omnipotence, and thus enthroning the "bearer" of the State-authority as a mortal god. . . . A previous sovereignty of the individual was the ultimate and only source of group authority.[19]

But the similarities between Hobbes's contract and Israel's covenant are even more remarkable than the differences between them. No less allegiance was due the living God of Israel or less sovereignty asserted by the covenant God enjoined upon the slaves and wandering tribesmen whom he consituted one people. Before God called them into being, they were not a people already able, by some previous multilateral contract with one another, to attach conditions to their acceptance and "ratification" of covenant with him. God's creation of the nation, his assertion of lordship, and the acknowledgment of his sovereignty took place with absolute simultaneity. Before the people heard God's voice, they had no common voice, nor had they any but his voice or their own rebellion afterward. The nation did not exist for a single

[18]*Ibid.,* Part II, chap. xvii, p. 177. [19]Gierke. *op. cit.,* I, 61 and 106.

instant in the absence of their ruler; the people never existed as a unity side by side with the ruler bargaining effectively with him, from which slender basis alone there grew up in the modern period notions of the rights of the people against their rulers. Human "righteousness" had no other primary definition for the Hebrews than *the performance of covenant;* "unrighteousness," "the not performance of covenant"; or "peace," any other definition than "the harmonious operation of covenant."[20] One law only was "above" the sovereign: the *salus populi,* the welfare of the people; and this was not above but *within* his will: no one need force his compliance. For Hobbes's and Israel's ruler alike, there could happen no breach of covenant on the part of the sovereign.[21] The endurance of the covenant depended on God's faithfulness alone. He might renounce sovereignty and let his people go, but in that case the covenant would not really be violated; it would simply cease to be. God did not depend on the fate of the nation or on his recognition and guaranty of the rights of the people; these depended on him.

The distinctive thing about the Hebrew covenant, therefore, was God's transcendence over it, not democratic ratification or constitutional contracting. "To cut a covenant" ordinarily brought about such intermingling and identification of one life with another that thereafter both parties depended for what they were upon their common bond. People were not one people without their god, but neither were gods gods without a people.

> Such blood covenants existed by the hundreds in the ancient world of the Hebrews. What marks the Hebrew covenant as unique is the appearance of a new conception, which may be negatively stated—that God was not automatically obligated, upon request, to help his people. His proffer of help depended upon the merits of each case, which were determined by a standard of measurement derived from the objectively righteous will of God.[22]

20 Scott, *op. cit.,* p. 24.
21 Hobbes, *op. cit.,* Part II, chap. xviii, p. 178.
22 Baab, *op. cit.,* p. 136. *Cf.* Snaith, *op. cit.,* p. 137: "The great barrier to religious progress was the belief that a god could not exist without a people, and that he must in the last resort rescue his people for his own credit's sake. Nay, he must save them, if he himself was to continue to exist, or to have any place in the dwelling-houses of the gods."

In "social-contract" language, this means that the God of the covenant was precisely the opposite of a constitutional monarch. What he promulgated was legal and righteous altogether; there was no law external to himself or whose source was the people's voice in accord with which he must rule in order to remain truly a lord. The people might break, they could not destroy, the covenant by rebelling against him. Much less could their action destroy God's nature as king. Instead, God himself might with impunity declare, "I am your destruction, O Israel." Whenever Israel turned aside and "cut a covenant" of one sort or another with some other god, the people were left in the condition they were in before *the* covenant and might without injustice have been destroyed (as Hobbes and Josh. 24:20 both say) but for the fact that God's justice proves not the same as Hobbes's justice, or, for that matter, Joshua's either. God's justice was *his* performance of covenant.

In similar fashion Rousseau ascribes an unqualified sovereignty to the general will. By a single contract there takes place a "total alienation of each associate, together with all his rights, to the whole community. . . . Moreover, the alienation being without reserve, the union is as perfect as it can be and no associate has anything more to demand."[23] "Each man alienates," he admits, "by the social compact only such part of his powers, goods and liberty as it is important for the community to control; but it must also be granted that the Sovereign is sole judge of what is important,"[24] and it would be "against the nature of the body politic for the sovereign to impose on itself a law which it cannot infringe."[25] The sovereign by its very nature is inalienable and indivisible: "The Sovereign cannot be represented except by himself: the power indeed may be transmitted, but not the will. . . . The Sovereign may indeed say: 'I now will actually what this man wills, or at least what he says he wills'; but it cannot say: 'What he wills tomorrow, I too shall will.' "[26] This would be a

[23]*The Social Contract*, Book I, chap. vi (Everyman edition), p. 16.
[24]*Ibid.*, Book II, chap. iv, p. 27.
[25]*Ibid.*, Book I, chap. vii, p. 17.
[26]*Ibid.*, Book II, chap. i, p. 23.

self-limitation to which by its nature sovereignty cannot submit. The sovereign is also infallible: "The general will is always right and tends to the public advantage," although it does not follow that deliberations which seek to determine what the general will is are always equally correct.[27]

Besides this covenant there can be none other. The institution of particular forms of government takes place by appointment, not by contract which would shift over to the government any, even a limited, degree of the people's sovereignty. "It is impossible to conceive of any public contract that would not be a violation of the first."[28] How then was the first government appointed? Since appointment is a particular act, it is an act of government executing law and not of the general will making law. How can there be "a governmental act before government exists"? This difficulty Rousseau resolves by a device comparable to the parliamentary procedure in which a legislative body transforms itself into a "committee of the whole" and, acting as a committee, reports back to itself as a legislature. The appointment of the first government "is accomplished," says Rousseau, "by a sudden conversion of the sovereignty into democracy [*i.e.*, into a democratic *government*], so that, without sensible change, and merely by virtue of a new relation of all to all, the citizens become magistrates, and pass from general to particular acts, from legislation to the execution of the law."[29]

Again there are differences between this social contract and Israel's covenant, differences arising mainly from the fact that Rousseau constructs a sovereign while Israel recognizes one. Rousseau's ersatz sovereign has also the further complication that Rousseau sets himself the task of finding "a form of association . . . in which each, while uniting himself with all, may still obey himself alone, and remain as free as before . . . [a form of association in which] each man, in giving himself to all, gives himself to nobody."[30]

27 *Ibid.*, chap. iii, p. 25.   29 *Ibid.*, chap. xvii, p. 87.
28 *Ibid.*, Book III, chap. xvi, p. 86.   30 *Ibid.*, Book I, chap. vi, pp. 14, 15.

Nevertheless, in the midst of wide analogy there is much in common between this social compact and the biblical idea of covenant. The obedience claimed through the latter was all the more unreserved precisely because in the covenant men give themselves to somebody and make his will their own, the sovereign himself being the sole judge of what is important. From Egypt on through desert wanderings Israel was rather "forced to be free."[31] The will of the covenant God was always right and tended always to the public advantage: "So the Lord commanded us to observe all these statutes, by standing in awe of the Lord our God for our good always, that he might keep us alive, as at this day" (Deut. 6:24). Nevertheless, the succession of prophets and a growing oral tradition indicate that deliberations which sought to determine the will of God were never equally correct or entirely finished and adjourned.

Beside the covenant there could be none other. It was impossible to conceive of any public contract with other gods or rulers that would not be a violation of the first. Some concluded from this that there should be no kings in Israel; others, that kings should rule under the suffrance and sovereignty of God. The institution of kings in Israel was always by appointment; no sovereignty, not even a limited degree, was contracted to them. It is true that we are told "all the elders of Israel came to the king at Hebron, and King David made a covenant with them in Hebron before the Lord, and they appointed David king over Israel" (II Sam. 5:3). This "covenant before the Lord" between David and the elders of the tribes was more like praying a blessing or taking an oath before "the God of truth" (Isa. 65:16) than like a second contract establishing government. Only the Lord could say, "You shall shepherd my people Israel, and you shall be a leader over Israel." Accordingly "David realized that the Lord had established him king over Israel; for his kingdom had been exalted for the sake of his people Israel" (II Sam. 5:2b, 12). It is significant that the prophet Nathan made no mention of David's

[31] *Ibid.*, chap. vii, p. 18.

violating the constitution prescribed and consented to by repre-
sentatives of the tribes, which surely would have been appropriate appeal on that occasion, but only of his having "despised
the Lord by doing that which is evil" in his sight. And David
confessed that he had broken the only covenant binding upon
him: "I have sinned against the Lord" (II Sam. 12:9, 13).

In God's hands also was the overturning of kings: "Because you
have rejected the word of the Lord, He has rejected you from
being king," said Samuel to Saul; and in this instance the source
of the trouble was, according to Saul's reply, too much attention
to the momentary will of the people: "I have sinned; for I have
transgressed the command of the Lord and your words, because
I feared the people and listened to their voice" (I Sam. 15:23b,
24). There is a single case in which a popular right of revolution
seems to have been exercised under the leadership of Jeroboam
against Solomon's successor, Rehoboam. "When all Israel saw that
the king had not listened to them," the cry went out: "To your
tents, O Israel!" But the fact that the king did not listen to the
people "was a thing brought about by the Lord to establish his
word," and the people were really on the Lord's side (I Kings
12:15, 16).

Two hundred years after the coronation of David when the
child-king Jehoash was crowned, the priest "made a covenant between the Lord and the king and the people, that they should
be the Lord's people; likewise between the king and the people"
(II Kings 11:17). The second covenant referred to here simply
bound the king to carry out all the obligations he and the people
together were responsible for by their primary covenant with
God. "This was first of all a renewal of allegiance to Yahweh, and
the public acknowledgment of Yahweh's justice and mercy as the
'custom and right' of the community to be upheld by the king."[32]
It was, in short, no "second contract" establishing government
with any sort of sovereignty, limited or unlimited.

Paraphrasing Rousseau, the sovereign God cannot be represented except by himself: the power, indeed, he may transmit but

[32]Scott, *op. cit.*, p. 63.

not the will which remains forever his. He may, indeed, say, "I now will actually what this man wills, or, at least, what he says he wills"; but without giving up his lordship God cannot say, "What he wills tomorrow, I too shall will." This would be a self-limitation to which, by his nature as sovereign, God cannot submit. The "ratification" or popular consent given the original covenant which God "commanded" resembles rather an assemblage of people transforming themselves by sudden conversion into a "committee of the whole" in order to do what no self-governing people can do, namely, acknowledge another to be their lord.

To find a closer parallel to Israel's covenant, we should not go to John Locke's limitation of sovereignty but to Jean Bodin and Hugo Grotius, who first formulated the concept of sovereignty in the modern period. Having on his hands the notion of earthly sovereignty, Locke was, of course, right in limiting the claims of monarchs who are "but men."[33] His statement cannot be challenged that any *man* "who attempts to get another man into his absolute power does thereby put himself into a state of war with him; it being to be understood as a declaration of a design upon his life. . . . He that . . . would take away the freedom that belongs to any one . . . must necessarily be supposed to have a design to take away everything else."[34] However, this hardly applies with equal force to the sovereign God of Israel whose judgments are righteous altogether.

Jean Bodin and Hugo Grotius were concerned not so much to limit as to justify sovereignty. As a consequence, what they say about the social contract and the authority of the ruler borders closely upon what an ancient Jew would have said in tribute to his ruler. Indeed, the two sources upon which political theory drew in formulating the idea of sovereignty were, first, the idea of the Roman imperium, which was traditionally the power of the Roman people, and, second, religious views as to the sovereignty of God strongly revived in the Reformation period, close to which

[33] *An Essay Concerning the True Original, Extent and End of Civil Government,* chap. ii, sec. 13, in *The English Philosophers from Bacon to Mill* (Modern Library Giants), ed. E. A. Burtt, p. 408.
[34] *Ibid.,* chap. iii, sec. 17, p. 410.

in point of time these men stood.[35] "The Prince," says Bodin, "is the image of God," and "the law of the Prince is made on the model of the law of God."[36] The primary mark of such sovereignty is the power of "giving the law to the subjects without their consent."[37]

> ... when the "estates" of the whole people are assembled, presenting their pleas and supplications to their Prince in all humility, without having any power to command him in the matter nor to decide anything nor any voice in the deliberations; and so whatsoever it pleases the king to consent to or dissent from, to command or to prohibit is taken to be law or edict, or ordinance. . . . The primary mark of the sovereign Prince is the power to give law to all in general, and to each one in particular; but this is not enough, for it must be added, without the consent of the majority nor of any equal nor of any one whatsoever, other than oneself alone . . . very often against the wishes of the subject.[38]

Bodin based his views on the possibility that there might be some *recognized* authority to give law without consent. The ruler rules by a kind of implicit "consent," but consent is not necessary to his laws. He is that person who has proved himself to be creative of national unity and peace; and on account of his recognized competence, his personal, proved power of achievement, he possesses authority with the people.

All this may also be said of Israel's king. "The Lord brought us out of Egypt by a strong hand. The Lord displayed before our eyes great and ominous signs and portents against Egypt" (Deut.

[35]Cf. J. Neville Figgis, "Political Thought in the Sixteenth Century," in *Cambridge Modern History*, Vol. III, article on "The Wars of Religion," chap. xxii, pp. 746–747: "With the sixteenth century law more and more takes on the nature of embodied will, and discards other elements. This was assisted by the strong sense of the sovereignty of God entertained by the Reformers, and by the doctrine of the arbitrary and irresponsible character of the Divine decrees. The Leviathan of Hobbes owed more of his non-moral attributes than the author knew to ideas of God which had been prevalent ever since the last phase of nominalism." These words betray the author's bias in favor of some form of natural-law theory of society. Nonetheless, they are correct in that the Reformation may be summed up as an effort to free the free will of God. This freedom the covenant first established.

[36]*Six Books of the Republic* (1583 ed.), Book I, chap. viii, p. 161.
[37]*Ibid.*, p. 142.
[38]*Ibid.*, pp. 137, 217, 222.

6:21b, 22). Therefore he possessed authority with them. By his personal, proved power of achievement, he gained recognition of his authority. This was Israel's acknowledgment of the covenant by which she consented not to have to consent to law or to have a part in determining what is just or what is "for our good always." "No man can oblige himself," says Bodin, "because, perforce, he must then be his own superior, which is impossible and absurd." Israel, accordingly, was under obligation *to God*, who himself was not made sovereign by contract but by his own strong hand.[39]

Hugo Grotius, not less than Jean Bodin, was concerned to establish sovereignty rather than, according to Tom Paine's influential misinterpretation, to put sovereignty under "natural right." "For when men are said to be by nature in a state of freedom . . . the freedom there meant is an exemption from slavery and not an absolute incompatibility with slavery: *i.e.*, no man naturally is a slave, but no man has a right never to become such, for in this sense no body living is free."[40] This is precisely what men do in the contract with a sovereign establishing government. The most powerful obligation arises out of their first free contract. In constituting him sovereign, the people are not thereby demonstrably superior to the person so constituted, since he gains "a power which though at first one was at liberty to confer it or not, cannot afterwards be revoked by him that has once conferred it."[41] "Why should it not therefore be lawful," Grotius asks, "for a people that are at their own disposal, to deliver up themselves

---

[39]Bodin believed, however, that the prince "ought" to keep whatever secondary promises he makes to the people (*ibid.*, pp. 414, 802). There are, in his view, "contracts" which are obligatory without any superior power to enforce them. In case "agreement or convention or contract is made mutually between the Prince and his subjects . . . it obliges the two parties reciprocally and no one of the parties can contravene it to the prejudice of or without the consent of the other, and the Prince in this case has no advantage over his subjects" (*ibid.*, p. 135). But this simply means that the sovereign had better not make many specific promises, which have certain moral force and somewhat delimit his freedom in exercising rulership.

[40]*Notes on the Rights of War and Peace in Three Books, Wherein Are Explained the Law of Nature and the Principal Points Relating to Government* (Barbeyrac ed., Eng. trans., 1738), Book II, chap. xxii, sec. xi, p. 478. This statement Rousseau indignantly criticizes (*op. cit.*, Book I, chap. ii, pp. 6–7).

[41]Grotius, *op. cit.*, Book I, chap. ii, p. 69.

to any one or more persons, and transfer the right of governing them upon him or them, without reserving any share of that right to themselves . . .?"[42] By the contract the people keep possession of themselves and their personal liberty, but their civil liberty and "the perpetual right of governing them, as they are a people," these are alienated.[43] The people retain no rights *of a governing kind;* what alone the sovereign may not do is turn them over to the governance of another.[44]

May not the main elements of this conception of the social contract also be found in Israel's covenant if it is rightly comprehended? Insofar as "the people's consent" to the covenant is at all a proper manner of speaking, do they not consent to God's "perpetual right of governing them, as they are a people," themselves retaining no rights of a governing kind, nor yet the right of revoking what they have conferred?

Behind these sixteenth- and seventeenth-century thinkers who first formulated the modern doctrine of political sovereignty stood the Reformers with their insistence upon the divine sovereignty and human salvation *sola gratia.* In this respect the Reformation may be described summarily as an effort to free the free will of God. This freedom the covenant first established.

What follows from the foregoing study of Israel's covenant? Instead of attempting to derive democracy directly or by implication from scripture, we would be better advised to confront there the asserted and "ratified" sovereignty of God, whatever may be found to be the political relevance or irrelevance of this doctrine. In spite of the uses Calvin made of it, the issue as to the sovereignty of God is always at bottom the question, "Who shall be god in Israel?" juxtaposed to the Sidonian Jezebel's words, "Do you [Ahab] not hold sway?" (I Kings 18:36, 37, and 21:7). In a world whose creators or spokesmen are in large meas-

---

[42]*Ibid.,* p. 64.

[43]*Ibid.,* p. 77. Compare Grotius' view with Hobbes's definition of personal liberty as "the absence of opposition" or "the silence of the laws" (*op. cit.,* Part II, chap. xxi, pp. 196 and 201). Rousseau denies that there can be personal freedom in any significant sense without civil liberty.

[44]In these and foregoing comments I am greatly indebted to studies pursued under the direction of Professor Charles W. Hendel of Yale University and to his own illuminating interpretation of the social philosophers examined above.

ure men like Bodin and Grotius, Hobbes and Rousseau, we have learned, Emil Brunner remarks, that "sovereignty is a concept which cannot with impunity be transferred from God, to whom alone it belongs, to men or human things. . . . The theory of human sovereignty, even when it is not so intended, is the beginning of political atheism."[45] Covenant religion stood against this development. The biblical covenant stood, and stands, against both politically atheistic worlds, both the modern world of monolithic dictators and omnicompetent states and the Roman Catholic world in which the pope claims to be, if he does not always act like, Christ's vicar on earth in such fashion as to make Christ his vicar in heaven.[46] Not without cause does Bodin expressly say that Innocent IV understood the nature of sovereignty better than any one else before the sixteenth century. The current conflict between these two politically atheistic worlds is a war of religions which are not ours.

As for the covenants modern men have cut with other gods,

> There is only one limit to the sovereignty of the state; it is the knowledge of the sovereignty of God. . . . Thus the old doctrine that the state needs religion is no crafty device of princes who imagine that religion gives them a better hold on their subjects, but the basis of all true statesmanship. Where it is lacking there is no limit to the *superbia* of the state, for there is only one remedy for *superbia*—the fear of God. How else shall the power which claims for itself the title of "supreme" realize its limits save in that most supreme power? By the will of the people? As if the will of the people could not itself fall victim to that *superbia!* The unlimited sovereignty of the people and the unlimited sovereignty of the state are simply two forms of *superbia,* the one individualistic, the other totalitarian.[47]

Three centuries ago it was found that nothing could remove the divinity that hedged a king save the divinity of religion when religion was ranged against him. Religious freedom was the first

[45]*Justice and the Social Order,* Harpers, 1945, p. 74.
[46]*Cf.* the Italian proverb "God is everywhere except at Rome; there He has a vicar" (quoted in a note to Luther's *Open Letter to the Christian Nobility of the German Nation,* in *Works* [Philadelphia: Muhlenberg Press], II, 113).
[47]Brunner, *op. cit.,* p. 213.

freedom. In our day again this proves true; or else, to the degree that it does not, there is live possibility that the first freedom may be the last. We in America who until now, except for occasional bad weather,[48] have lived (to borrow an expression of Chesterton's) in a patch of peace like a dog in a patch of sunlight—we are likely to suppose that the strongest bulwark against tyranny would be rationally clear and popularly agreed to notions of natural law and natural human rights. These, if available, may be of indispensable assistance. Yet in the thick of things men have, like Elijah, had recourse to the sovereignty of God as their court of first and last resort. Thus, European Christians have discovered in Paul's apparently ultra-conservative expression, "Every one must obey the authorities that are over him, for no authority can exist without the permission of God" (Rom. 13:1), a most powerful stimulus to resistance against tyrants who ordain themselves and live by their own permission. They have understood that this justification of earthly authority, rightly grasped, must be reduced to a simple corollary of the idea of "covenant." With Paul they have seen that political power must be "God's agent to do you good" (Rom. 13:4). Consequently, the cry has gone out: "To your tents, O Israel!" It remains impossible to conceive of any public contract with other gods or supreme rulers that would not be a violation of our first covenant.

How to determine as basis for practical, day-to-day decisions whether God or Ahab holds sway in the political arena or in relationships among nations places upon us all a most terrifying responsibility, especially in democratic countries. The covenant means unconditional obedience. Nevertheless, "obedience to God" does not in itself contain adequate directions for an entire social policy. When compared with one of the legal codes "written in" to the covenant by the ancient Hebrews, covenant-obedience

---

[48]Hobbes's famous definition of war and peace still holds true: "For *war* consisteth not in battle only, or the act of fighting, but in a tract of time wherein the will to contend by battle is sufficiently known. . . . For as the nature of foul weather lieth not in a shower or two of rain, but in an inclination thereto of many days together; so the nature of war consisteth not in actual fighting, but in the known disposition thereto, during all the time there is no assurance to the contrary. All other time is *peace*" (*op. cit.,* Part I, chap. xiii, p. 161).

shows as a quite indeterminate standard. The same is true when the covenant is compared with any of the specific proposals for social enactment in which a modern Christian may happen to believe and, so far as he is concerned, "write in" to his own understanding of the covenant relationship. Compared with any full-blown legalism, the covenant means unconditional obedience in search of a social policy. Covenant-obedience contains abundant implications for social action, yet shows as a quite indeterminate norm in quest of a social policy when it is compared with specific stipulations for action. For all that may be said concerning the religious foundations of any tolerable community life, "obedience to God and not to man" is not all Christians need to know for their practice in actual life.

Nevertheless, covenant-obedience holds firmly onto the conviction that man's ultimate loyalty transcends every earthly system or center of human power. This gives man whereon to stand in opposing the present shape of the world; it provides at least some indication of how big tyrants ought not to be and places an ultimate limit on the totalitarian demands of the state. Here are the main lines of a covenant-centered social policy seeking to determine in every age the meaning of "obedience to God." Man's proximate political allegiance calls for selecting among relative degrees of political idolatry and political atheism or degrees of *superbia,* by making reference to the absolute sovereignty of God disclosed, or so Christians believe, in the old and new covenants. However admittedly problematic this may be, it has yet to be shown more difficult or less reasonable than gauging relative justice, relative natural law, relative degrees of value, and degrees of perfection against an as yet undisclosed absolute justice, absolute natural law, *summum bonum,* or final perfection of a secular sort. If "value judgment" may do the one, "religious judgment" centering in the covenant may be counted competent to do the other of these things. For biblically grounded thought argument for democracy can never take the form of divinizing the will of the people or of *primary* reference to abstract values, standards of justice, or natural rights independent of the cove-

388   *The Religious Foundation for Community Life*

nant in terms of which both God and men are supposed to rule when they rule legitimately. It may be that the experience of the race enables us now to conclude that justice can rarely be achieved for long except through the exercise of creative intelligence and by implementing popular consent with the procedures of democracy. However, while justice may seldom arise except *with* these, it does not arise *from* them. It arises from conformity to covenant conditions commanded by the God of truth and righteousness by which measurement alone human consent and intelligence become right.

These covenant conditions are summed up in the biblical notion of righteousness or justice. The covenant means unconditional obedience; it means unclaiming love. In this book, the basic norm for Christian ethics has been called "*obedient* love" because of its intimate association with the idea of "covenant" and with the "reign" of God. Covenant-centered "theologico-political" judgment finds guidance not only in the principle, "You shall have no other gods before me or beside me." This would be a purely negative "protestant principle." Political decision also should be guided by the righteousness of the God we know through the covenant, especially through the restoration of the covenant in Jesus Christ. It is he "in whom all things cohere"; and, as we have seen, Christian love does the work of creating and preserving community where other sorts of love fail. The command of God that we love one another as we have been taught by Christ provides the religious foundation for community life. As long as God's covenant endures, human community cannot rightly be grounded in anything else. Rightly grasped, the biblical idea of justice or Christian love may also be reduced to a simple corollary of the idea of covenant. And "consenting" to the sovereignty of God manifestly means acknowledging his righteousness or justice to be the sovereign rule of life. These two are, in fact, the same thing: obeying the covenant and doing justice, love for neighbor and fulfilling the law.

SUGGESTIONS FOR FURTHER READING

For personal study as well as for use in classes and other study groups it may be found useful to correlate selections or assignments from this volume with readings from the Old and New Testaments, and from St. Augustine's writings or other definitive statements of Christian ethics, such as Martin Luther's *Treatise on Christian Liberty,* Soren Kierkegaard's *Works of Love* and Anders Nygren's *Agape and Eros,* Pt. I, Vol. I.

*

CHAPTER I. THE TWO SOURCES OF CHRISTIAN LOVE
and CHAPTER X. THE RELIGIOUS FOUNDATION FOR
COMMUNITY LIFE

Baab, Otto J., *The Theology of the Old Testament,* Abingdon-Cokesbury, 1949, Chs. V, VI.
Burrows, Millar, *An Outline of Biblical Theology,* Westminster, 1946, Chs. III, VII, VIII.
Dibelius, Martin, *Jesus,* Westminster, 1949, Chs. V–VIII.
  The Sermon on the Mount, Scribners, 1940, Chs. II–IV, VI.
Manson, T. W., *The Teachings of Jesus,* Cambridge, 1943, Chs. V–VIII.
Minear, Paul S., *Eyes of Faith,* Westminster, 1946.
Otto, Rudolph, *The Kingdom of God and the Son of Man,* Lutterworth, 1943.
Scott, R. B. Y., *The Relevance of the Prophets,* Macmillan, 1944, Chs. IV, VI–VIII.
Snaith, Norman H., *The Distinctive Ideas of the Old Testament,* Westminster, 1946, Chs. III–VI.
Wilder, Amos N., *Eschatology and Ethics in the Teaching of Jesus,* Harpers, 1939.

*

CHAPTER II. CHRISTIAN LIBERTY

Abrahams, Israel, *Studies in Pharisaism and the Gospels,* Macmillan, first series, 1917.
Dibelius, Martin, *Jesus,* Westminster, 1949, Ch. VIII.
  The Sermon on the Mount, Scribners, 1940, Ch. V.

389

Fosdick, Harry Emerson, *The Man from Nazareth,* Harpers, 1949, Chs. III–V.
Herford, R. Travers, *The Pharisees,* Macmillan, 1924.
Major, H. D. A., Manson, T. W., and Wright, C. J., *The Mission and Message of Jesus,* Dutton, 1946.
Manson, T. W., *The Teaching of Jesus,* Cambridge, 1943, Ch. IX.
Moore, George Foot, *Judaism in the First Centuries of the Christian Era: The Age of the Tannaim,* Harvard, 1927.
Niebuhr, Reinhold, *Faith and History,* Scribners, 1949, Ch. XI.
Scott, C. A. A., *New Testament Ethics,* Macmillan, 1930.
Scott, Ernest F., *The Ethical Teachings of Jesus,* Macmillan, 1936.
Tillich, Paul, *The Protestant Era,* Univ. of Chicago, 1948, Chs. VIII–XI.

✻

CHAPTER III.   THE MEANING OF CHRISTIAN LOVE

Aristotle, *Nicomachean Ethics,* Bks. VIII–IX.
St. Augustine, *The City of God,* Bks. XI, XIV, XIX.
     On Christian Doctrine, Bk. I.
     On the Trinity, Bk. VIII.
     On the Morals of the Catholic Church.
Brunner, Emil, *The Divine Imperative,* Macmillan, 1942, Chs. XIX–XXVI.
Burnaby, John, *Amor Dei,* Hodder and Stoughton, 1938, Chs. IV–VI, IX.
D'Arcy, M. C., *The Mind and Heart of Love,* Holt, 1947.
Fromm, Erich, *Man for Himself,* Rinehart, 1947, Ch. IV.
Hirst, Edward W., *Studies in Christian Love,* Epworth Press, 1944.
Kierkegaard, Soren, *Works of Love,* Princeton, 1946.
Knudson, A. C., *The Principles of Christian Ethics,* Abingdon-Cokesbury, 1943, Chs. VI–VII.
Lewis, C. S., *Christian Behaviour,* Macmillan, 1943, Chs. VII, IX.
Luther, Martin, *Treatise on Christian Liberty, Works,* Muhlenberg, 1943, Vol. II.
Moffatt, James, *Love in the New Testament,* Richard R. Smith, 1930.
Nygren, Anders, *Agape and Eros,* Society for Propagating Christian Knowledge (Macmillan), 1941, Vol. I.
Plato, *The Symposium.*
de Rougemont, Denis, *Love in the Western World,* Harcourt, 1940.
St. Thomas Aquinas, *Summa Theologica,* II–II, QQ. 23–33, 44.

✻

Chapter IV. FAITH'S EFFECTIVENESS
and Chapter V. CHRISTIAN VOCATION

St. Augustine, *On Christian Doctrine*, Bk. I.
On the Morals of the Catholic Church.
Brunner, Emil, *The Divine Imperative*, Macmillan, 1942, Chs. XV–
XVIII, XX–XXII, XXVII–XXIX.
Geren, Paul, *Burma Diary*, Harpers, 1943.
Kierkegaard, Soren, *Works of Love*, Princeton, 1946, Vol. II.
Knudson, A. C., *The Principles of Christian Ethics*, Abingdon-Cokes-
bury, 1943, Ch. IX.
Luther, Martin, *Treatise on Christian Liberty*, *Works*, Muhlenberg,
1943, Vol. II.
Secular Authority: To What Extent It Should be Obeyed, *Works*,
Muhlenberg, 1943, Vol. III.
Tolstoy, Leo, *On Life*, World's Classics edition, Oxford, 1934, Chs.
XV–XXV.

*

Chapter VI. CHRISTIAN VIRTUE

Aristotle, *Nicomachean Ethics*, Bks. I–VII.
St. Augustine, *On the Morals of the Catholic Church.*
The City of God, Bks. V, XIX.
Brunner, Emil, *The Divine Imperative*, Macmillan, 1942, Chs. XV–XVI.
Kierkegaard, Soren, *Works of Love*, Princeton, 1946, Vol. II (esp. Ch.
II).
Knudson, A. C., *The Principles of Christian Ethics*, Abingdon-Cokes-
bury, 1943, Ch. VIII.
Lewis, C. S., *Christian Behaviour*, Macmillan, 1943, Chs. I, II, IX–XII.
Ross Williamson, Hugh, *The Seven Christian Virtues*, S. C. M. Press,
1949.
Sayers, Dorothy L., *Creed or Chaos*, Harcourt, 1949, Ch. VII.
St. Thomas Aquinas, *Summa Theologica*, I–II, QQ. 50–70.

*

Chapter VII. THE WORK OF CHRISTIAN LOVE

Bentham, Jeremy, *Introduction to the Principles of Morals and Legis-
lation*. (Cf. E. A. Burtt, ed., *The English Philosophers from
Bacon to Mill*, Random House, Modern Library, 1939.)
Brunner, Emil, *The Divine Imperative*, Macmillan, 1942, Bk. III.

Kierkegaard, Soren, *Works of Love*, Princeton, 1946, Vol. I, Ch. IV; Vol. II, Chs. VII, VIII.

Mill, J. S., *Utilitarianism.* (Cf. E. A. Burtt, ed., *The English Philosophers from Bacon to Mill*, Random House, Modern Library, 1939.)

Nygren, Anders, *Agape and Eros*, Society for Propagating Christian Knowledge (Macmillan), Part I, Chs. II, VII.

*

CHAPTER VIII. THIS HUMAN NATURE

Aristotle, *de Anima*, Bk. II.

St. Augustine, *The City of God*, Bks. XI, XII, XXII.
   The Confessions, Bk. XIII.
   On the Grace of Christ and Original Sin, Bk. II.
   On the Morals of the Catholic Church.
   On the Nature of the Good.
   On the Trinity, Bks. VIII, XII, XIV, XV.

Barth, Karl, *The Knowledge of God and the Service of God*, Hodder & Stoughton, 1938, Chs. IV–V.
   "No!" in *Natural Theology*, by Karl Barth and Emil Brunner, Geoffrey Bles, 1946.

Brunner, Emil, *The Divine Imperative*, Macmillan, 1942, Chs. V, VII.
   Man in Revolt, Scribners, 1939, esp. Chs. IV–VIII.
   "Nature and Grace," in *Natural Theology*, by Karl Barth and Emil Brunner, Geoffrey Bles, 1946.

Dostoyevsky, Fyodor, *Letters from the Underworld*, Dutton (Everyman), 1938, Part I.

Huxley, Julian S., *Man Stands Alone*, Harpers, 1941.

Huxley, Julian S., and Huxley, Thomas H., *Touchstone for Ethics*, Harpers, 1947.

Kierkegaard, Soren, *The Concept of Dread*, Princeton, 1944.
   Sickness unto Death, Princeton, 1941.

Knudson, A. C., *The Principles of Christian Ethics*, Abingdon-Cokesbury, 1943, Chs. III–VI.

Maritain, Jacques, *True Humanism*, Geoffrey Bles, 1946, Chs. I–II.

Niebuhr, Reinhold, *The Nature and Destiny of Man*, Vol. I: *Human Nature*, Scribners, 1941, Chs. I, V–X.

Rousseau, Jean Jacques, *Discourses*: "The Origin of Inequality," and "The Moral Effects of the Arts and Sciences," Dutton (Everyman), 1938.

Royce, Josiah, *The Problem of Christianity*, Macmillan, 1913, Vol. I.

*

CHAPTER IX. CHRISTIAN LOVE IN SEARCH OF A
SOCIAL POLICY

The Amsterdam Assembly Series, *Man's Disorder and God's Design.*
Vol. III: *The Church and the Disorder of Society.*
Vol. IV: *The Church and the International Disorder,* Harpers,
1948.
Bennett, John C., *Christian Ethics and Social Policy,* Scribners, 1946.
Brunner, Emil, *The Divine Imperative,* Macmillan, 1942, Bk. III.
Justice and the Social Order, Harpers, 1945.
Green, T. H., *Lectures on the Principles of Political Obligation,* Long-
mans, Green, new impression, 1937.
Maritain, Jacques, *The Person and the Common Good,* Scribners, 1947.
The Rights of Man and Natural Law, Scribners, 1943.
Rousseau, Jean Jacques, *Social Contract,* Dutton (Everyman), 1938,
Bks. I–II.
Visser't Hooft, W. A., and Oldham, J. H., *The Church and Its Function
in Society,* Willett, Clark, 1937.
Williams, Daniel Day, *God's Grace and Man's Hope,* Harpers, 1949.

*

CHAPTER X. THE RELIGIOUS FOUNDATION FOR
COMMUNITY LIFE

(*See* CHAPTER I)

INDEX OF SCRIPTURE PASSAGES

OLD TESTAMENT

NEW TESTAMENT

INDEX

OF AUTHORS AND SUBJECTS

399

Conventional morality. *Cf.* Law.
Copernicus, 266 f.
Counsels of perfection, 188
Courage (virtue of), 203 ff., 210 f., 214, 229
Covenant, 4 ff., 367 ff.
Custom. *Cf.* Law

Darwin, C., 266, 268
Davidson, A. B., 5
Decision, 218, 220 f., 338 f.
Democracy, 330 ff., 358 ff., 363 ff.
Dewey, John, 276. *Cf.* Instrumentalism
Dibelius, Martin, 29, 31, 43
Divorce. *Cf.* Marriage and divorce
Donne, John, 281
Dosetai ben Judah, Rabbi, 67
Dostoyevsky, Fyodor, 94 f., 139, 152, 179 f., 226, 308 ff.
Dread. *Cf.* Anxiety
Dualism, 107 ff.
Duty
  Duties to oneself, 157 ff.
  Rights and duties, 353 ff.
  Cf. Obedient Love; Vocation

Edwards, Jonathan, 146, 151
Egotism, 296. *Cf.* Self-love, Idolatry
Eliot, T. S., 247
Ellul, Jacques, 345, 371
Enlightened unselfishness, 160 ff.
Epictetus, 252
Eschatology
  in Jesus' teaching, 26 ff.
  and ethics, 29 ff.
Existentialism, 307 ff.

Faith
  and love, 128 ff.
  and works, 133 ff.
  and "virtue," 214 f., 220 ff., 229
Fall (of man), 262 ff. *Cf.* Original Sin
Figgis, J. N., 382
Flesh, 107 ff.
Forgiveness, 69, 219 ff. *Cf.* God; Love
Fosdick, H. E., 29
Francis, St., 244
Freedom, 213 ff.
  religious, 356 ff.
  social, 356 ff. *Cf.* Rights
  of speech, 359 ff.
  spiritual, 307 ff.
Freeman, Douglas S., 234
Freud, S., 266, 271, 272
Friendship and Christian love, 20, 96 f., 120, 245 f. *Cf.* Aristotle
Fromm, Erich, 94, 103 ff., 352

Gabriel, Ralph, 357
Garrard, L. A., 43, 170
"General will," 331 ff.
Geren, Paul, 161 f., 164 f., 178 f., 183 f., 336 f.
Gierke, Otto, 369, 375
God
  Condescension, 19 f., 22, 129, 225
  Faithfulness, 370 ff.
  His love, 16 ff., 24 f., 44 f., 100, 126 ff., 141
  In Christ, 17 ff., 21 f., 126 f., 198 ff., 225
  Kingdom of, 24 ff. *Cf.* Covenant
  Power, 22, 26
  Righteousness, 2 ff., 40, 295, 349
  Sovereignty, 22 ff., 367 ff., 384 ff. *Cf.* Obedient Love
Good, 112 ff. *Cf.* Value
Grace, 213 ff., 215 f., 220
Green, T. H., 187, 359 ff.
Grotius, Hugo, 381, 383 f.
Guignebert, Charles, 58

Haeckel, Ernest, 267 f.
Happiness. *Cf.* Hedonism; Utilitarianism
Harnack, Adolph von, 143
Hedonism, 112 f., 145 f., 202 f.
Hegel, Georg W. F., 301 ff., 304
Hillel, Rabbi, 48, 61
Hobbes, Thomas, 369, 373 ff., 384, 386
Holloway, Vernon, 334
Holmes, Oliver W., 357

Holy Spirit
  inspiration, 82 f.
  spirit of Christ, 339 f.
  works of, 107 ff.
Hope, 230 ff.
Humanism, 219, 265 f., 277
  Christian humanism, 352 ff.
Humility, 129, 200 f., 220 ff.

Idealism, 276, 301 ff.
  theory of democracy, 331 ff.
  view of sin, 313 ff.
Idolatry, 295 ff.
Image of God, 249 sq.
  Relational conceptions, 254 ff., 277
    ff., 354
  Reformation views, 261, 282 ff.
  Substantialist conceptions
    Aristotelian, 250 f., 253
    Catholic, 260 ff., 282
    Personalist, 253 f.
    Stoic, 250, 252 f.
Incarnation, 132. *Cf.* Jesus Christ
Infused grace, 213 ff.
Infused virtue, 213 ff.
  moral virtues, 214 f., 217, 228
  theological virtues, 213, 228, 260
    Cf. Faith, Hope, Love
Instrumentalism, 268 ff.
Intuition, 88 f., 338 ff.

Jesus Christ
  divinity and humanity, 21 f., 198 ff.
  eschatological teachings, 24 ff., 57
  humility, 129
  kenotic love, 19 ff., 225
  measure of Christian love, Intro-
    duction, 17 ff., 44
  measure of Christian virtue, 195 ff.,
    225 f.
  righteousness and love of God, 16
    ff., 126
Justice
  and love, 2 ff.
  as moral virtue, 206 f.
  biblical view of, 2 ff., 244 ff.

human and divine, 2 ff.
  political, 330 ff.
Justification. *Cf.* Salvation
justitia originalis, 311 ff.

Kafka, Franz, 225
Kant, Emmanuel, 123, 251, 306, 352
Kenoticism, 19 f. *Cf.* God, condescension; Jesus Christ
Kierkegaard, Soren
  anxiety or dread, 307 f.
  despair, 297
  duty to self, 161
  freedom, 307 f., 324
  hope, "always hoping," 231
  humility, 225
  idolatry, 297
  image of God, 225, 257 ff., 277 f.
  love for self, 102, 161
  meaning of Christian love, 92, 93,
    97 f., 102, 246
  sin
    one's own, 288 f.
    and idolatry, 297
    and anxiety, 307 f.
  teleological suspension of ethics,
    338 f.
Kingdom of God, 24 ff., 57
Klausner, Joseph, 66
Knox, John, 37, 170 f.
Knudson, A. C., 119, 254, 287
Kroner, Richard, 264

Law
  Jesus and the law, 51 ff., 54 sq.
  Jewish law, 13, 33 f., 46 sq.
    divorce, 48, 70 ff.
    lex talionis, 52, 67 ff.
    Sabbath, 48 ff., 55 ff., 63
    summaries, 61 ff.
  Legalism, ch. II *passim*
  St. Paul and the law, 74 sq.
  Cf. Natural law; Love, Christian,
    and law
Legalism. *Cf.* Law
Leon, Philip, 300
Lewis, C. S., 111, 131, 329